Business, Globalization
and the Common Good

Frontiers of Business Ethics

Series Editor

LÁSZLÓ ZSOLNAI
Business Ethics Center
Corvinus University of Budapest

VOLUME 6

PETER LANG

Oxford · Bern · Berlin · Bruxelles · Frankfurt am Main · New York · Wien

Business, Globalization and the Common Good

edited by

HENRI-CLAUDE DE BETTIGNIES

and

FRANÇOIS LÉPINEUX

PETER LANG

Oxford · Bern · Berlin · Bruxelles · Frankfurt am Main · New York · Wien

Bibliographic information published by Die Deutsche Bibliothek
Die Deutsche Bibliothek lists this publication in the Deutsche National-
bibliografie; detailed bibliographic data is available on the Internet at
‹http://dnb.ddb.de›.

A catalogue record for this book is available from The British Library.

Library of Congress Cataloguing-in-Publication Data:

Business, globalization, and the common good / [edited by] Henri-Claude de
Bettignies and François Lépineux.
    p. cm.
    Includes bibliographical references and index.
    ISBN 978-3-03911-876-2 (alk. paper)
    1. Social responsibility of business. 2. Globalization--Economic aspects. 3.
Globalization--Social aspects. 4. Common good--International cooperation. 5.
International economic relations--Moral and ethical aspects. I. Bettignies, Henri
Claude de. II. Lépineux, François, 1968-
    HD60.B884 2008
    658.4'08--dc22
                            2008041498

Cover design: Judit Kovacs, Createch Ltd, Hungary

ISSN 1661-4844
ISBN 978-3-03911-876-2

© Peter Lang AG, International Academic Publishers, Bern 2009
Hochfeldstrasse 32, Postfach 746, CH-3000 Bern 9, Switzerland
info@peterlang.com, www.peterlang.com, www.peterlang.net

Printed in Germany

Contents

Introduction

1. "Raison d'être" of the book

Globalization does not make the world flat but only more interdependent. Business does make the world better, but only for a minority. Concern for the common good could make the world wiser and our planet sustainable, but we are not there yet. This is why we put this book together.

Globalization was supposed to create a borderless world, a seamless market, while the internet and other planet spanning technologies were absorbing distance making international exchanges easier and cheaper, fostering economic growth and nurturing better inter-cultural understanding. It did not happen. Over a decade ago naive expectations led us to believe that the fall of the Berlin Wall would open a new era and that with the "end of history" we were entering in a safer world. The world today is more dangerous and less orderly with more international terrorism and more nuclear proliferation, weaker international institutions, with threats of climate change increasingly more visible. Cleavages of religious and cultural ideology are more intense while our complex global financial system today shows its vulnerability more than ever. Science and technology – blind as to where they are leading – are racing ahead, ahead of our capacity to master their development. We call this "progress" but, as the philosopher Michel Serres says: "l'homme ne maîtrise plus sa maîtrise".

Business is the most effective institution to create value through its multiple outputs – products and services (including money out of money), jobs and taxes, innovation and community or societal contributions – but society is ineffective in inducing it to internalize its many negative externalities. Its dominant paradigm of shareholder value maximization is based on a concept of man as a rational animal guided by self-interest whose mimetic desire can be manipulated and turned into purchasing behavior. It trusts the divine hand of the market supposed to ensure a smooth functioning of the system, thanks to competition – if not too hampered by the regulatory hand of the government. However, we realize today how this dominant model that privileges one stakeholder (the shareholder) among many is conducive to the creation of an unsustainable world leading our planet to a catastrophe, particularly for future generations.

A couple of years ago business leaders in their annual get-together celebrations of Davos were still surprised to hear surveys results from around the world showing that society did not like them. Seen as greedy, exploiting, corrupting and polluting, their multiple and obvious contributions to society seem to have been forgotten by public opinion that wanted to remember only Enron failures, corruption cases, over-compensated CEOs, growing inequalities, gambling with other people's money, environmental and industrial accidents ... in short the fuel of the anti-globalization movements, offspring of the so called "Seattle Crowd". To blame politicians, in advanced democracies (for their short-termism and quasi exclusive concerns for the next election) and in developing economies (for their corruption and ineffective use of power) could not be an effective alibi. The most enlightened leaders realized that respecting the law of the land and pursuing their business to maximize shareholder value was not enough to improve their image. Aware of the fact that they should be careful not to do the job of the government, of those elected by the people for that purpose and for caring for the common good, they had to broaden their concept of responsibility and – perhaps with compassion – engage further on the CSR road. But the fashionable trend of Corporate Social Responsibility that percolates slowly through large corporations – and advertised in their annual reports – around the world (now also in China) is however no substitute for the concern for the common good.

The common good, an ambiguous concept not traditionally associated with globalization is also not part of the daily business jargon or management buzzwords. Board discussions and decisions have more to do with return on investment and earning per share than with "common good". Though – as we will see in this book – defining "the common good" requires clarifying conceptual differences between "common goods", "collective goods", "public goods", and "global common good". For us "the common good" implies the dimension of *community* and can be defined as "the good realized in the mutual relationships in and through which human beings achieve their well-being".[1] It is more than the good of individuals; it is attainable only by the community, yet individually shared by its members. Furthermore, concern for the common good will contribute to create for the community and for the individual, today and tomorrow, conditions for a better human well-being. This is also the function of the "global public goods" so necessary in today's globalization process. Global public goods (i.e. "commodities which contribute to giving better opportunities for each individual to live a life he chooses to live")[2] contribute to respond to the global challenges of our times which national governments alone cannot secure (e.g. financial stability, peace, environment, scientific knowledge, cultural heritage) and for which international cooperation among governments is necessary. It assumes that the good life of the community to which we belong is constitutive of the good life of the individual. My well-being needs the good life of the community, contribution of the common good to my own well-being.

In corporate life reference is seldom made to the common good and when it is, it often refers to "public goods", a non-market issue, easily outsourced to government, to international organizations and/or to NGOs. This outsourcing process stems from Milton Friedman's concept of the firm which emphasizes that the main duty of business leaders is not to concentrate on CSR or the common good, but simply on the maximization of shareholders' return. This lack of interest of the corporation in the common good is changing, albeit too slowly. Many drivers – beyond biosphere deterioration, civil society pressure and the need to invent a new social contract (or to redefine the purpose of the enterprise) – explain this evolution. The obsolete power structures and operational mechanisms of

---

1   Hollenbach, D., 2002, *The Common Good and Christian Ethics*, Cambridge: Cambridge University Press, p. 81.
2   Deneulin, S. and Townsend, N., 2007, "Public Goods, Global Public Goods and the Common Good", *International Journal of Social Economics*, 1–2, p. 34.

our global organizations (UN, IMF, World Bank, WTO) – for whom common good was in the agenda; the evidence of global warming and the disturbing reports about deforestation, melting polar ice caps, the diminishing capacity of oceans and the increase in carbon dioxide emissions – with their impacts on our common good; the vulnerability of our global financial system – as a threat to many domestic economies; all are symptoms of the fragility of our commons and a pressure on firms to internalize responsibility in their corporate behavior.

As President Michel Albert said recently addressing a large audience of business leaders in China: "We are meeting a double crisis: a crisis of Nature, which manifests itself by the exhaustion of natural resources and a growing number of natural disasters; a crisis of Culture, which manifests itself by the rise of terrorism, the closing down on one's identity, the rise of xenophobic behaviors on the basis of which other people are rejected and despised ..."[3] Prisoners of globalization – but fueling its process –, watched by civil society, corporations will have no choice but to internalize responsibility through actively contributing to sustainable development and to do so in a world where diversity (biological, human and cultural) is continuously threatened by homogenization. This will require efforts and investments to maintain and develop the capacity to invent, which in turn is built upon the capacity to remember, hence the critical importance of cultural diversity (variety contributes to create durability – as we know from biology). By protecting cultural diversity, we keep memory and as we have learnt our innovation potential is enriched by diversity more than by homogeneity.[4] It is thus useful to remember that our human diversity is part of our common good and should be carefully maintained against the threat of the globalization process. It is one of our natural resources to be respected and it is also part of the rights of the generations to come that we must preserve to allow them to continue making history.

---

3   Albert, M., 2008, "Culture and Sustainable Development", *International Symposium: Cultural Resources for Sustainable Development*, Shanghai, 25 April, p. 42.
4   De Bettignies, H.-C., 2000, "The Corporation as a 'Community': An Oxymoron? Can Business Schools Re-invent Themselves?", *Concepts and Transformation*, 5–2, pp. 165–211.

Globalization, business and the common good may not be jovial bedfellows, today, but they will have to appreciate each other's company, and pretty quickly. Otherwise, sustainable development, diversity and responsibility will not be attainable and it will make the well-being of our grandchildren a remote possibility. Business schools thanks to the knowledge they produce through their research, thanks to the education they provide through their teaching, thanks to the information they share through their publications and networking, have a critical role to play to accelerate this promiscuity, influencing decision makers to embed responsible leadership throughout their organizations. The promotion of "globally responsible leadership" will contribute to advance the new contract that will make the common good not the packaging of CSR, but its very essence. So doing, we will help leaders to leverage complexity, to develop true solidarity, not the one imposed upon people but the one they feel within themselves and experience as fraternity. We will have made them more aware. They will also realize that if history teaches us that sometimes the possible becomes impossible, it also tells us that hopeless dreams can come true. This is what this book would like to explore.

2. Structure of the book

In so far as the first chapter can also be considered as a general introduction to the whole book, this introduction will remain short, presenting briefly the different contributions. The book is divided in three parts; each part is composed of five chapters, organized in a logical order. The first part concentrates on the very notion of the common good, and strives to determine to what extent business is responsible for it in the globalization era. It develops various approaches, shedding on these issues theoretical, ethical and spiritual lights. Chapter 1 (Business and the Global Common Good: An Interdisciplinary Approach) starts by recalling some objections commonly waved against the idea that business should be concerned with the common good, and suggests a possible refutation for each of them.

To explore the interplay between business and the global common good, it proceeds in two steps, and mobilizes several disciplines or schools of thought which tackle this complex issue from different standpoints. Firstly, it examines some fundamental reasons why it is likely that the business sphere will not be in a position to disregard the global common good much longer; the main arguments supporting this position are either theoretical, or related to contemporary ethical problems. Secondly, it analyzes three models of the common good that are prevailing today and competing with each other on the global scale: the teleological model, the utilitarian model, and the relational model. It eventually raises a question for future research: which conception of the common good should business be concerned with in the globalization era?

In Chapter 2 (Corporate Social Responsibility and Common Good), Helen Alford and Yuliya Shcherbinina point out that CSR has become a major movement, especially in Europe. Much time and energy have been invested in creating consensus around this and related terms regarding the need for businesses to take a broader view of their responsibilities other than that of producing a profit for owners in accordance with the law. However, the academic writings on the nature and purpose of CSR reveal that its ethical foundations are not yet secure. This leaves CSR vulnerable to manipulation and ultimately to instrumentalization towards limited profit-maximizing goals. This chapter thus develops the fundamental idea that could underpin and strengthen CSR – the idea of the common good. It outlines briefly the nature and purpose of business within the common good perspective and discusses how the common good idea can influence the way we think about and practice CSR.

In Chapter 3 (The Common Good as a Global Wealth: Preventing Globalization from Leading to an Ethical Decay of the Common Good), Hendrik Opdebeeck analyzes the threat that globalization poses to what the French philosopher Paul Ricœur calls "the longing for being and collaboration with the other(s)", which can be seen as the foundation of the common good. In the present economy, people are no longer regarded as individuals but as human resources, comparable to natural, technological and financial resources. Reducing human persons to economic agents is increasingly making us lose our sense of being, working and living together with the others. Therefore, if one wants to put a stop to the decay of the common good, the urgency of a broader ethical (i.e. more just) dimension in the globalization process is more apparent than ever before. Appropriate global institutions are urgently needed; and the purpose of institutions is that they should serve people and the common good – otherwise they are entirely meaningless. In this respect, the concept of a global social contract seems to be an important basis to establish the common good as a global wealth.

At the beginning of Chapter 4 (Stakeholders and the Common Good: A Polarity within Corporate Conscience), Kenneth Goodpaster reminds us of a relevant question asked by Peter Drucker almost 15 years ago: "In the society of organizations, [...] who, then, is concerned with the common good?" He firstly underlines that careful reflection on the meaning of conscience reveals an important polarity. In the case of organizations, this polarity may help us to understand the relationship between "stakeholder thinking" and reflections on CSR, and the Catholic Social Tradition, which often focuses on more comprehensive themes like human dignity and the common good. In relation to corporate decision making, the tension may help us to appreciate both the necessity and the insufficiency of stakeholder thinking: by focusing on what might be called the ethics of engagement (towards multiple constituencies), stakeholder thinking can overlook the ethics of participation (in the common good). To develop his argument, Kenneth Goodpaster draws upon the writings of philosophers (Josiah Royce, Thomas Nagel), management theorists (Peter Drucker), and Catholic social thinkers (John Paul II and Joseph Cardinal Ratzinger before he became Benedict XVI).

In Chapter 5 (Business Ethics and Inter-Religious Contribution in the Age of Globalization), Noel Keizo Yamada intends to describe the role and contribution of religious people to business ethics. As a member of the Japanese Committee of the World Conference on Religion and Peace, whose eighth Assembly took place in Kyoto in August 2006, he is convinced that people belonging to all religious traditions have a role to play in the age of globalization, especially to reduce its negative aspects, to identify its lights and shadows, and to generate the dynamism for a value shift. He calls for the cooperation of people involved in inter-religious dialogue to promote business ethics, i.e. to respond to the challenge of the Spirit of God, through innovative thinking and moral commitment to justice. He proposes the idea of the "Common Living" (*Kyosei*) as a key word for business ethics and global leadership through the 21st century. He introduces and develops the contents of *Kyosei*, which are the treasures of Asian and Japanese traditional religions like Buddhism and Shintoism, by defining the word and giving the conditions more in detail. His dream is that putting the spirit of *Kyosei* into practice in business ethics may be the contribution of Japan to Justice and Peace in the World, i.e., Justice for All, Peace for All Nations (J-A-P-A-N).

The second part of the book is more focused on empirical aspects, and develops a variety of initiatives involving business at different levels – initiatives that aim at realizing the common good in the globalization context. In Chapter 6 (Nature, Society and Future Generations), László Zsolnai suggests that business should contribute to the common good by achieving ecological sustainability, pro-socialness and respect for future generations. In so far as business organizations affect the fate and survival of natural ecosystems and the life conditions of human beings presently and in the future, nature, society and future generations are primordial stakeholders of business. László Zsolnai uses Hans Jonas' theory of responsibility to show that business has a non-reciprocal duty of caring for the beings which are under the impacts of its functioning. He presents the activities of progressive companies like outdoor clothing company *Patagonia*, retail business firm *Ishka*, natural health care company *Blackmores*, skin care specialist *Jurlique*, and organic food company *Whole Foods*, which are good illustrations of how business can be successful by serving the common good. By acting for the conservation and restoration of the natural world, for the development of human capabilities and for the freedom of future generations, business can serve the common good and regain its legitimacy in today's globalized world characterized by ecological degradation and human disintegration.

Chapter 7 (*¡Ay mi Nicaragüita!* The construction of the Common Good in Nicaragua as a "Work of Translation") studies the case of one of the poorest countries in Latin America: Nicaragua. After the dictatorship of the Somoza dynasty, the Sandinista Revolution in 1979 and the Civil

War during the 1980s, it appears that since 1990 the economic, political and cultural situation has not improved. The country has assumed a fatalist culture that keeps in many Nicaraguans the idea that their future is not in their hands: Nicaragua will be saved by foreign investment, by international cooperation ... or, perhaps, by the support of the Venezuelan President Hugo Chavez. There are however people and organizations in Nicaragua that are working to set positive deals among political groups, grassroots NGOs, and local economic organizations that may lead to change the fatalist culture, develop the conscience of citizenship in the population, and foster a dialogue among the different sectors of society directed to the common good. Josep Mària identifies this new vision with the sociological approach of Boaventura de Sousa Santos, who criticizes the hegemonic globalization as an approach of the social reality that prevents from discovering emerging ideas and organizations that work for the common good at the local level. Santos' proposal to build the common good consists in a "Work of Translation", i.e. a dialogue among different organizations (beginning with grassroots groups) aiming at human development for all citizens. Josep Mària thus analyzes successively some examples of organizations that work in the perspective of this "Work of Translation" in Nicaragua today: the international cooperation NGO *Intermón Oxfam*; the political party *Alianza MRS*; the local development fund *FDL (Fondo de Desarrollo Local)*; and the national federation of cooperatives working with a non-capitalistic logic *FENACOOP*.

In Chapter 8 (The Common Good as a Criterion for a Globalization in the Service of Mankind), Jean-Marie Fèvre underlines that the notion of common good, elaborated over centuries within the frame of Christian Social Teaching, is neither vague nor outdated if one formulates accurately its assumptions, limits and aims. Therefore, he provides a clear presentation of the common good concept with a resolute reference to St Thomas Aquinas and two scholars of the 20th century: Arthur-Fridolin Utz and Leo Elders. Today, the world needs more harmony and coordination of efforts to reach a global synergy rather than a chaotic and potentially lethal struggle for short-term wealth and power. Some firms and international organizations already show that it is possible to make profit and get a positive image by contributing to a sustainable development respecting the environment and promoting people within the frame of the common good, which appears as a useful criterion of knowledge, judgment and action for a globalization in the service of mankind according to the Declaration of Human Rights of 10 December 1948. In this respect, Jean-Marie Fèvre provides two examples: the global company *Villeroy & Boch*, flourishing and performing for the common good through responsible and solid entrepreneurship, and the International Standardization Organization *ISO*, whose work and influence benefit the whole world.

In Chapter 9 (Ethical Infrastructure for Business with Special Emphasis on Poland: Designing for the Common Good), Wojciech Gasparski discusses openly or implicitly adopted premises concerning business activity that form its intellectual structure, with a special focus on their relation to the common good. He recounts the demands of business ethicists addressed to the business community regarding mechanisms fostering the ethical conduct of the stakeholders that form business organizations in a broad sense (companies *sensu largo*). He analyzes issues of solution design that are important for the transparent development of elements that constitute the material ethical infrastructure of business. Examples of solutions applied in Polish economic practice – based on European and worldwide, chiefly American, models from a world undergoing globalization – illustrate the business community's response to these demands as well as the community's own initiatives, such as ethics programs, codes of conduct, codes of good practice, corporate responsibility, responsiveness and citizenship, social audits, and others.

In Chapter 10 (Profit, Partnerships, and the Global Common Good), Laura Hartman, Scott Kelley and Patricia Werhane break free from what they identify as a mental model that permeates the understanding of the common good and CSR practices on a global scale: a model which favors public sector projects and pure philanthropy over a profit-maximizing perspective as the only means by which to address global poverty. In order to escape this way of thinking, they contend that the common good, as a positive idea, cannot be articulated so as to fit across cultural or political domains. Secondly, they argue that, to the contrary, a focus on common "bads" is more properly within the domain of possibility; considering endemic poverty for instance, the alleviation of economic distress is served more effectively by reducing patterns of neglect or exclusion than by pursuing a common, clearly articulated shared notion of "public or common goods". Thirdly, economic distress can be reduced not merely by public works or philanthropy but, counter-intuitively, through commerce. When a corporation's profit-maximizing incentives are aligned with the alleviation of extreme poverty, strategic convergence can emerge through profitable partnerships. Three examples of sustainable and profitable partnerships between for-profit corporations and communities are used to illuminate the value of this strategic convergence: *Manila Water* in the Philippines, *Cemex* in Mexico, and *Hindustan Lever Limited* in India.

Eventually, the last part of the book deals with the relationship between the business sphere and the emerging global civil society: to what extent could a global social contract be established in order to respond to the challenges brought about by the globalization process? In Chapter 11 (Reflections on Global Civil Society), Jean-François Petit strives to determine under which conditions a global civil society could be constituted, in particular to foster the creation of a global government; he defends the view that a true global civil society cannot exist without the implementation of a real global citizenship. In a liberal society, market and State must be counterbalanced by a civil society. The plurality of private initiatives and associative relations prevent societies from being too polarized by the economic sphere or by the State. Only a democratic State can create a democratic civil society, which will be able to train citizens to act beyond their self-interest, to develop gratuitously associative relationships, and to take care of political life with equity. But can this model be extrapolated at the world level? World government and civil society must be thought in reciprocity on the basis of certain values. A world government would precisely have the responsibility to foster association forms based on moral consensus, to encourage the right and dignity of their members, and to care for equity, justice and transparency of procedures. A world citizenship is not impossible, provided that personal aspirations and specific needs are taken seriously into account; the wish to avoid dissolution in globalization implies that this world citizenship cannot be created without a strong rehabilitation of politics.

In Chapter 12 (Can Governance Structures and Civil-Corporate Partnerships Manage the Global Commons?), Zsolt Boda argues that the lack of a global government, on one hand, and the need to sustain the global commons, on the other, render necessary the development of alternative governance forms. Some promising examples of civil-corporate partnerships, such as the *Forest Stewardship Council* or the *Marine Stewardship Council*, and the growing number of multi-stakeholder management standards and codes based on the cooperation of different stakeholders – including companies, trade unions and/or civil society organizations, raise the hope that governance without government could be possible, and that social and ecological sustainability could be achieved through agreement among the different social actors, even without state regulation. Zsolt Boda raises the issues of the legitimacy and effectiveness of those governance structures. He suggests that the Habermasian discourse ethics and the theory of deliberative democracy could serve as normative underpinnings to found the legitimacy of these structures, and may as well have a positive influence on their effectiveness. He concludes that participatory decision-making should be a basic model for the global economy, as it has the merit of helping to define the meaning of global commons and to envision the practical implications those definitions might bring about.

In Chapter 13 (Legal Aspects of the Respect for Environmental Commons Goods: On What Foundations Does it and Should it Rely?), Isabelle Cadet concentrates on a particular common or public good: water, and explores how this good is dealt with in the field of law. She suggests that the legal categorization of "Blue Gold", by determining both its legal status and the system of management appropriate to that status, is an essential move in the attempt to prevent the "water wars" which represent one of the greatest threats of the 21st century. This crucial issue provides a window through which not only a redefinition of property, but also the increasing importance of international human rights can be envisioned. Water is legally defined in a host of ways; some are far from neutral. But the term "environmental good" makes little to no sense, since it can be argued that a) water is not a good; b) water is a common good; and c) water is more than a good. In the interest of being precise and getting quickly to the heart of the matter, Isabelle Cadet uses the original French legal stance as a reference point. In environmental matters, this system is greatly influenced by European Union's law, a mixture of hard and soft law, and particularly by a resolutely modern conception of human rights. It is time, she concludes, to dare to create an international constitutional right, which could constitute a foundation stone of global governance; such an initiative could lead to implement procedures to prevent pollution and shortages, to repair the damage already caused, and to guarantee a universal access to this vital resource.

In Chapter 14 (Business, Society and the Common Good: The Contribution of Paul Ricœur), Jacob Dahl Rendtorff intends to propose a foundation of the common good concept based on the philosophy of Paul Ricœur. His analysis is grounded on the theory of republican democracy with respect to basic rights of citizens as the framework for theories of values-driven management, business ethics and corporate social responsibility. Republicanism emphasizes the importance of the common good for the development of the best society, as well as the need for citizenship based on liberty and civic virtue; republican business ethics thus refer to the engagement of the corporation as a good citizen that actively contributes to the common good with civic virtue, and respects the laws of political democracy. Ricœur defines the ideal of politics as the realization of "the good life with and for the other in just institutions". The philosophy of Paul Ricœur helps to renew the concept of republicanism as the foundation of the common good concept in the international society. Jacob Rendtorff starts by defining the concept of the common good on the basis of Ricœur's political philosophy; he then relates this concept to the idea of a global civil ethos as the basis of the common good in a global context; eventually, he shows how a concept of ethical judgment can be the basis for the realization of the common good in international business and society.

In the same way that the first chapter can be viewed as an introduction, the last chapter serves as a general conclusion for the whole book, and develops its programmatic character; that is why its presentation will be longer than that of the others. In Chapter 15 (Corporate Responsibility and Global Social Contract: New Constructivist, Personalist and

Dialectical Perspectives), Jean-Jacques Rosé attempts to summarize and expand upon a recent collection of essays entitled *Corporate Social Responsibility. Towards a New Social Contract* (J.-J. Rosé, ed., 2006, in French), which may be considered as a starting point to show the necessary links between Responsibility, Social Contract and Justice. This title could be understood as a paradox or even an epistemological transgression; how and why is it possible to reconnect, in a research project, an ordinary management science's concept (corporate social responsibility) with the founding notion of modern political philosophy (the social contract) and an ancient concept of Greek and medieval metaphysics and ethics (the common good)? This may be a paradox, but if it is a transgression, it is voluntary and out of necessity. The purpose of this final chapter is to demonstrate this statement. To that end, it interrogates some major works by such authors as Rousseau, Durkheim, Donaldson and Dunfee and Ricœur. Jean-Jacques Rosé has thus assembled texts produced in seemingly historically and culturally heterogeneous spheres, but whose aim is common: to connect what was separated by Hume's epistemological rupture (between the "is" and the "ought") as well as to find a possible foundation for transcendence (without which there is no ethics).

In other words, he develops a critique of the "modern" paradigm which is epistemologically split into economics and management on the one hand, and ethics and politics on the other. The reading of Donaldson and Dunfee's *Ties That Bind – A Social Contracts Approach to Business Ethics* as an application of Rawls' procedural theory of justice in the field of economics is the cornerstone of his thesis. Ricœur's very subtle analysis is used to claim that all forms of procedural and deontological ethics presuppose or imply finality as a hidden principle or assumption. Rousseau's *The Social Contract* explicitly permits the general will to define the common good: "Only the general will can direct the powers of the state in accordance with the purpose for which it was established, which is the common good". This movement is the opposite of mainstream 20th century ethics, which tends to push the idea of Good out of Philosophy. Today, the key challenge for the peoples of the earth is to rapidly find the means to build the general will for the common good not for a single nation, but for all states; this is role of politics. However, who can assert that business would not be a decisive agent in the now urgent construction of a new global social contract?

The analysis conducted by Jean-Jacques Rosé begins with Durkheim's reading of Rousseau's social contract which establishes social bonds as the new foundation of moral transcendence (1). With Donaldson and Dunfee, a contractarian approach is mobilized to respond to the challenge resulting from the relative failure of business ethics attributed by them to the insurmountable separation between works of normative dimension and empirical research (2). To evaluate the aptitude of the "Integrative Social Contracts Theory" (ISCT) to truly overcome this challenge, Rosé follows Ricœur in his reading of John Rawls, who shows how the idea of good is preconceived in the theory of justice (3). On the contrary, the interpretation Ricœur gives of finality in *The Nichomachean Ethics* allows for the validation of Donaldson and Dunfee's central idea of coexistence between the micro-social contract and the macro-social contract (4). A close rereading of a few passages from Rousseau's *The Social Contract* leads from the foundation of individual ethics in Aristotle's and Ricœur's works to the foundation of just institutions for modern society (5). Since any affirmation of a teleological phenomena approach is justly suspected of masking forms of manipulative ideologies, it is necessary to disarm this trap before designing any new perspective today of a social contract on a global scale by mobilizing in particular the results of empirical studies conducted to test the feasibility of ISCT theories (6). To conclude, by referring to a certain number of contemporary works within several disciplines, this final chapter attempts to trace the axis of research that redefines corporate social responsibility in a global social contract.

PART I

Business and the Common Good
in the Globalization Context:
Theoretical, Ethical and Spiritual Perspectives

CHAPTER I

Business and the Global Common Good: An Interdisciplinary Approach

HENRI-CLAUDE DE BETTIGNIES AND FRANÇOIS LÉPINEUX

"Utopias are only premature truths"

— ALPHONSE DE LAMARTINE

Introduction

Today, a growing number of voices are expressing deep concerns about the consequences of the globalization process as it currently unfolds. Nation-States, which had been the traditional guarantors of the common good, find themselves overwhelmed by the globalization process. Companies of all kinds, and especially multinational corporations, owing to their huge economic power, to their influence capacity and to the multiple consequences of their activities, are the focus of much interest among those who strive to devise new ways to serve the common good – and more precisely, the global common good. Civil society exerts increasing pressures on business to act more responsibly. In order to respond to these demands, and despite the forces that push them to meet short-term financial goals, numerous enlightened business leaders have already started to integrate the societal and environmental dimensions in their corporate policies, and to make their stakeholders more aware of sustainability issues. In this regard, examples of proactive and pioneering businesses can now be found in the energy sector, in the financial sector, or in various industrial sectors ... Although most of these business leaders do not explicitly refer to the common good, their actions raise the question of the relationship between business and the common good – and more specifically, between *international* business and the *global* common good. Besides, the globalization process itself brings to the fore the issue of the *responsibility* of corporations – whatever the sector in which they operate – towards the global common good.

To the idea that business could or should be concerned with the common good, however, many would object, and use for that purpose a variety of counter-arguments. We have selected five commonly put forward, and propose a possible refutation for each of them. The first counter-argument could be stated as follows: *globalization is wonderful.* The globalization process, which is now expanding the capitalist system worldwide, is a source of benefits for all the countries of the world thanks to the *invisible hand,* which ensures an efficient allocation of available resources, the successful matching of supply and demand, and the optimal functioning of markets. Consequently, the common good will be attained *automatically*, and corporations do not need to care about it. Besides, there is no alternative to economic liberalism and global capitalism. To tackle this first objection, it may be said that globalization brings benefits to some and misdeeds to others; it is a multi-consequences process. The environmental degradation is one of its major consequences; besides, it has entailed the rise of social inequalities to unprecedented levels, aggravating the divide between the richest countries and the less developed ones that are unable to join the movement, and widening the income disparities in almost every nation. Therefore *the attainment of the common good is far from being automatic,* and globalization cannot but induce a reflection on the responsibility of the business sphere in this regard. Critics of global capitalism rightfully question the TINA doctrine;[1] they are especially interested in knowing who rules, in whose interests, to what ends, and by what means (Held and McGrew, 2002).

---

1   TINA: There IS No Alternative.

Second counter-argument: *the firm is accountable only to its share-holders for its financial results*. Business objectives are purely economic by nature. This flows from the very essence of the firm within the capitalist system: it is an economic entity designed to create private wealth for its shareholders. Hence, corporations simply do not have to care about non-economic considerations such as ethics, social issues, or the common good. Besides, why should corporations be granted the right to decide what the common good consists in and how they should contribute to it, since corporate leaders and managers – being agents for a principal – are not elected by the people? This objection is just the continuation of Milton Friedman's assertion that the social responsibility of business is to make profits while abiding by the laws. However, corporations exist and flourish thanks to a legal and institutional system that ensures ownership rights and the security of business transactions. The market mechanism itself is an institutional arrangement agreed upon by society in the name of the public interest; the very possibility for corporations to pursue their private good originates in the concern for society's common good. Therefore, *it can be said that corporations bear a responsibility to support and promote the common good, since this is a condition of their perpetuation*. And as regards the problem of the legitimacy of corporate leaders and managers, the argument is easy to reverse: who, in society, knows better than them what corporations can effectively do to pursue the global common good?

The third counter-argument is probably the most often mentioned objection: *competitors prevent any progress*. A given corporation could probably care about the common good, but if its competitors don't follow this stance, it will put itself at a competitive disadvantage. Since this corporation doesn't know what its competitors will do, it will not get involved toward the common good. This objection dovetails with the argument advanced by Velasquez (1992), which will be examined below; it can be handled by considering the situation modeled by the Prisoner's Dilemma. In a non-repeated game (a one-time event) involving two players A and B who both have the choice between cooperating and not cooperating, the most rational[2] strategy for both players is not to cooperate, since whatever the other player may do, each player gets a greater payoff if he does not cooperate.

Relating to our subject, not to cooperate means disregarding the issue of corporate responsibility toward the common good – and thereby trying to take advantage of those that are involved in it, whereas to cooperate implies an effective contribution to the global common good on the part of the concerned players. However, in the real world, multinational corporations *do have repeated dealings* with one another on the global scale; and in repeated Prisoner's Dilemma interactions, each player is able to retaliate against the other if the latter has failed to cooperate in the previous meeting, so that the costs of non-cooperation can make cooperation the more rational strategy for the rest of the game. Besides, the no-negotiation and rationality hypotheses that lie at the basis of the game can be released, thus enabling the players to freely choose to cooperate in order to reach an optimal outcome.

Fourth counter-argument: *States should create appropriate regulations.* It is the mission of governments and international organizations to establish rules that will improve the course of globalization, and notably to set higher standards in the social and environmental areas. The safeguard of nature and the fight against poverty are a matter of political will and courage; corporations do not have to take initiatives in this regard. Governments have proved their ability to regulate business in the interest of the common good on a national basis through legislations regarding worker safety, child labor, toxic waste, or affirmative action programs. They should now negotiate international agreements and enforce compliance with the new regulations. How can this objection be refuted? Obviously more constraining international regulations in the social and environmental fields would help alleviate the negative side effects of globalization. But isn't it rather paradoxical to see corporations call for more and more liberalization, and rely on the State to solve the problems

---

2   Rational in the sense that is standard in social theory: the maximization of one's utility, or the exclusive concern for the defense and promotion of one's own interests.

caused by that same liberalization? Furthermore, there is also a certain amount of hypocrisy on the part of multinationals that allegedly expect the international community to adopt new rules, whereas at the same time business lobbies are opposing any form of new constraint on their activities. However, on the side of government, a number of political leaders have already and repeatedly called on business to act more responsibly. Consequently, isn't it in the interest of corporations to respond to society's expectations in a proactive way before new constraining regulations are imposed on their actions?

The last commonly used counter-argument is the following: *consumers and NGOs carry the burden of the responsibility*. Corporations are not responsible for the damage caused by economic activities, as they only respond to their customers' expectations. It is the consumers who pollute the environment by their way of life; in the last resort, it is them who command the course of globalization by their consuming behavior. Therefore they are liable for the negative side effects of the globalization process, and corporations are not – or to a lesser extent. To overcome this objection, a question may be asked: if consumers bear a part of the responsibility for the misdeeds of globalization, why do they behave the way they do? Corporations never stop creating new and artificial needs through advertising; they psychologically condition citizens to become consumers and get them to buy more and more products; they fuel the *mimetic desire* that the philosopher René Girard sees as a key paradigm to explain human behavior. In this light, consumers look like easy scapegoats.

Should the responsibility for the common good, then, be attributed to NGOs? Indeed, some non-governmental organizations are implicitly engaged in activities geared to serve the public interest or explicitly pursuing the "common good". Corporations can therefore "outsource" concern and action to promote the common good to NGOs, rationalizing that each institution is purposeful: the corporation aims at profit, NGOs deal with the common good. This argument looks like an easy way out, but it does not hold water. NGOs cannot be used as a proxy to care for the common good on behalf of corporations that would have subcontracted their responsibilities to "specialists" in negative externalities alleviation.

The road should be – and already is – toward the development of cooperative relationships between NGOs and companies of all kinds, associating – when necessary – the public sector or international institutions as well, thus enhancing the effectiveness of all actors in managing their own responsibilities.

This chapter intends to explore the relationship between business and the global common good through an interdisciplinary approach – that is, by mobilizing several disciplines, traditions or schools of thought, which shed various lights on this complex issue. It proceeds in two steps. Firstly, it examines some fundamental reasons why it is likely that the business sphere will not be in a position to disregard the global common good much longer; the main arguments supporting this position are either theoretical, or related to contemporary ethical problems. Secondly, it analyses three models of the common good that are prevailing today and competing with each other on the global scale: the teleological model, the utilitarian model, and the relational model. It eventually suggests a question for future research: which conception of the common good should business be concerned with in the globalization era?[3]

I. Could or Should Business Serve the Global Common Good? Identifying Some Fundamental Arguments

The traditional conception of the common good as the supreme good of the community can be applied to a number of different levels: the family, the organization, the local community, all the intermediate social entities, the nation, and in its largest extension, the totality of mankind. In what follows we will concentrate on the planetary level – that is, on the

3   The authors would like to thank Luk Bouckaert (K.U. Leuven) and Arnaud Pellissier-Tanon (University Paris I Panthéon-Sorbonne) for their insightful comments on a draft version of this paper.

global common good, which can be characterized as *the supreme good of humanity as a whole*. Although very general in its essence, this concept can be approached through a variety of ways, material and immaterial: peace among nations, scientific knowledge, philosophical works, artistic heritage, biodiversity, a healthy climate, the quality of life, shared economic prosperity ... all these elements represent as many conditions, aspects or partial expressions of the global common good, which exceeds and includes them in its universal perspective. Following Petrella (1996, p. 75), we consider that the global common good embraces two general categories of common or public goods:

– access to the means of human *existence*, such as water, energy and health;
– access to the means of *coexistence* between all members of the world community, such as information, culture, civil and political rights.

Could or should companies of all kinds and especially multinational corporations, then, be concerned about the global common good? This question has drawn special attention today, as it arises in the context of a profound societal change characterized by the globalization phenomenon and the spreading of information technology, whose combined effects are driving the world into a new era. With the spreading of the global economy, national boundaries tend to become irrelevant for a number of corporations aiming at the world market; multinationals have become leading players in contemporary society, and exert a great influence in shaping our conditions of life. But precisely, *it is the combination of their considerable power and of their ability to escape national laws, which represents a threat to the global common good.* After questioning the provocative thesis defended by Velasquez some fifteen years ago, this first part identifies three major determinants that are likely to drive the business community to take the global common good into account.

I.1. Questioning the Thesis of Velasquez

In a thought-provoking article published in 1992, Velasquez has provided a rigorous and stimulating basis for the discussion of the relationship between international business and the global common good. Striving to determine whether or not companies that are operating in a competitive international environment have any obligations to contribute to the global common good, he examined the problem in the light of the realist objection, which holds that in the case of non-repeated interactions and without signaling mechanisms, in the absence of a third-party authority than can enforce compliance with the principles of morality, individual agents – like corporations – have no moral obligations on the international level. The classical statement of this view, which Velasquez calls the traditional version of realism, is generally attributed to Hobbes: without a sovereign power that can force every man to behave civilly with each other, men are in the "state of nature", a state Hobbes characterizes as a "war of every man against every man" – and in such a state, moral terms have no meaning and moral obligations are nonexistent.

Velasquez derives from his analysis that it is not possible to make the claim that multinationals have a moral obligation to pursue the global common good, since if some multinationals decided to contribute to the common good in the highly competitive arena of globalization while the others refused to act likewise, the former would put themselves at a significant disadvantage, and this decision would negatively impact their profits. The reasoning would be different, he argues, if the interactions between multinationals were repeated, and if signaling mechanisms did exist, so that each player could be informed of the others' intent to cooperate; in that case, the players would mutually enforce their cooperative agreements, and no third-party enforcer would be needed. But in his view, these two conditions are not met, which leads him to the following conclusion (1992, p. 27):

> In the absence of an international enforcement agency, multinational corporations operating in a competitive international environment cannot be said to have a moral obligation to contribute to the international common good, provided that interactions are non-repetitive and provided effective signals of agent reliability are not possible.

He then logically utters a plea for the establishment of an international authority capable of ensuring that all agents contribute to the global common good: this is, he suggests, the necessary and sufficient condition so that moral obligations can legitimately be demanded from multinational corporations worldwide. However, there seem to be some weaknesses associated with the demonstration conducted by Velasquez, and with his conviction that a third-party enforcer will be powerful enough to drive all the economic agents toward the global common good. Three reasons cast doubt on the success of such an international institution intended for global decision-making. Let us examine them in turn.

First, only governments can create an international authority of that kind. But how can so many distinct governments agree to set up an international agency to regulate the supply and use of global public goods? Instead of supporting the establishment of a supranational entity devoted to this mission, it is rather likely that many States will choose to free-ride, and that they will thwart the others' efforts to find durable collective solutions to transnational problems, pressing though they may be (Kaul, Grunberg and Stern, 1999). The national interests involved are too remote from one another. Governments of the dominant countries (e.g. G7 or OECD countries) are very likely to defend their own business interests, to the detriment of the global common good – as evidenced by the WTO negotiations on the dismantling of agriculture subsidies or by the global warming issue. Conversely, less developed countries could agree to promote their own economic development exclusively, arguing that they see no reason why they should endure restraints on their industrialization process, since rich countries themselves did not endure any restraints during their lift-off stage. And if some of the rich countries decided to join their efforts with some of the poor countries to establish the agency, then the process would be thwarted by the free-rider problem, since the interests of the reluctant governments would merge with those of multinationals that are seeking competitive advantages over others, and that are ready to move to countries where they will not have to contribute to the common good. As a result, the creation of the agency might prove difficult.

But, and secondly, let us suppose the problems stated above have been solved, and this international authority dedicated to the global common good exists, with a large number if not all nations involved in it. How can we be sure that this agency will effectively serve the global common good and not distort its original mission? Can we be sure that a global entity of that kind will never become either a petrified and crippling bureaucracy, or the tyrannical instrument of a dangerous ideology, instead of being effective and responsive to the critical problems of the time? Since there would be no counter-power or control mechanism, and the agency would be run by human beings, a drift cannot be excluded. In particular, there is no guarantee that it will remain free from the multinationals' influence. Again, experience shows that large corporations are very efficient in protecting their vested interests, and that their lobbying efforts can be successful against laws designed to promote the common good. The American Congress in Washington, as well as the European Commission in Brussels, are literally besieged by a crowd of business lobbyists, quite skilful to influence official decisions in a way that meets their interests.

Last but not least, let us now assume this agency exists and effectively serves the global common good. How can we imagine that it will be able to force all agents to behave morally?

In fact, an agency of that kind exists already in the form of the United Nations, which was created, among other reasons, to promote and maintain peace among nations; but for more than fifty years, it has failed in many instances to put an end to international conflicts (though it has also been successful in some cases). Why should we then believe that the creation of a new institution will drive all agents to suddenly start to cooperate in a common search for the common good, as if by the wave of a magic wand? Besides, there are some reasons for doubting that it will ever be possible for any external authority to force all agents – whether an individual or a corporation – to behave morally. On the contrary, human history and all spiritual traditions provide reasons to believe that the only authority which can surely drive an individual to respect moral rules – including beyond the scope of laws – is an internal authority: his/her conscience, his/her *inner voice*.

This does not mean, however, that new global institutions are not needed. International law and supranational organizations are necessary to enforce rules for the global economy (Drucker, 1997). But *the pursuit of the common good is not only a matter of abiding by the laws; it also and essentially consists in a personal attitude, in a voluntary commitment, in a freely chosen ethics.* Therefore, there are serious reasons to believe that the fundamental motivation that will drive multinationals toward the global common good is the rising awareness of corporate leaders and managers, more than – and in parallel to – the hypothetical constraints imposed by a third-party. But there is no need to choose between these two motivations, the internal and the external; they are complimentary and mutually reinforcing.

So the establishment of a Hobbes-inspired sovereign authority might not be the unique solution. Therefore, *it seems more appropriate to consider that multinational corporations can voluntarily contribute their fair share to the global common good, and not only that they can, but also that they should do so*: we share this view with Fleming (1992) and some other authors. As a matter of fact, empirical studies extensively demonstrate that multinationals do not always act as a Hobbesian agent in the state of nature does. There are many examples of enlightened, wise corporate leaders, who pay attention to the demands of their multiple stakeholders, and who behave in ways that further the common good. The fast development of the corporate social responsibility (CSR) movement since the mid-1990s, illustrated by the mushrooming of business-led networks such as the Global Compact, the World Business Council for Sustainable Development (WBCSD), Business for Social Responsibility (BSR) in the US, or CSR Europe, arguably supports this assumption; and in the financial arena, the socially responsible investment (SRI) trend is also gaining momentum worldwide, as exemplified by the work of the UNEP Finance Initiative and the launch of the Principles for Responsible Investment (PRI) by Kofi Annan in April 2006.

I.2. Three Major Determinants

This section underlines three major determining factors that are likely
to drive corporations to take the global common good into account: the
deterioration of the biosphere, the rise of an anti-globalization sentiment,
and the necessity to invent a global social contract. In so far as these
factors have been extensively developed in another paper,[4] they will be
briefly summarized here.

First determinant: the biosphere, which is the physical basis of life,
is deteriorating at a rapid pace. In particular, *the global warming phenomenon is a major and growing cause of concern.* Global warming has many
effects, including the melting of glaciers and polar ice caps, the reduction
of ocean salinity, animal species losing their habitats, and an increasing
number of people trying to cope with the rise of the sea level. For more
than 15 years already, scientists from all around the world have worked
together within the Intergovernmental Panel on Climate Change, and
have reached a consensus: *climate change is a reality and it is caused by
human activities* (IPCC, 2007). The question is not about the *existence*
of global warming but about its *magnitude:* by the end of the twenty-first
century, will the average temperature at the surface of the Earth have risen
by 2°C, 4°C or 6°C? And what will be the regional variations?

Desertification, deforestation, the depletion of natural resources,
the pollution of soil, atmosphere, water, etc., are other facets of the environmental devastation. *Biodiversity is vanishing:* the expansion of human
activities is causing the destruction of ecosystems and the loss of species of wild flora and fauna at an extremely high rate (UNEP, 2005).
The "Millennium Ecosystem Assessment", a major UN Report released
in March 2005, confirms that 60% of the world's ecosystems are being
degraded by a variety of causes. It has concluded that *human activities
exert such a pressure on the natural functions of the Earth that the ability of ecosystems to support future generations is not guaranteed anymore.*

---

4   De Bettignies, H.-C. and F. Lépineux, "Can Multinational Corporations Afford to
     Ignore the Global Common Good?", *Business and Society Review*, forthcoming.

The economic activities of man have already caused irreparable damages to the Earth. *In many respects, thresholds of irreversibility have been crossed.* Should these activities stop at this point, or at least be markedly reduced, their enduring effects would continue to harm the environment for decades, due to the *inertia effect.*

But ecologically harmful activities, far from being reduced, are still increasing; quite logically, the negative ecological impact can't but worsen in proportion. According to Lovelock (2000, 2004), the Earth functions as one great life-sustaining organism; the atmosphere, the oceans, the land and all the species are components of a single complex system, wherein the biological processes of the Earth change environmental conditions in order to enable survival. Living matter is not passive in the face of threats to its existence; therefore, the damage human economic activities are causing to the integrity of the planet can't but entail defense reactions that will eventually backfire on humankind. *What is at stake today is nothing less than the very possibility for future generations to live on this planet in the long run.* Many signs suggest that the blind race for economic growth is *not sustainable* any more, and the time will come soon when *drastic revisions* will be unavoidable. Given the current state of the planet and the existing trends, it seems that we are now close to the point when not only political leaders, but also business leaders, will widely acknowledge that *the biosphere must be treated as an end in itself.* The only way to solve environmental plagues is to change our energy-intensive way of life into an *environmentally-friendly lifestyle;* in this regard, both consumers and corporations have a great role to play.

Second determinant: an anti-globalization sentiment has been loudly expressed over the past few years by protesters in Washington, Prague, Nice, Quebec, Genoa and elsewhere, since the December 1999 meeting of the WTO in Seattle. The constellation of social movements that protest in the streets are opposed to the *planetary extension of neo-liberal capitalism* pursuing short-term financial objectives through financial markets imposing their rules all over the planet. They express a revolt against a global economic system that they deem *unfair and destructive,* and which, they say, institutes the universal dictatorship of profit-maximization to satisfy the greed of shareholders and top executives. These campaigners are concerned with the global common good, with protecting human rights and the natural environment, and with social inequalities; they call for a greater corporate responsibility. Anti-globalists claim that instead of reducing poverty, globalization leads to the exclusion of millions of people who are unable to join the world economy, and to the marginalization of the world's poorest nations. *The gap between the North and the South continues to widen*: of a global population of more than 6 billion people, approximately one fifth, or 1.3 billion, live on less than $1 per day, and nearly half, or 2.8 billion, live on less than $2 per day. This means that in spite of decades of economic development, prosperity has not filtered down to the poorest, and that a situation of "economic apartheid" (Mofid, 2003) is prevailing both between and within countries.

Since economic globalization enhances the domination of less developed countries by rich nations and global firms, some authors consider it as a new form of *imperialism* (Petras and Weltmeyer, 2001). Moreover, detractors of global capitalism argue that its extension *undermines cultural diversity by eroding local cultures*. The alignment of lifestyles on the Western standard generates a threat to cultural identities. Globalization conveys a danger of uniformity: Ritzer (1996) speaks of "McDonaldization" to point at the homogenization of society throughout the world. The goods and services we buy or use, from petrol and crops to health and education, are increasingly provided or controlled by a small number of corporations; *this* "corporate takeover" *on many aspects of our lives endangers democracy* (Heertz, 2002). Critics of global capitalism reject a world in which corporations define the very vision of the good life, and in which the acquisition of wealth has replaced real human ends such as self-realization and the pursuit of happiness. They reject the primacy of the market over politics, the advent of a *market society*, and the extension of the market logic to every aspect of life, turning everything into a *commodity* that can be sold and bought.

Besides, this mounting anti-globalization sentiment *is not unconnected with the generalized bursting of violence* throughout the planet: in so far as globalization is viewed as conveying injustice, destroying communities and damaging the environment, it nurtures despair and violence on the side of those that are excluded and pushed to a withdrawn attitude centered on their cultural identity (Bauman, 1998). *The confrontation depicted by Barber (1995) between "Jihad" and "McWorld" is now widespread throughout the planet.* Terrorist groups are now included in the stakeholder list by some management scholars: Phillips (2003) conceives of them as "derivative stakeholders", capable of harming either the organization or its normative stakeholders. Corporations can certainly *try* to protect themselves against this peril, as many of them do for example in Saudi Arabia; but the cost is very high, in terms of security expenses, risk premiums, wage rises, etc. As a result, it is only through the integration of the global common good perspective in their operations and policies that corporations will be able to overcome this *ideological hostility*, and to pave the way for a *pacified development*, respectful of cultural identities and of human dignity.

The third determinant is of socio-political nature: *the social contract is being redesigned*, and new institutional devices are to be implemented, not only within nations, but also *on a worldwide scale. Globalization entails the moving up to the universal level.* The development of IT brings about major scientific, technological, economic and social change: it leads the world out of an era based on the use of energy – a material resource, into a new era based on the use of information – an immaterial resource (Robin, 1989). Technology has overcome distance, and the revolution in communications has created a global audience. *A planetary patriotism is appearing, through the rising awareness of a global community of destiny of mankind* (Morin and Kern, 1993). Nation-States, which were traditionally the guarantors of the common good, find themselves overwhelmed by the globalization process. Global economy has gradually escaped political control, and by an interesting turnaround, is now imposing restraints on government. A power shift has taken place: whereas the growth of global capitalism has induced a decline in the power of Nation-States over the past thirty years, global corporate power has risen dramatically.

The new reality of the global village questions the significance of national boundaries. The traditional conception of State sovereignty that has prevailed in Europe since the Treaty of Westphalia in 1648 is challenged by the relentless integration of the world economy, and by the fact that as more and more issues call for global solutions, the extent to which any State can act independently is diminishing. The very term "globalization" conveys the idea that we are moving out of the era of inter-national relations and that a new historical stage is beginning, in which new forms of global governance are to be developed. The rising number of transnational issues and problems has involved an increase in the levels of governance both within and across political boundaries, and undermines the relevance of territorially-based political decision-making. More sophisticated, developed systems of regional and global regulation are required so as to accomplish *the shift from national government to multilevel governance* (Held, 2004).

For an increasing number of problems, national policies, piecemeal approaches are inadequate; *new tools, new mechanisms are needed*. The nature of global problems such as poverty, climate change, the ozone hole, Aids, drug trafficking, etc., calls for new strategies and forms of action that go beyond traditional lines. In most cases, the provision of global common goods also requires *a linkage of the local, national, regional and global settings* – a view now widely held by political scientists. In order to be more effective, the provision of public goods requires *the collaboration of various actors*, belonging to the spheres of government, business or civil society. After the adoption of the Agenda 21 in 1992, the recent UNEP Annual Reports insist on the importance of such multi-actor collaborations to protect the environmental foundations on which human society stands and to promote sustainable development. Businesses and not-for-profit organizations (social sector and government) *need to develop partnerships to serve the global common good, and this collaboration can be fruitful for all the parties*: this idea is gaining audience (Sagawa and Segal, 1999).

To summarize, we see three major evolutions that are likely to induce multinational corporations to take the global common good into account: a) the imperative of the preservation of our biosphere; b) the rise of an anti-globalization sentiment with its potential consequences; and c) the necessity to design new mechanisms of global governance. Besides, *these three phenomena are interconnected, and this adds to the pressure on MNCs to change their policies and practices*. In particular, b) is partly fueled by a) and all the ecological disasters; among the growing number of issues that call for c), the environmental crisis and the widening planetary social gap are certainly critical; and it doesn't seem unreasonable to think that it is only by understanding c) that humankind will be able to match a).

II. Divergent Interpretations of the Common Good: Which Conception Should Business Be Concerned With?

This second part intends to analyze three different models of the common good that are prevailing today – and competing with each other. For that purpose, and in so far as the common good concept is widely ignored by management scholars, it will solicit the lights of three other disciplines: philosophy, Christian theology and economics. In a philosophical perspective, the issue of the common good – under different names – stands at the confluence of ethics and politics. We mention hereafter a few authors whose works seek to embrace the two dimensions of moral analysis and political thinking in a unified intention; their will to link together the questioning on the axiological foundations and the reflection on the organization of life in society seems especially appropriate, at a time when the two fields of ethics and politics tend to become separate and distinct spheres. More recently, theologians have developed the Christian interpretation of the "Common Good". Economists have also constructed a specific approach, concentrating on "public goods". *This interdisciplinary approach will help us understand three divergent interpretations of the common good on the global setting today: the teleological model, the utilitarian model, and the relational model.* These three conceptions of the common good will now be examined in turn.

II.1. The Teleological Model

The first model of the common good that will be presented here may be called "teleological" (or "perfectionist"), because it is based on *a teleological view on human nature*: some philosophers, and most religions in the world, do promote such a model (even if each spiritual tradition has its own approach). As we lack space to study a great number of religions, we will concentrate on the Christian doctrine only; but before that, we will say a few words about the philosophical conceptions of Plato and Aristotle.

According to Plato (2000), ethics and politics are subordinated to the theory of Ideas; the philosopher, having contemplated the beauty of Ideas, deduces from it the principles of ethics and the rules of politics. Plato's ethical thinking rests on the premise that men are fundamentally yearning for happiness, considered as the Supreme Good. The quest for happiness implies the knowledge of the Good, which determines access to a genuinely spiritual life and to the satisfactions that the contemplation of Ideas gives to the soul. Man must recognize himself as a spiritual being, aspiring to transcendence and to the Absolute. Those who do not know things in their intelligible essence, that is, in the light of the Good, are comparable to Plato's inhabitants of the cave who do not see tangible objects in daylight, but only the shadows of these objects in a semi-darkness, cast on the wall by a fire burning behind them; they remain prisoners of their delusions. Through this allegory, Plato means that it is necessary to go beyond the surface of things, and to pass the tangible appearances in perpetual change, in order to reach the timeless reality, the world of immutable ideas and the inner harmony of the soul.

Rising above sentient observation up to the Idea of the Good, the philosopher – according to Plato – is able to grasp the organization principle of the Universe; once he has understood it, he strives to realize its image in his own conduct, in his inner life and in the government of the City. Plato's politics are thus closely linked to his idealistic ethics: trying to build the ideal City, he aims at social harmony through the moral perfection of citizens. The finality of the State is *to make people better, to establish an order in which every citizen could have a share in the common good, lead a just and wise existence in so far as he is able to do so, and in which freedom would be ensured for those who deserve it.* But Plato's ideal City is ruled by a dominant class composed of philosophers, for in his view, only philosophers are able to govern; as a result, his republic is authoritarian by nature and tends to sacrifice the individual to the good of the State.

Similarly to Plato, Aristotle (2004) is convinced that politics, being the science of the City, are not separable from ethics; he also develops a *eudemonist* ethical doctrine, in which moral activity consists in the pursuit of happiness considered as the Supreme Good. All men aspire to happiness, which is the most desirable of all things, in so far as it is the end to which other ends are only means, and which is not itself a means to another end. Happiness is the perfect end, since it is always desirable *per se*, and never with a view to something else; Aristotle identifies happiness as the ultimate purpose of life, a state that perfects or fulfills the human being. But the two philosophers diverge at this point: Aristotle does not endorse the Platonic conception that hypostasizes the Good in general. By contrast, he seeks in the *praxis* the foundation of the ethical aim; in his view, the supreme good is realized in particular situations that are every time different. In Aristotle's philosophy, what brings happiness is the exercise and development of one's abilities, as long as they remain compatible with life in society. Happiness is not a matter of being, but a matter of doing. It flows from a reasonable activity in accordance with virtue.

Aristotle conceives virtue as a happy middle, as a central point on a line whose extremes are vices; virtue is always relative to a context, it is a particular balance corresponding to a specific situation. His ethics are realistic; for him, the virtuous man is one who keeps within bounds, who has a sense of moderation. In Aristotle's view, the aim of the City is happy life, which is identical to virtuous life; precisely, the real purpose of government must be to enable citizens to reach this full and happy life that he describes in his ethics. Being a "political animal", the individual cannot live harmoniously except in society, for happiness and self-actualization – as we will see later – are not to be found in isolation; a happy life necessarily rests on a social and political basis. More than with the absolute Good,

Aristotle is concerned with external conditions that enable man to be virtuous and happy; it is the problem of politics to create those conditions. Good government implies a constitution which looks after the interests of all citizens, and which can provide everyone with the opportunity to blossom while contributing to the happiness of the City.

Closer to us and in another perspective, Christian theology has also developed a teleological view of the common good. The Catholic social doctrine has been elaborated through a number of encyclicals and other papal documents over the whole 20th century; its origin dates back to 1891 when Pope Leo XIII promulgated *Rerum novarum*. This pioneering text has been commemorated by other encyclicals, which applied its spirit to more specific issues in accordance with the circumstances.[5] All these documents deal with the concept of the common good, which has been defined as follows by the Second Vatican Council:

> The overall conditions of life in society that allow the different groups and their members to achieve their own perfection more fully and more easily.

This definition differentiates and at the same time embraces the individual and the collective dimensions. Groups include any kinds of organizations, notably business organizations; and the phrase "the overall conditions" may suggest political as well as socioeconomic conditions. In the perspective of the Church's social magisterium, the common good, being the supreme good of the community, is also and inseparably the supreme good of the person: far from contrasting the two ideas of individual and society, the design of the common good considers them simultaneously; *it unites in a single intention the person with the community*. For the person assumes its responsibility toward others only by serving the community, and by contributing to the construction of a more equitable

---

5   *Quadragesimmo Anno* by Pius XI in 1931 (for the fortieth anniversary of *Rerum Novarum*); *Mater et Magistra* by John XXIII in 1961; *Populorum Progressio* by Paul VI in 1967; *Laborem Exercens* by John Paul II in 1981 (for the ninetieth anniversary, on human work); *Sollicitudo rei socialis* in 1987 (on the development of individuals and peoples) – and *Centesimus Annus* in 1991 for the centenary, still by John Paul II.

and more human society; conversely, the community doesn't represent an end in itself, but its finality resides in this, that it enables the persons to develop their talents and to blossom.

The Church's social teaching is above all interested in the individual person, considered as a social and spiritual being; it focuses on the integral human development of each individual. This implies that individual persons should not be considered as parts or elements within society, or as instruments for other ends: they are ends in themselves, and the fulfillment of each person as a person remains the ultimate aim of the common good (Maritain, 1966). However, the integral human development of each person is interlaced with the good of others, and the individual person's fulfillment follows from participation in the common good. Alford and Naughton (2001) insist on this dimension of shared ends (p. 41):

> Historically, a common good is considered to be a human perfection or fulfillment achievable by a community, such that the community's members all share it, both as a community, and singly, in their persons. A common good, then, is neither a mere amalgam of private and particular goods nor is it a good of the whole that disregards the good of its members.

Besides, *the common good is at once material and spiritual.* It is spiritual in so far as it aims, at its highest point, the accomplishment of the divine nature of man; that is why St Thomas Aquinas (2000), with many other theologians, asserts that man can only find full happiness in God, as human fulfillment resides in the union with God. But the common good also includes the material – or temporal – dimension: it comprises the economic, social and physical conditions necessary to lead a virtuous life and to tend toward that spiritual accomplishment. And the search for the common good on the material level itself will only be fruitful if it is inspired by a spirit of justice, solidarity and truth that is ultimately rooted in the spiritual level. The purpose of the common good is thus universal in its essence, and it definitely stands apart from the classical, dualistic oppositions between individual and society on the one hand, and between the material level and the spiritual level on the other.

Finally, it seems useful to insist on the fact that the Christian theological approach of the common good *calls on all human groups – including business organizations – to contribute to the good of the community and to reach their own perfection*. The word perfection makes sense for all men, whatever their tradition and culture, believers and non-believers alike; and the theory of the common good is accessible to all, which means that it is a truly universal theory. It is no surprise then if the Christian theological interpretation echoes other spiritual traditions that have developed their own reflections on human fulfillment and perfection; *the common good concept has equivalents in other cultural contexts*, and even if the words differ, other traditions (from the East or from the West) can bring their own contribution to the understanding of its nature. For instance Yamaji (1997) explains how the implementation of a *kyosei* approach in the management of Canon has been the source of a significant competitive advantage for the company and of progress for society as a whole.[6]

II.2. The Utilitarian Model

Another model of the common good that can be identified today is the "utilitarian" (or "welfarist") model: it envisions the common good as *a welfare function maximizing individual preferences*. With their own approach, utilitarian philosophers have strived to interweave ethical and political considerations. Founded by Bentham in the 18th century and further developed by John Stuart Mill in the 19th century, utilitarianism – a doctrine based on the principle of utility – aims at *the greatest good for the greatest number*. All that counts here is the sum total of satisfactions obtained in society as a whole; the purpose of the greatest good for the greatest number of individuals should serve as a basis for government. Hence, it is necessary to balance the satisfactions and dissatisfactions of the various individuals who compose society, in order to reach the greatest possible good in total. This theory of maximum contentment extends to society the choice of individuals, and posits that social harmony stems

6   The Japanese term *kyosei* was popularized by Ryuzaburo Kaku (1997), chairman
     of Canon Inc., to describe the purpose of this company.

from an arithmetic of pleasure and enjoyment. But *the conception of the common good conveyed by utilitarianism is a reductive and simplistic one.* The common good is considered here as an aggregate of the utilities of each member of a society; following Bentham's view, it would boil down to the sum total of the pleasures of all individuals, minus the sum total of their pains ....

Quite logically, the utilitarian doctrine has been criticized by a number of philosophers. Firstly, because it does not care about the well-being of each individual; it takes only into account a general, collective well-being, but takes no interest in the individual as a person. Secondly, it is not concerned with the quality of satisfaction, but only with the maximum amount of contentment, and with the usefulness of things regarding this quantitative goal. But it lacks instruments to measure utility; besides, the meaning of human life does not reside in the accumulation of quantitative satisfactions. Such an orientation may lead to the exclusion of important dimensions of life such as culture, spirituality, rights and duties for instance – and more generally of all that is not apparently useful. Thirdly, when applied to the organizational context, this doctrine has been criticized for failing to identify all the stakeholders of a given company. *Therefore, when referring to utilitarian theory, it seems more appropriate to speak of a common interest than of a common good, since society is considered here as a conglomeration of individuals, as an abstract social order.*

If we now consider the economic approach of the common good concept, the political economy debate on this issue can be traced back to Adam Smith (1998/1776), who stated in *The Wealth of Nations* that the invisible hand of the market transforms the self-interest of many individuals into the common good. A profuse branch of economics called *welfare economics* has flourished since then. In the recent decades, it has developed a modern interpretation of the common good based on the criterion of *Pareto optimality:* a situation is said to be Pareto optimal if there is no feasible alternative that makes everyone better off. In other words, if in a situation B all agents except one are better off than in a situation A while one agent is worse off, then situation B is not Pareto-optimal. Which does not mean that situation A is Pareto-optimal either;

there could exist a situation C, in which all agents without exception would be better off than in situation A, or in which at least one agent would be better off than in situation A while all the others would see their endowments unchanged; and if no situation is superior to situation C according to this same criterion, then it can be said that situation C is Pareto-optimal. Hence, Pareto optimality is an ethical criterion requiring that all exchanges should be made which can make at least one agent better off without at the same time harming another.

Much of the reflections of welfare economics rely on the fact that competitive markets are not always capable of ensuring the best allocations with regard to this criterion of Pareto optimality. There are many cases of goods and services that are not efficiently allocated by markets: national defense, basic scientific research, clean air and water, or lighthouses, for instance. These goods have come to be known as *public goods* or *collective goods*; they are characterized by the fact that, contrary to private goods, they are not used up in the process of being consumed or utilized as an input in a production process by a given agent: the consumption possibilities of the other agents are not affected. The consumption benefits of any one individual do not depend on the benefits enjoyed by others: simply put, "more for you means no less for me". This property is usually referred to as non-rivalry in consumption. The fact that these goods are not used up in the process of consumption – and consequently that the marginal cost of extending provision to additional users is zero – is itself sufficient to generate what economists call a *market failure*, as public goods create a conflict between the maximizing behavior of individual agents and the attainment of a Pareto-efficient allocation of social resources.

Markets fail for one fundamental reason: whereas a cooperative behavior between agents is often required for beneficial trading, the market mechanism cannot force them to cooperate, thus resulting in inefficient outcomes. The essence of the market failure problem has been captured in the well-known game of the Prisoner's Dilemma, which represents two individuals who fail to cooperate even when cooperation is in their joint interest. The game can be modeled in various ways and has been used to illustrate a number of situations, but in a *non-repeated* game the conclusion remains the same: since non-cooperation is the dominant strategy for both rational, self-seeking, utility-maximizing players, the end result is worse for each of them than if they cooperated. Yet both players would prefer the cooperative outcome to this result. But no one will play cooperatively, for fear of suffering large losses if the other player doesn't.

A host of game theorists have tried to identify the necessary conditions for voluntary cooperative behavior to emerge in repeated Prisoner's Dilemma games; under certain assumptions, they have reached a positive conclusion. But the smaller the number of iterations, and the greater the number of players, the more non-cooperation is likely to be the outcome of the game. Therefore, the Prisoner's Dilemma may be viewed as a generic model of strategic interactions in a market economy: *just as the players in the game lack the means to enforce the cooperative solution, the market mechanism fails to ensure cooperative behavior among economic agents when they have an incentive to act independently*. It provides a striking illustration of the tension that exists between individual interests and the common good.

In sum, the economic analysis of market failures challenges the "invisible hand" model: in many instances, the behavior of everyone-pursuing-his/her-own-interest produces a result for everyone worse than would have produced a cooperative behavior. *This means that the common good is not automatically attained when all agents pursue their own interest, and that cooperation among them is often required to reach efficient social outcomes; this cooperation can be either imposed by a superior authority such as the hand of government, or freely implemented by economic agents – such as corporations – themselves.*

II.3. The Relational Model

The last model of the common good that we will present here is the "relational" (or "deliberative") model, which views the common good as *a set of shared responsibilities*. Many contemporary thinkers or philosophers could be mentioned to illustrate this approach; we have selected three of them – Rawls, Ricœur and Misrahi.

Rawls' book *A Theory of Justice* (1999/1971) is indivisibly a work of ethics and political thinking; it underlines that political principles require moral foundations. Taking as a starting point the principle of justice, Rawls is particularly interested in the issue of the distribution of social advantages and the allocation of rights and liberties. Justice is for him the first virtue of social institutions: he postulates that socioeconomic inequalities are just if they produce, to compensate, advantages for everyone *and* if they are beneficial to the least favored individuals. There is no injustice in the fact that a small number of people obtain advantages above the average, as long as the situation of the underprivileged is improved. *He aims at mutual advantage of social actors through a system of cooperation, and proposes a new social contract between free and rational persons.*

Rawls adopts a deontological framework, excluding the reference to a Supreme Good; he moves away from the Greek tradition and particularly from Aristotle, who develops a teleological, finality-oriented perspective. Rawls does not place the emphasis on the good, but on the *just*, or the *fair*. Nevertheless the good is not completely absent in his doctrine, for if the concept of justice comes before the concept of the good, the first eventually integrates the second: there is congruence between justice and the good. *Just devices contribute to the good of the citizens, and happiness is to be found in a just collective activity.* Rawls' contractualist doctrine is rooted in an ethical reflection; he attempts to elaborate a systematic conception of justice, placed under the sign of Kant. Like Kant, Rawls cares about persons, and presents the principles of justice as analogous to categorical imperatives; in his theory, political principles are grounded in moral principles.

After Rawls, and echoing his concern for persons and for justice, Ricœur (1990) is also concerned by the common good. He is interested in the will to live together, and in the desire of the good life which animates everyone. He defines as follows what he calls the "ethical aim" (p. 202): "The aim of the 'good life' with and for others within just institutions."

The concept of the "ethical aim" thus comprises three components. The "good life" is the very object of the ethical aim. Whatever image one has of an accomplished life, it is the ultimate achievement of one's efforts. "With and for others": Ricœur stresses the importance of solicitude, of caring about others. He points at the intrinsic value of all human beings which renders each person irreplaceable in our affection, and which reveals by a mirror effect the irreplaceable value of our own life. *One cannot esteem oneself without esteeming the other as oneself*, that is, without recognizing that the other also is able to undertake something in the world, to prioritize his/her preferences, to value the goals of his/her actions – and in so doing, to esteem him/herself as one esteems oneself. Therefore, the esteem of the other as oneself is equivalent to the esteem of oneself as the other. "In just institutions": the aim of the good life embraces the sense of justice, which is not limited to interpersonal relationships, but extends to the life of institutions. By institution, Ricœur understands the structure of the living-together in a historical community (a nation or a people for instance). By justice, he understands a virtue that conveys a demand for equality; in his view, *equality is the ethical content of the sense of justice*. Justice adds to solicitude, since the range of application of the concept of equality extends to the whole of humanity. Ricœur thereby ensures the transition between the interpersonal level and the societal level, between ethics and politics.

Similarly to Rawls and Ricœur, Misrahi (1983, 1997) is concerned with the fairness of institutions, and points at the quality of a fully human life, at the unification of man recovering peace with himself. The search for happiness, says Misrahi, provides the content, indeed the core of ethics. Beyond pleasure and joy, happiness regards the whole of life, and aims at the unified nature of an active project in the world; the pursuit of happiness rests on the personal will to build a free and responsible life, whereby the exercise of one's profession turns into a meaningful and gratifying activity. Misrahi also stresses the importance of establishing substantial relations to others and to the world: *it is by a constructive design that the individual gets organized and fulfils himself, within a network of social relationships*. Thus, happiness is to be invented by each individual, and is always formed by a freely chosen synthesis of freedom, plenitude and meaning.

But if ethics recommends the construction of happiness, according to Misrahi, it must also say where the obstacles to happiness reside, and so devise the means to fight social misfortune and the pain deriving from institutions. Ethical reflection leads to the institutional problem of the best society. Ethics necessarily have political prolongations: ethics as a quest for happiness for all individuals is the foundation of politics. *There is a need to elaborate an organization of society that corresponds at best to the search for happiness, making it possible for everyone.* Misrahi looks for a convergence between the end – the construction of happiness – and the means – the political regime and the socioeconomic system: the former and the latter are closely intertwined.

To conclude this interdisciplinary – and necessarily selective – presentation, it appears that the three disciplines – philosophy, Christian theology and economics – that have been mobilized *provide divergent interpretations of the common good concept.* Three main models have been examined: the first one, *the teleological model,* refers to Plato, Aristotle, and the Catholic social teaching; the second one, *the utilitarian model,* is based on the ideas of Bentham, Stuart Mill and the branch of welfare economics; and the third one, *the relational model,* is grounded in the works of contemporary philosophers such as Rawls, Ricœur or Misrahi. In other words, in the second part of this chapter, we have developed what could be called *a pluralist view of the common good,* which at least partly reflects the different approaches of this notion that exist in the contemporary world – be they philosophical, economic or religious – and that are often conflicting which each other. Bearing in mind that the purpose of this study is to explore the relationship between business and the global common good, a question eventually arises: *which conception of the common good should business be concerned with in the globalization context?*

Whereas the first part of this chapter has identified some fundamental arguments accounting for the fact that businesses (especially multinational corporations) could – indeed, should – turn their attention towards the global common good, the second part, through the confrontation of the three models of the common good that have been analyzed, ends with a difficult question; it seems that another study would be required to tackle it in greater detail. In this chapter, however, our intention was not to answer this question, but *to bring it out, to shed light on it.* This being said, we can nevertheless try to discover some clues that could contribute to the solution:

a) The major risk associated with the teleological model of the common good is that it can generate a fundamentalist conception of the good society, or an authoritarian praxis – as it is the case in Plato's philosophy (according to which the City should be governed by the sages), or in the real world and closer to us, in theocratic political regimes such as Iran. Therefore, this model is intrinsically dangerous.

b) The utilitarian model is dangerous as well: it is the drive behind the neo-liberal vision of globalization, and it determines the utility-maximizing behavior of individualist economic agents that are eager to reap maximum profits in the short term, whatever the consequences. In this perspective, the common good is instrumentalized according to the preferences of the most powerful groups in society.

c) Contrary to the two others, the relational model doesn't seem to convey any danger: as it broadly considers the common good as a set of shared responsibilities without defining a priori and precisely the concept, its potential for conflict seems limited. Here the global common good is approached and discussed through a process of intercultural and inter-spiritual learning and deliberation; it is only after this process that a possible consensus could emerge regarding the definition and its consequences. Of course this model works only if all participants accept the logic of dialogue, which is not guaranteed at all; besides, the will to seek a consensus entails the risk that the common good can be completely emptied of its substance. However, the recent creation of new concepts such as "transnational democracy" or "global civil society" is in line with this model. And we can legitimately suggest that this model is also the most appropriate for business to consider in the globalization context, as it is consistent with the stakeholder theory literature in general and with the stream of research dealing with corporate citizenship in particular. Besides, it echoes the third determinant (the redesigning of the social contract) that has been examined previously.

Conclusion

There are some crucial reasons why corporations should nowadays be concerned about the common good, probably more than ever before in history. Whereas the common good was traditionally the prerogative of the States, this is not true anymore: other actors such as international institutions, businesses, NGOs or civic constituencies, are becoming co-responsible with governments for seeking the global common good. In this regard, multinational corporations – and companies of all kinds – have a great role to play: given the extent of their economic and social power, the global social contract – now called for by the advent of the new era – cannot be established without their active participation, and without their willingness to cooperate with other actors. Conversely, as long as this global social contract has not been set up, they will suffer a lack of legitimacy and understanding of their role by governments and civil society, and run the risk that hostile steps be taken against them. More generally, it may be said that by its very activity, business is in permanent interaction with society; and society cannot be maintained without a strong concern for the common good. Therefore, business and the common good are interdependent.

An important aspect of the relationship between international business and the global common good derives from the fact that globalization calls for a global business ethics. As global economic integration and the progress of information technology foster the emergence of a single world community, we urgently need to take a global ethical viewpoint. We need to develop the ethical foundations of the coming era (Kung, 1997; Swidler, 1999; Booth, Dunne and Cox, 2001; Singer, 2002; Morin, 2004). Beyond cultural differences, there is a growing need for a set of shared principles, rules and standards of behavior in the international business arena. Even if moral divergences, which are logical expressions of cultural diversity, can be observed among nations, much research speaks in favor of the possibility of a unified set of core principles: conceptions and practices of business ethics around the globe tend to overlap one another and to converge around some basic rules and standards (beyond the Universal Declaration of Human Rights and the UN Global Compact's 10 Principles). The interfaith declaration of the Parliament of the World's Religions in 1993, entitled *Toward a Global Ethic* (Kung and Kuschel, 1993), as well as the *Principles for Business* issued in 1994 by the Caux Round Table, which combine Eastern and Western views, the *Global Sullivan Principles* elaborated in 1999 with the participation of several corporations, and the *OECD Guidelines for Multinational Enterprises* revised in 2000, lend support to the convergence thesis and to the global ethics hypothesis.

The applied ethicist Peter Singer, as he illustrates how the globalization process creates one atmosphere, one economy, one law and one community, makes explicit that globalization alters the material basis of life by establishing "interconnectedness" as a new reality, and foresees the ethical consequences of this alteration (Singer, 2002, pp. 12–13):

> Our newly interdependent global society, with its remarkable possibilities for linking people around the planet, gives us the material basis for a new ethic. [...] How well we come through the era of globalization (perhaps whether we come through it at all) will depend on how we respond ethically to the idea that we live in one world.

In a similar vein, Donaldson and Dunfee (1994, 1999), defending a pluralistic view of business ethics that lies in the middle of the relativism/universalism continuum, explore the concept of "hypernorms", i.e. overriding principles which limit the "moral free space" of all social actors (1999, p. 50):

> Hypernorms constitute principles so fundamental that, by definition, they serve as "second-order" norms by which lower order norms are to be judged. Defined in this way and reflecting the deepest sources of human ethical experience, hypernorms are discoverable, we have reason to hope, in a convergence of religious, political and philosophical thought.

The authors of *Ties That Bind* draw a distinction between three categories of universal principles: procedural hypernorms, that specify and protect the rights of voice and exit within communities; substantive hypernorms, relating to the respect of human dignity and dealing with workplace safety or gender discrimination for instance; and structural hypernorms, that are necessary for political and social organization, such as property rights or "necessary social efficiency", aimed at providing basic social goods to all people. The authors do not, however – and for good reasons – delineate a list of these principles; they only present a list of sources and foundations – but this set is rather heterogeneous, and they acknowledge that they don't tackle the issue of the source of these sources.

Thus, relevant as the distinction made by Donaldson and Dunfee between far-reaching hypernorms and community-related norms may be, the question of the ultimate justification remains open. Now, *the concept of global common good is universal by nature; therefore, it could represent an adequate foundation for a global business ethics.* Eastern cultures, such as, for instance, the Japanese culture that has developed the *kyosei* approach, could recognize the validity of this foundation: the word *kyosei* can be roughly translated as "working and living for the common good". The search for perfection and fulfillment of both persons and communities conveyed by the common good concept echoes the fundamental values of all civilizations. The common good may be considered as a *mediating concept* between the core principles of various traditions; it makes it possible to discover correspondences among diverse norms generated within different cultures. Therefore, it seems that *the concept of global common good is a good candidate to occupy the third level in the hierarchy of ethical norms, the level of the ultimate justification; it provides a solid foundation for the elaboration of universal principles of business ethics, which themselves override community-based norms.*

References

Alford, H. and Naughton, M., 2001, *Managing as if Faith Mattered. Christian Social Principles in the Modern Organization*, Notre Dame: University of Notre Dame Press.

Aristotle, 2004, *The Nichomachean Ethics*, London: Penguin Books.

Barber, B., 1995, *Jihad vs. McWorld: How Globalism and Tribalism are Reshaping the World*, New York: Times Books.

Bauman, Z., 1998, *Globalization – The Human Consequences*, London: Polity Press and Blackwell Publishers.

Booth, K., Dunne, T. and Cox, M., eds, 2001, *How Might We Live? Global Ethics in the New Century*, Cambridge: Cambridge University Press.

Donaldson, T. and Dunfee, T., 1994, "Toward a Unified Conception of Business Ethics: Integrative Social Contracts Theory", *Academy of Management Review*, Vol. 19, n°2.

——and ——1999, *Ties that Bind – A Social Contracts Approach to Business Ethics*, Boston: Harvard Business School Press.

Drucker, P., 1997, "The Global Economy and the Nation-State", *Foreign Affairs*, Vol. 76, n°5, pp. 159–71.

Fleming, J., 1992, "Alternative Approaches and Assumptions: Comments on Manuel Velasquez", *Business Ethics Quarterly*, Vol. 2, n°1, pp. 41–3.

Heertz, N., 2002, *The Silent Takeover – Global Capitalism and the Death of Democracy*, London: Arrow Books.

Held, D., 2004, "Becoming Cosmopolitan: The Dimensions and Challenges of Globalization", in P. Heslam, ed., *Globalization and the Good*, London: Society for Promoting Christian Knowledge.

——and Mcgrew, A., 2002, *Globalism/Anti-globalism*, Cambridge: Polity Press.

Intergovernmental Panel on Climate Change, 2007, *Fourth Assessment Report*, IPCC.

Kaku, R., 1997, "The Path of Kyosei", *Harvard Business Review*, Vol. 75, n°4, pp. 55–63.

Kaul, I., Grunberg, I. and Stern, M., eds, 1999, *Global Public Goods: International Cooperation in the Twenty-First Century*, Oxford: Oxford University Press.

Kung, H., 1997, "A Global Ethic in an Age of Globalization", *Business Ethics Quarterly*, Vol. 7, n°3, pp. 17–32.

—— and Kuschel, K., eds, 1993, *A Global Ethic – The Declaration of the Parliament of the World's Religions*, London and New York.

Lovelock, J., 2000, *Gaia: A New Look at Life on Earth*, Oxford: Oxford University Press.

—— 2004, *The Ages of Gaia*, Oxford: Oxford University Press.

Maritain, J., 1966, *The Person and the Common Good*, Notre Dame: University of Notre Dame Press.

Misrahi, R., 1983, *Traité du Bonheur*, Paris: Editions du Seuil.

—— 1997, *Qu'est-ce que l'éthique*, Paris: Armand Colin.

Mofid, K., 2003, *Globalization for the Common Good*, London: Shepheard-Walwyn Publishers.

Morin, E., 2004, *La Méthode 6. Ethique*, Paris: Editions du Seuil.

—— and Kern, A.B., 1993, *Terre-Patrie*, Paris: Editions du Seuil.

Petras, J. and Weltmeyer, H., 2001, *Globalization Unmasked: Imperialism in the Twenty First Century*, London: Zed Books.

Petrella, R., 1996, *Le Bien Commun. Eloge de la Solidarité*, Brussels: Labor.

Phillips, R.A., 2003, *Stakeholder Theory and Organizational Ethics*, San Francisco: Berrett-Koehler.

Plato, 2000, *The Republic*, Cambridge: Cambridge University Press.

Rawls, J., 1999 (1st ed. 1971), *A Theory of Justice*, Oxford: Oxford University Press.

Ricoeur, P., 1990, *Soi-même comme un autre*, Paris: Editions du Seuil.

Ritzer, G., 1996, *The McDonaldization of Society*, Thousand Oaks: Pine Forge.

Robin, J., 1989, *Changer d'ère*, Paris: Editions du Seuil.

St Thomas Aquinas, 2000, *Summa Theologica*, Notre Dame: Christian Classics.

Sagawa, S. and Segal, E., 1999, *Common Interest, Common Good: Creating Value Through Business and Social Sector Partnerships*, Boston: Harvard Business School Press.

Singer, P., 2002, *One World: The Ethics of Globalization*, New Haven: Yale University Press.

Smith, A., 1998 (1st ed. 1776), *The Wealth of Nations*, Oxford: Oxford University Press.

Swidler, L., ed., 1999, *For All Life – Toward a Universal Declaration of a Global Ethic*, Ashland: White Cloud Press.

United Nations, 2005, *Millennium Ecosystem Assessment General Synthesis Report*, UN.

United Nations Environment Programme, 2005, *2004 Annual Report*, UNEP.

Velasquez, M., 1992, "International Business, Morality, and the Common Good", *Business Ethics Quarterly*, Vol. 2, n°1, pp. 27–40.

Yamaji, K., 1997, "A Global Perspective of Ethics in Business", *Business Ethics Quarterly*, Vol. 7, n°3, pp. 55–70.

CHAPTER 2

Corporate Social Responsibility and Common Good

HELEN ALFORD AND YULIYA SHCHERBININA

> – Cheshire Puss, asked Alice, – Would you tell me, please,
> which way I ought to go from here?
> – That depends a good deal on where you want to go.
> – I don't much care where.
> – Then it doesn't matter which way you go.
>
> — LEWIS CARROLL, *Alice's Adventures in Wonderland*

Introduction

In his *Comment on the Doctrine of Social Responsibility* (1972) D. Votaw writes that "corporate social responsibility means something, but not always the same thing to everybody. To some it conveys the idea of legal responsibility or liability; to others, it means socially responsible behavior in the ethical sense; to still others, the meaning transmitted is that of 'responsible for' in a casual mode; many simply equate it with a charitable contribution; some take it to mean socially conscious; many of those who embrace it most fervently see it as a mere synonym for legitimacy in the context of belonging or being proper or valid; a few see a sort of fiduciary duty imposing higher standards of behavior on businessman than on citizens at large" (p. 25). More than thirty years later the situation has not been simplified but on the contrary overloaded with new theories, approaches and concepts. These new arrivals are usually justified by the necessity to clear up the field of the debate but often the real reason is nothing but marketing efforts to better "sell" the CSR idea. In the face of such a proliferation of terminology (CSR, stakeholders approach, sustainability, durability, social performance, social responsiveness, corporate citizenship among the most popular but this list is not exhaustive) and the mushrooming of the various positions (from that of *The Economist*, 2005 to those of the NGOs), an instinctive Alice-like question arises: where do we want to go from here?

Some scholars have tried to clarify the situation by setting different classifications of CSR (Frederick, 1987) or "mapping the territory" of CSR theories (Garriga, Melé, 2004). Others have sought to simplify the field by getting rid of the "failed" concept of CSR, insisting on the definitional and normative superiority of other terms, such as corporate citizenship (Whitehouse, 2003) or stakeholder theory (Siebens, 2006). While such endeavors contribute to the further development of thinking on CSR, they do not seem to resolve the main problem, marking time rather than making any real breakthrough. A quite different attempt has been made by Wheeler, Colbert and Freeman (2003). They try to reconcile the three most widely-used concepts – CSR, sustainable development and the stakeholder approach – into a hierarchic pyramid built on the idea of value creation. Despite the ambiguity in determining what counts as value, a problem recognized by the authors themselves, this attempt is the fruit of an important intuition: there is something that can underpin and bind together the different concepts in the field that have been produced during the half-century of academic reflection on CSR.

We agree that CSR and its related terms (corporate citizenship, sustainability, stakeholder approach) are in need of a fundamental idea to root them and integrate them (Davies, 2003). These various concepts seem to grasp different aspects of the foundational idea, that is, of business participation in the good living of the society, or, in words of the Thomistic personalist tradition we would like to present here, of business participation in the common good. Thus, what this paper aims to do is not to go *around* sketching out the boundaries and limits of the CSR discussion field but to go *deeper*, down into the idea underpinning CSR, the idea of the common good. This permits us to do two things: firstly, to offer solid normative foundations for the concept of CSR and secondly, to provide an integrative ground for some interwoven concepts, such as CSR, sustainability, citizenship and the stakeholder approach.

1. Some General Premises

Going deeper into the idea of the common good will require us to adopt two important interrelated premises. The first relates to the image of the company, while the second concerns the anthropological vision presupposed. Modern liberalism offers us basically two images of what business is about. The first one sees the enterprise as "a piece of property" that must render the maximum profit to the owners. Profit-maximization is the only guiding principle and value judgment criteria for those who manage this property, be they managers or owners. In this model of business as "a profit-machine", human beings are but a piece of the mechanism, alongside other company assets, designed to serve the maximization of shareholder value. The other model sees business as "a nexus of contracts" between different groups of people: employees, customers, owners, managers, suppliers etc. The final products of an enterprise are a result of agreements between these groups, and a company itself is nothing more than a mere place of negotiating and trade-offs between competing interests or, thanks to Freeman's initiative, stakes. Such an approach presupposes an extremely individualistic anthropological vision where people are linked primarily (if not exclusively!) by relationships of competition and rivalry, excluding the possibility of creating a community.

If the first model presents an enterprise as "a society of shares", the second makes of it "a society of interests" (Naughton, 2006), and neither of the two recognize that by working together people may form a "community of work" aimed at the common good, and in which individual rights and identity are not destroyed. But before going further, we should deal with an objection: one could argue that the common good may be a good idea for the spheres of activity in which it was developed – politics, philosophy, theology or law – but is it applicable to business? Does an enterprise have features that make it a community in relation to the common good in an analogous way to the traditionally accepted communities of state or the family? In his *Philosophy of Democratic Government* Yves Simon (1951) suggests three criteria that make a community a relevant actor in the creation of the common good: collective causality, communion in immanent actions, and communion-causing communication (pp. 64–6). Do we see these in the business? Business consists of decisions taken and activity pursued together in order to create products or services. It is usually practically impossible to attribute to any particular member of a company the entire responsibility for a decision or activity, as might be possible in the case of craftsmen or work done by artisans. The direct act of producing may not involve all the members of the company; but it still remains the act of the whole company for it is always supported by human resources, marketing, logistics etc. indirectly. Collective causality, thus, is a typical feature of modern companies.

Working in common is possible because people in a business usually know why they are gathered together and what the objectives of their cooperative actions are, and can then strive to achieve these goals. Knowledge of the same object and desire to achieve it can be called "immanent action" in philosophy. Furthermore, there should be a kind of "fabric of sharing" of this knowledge and desire with others, of trusting that others know and want the same thing and are willing to cooperate in its achievement. In other words, there needs to be a minimum of social capital, otherwise no enterprise could survive. Finally, coordination and cooperation at work is unthinkable without communication. Modern business literature is weighed down with advice on how to build efficient communication that build up team spirit, corporate identity and unity. Thus, we may say that a modern enterprise corresponds to all the three criteria that make it responsible for the common good promotion.

Before we turn to the closer analysis of what common good precisely means, let us note that its idea is inherent to a personalist understanding of the human being. In fact, in the Thomistic personalist tradition the idea of the common good flows naturally from the understanding of human nature as essentially relational.[1] J. Maritain (1948), one of the main proponents of the Catholic personalism, gives two reasons for our relationality:

> [...] first, because of its very perfections, as person, and its inner urge to the communications of knowledge and love which require relationship with other persons. In its radical generosity, the human person tends to overflow into social communications in response to the law of superabundance inscribed in the depths of being, life, intelligence and love. It does so secondly because of its needs or deficiencies, which derive from its material individuality. In this respect, unless it is integrated in a body of social communications, it cannot attain the fullness of its life and accomplishment (pp. 37–8).

There are two important moments to be highlighted in this passage. Firstly, the importance of relationality is underlined by the order of the given reasons, where the need to share and to grow in knowledge and love with others precedes the biological needs and material deficiencies.[2]

---

1 In this key see how P. Koslowski links the critical position of renouncing the concept of the common good to a Protestant tradition of the inability of the sinner to do good things, and, at a deeper level, to different anthropological visions (including the conception of original sin) (Koslowski, 2004).

2 This seems to be confirmed from other areas of knowledge. For instance, Lewis Mumford in *Technics and Civilisation*, argues that early human beings developed technical equipment more because of the overabundant psychic energy and capacity that they wanted to use, even if they were also driven by physical need. He argues that this is demonstrated by the fact that human artifacts such as dance, ritual and imagery are far more advanced amongst early human groups than are their tools, precisely because the former are more important in relating and communicating. Similarly, modern research on the link between economic wealth and happiness tends to show that at after a relatively low level of income has been reached, happiness starts to decline as income increases. One of the most plausible theories for explaining this is that at a certain point, we start to buy things that in the past we would have obtained through relationships with others, and, since it is primarily the relationships that make us happy, when we start to substitute things for relationships, our level of happiness starts to decline. For more on the relationship deprivation as a serious obstacle to human well-being see Frey and Stutzer, 2002; Bruni, 2004; Bruni and Porta, 2005.

Secondly, it is accentuated by the immanent presence of such an urge. While the second aspect of relationality relates to physical needs which disappear once they have been fulfilled, at least temporarily, the first aspect is never exhausted, revealing the depths of the richness of being and goodness to be communicated and its ontological characteristic. And since it is connatural to the human being to search for happiness in relation with others, the context of the common good is essential for acting, living, and especially working together for it occupies a large part of our active time.[3]

2. Developing the Idea of the Common Good

The definition of the common good that we introduce here emerges from the Aristotelian-Thomistic tradition, and has been carried forward into our own day through the tradition of Catholic social thought (Alford and Naughton, 2001; Melé, 2002). Firstly, we need to say something about the idea of "good". What is "good", or "a good"? In this tradition,

---

3   Such an anthropological vision is very different from the individualistic idea, where, to put it crudely, relationships are based on mutually convenient agreements and contracts for the sake of avoiding a permanent state of war among competing interests and rights. It has been pointed out to us that modern sociological reality suggests much easier that a human being is moved by purely egoistic interest than that the common good idea flows from our natural capacity to operate for the common good. It is easy to reject such an approach as "idealistic" or naïve. But if then, one is consistent with such a "realistic" observation of the pure natural egoism of human beings, it will bring him to describe a society which does not exist in reality, and even if it does, it would be condemned by everyone. As Millon-Delsol (1995) once noted, XIX-century liberal society based on such an exclusive self-interest search conviction proved to be so uninhabitable that XX century did everything to recover the common good notion even at the excessive price of dictatorships and forced solidarity. To say, therefore, that human beings are naturally inclined to common good does not seem so naive as it could have.

a good is directly connected with life – life itself is good, and the development of a living being towards its fullest expression is also good. The basic approach here is twofold; firstly, living beings, like human beings, have the capacity to develop – they are beings with "potential", always with new possibilities for development that are never fully expressed but towards the full expression of which they can direct their activity. We can identify different kinds of good, a point to which we will return later. Secondly, it is through action that this development takes place – we grow and develop through what we do. Action and growing into the fullness of being are inextricably linked. One can see signs of some influence of this idea of "good" in the way in which the term is used in economics, but in the latter case, its meaning is reduced in comparison to the fuller idea of good we are discussing here.

Where does this leave us in terms of the common good? Insofar as we are talking about something "good", we are talking about something that supports and adds to the development of those who are part of the group, those to whom the good is common (which can be a family, a local community, the whole of the human race, or – especially important for us here – a business or a business in communication with its environment). The more complex bit is how this good can be common. Only totalitarian theories can hold that the group is some kind of living being in itself of which human beings are only parts (like the hand is a part of the human body) and for whom the parts, the human beings, can be sacrificed without too much ado. According to such theories, there is only the good of the group, in which, in some way, each human member of that group participates. Individualistic theories also have a problem with this idea, since they do not have any way of seeing that there could be a good that could really exist in any way other than at the level of the individual human being. The idea of the common good in these theories, such as utilitarianism, is not much more than a convenient shorthand for referring to the sum of the goods of each individual member of the group. If we want to have a serious and helpful idea of the common good, we have to avoid these two extremes (Sulmasy, 2001).

Within the Thomistic personalist tradition, the common good is not the only real good in which each individual participates (a reminiscent

of Mussolini's "In state, for state, through state") neither it is a sum of
individual goods. Instead, it arises out of common, shared activity, just as
the good of each human being (i.e. development towards full maturity)
arises through his or her own activity. "The" common good is ultimately
the result of shared activity across the widest possible group of human
beings, much of which is shared between us not because we have worked
directly on it, but because it "overflows" from its source out to others (we
could say it is a positive externality). Since much of my activity is carried
out with others, there is going to be a close link between what is good for
me and what is good for others around me, and from this we can deduce
that there is going to be a close link between the good of each human being
and the common good, but that they are not the same. There is a relationship of "mutual implication and reciprocal subordination" between the
good of each one of us and the common good (Maritain, 1948, p. 46).[4] In
a certain sense, the common good provides the "humus" or the context
within which personal or private good can be developed, but it is also
only through the development of persons that the common good may be
created and be strengthened.[5] The common good is something created

4   Another way of looking at this relationship is to take the analogy of friendship.
     When two friends are together, they "naturally" act in such a way as to develop
     the good of their friendship. This means, for instance, that they look for things
     to do which are good for both of them, the needs of neither one dominating over
     the other, but where they can both find fulfillment. In a way, the friendship itself
     is an analogy to the common good. The friendship exists "between" the friends
     – if they were separated from each other, the good of their friendship could not
     continue, since it cannot be parceled up into two pieces, one for each of them. It
     either exists between them or it does not exist at all. Analogically speaking, the
     common good exists between people – it is something shared or it is not there
     at all. Both in the case of friendship and of the common good, we can talk about
     the idea of a "third viewpoint" (Finnis, 1980), which is not that of either of the
     friends alone or of any member of the group participating in the common good,
     but is their shared, common viewpoint – the point from which they see what is
     good for both or all of them.
5   The modern idea of the "public good" in economic thought goes some way towards
     the same idea of the common good, though in the latter case, the relationship
     between personal or private good and the common good is more subtle (and here,

and shared by *all* members of the community but at the same time it underpins and permits their perfection and growth.

Since the common good is the result of the activity of particular human beings in particular historical contexts, and of the output and activity of their forebears that has come down to them, it is always historically conditioned, and its interpretation depends on cultural and social context under consideration. The historical singularity of every realized common good is particularly clear in the modern world, with so many possibilities thanks to the complex technological and institutional resources at hand, and so many cultures and religions in contact with each other, it is more often than not a complex process to arrive at a genuine idea of the common good. That's where the dialogue and common search plays a paramount role. The lesson of the discursive ethics of K.-O. Apel comes to mind here. In its terms we may say that the common good idea belongs somehow to the ideal community of communication, and is among or more precisely, embraces already recognized moral norms (as justice, solidarity and co-responsibility). Common good humus is essential for the dialogue between stakeholders of the company and conflict resolution an enterprise faces in everyday real business life, for it provides a necessary solid shared foundation rooted rather in the nature of the human person, her blossoming and developing embedded in a certain framework of culture and history, than in power and relativist interests as in case of the stakeholder theory.

Some of the examples of changes in the articulation of the common good today would be the very different educational system compared, say to ancient Greece, or the role of women, compared, say, to medieval Europe, or the evaluation of cultural diversity, compared to quite recent times. The complexity involved in finding out the true nature of the common good in a particular set of concrete circumstances does not mean that it is an impossible task. We are conscious of the fact that implementation of the common good idea makes management more complex. It

---

this means also more realistic) than is that between the ideas of private and public good in economics (Alford, 2005).

is definitively more complex than business case but at the same time it could be argued that it is less complex than the stakeholder theory, including as it does a myriad of interests that the company should consider when making decisions. It is, however, more realistically grounded than stakeholder theory, which leaves in the air possible trade-offs between stakeholders' interests.

If we say that the common good concept is rooted in human nature but is worked out historically in every age and place, we need to look realistically at the period, with its loss of the organic sense of life characteristic of the Middle Ages, when the concept of the common good notion received its form. If we want to try to recover this idea, one of the challenges we need to face is how to incorporate the processes of competition and of "win-lose" situations, which make up an undeniable part of economic life: if I take a job or a promotion, someone else won't be able to have it; an increase in my company's share in the market means less market share for other companies. How would a Thomistic personalist perspective, then, treat this tension present, for example, in the allocation of foundational goods between different stakeholders of a company?

Paradoxically, particularization of interests and diversification of activities is itself an element of the common good. Consider an example of a Latin teacher cited by Y. Simon in order to illustrate the tension inherent to the common good. Let us imagine a Latin school teacher who spares no effort to promote the Latin culture by trying to increase the number of Latin classes in the school curriculum. His purpose, the good he pursues is particular but at the same time pertains to the common good of the school, as the school is one of its dimensions. In fact, his efforts could enter into conflict with a teacher of biology, a teacher of Mathematics and others but not because he lacks common good sense or respect for other disciplines. On the contrary, the very common good demands him to promote and defend faithfully the importance of classics. Thus, the good pursued by the passionate Latin teacher is obviously a good whose subject is beneficiary for the whole of society. But at the same time it is not the whole of the common good but just an important part or aspect.[6] The school board or other decision-making body responsible for the school curriculum will be where priorities are established and programs fixed.

The objective of a Latin teacher (promotion of classical culture) is a particular good[7] but this good underpins, supports and enables the common good of the human community to which he belongs. In a similar way, in the business environment there are different particular goods, the pursuit of which is required by the common good but which at the same time, may (and we even dare to say, should) enter into competition. The autonomic goodness of particular goods requires, then, the presence of a virtuous manager able, first, to direct private interests towards the common good, and, secondly, to order, prioritize and manage particular goods so as to direct them towards the whole common good.

The point that we seek to underline here is that the common good embraces and even requires the co-existence of cooperation and competition for the human person development. As Viola (2004) rightly notes, in order to be fulfilled an action in common needs both persons' intentional competition (*concorso*) and interpersonal relationships that guarantee a certain level of union of efforts. In fact, this is just the re-discovery of the old idea of "civic economy" developed during the 1700s in Italy, which is also echoed in the works of A. Smith when he observes that narrow self-

6   As Simon describes vividly: "He may be fully aware of the modesty of his job; his occupational conscience may be pervaded with humility. But one day he realized that his unglamorous job, rather thankless, poorly paid, and not too highly considered, was needed for the common good and that a society in which a few men appreciate Virgil is, all other things being equal, better than a society in which Virgil is entirely unknown; and, because there is something divine about the common good, his vocation, from that day on, was animated with a sense of fervour whose expressions were rough and tough, like everything that is concerned with the absolute. Society is well served by such individuals" (p. 46).

7   We should note though that Simon distinguishes two ways in which a good may be called particular: (1) as opposed to common, the good of a part of society, private or individual; (2) as opposed to "whole" or "general", a part, an aspect, a dimension of the common good, specific or particular (cf. Simon, pp. 55–6). The good of a Latin teacher is used in a second sense.

interest could never be sufficient for the good functioning of the market.[8] In fact, some scholars argue Smith's thinking has been oversimplified and impoverished by his followers who rid it of any relational fabric, such as "sympathy" or "fellow-feeling" (Bruni and Zamagni, 2004; Sparkes, 2005). Such a partial reading could probably explain why the "invisible hand" metaphor (mentioned by the way just one in the "Wealth of Nations") is cited much more widely in the modern literature than Smith's condemnation of the limited-liabilities companies, that in his opinion may "do more harm than good" (cited in Sparkes, 2005, p. 11).

This particularization of the common good makes us think of another mechanism necessary for its realization in a pluralistic individualistic society – the principle of subsidiarity. Its negative aspect (the duty of non-interference) usually is easily accepted: the human search for self-determination is rooted into the modern mentality. Its positive aspect (the duty of interference), which is usually less spoken of, finds its unique justification in the common good principle understood as the promotion of human development. What subsidiarity basically says is that human flourishing is to be found in the opportunity to act on one's own initiative (negative aspect of subsidiarity) but also in the light of common goals (positive aspect).

On the one hand, the common good is everything that enables and promotes the good human life, or, as Maritain puts it, "communion in good living", in concrete historical and social conditions. So it cannot be defined in static terms and represents an achievement and an aim of continuing to promote the fullest human development of the members of the group that participate in this good.[9] On the other hand, we can

---

8   Non-European cultures provide us with the similar insight where the very word "economy" (*Kei Zai* in Japanese or *Ching-Chi* in Chinese) means "governing in harmony to bring about the well-being of the people" (Lu Xiaohe).

9   As Maritain puts it: "The common good is something ethically good. Included in it, as an essential element, is the maximum possible development, here and now, of the persons making up the united multitude to the end of forming a people, organised not by force alone, but by justice. Historical conditions and the still inferior development of humanity make difficult the full achievement of the end

identify some of its elements, five of which often show up in contemporary literature (De George, 2004). The modern idea of "public goods" (parks, roads, armies etc.) in economic thought goes some way towards the same idea of the common good, though in the latter case, the relationship between personal or private good and the common good is more subtle (and here, this means also more realistic) than is that between the ideas of private and public good in economics (Alford, 2005). But there are also common goods that do not require government provision, such as air or water.

A third component of the common good is of immaterial nature. It is presented by relations, conditions, systems and structures existing in a human community. Examples of such types of common goods in business organizations include internal and external policies, effective organizational and production structures, safe working conditions, environment-friendly technologies, high levels of social capital, and so on. All of these are used without being diminished by each person who works there, and they benefit both the community of work as a whole and each of its "constituent wholes" (i.e. the human persons working in it). The fourth aspect of the common good includes moral values and virtues, all that enhances human life and flourishing, such as solidarity, freedom, peace, justice, respect for human life and so on. Finally, important preconditions of the common good refer to goods and services produced and traded in the marketplace, which we call "foundational goods".

While at a first glance, this last aspect of the common good may seem the most obvious area of business responsibility, we argue that it should be pursued in the framework of the other four aspects. Moreover, very often the common goods of business organizations embrace several of these aspects. Take, for example, the idea of "core competences", widely

---

of social life. But the end to which it tends is to procure the common good of the multitude in such a way that the concrete person gains the greatest possible measure, compatible with the good of the whole, of real independence from the servitude of nature. The economic guarantees of labour and capital, political rights, the moral virtues and the culture of the mind, all contribute to the realisation of this independence" (Maritain, 1948, pp. 38–9).

recognized in the business literature as one of the most important sources of a company's uniqueness (Prahalad and Hamel, 1990). As a complex of concrete people-embodied skills and "embedded" work relationships (internal cooperation, collective learning and coordination), core competences are not only difficult for competitors to imitate, but also cannot be "hired out" through outsourcing. They are something that is not just created within a certain community of work but also that can exist and bring benefits only within that community, just as the classical example of Sony's capacity of component integration and miniaturization shows.

Before we move to the application of the common good idea to CSR, there is one more important point about the common good to be underlined. We think it is essential to recognize that we can make bad judgments about what is good in the sense defined here. This means that we can make mistakes about what contributes to the development of human beings. History is full of examples where mistakes of this kind have been made, and we know from our own lives that we often choose to do things which afterwards we regret or later judge to have been a waste of time or a distraction from doing something really fulfilling. Thus, it is important to add another criterion here: for the common good to be genuine, it must be *really* good, not just apparently so. This criterion, while it may be difficult to apply in many cases, is still essential to include, since it allows us to exclude the kind of "good" that holds together rogue organizations, terrorist groups and mafia-style "communities", as well as excluding that otherwise acceptable groups may engage from time to time in acts which could be *useful* for them at the time, but which are not *really* good (such as exploiting the weak position of poor workers, even if only for a relatively short time until, perhaps, general economic development gives such workers more power in the marketplace).

3. CSR and the Common Good

We suggest that the common good idea is able not only to offer a new wider model of business but to integrate CSR "naturally" into business practice and not in a residual way. In fact, we may say that an enterprise works in order to achieve many goals, not just maximization of the shareholders' value, commonly ascribed as the main goal of business, but also products for consumers, jobs and good wages for employees, improvements in the quality of life, and so on. The fundamental point consists in determining the nature of these goals and the priorities that enterprises need to assign to them. In order to do this, we will need to distinguish between two types of good that can be pursued by a firm: "foundational goods" or "instrumental goods" (such as profit, capital, technological development) and "excellent goods" or "intrinsic goods" (such as the human development, in all its forms, in harmony with the development of the society as a whole) (Alford and Naughton, 2001 and 2002).

The distinction between foundational goods and excellent goods is based on the fact that the first are what we need and work for in order to obtain other things, while the second are goods we need and aim for because of their intrinsic value, not as instruments or means in order to obtain something else, even if they may also have instrumental value (Alford and Naughton, 2002). The market requires that in order to be competitive it is necessary to guarantee the pursuit of foundational goods, so it is not difficult to see how the current focus on this level of good has come to be seen as the only goal or good that the enterprise pursues. These goods are obviously necessary to the operation and the survival of the enterprise in the same way in which air, water and food are indispensable goods to the life of human persons (idem). They are goods that an enterprise must realize for its development and its survival, but cannot be considered as the ultimate aim of its activity, just as to breathe, to drink or to eat cannot be considered the ultimate aim of the human life.

The aim of human labor, in each organization composed by persons, is not merely to create a product, provide a service, or to become rich, but while it may well achieve these and other foundational goods, its ultimate goal is to be the means of the fullest development of human persons in that community. In other words, it is ultimately about creating excellent goods on a solid base of foundational goods. Excellent goods contribute to the development and progress of humanity in all its forms, for example, through respect for human dignity and the extension of fundamental rights to all, the pursuit of social and spiritual well-being, safety, justice and peace (Melé, 2002). In the case of the business, promoting excellent goods will mostly mean taking due care of employees – the organization of their work, safety, training for future new work tasks – and, to a greater or lesser extent, all those people on which an enterprise has an influence (for example, families, local and national communities, consumers, etc.). This, however, contrary to the position expressed by the stakeholder approach, should not be seen as a sort of exchange of mutual interests, but as an acknowledgment of the important function and responsibility of the enterprise in promoting the well-being of the human community as a whole, and not the individual interests of a part, based on the different force and power relation of each within the enterprise.

What can then be said about the relationship between the concepts of common good and CSR? It is possible in the first place to define CSR within this perspective: "the socially responsible enterprise considers the pursuit of the common good as the final goal of all its actions and activities, meaning by common good the development and the well-being of humanity as a whole and in all its aspects, consistent with the production of a sustainable level of foundational goods". Therefore, the socially responsible enterprise must pursue profit in accordance with the law, and try to survive and to remain competitive in the market, but at the same time, it keeps in mind that all this must be considered as an instrument, as a useful means, for the attainment of "higher" goods, *principally* human development and the progress of the human condition, and *not only* pursuit of the mere interests of shareholders and managers. The difference between the definition we have here and other conceptions of CSR emerges here, for excellent goods are not merely instruments for achieving the business goals of obtaining more foundational goods, as can be seen in literature on CSR. On the contrary, the foundational goods are the means for the production of excellent goods, without which we can have no genuine common good.

Concluding Thoughts

While theorists have been trying to articulate the responsibility of business in terms of commitment to share- or stakeholders' interests, practitioners a long time ago intuited that the search for the ethical foundations of business should embrace service to the "good life of the community" as Oliver Sheldon, manager of Rowntree & Company, an English producer of chocolate, wrote in 1922 in his *A Professional Creed for Management*.[10] But historical antecedents of CSR reasoning may be found even earlier from quite another source: papal encyclicals. In 1891 the encyclical letter of Leo XIII *Rerum Novarum* came out, where we may perhaps find the first prototype of modern codes of conduct. Deeply worried by the unequal accumulation of wealth and unequal access to resources between owners and those without, the Pontiff attributes special responsibilities to property owners. Among them there are both negative (e.g. not to exploit workers, not to destroy their savings by fraud or usury) and positive precepts (e.g. to treat the workers in a just way, to create conditions for developing other spheres of their lives, as family and religious life, to treat them according to their age and sex etc.) (RN 20).

---

10   Ten years earlier a management consultant, Harrington Emerson, in his *The Twelve Principles of Efficiency* wrote about the importance for an enterprise to have "a clearly defined ideal" meaning providing job, just wages, development of workers, sustainability of the community's life, consolidation of workers' family life etc. for, as he explains, "in corporations as in individuals, what is the profit of gaining the whole world if the soul is lost?" It seems that the sense of a greater social good typical for all those who call their occupation a profession has been significantly lost among modern managers.

The duties of owners are summed up in a short expression: "to respect in every man his dignity as a person". This statement, over 100 years old, impressively precedes and is echoed by modern reflection on CSR (see, for example, Global Compact initiative of the UN). In fact, we may say that in the modern situation where, by concentrating wealth, large corporations divide the modern economy between the propertied and the property-less, between few and many in an even more stark manner than at the time of Leo XIII, CSR may be viewed as a logical historical extension of the social responsibility of owners as indicated by *Rerum Novarum*. Although the common good idea just enters the debate field of CSR, we believe it has the potential to breakthrough the CSR definitional and normative impasse for those who, unlike Alice from Wonderland, care which way CSR will go.

References

Alford, Helen, 2005, "Equitable Global Wealth Distribution: A Global Public Good and a Building Block for the Global Common Good", in H. Alford, C. Clark, S.A. Cortright and M. Naughton (eds), *Rediscovering Abundance: Interdisciplinary Essays on Wealth, Income and Their Distribution in the Catholic Social Tradition*, Notre Dame: University of Notre Dame Press.

—— and Naughton, Michael, 2002, "Beyond the Shareholder Model of the Firm: Working toward the Common Good of a Business", in S.A. Cortright and M.J. Naughton (eds), *Rethinking the Purpose of Business*, Notre Dame: University of Notre Dame Press, 27–47.

—— and —— 2001, *Managing As If Faith Mattered: Christian Social Principles in the Modern Organization*, Notre Dame: University of Notre Dame Press.

Apel, Karl-Otto, 1992, *Etica della comunicazione*, Milano: Jaca Book.

Bruni, Luigino and Zamagni, Stefano, 2004, *Economia civile: efficienza, equità, felicità pubblica*, Bologna: Il Mulino.

—— and Porta, Pier Luigi, 2005, *Economics and Happiness*, Oxford: Oxford University Press.

—— 2004, *L'economia, la felicità e gli altri*, Rome: Città Nuova.

Davies, Robert, 2003, "The Business Community: Social Responsibility and Corporate Values", in Dunning, John (ed.), *Making Globalization Good: The Moral Challenges of Global Capitalism*, Oxford: Oxford University Press, 301–19.

De George, Richard, 2004, "The Invisible Hand and Thinness of the Common Good" in Hodgson, Bernard (ed.), *The Invisible Hand and the Common Good*, New York: Springer, 38–47.

Emerson, Harrington, 1912, "The Twelve Principles of Efficiency", reprinted in Miner J.B. (ed.), 1995, *Administrative and Management Theory*, Dartmouth: Aldershot.

Finnis, John, 1980, *Natural Law and Natural Rights*, Oxford: Clarendon Press.

Frederick, W.C., 1987, "Theories of Corporate Social Performance" in Sethi, S.P. and C.M. Flabe (eds), *Business and Society: Dimensions of Conflict and Cooperation*, New York: Lexington Books, 142–61.

Frey, B. and Stutzer, A., 2002, *Happiness in Economics*, Princeton: Princeton University Press.

Garriga, Elisabet and Doménec Melé, 2004, "Corporate Social Responsibility Theories: Mapping the Territory", *Journal of Business Ethics* 53, 51–71.

Koslowski, Peter, 2004, "Public Interest and Self-Interest in the Market and the Democratic Process" in Hodgson, Bernard (ed.), *The Invisible Hand and the Common Good*, New York: Springer, 13–37.

Leo XIII, Pope, 1891, *Rerum Novarum*.

Lu Xiaohe, *On Economic and Ethical Values*, in http://www.stthom.edu/ academics/centers/cbes/economic.html (last access – June 2006)

Maritain, Jacques, 1948, *The Person and the Common Good*, London: Geoffrey Bles.

Melé, Doménec, 2002, "Not Only Stakeholder Interests. The Firm Oriented toward the Common Good", in S.A. Cortright and M.J. Naughton (eds), *Rethinking the Purpose of Business*, Notre Dame: University of Notre Dame Press, 190–214.

Millon Delsol, Chantal, 1995, *Lo stato della sussidiarietà*, Gorle: CEL.

Mumford, Lewis, 1963, *Technics and Civilisation*, Florida: Harcout Brace and Company.

Naughton, Michael, 2006, "The Corporation as a Community of Work: Understanding the Firm within the Catholic Social Tradition", *Ave Mara Law Review*, Vol. 4:1, 33–76.

Prahalad and Hamel, 1990, "The Core Competence of the Corporation", *Harvard Business Review*, (May–June), 79–91.

Sheldon, Oliver, 1922, "The Professional Creed for Management", reprinted in Miner J.B. (ed.), 1995, *Administrative and Management Theory*, Dartmouth: Aldershot.

Siebens, Herman, 2006, "As Simple as It Seems? A Critical Reading of the CSR Concept", paper presented at the *EBEN 2006 Research Conference "Normative Foundations of Corporate Responsibility"*.

Simon, Yves, 1951, *Philosophy of Democratic Government*, Chicago: The University of Chicago Press.

Sparkes, Russel, 2005, *From Mortmain to Adam Smith: Historical Insights on the Problem of Corporate Social Responsibility*, mimeo.

Sulmasy, D.P., 2001, "Four Basic Notions of the Common Good", *St John's Law Review* 75 (2), 303–11.

The Economist, 2005, "The Good Company. A Survey of Corporate Social Responsibility", 22 January, 3–18.

Viola, Francesco and Giuseppe Zaccaria, 2004, *Diritto e interpretazione. Lineamenti di teoria ermeneutica del diritto*, Bari: Editore Laterza.

Votaw, D., 1972, "Genius Becomes Rare: Comment on the Doctrine of Social Responsibility", *California Management Review*, XV (2), 25–31.

Wheeler, David, Barry Colbert and Edward Freeman, 2003, "Focusing on Value: Reconciling Corporate Social Responsibility, Sustainability and a Stakeholder Approach in a Network World", *Journal of General Management*, Vol. 28, n°3, 1–28.

Whitehouse, Lisa, 2003, "Corporate Social Responsibility, Corporate Citizenship and the Global Compact: A New Approach to Regulating Corporate Social Power?", *Global Social Policy*, Vol. 3, n°3, 299–318.

CHAPTER 3

The Common Good as a Global Wealth: Preventing Globalization from Leading to an Ethical Decay of the Common Good

HENDRIK OPDEBEECK

Introduction

Authors such as M. Velasquez[1] suggest that since all citizens benefit from the Common Good, they all are willing to cooperate in order to establish and maintain the Common Good. However, numerous authors, including Velasquez, have identified a number of obstacles that hinder society from successfully doing so. One can think of the free-rider problem in an individualistic society and the problem of the incompatibility of the idea of the "common" good in our pluralistic society. In this paper, we intend to explore how one can prevent the social and economic change in the globalization process from leading to an ever-greater ethical decay of the Common Good. By ethical decay, we mean specifically the threat that globalization poses to what is referred to as the heart of the Common Good namely, in terms of the French philosopher Paul Ricœur, *the longing for being and collaboration with the other(s).*[2]

---

1   M. Velasquez, C. Andre, T. Shanks and M. Meyer, *The Common Good*, http://www.scu.edu/ethics/practicing/decision/commongood.html.
2   For a more extensive overview see H. Opdebeeck (ed.), *The Problem of the Foundation of Ethics*, Leuven: Peeters, 2000. Compare with H.-C. de Bettignies and F. Lépineux, "Should Multinational Corporations Be Concerned with the Global

Against the background of the question of whether universities and business schools are an effective instrument to promote the Common Good, one of the latest initiatives of R. Petrella's Lissabon Group, the launching of small-scale academic centers of the Common Good all over the world (already in Québec, Milano, Antwerp ...) seems to be an interesting challenge. In this paper, we shall therefore take as starting point Riccardo Petrella's *Grande conférence* at the "Musée de la Civilisation" in Québec with the title *Ecueils de la mondialisation – Urgence d'un nouveau contrat social.*[3] The prevailing globalization discourse manifests itself world-wide in political, socio-economic and scientific circles. It assumes both an explicative and a legitimizing position vis-à-vis the globalization process and its purpose. If one wants to put a stop to the decay of the Common Good or the longing for being and collaboration with the other(s), the urgency of a broader ethical (i.e. a more just) dimension in the globalization process, seems to be more apparent than ever before. The concept of a global social contract seems to be an important elaboration of the concern with institutionalizing more equality besides efficiency as the basis for the Common Good as a Global Wealth.

1. The Globalization Process

The current globalization of markets, enterprises and capital goes hand in hand with an ongoing revolution in information and communication technology based knowledge. We need to extrapolate in order to predict where these technological developments will lead. It is claimed in the globalization discourse, which manifests itself in all languages, and via all possible media, that globalization is an inevitability against

---

Common Good? An Interdisciplinary Exploration", Fontainebleau: INSEAD Working Paper Series, 2005, p. 8.

3   R. Petrella, *Ecueils de la mondialisation. Urgence d'un nouveau contrat social*, Montréal: Fides, 1997.

which nothing or no one can put up meaningful resistance. Thus, the key notion is adaptation: one appears to adjust at all levels to this process. Anyone who fails to adapt is excluded, if only on the basis of the hard rules of competition. The imperative of global competition of all against all is paramount. New technologies are put forward as the most powerful and efficient tools for guaranteeing competition in world markets and in knowledge.

The omnipresence of this discourse stems from the de facto economic power of the most developed nations, whereby the values and the criteria of the capitalist market economy are regarded as the exclusive global characteristics of what is good, useful and necessary. This is apparent not merely in the economic domain, but in any possible field. Hence, the purpose of the history of contemporary society is equated to a necessary, inexorable and inevitable evolution towards a single and self-regulating global market place. The nations of the world have set themselves the principal task of integrating their national economies as smoothly as possible into the global economy, or at least of not imposing obstacles to this integration. Thus, they have relinquished their own political accountability. Everything is subordinated to this finality: investment policy, technological innovation, labor market policy, education, trade regulations, tax policy, the process of European unification and of course knowledge. Scientific and technology policy, including the stimulation of R&D, is one of the most striking examples of this trend. Consequently, new alliances are forming between governments and private enterprises in the free market, with the purpose of realizing their common goal of a competitive integration of the national economy into the global economy.

The discourse of the inevitably integrated global market also explains how it has been possible over the past twenty years for the economic and socio-political system to experience a thorough reorientation on the basis of three principles: liberalization of markets, deregulation of the economy, and privatization (not only of banks and railways, but also of hospitals and knowledge producing centers such as schools). It is quite striking in this respect how political deregulation has made way for financial regulation. Today, finance is no longer controlled by politics, but by the money markets. This evolution has unfolded against the backdrop of an ever-greater divergence of the financial-economic and the real economic spheres. Only a small fraction of current financial transactions are aimed at the creation of real new wealth. The rest is purely speculative. A final important characteristic of today's globalization process as described by, among others, Petrella is the imposition by the greatest economic powers of social, democratic and environmental clauses in the new regulation of the World Trade Organization (WTO). These clauses concern the quality of labor, human rights and environmental standards respectively. While these are undoubtedly important clauses, the question remains whether the WTO is the most appropriate body for controlling global social, democratic and environmental standards.

2. The Ethical Decay of the Common Good

In order to ascertain whether or not the globalization discourse described above entails a decay of the Common Good, it is worth recalling what, according to Paul Ricœur, is the foundation of the longing for being. As mentioned in the introduction, this longing for being can be seen as the foundation of the Common Good. The starting point for Ricœur's theory of ethics is his assertion that the human being constitutes an original confirmation of being, which manifests itself in endeavor and longing. What Ricœur means by original confirmation of being is the act whereby we are placed in existence, which precedes our feeling, thinking, knowledge and acting, and underpins and guides them, but which is never given to us and can therefore never be beheld. One could, therefore, regard this original confirmation of being as an act of freedom; the basis of what we are and what there is for us to be. So Ricœur wishes to lay bare the human being's longing for being, in order to help him or her acquire a more adequate degree of self-understanding. This is the only way that a more authentic (co)existence can be attained that transcends alienation.[4] Ethics thus enables us to identify the meaningful history of our longing for being. Clearly, then, the notion of freedom is central to Ricœur's theory of ethics.

Certainly in the light of the constantly changing free market economy within the globalization process – as a kind of structural anchoring of the central ethical concept of freedom – Ricœur's perspective is extremely interesting. Note, however, that the notion of freedom is not so easily grasped. Therefore, reflection is required on its concrete expressions or manifestations. The above hermeneutics of the globalization process ties in with this interpretative process. Significantly, evil (as contested by the anti-globalist movements) is not equally original as the act of freedom. According to Ricœur, it is however the case that evil and freedom elucidate one another and, indeed, that evil not only mutilates ethical striving at individual level, but also within the structures in which we operate. Ricœur formulates this very clearly when he asserts that there is a specific evil of the institution, i.e. the evil of objectification that one encounters in all forms of organization. In the distribution of labor, for example, it assumes the subtle shape of drudgery, which slowly takes possession of hyper-specialized and monotonous work in industry.

Petrella's analysis of the erosion of the right to meaningful employment in the globalization process ties in with this view entirely. Those in charge of our economy are insisting that it is no longer possible to provide full employment, let alone meaningful and qualitative employment. In the European Union alone, there are close to 20 million unemployed. Worldwide, the number is estimated at around one billion. Fundamentally, what is at issue is that people are no longer regarded as individuals, but as a human resource, comparable to natural, technological and financial resources. If the cost of labor becomes too great, workers are made redundant and they are replaced with another economic resource, such as a machine. The evil within the globalization process is therefore an unfath-

4   Compare with E. Weil, *Philosophie politique*, Paris: Librairie Vrin, 1956.

omable manifestation of freedom that makes freedom itself unattainable, and that immediately restricts our ethical striving.

3. A Threat to Collaboration

If the starting point of the ethics of the Common Good is the free human being longing and striving for being, then one only attains actual ethical existence through the encounter with the other.[5] The recognition of the other as a person at once entails an obligation, creating an inclusive space in which everyone's motivations and energies are enlisted, even if they don't fit for instance a single obvious corporate mould. The freedom, with which everything started, is also recognized in the other person. Of fundamental importance here is that Ricœur extends this inter-subjectivity to the whole world through the process of norms and laws. He renounces individualist ethics, because man is not merely an individual, but constitutes various levels of the "we" or the "Common", which are embedded in the totality of structures and institutions. In this respect, one gets the opportunity to envision themselves, not as an object subjected to change, but as an agent of change.

Considered in this context, Petrella's warning that globalization increasingly threatens collaboration between the "I" and the "other(s)" is of great importance. He asserts that the phenomenon of growing poverty is not only an indication of the negation of the collaboration principle in the welfare state, but also of the negation of citizenship. Indeed, it is increasingly argued that citizenship does not imply social rights of the other. In the world's richest country, the United States, 1 in 5 people are living in poverty. In the European Union, the proportion is about 1 in 6, but in the UK it is as high as 1 in 4. This also manifests itself in an unequal income distribution. In the US, 1% of the population possesses 40% of

5   P. Ricœur, *Soi-même comme un autre*, Paris: Editions du Seuil, 1990, pp. 212–13.

the national wealth. This unequal distribution of wealth is manifesting itself in the emergence of more and more private neighborhoods in cities, where the rich can cut themselves off from the other(s), and enjoy extra protection against violence and crime. It is also striking that technology is one of the principal factors in the dynamics of social exclusion. With respect to work, for example, one sees how difficult it often is for the unemployed to re-enter the labor market, since the greatest possible number of jobs are being made redundant through technology.

Moreover, the present economy is increasingly making us lose our sense of being, working and living together with the other. In the light of the global competitive struggle, collaboration has become an obstacle and an unbearable cost for enterprises. This is partly why the value of the Common Good is being lost. Priority is given to individual careers ("my education", "my knowledge"), to individual survival strategies ("my job and income") and to individual possessions ("my home, my car") as fundamental and irreplaceable expressions of freedom. We have lost sight of the other. The logic of economic competition is made into the obligatory logic of society as a whole, which inevitably results in a victory of the one over the other, or, if you will, in the exclusion of the one by the other. Particularly the less developed countries are worse-off for by process of globalization. A mere 15% of global direct investment is not intended for the most developed economies. Entirely in line with the logic of globalization, investors are attracted to those places offering the highest and quickest return. At the same time, the liberalization of markets is compelling the less developed countries to orient their economies increasingly towards the production of export commodities (such as agricultural produce and textiles). As a result, the development of these countries continues to lag far behind.

4. The Need for Adequate Global Institutions

When a free individual enters into an ethical existence through the encounter with the other, he or she can only do so by mediation of organizations to ensure that collaboration is institutionalized. A third moment is required to speak about the Common Good, i.e. a neutral term, organizations or institutions in all their forms and manifestations. Hence, the threat that the globalization process poses to the longing for being and collaboration with the other(s) increasingly necessitates an appropriate global institution. An institution consists of a set of rules for acts in social life, whereby everyone can realize their freedom without impairing that of others. Therefore organizations will fail if they are not capable of learning, in a collective sense, as well as the individuals who spend their days at work there. It is within the framework of existing institutions that human beings act. These institutions or organizations are driven by culture. In direct contrast to the focus on system and structure in an earlier era when management was considered to be an exact science, they are not detached from value judgments. So organizations are already qualified ethically and, as such, can either bring forth freedom or not.

   Petrella points out that globalization, with its drive towards liberalization, deregulation and privatization has drastically reduced the significance of the Common Good as an institutionalization of freedom. This finds expression in, for example, the waning influence of parliament. Government is increasingly giving in to the demands imposed by the often-aggressive markets. The most detrimental aspect of this evolution is that, because of the growing tendency on the part of national economies to adapt to the global economy, the public authorities have failed to develop a global political authority; on the contrary, this international integration actually enhances private power at global level. This is also true at European level. The more the member states apply the principles of liberalization, deregulation and privatization, the further they appear to remove themselves from developing a federal European power. The fundamental question here is what is meaningful freedom?

Ethical mediation must ultimately be beneficial to the human person if one is to avoid bureaucratic stalemate. Indeed, the very purpose of institutions is that they should serve people and the Common Good. If not, institutions are entirely meaningless. Certainly in the light of the globalization process, the big question is whether specific ethical rules need to be established at institutional level, as it is difficult to extend those from the interpersonal sphere to institutions. This explains the great significance of justice as an institutional tool that allows different freedoms to co-exist. Following in the footsteps of Aristotle, Ricœur further elaborates this assertion by underlying the connection between justice and equality. However one interprets equality, it means to institutions what care-for-the-other or solicitude means to interpersonal relationships.

5. Justice Criteria

Justice has always been a moral characteristic whereby people grant others, with an inner self-evidence, whatever they have a right to. Justice relates not only to property, commodities and finance, but to all values that people must realize with and for each other, including safety, health, marriage, education, truth, freedom and life itself. The 18th century philosopher David Hume refers to four circumstances that make justice indispensable in our society.[6] It is remarkable how one can also refer to those four elements to understand why the common good is indispensable in a global society. First, the individual is required to cooperate with others in order to satisfy his personal needs. Surviving as an isolated individual is impossible. Second, the extent of man's benevolence is limited, so individuals are quickly inclined to claim everything for themselves, without taking account of the other. Third, goods are scarce, so that conventions are required that establish right of property. Finally, all human beings have

6   D. Hume, *A Treatise of Human Nature*, Oxford: Clarendon Press, 1978.

more or less the same basic needs. Satisfying these needs presupposes a reasonable distribution. Otherwise one will be reduced to inhumanity, as the anti-globalist movement argues forcefully.

This brings us to the confrontation between justice and excessive economic power, as in the present globalization context. Abuse of economic power at the level of communal justice is manifest in exploitation, consumer manipulation and market monopolies among other things. But economic power also plays a role in legal justice. Examples that spring to mind are various forms of tax evasion and the bypassing of government by, among others, multinational corporations. Since, as H.-C. de Bettignies and F. Lépineux[7] underline, the common good has as fundamental attribute that it is distributive, the issue of globalization mostly comes into play in the field of distributive justice. Distributive justice is concerned with a reasonable or equitable distribution of scarce commodities. There are two important principles of distributive justice in the economic domain, i.e. "grant everyone their share according to merit" and "grant everyone their share according to their needs". These two principles not only typify the age-old tension between liberalism and socialism, or between capitalism and communism,[8] but, as will become apparent, they also shed light on the origin of injustice in the present globalization process.

The notion of merit has different meanings and explains how the value of an organization is increasingly located in intangibles such as business systems, intellectual property and the human skills base, and in this sense, knowledge has become a factor of production. Merit can refer to a performance or a responsibility, as well as to a mental effort. The principle "grant everyone their share according to merit" always refers to the past, as merit is inevitably based on assets such as talent, skills, knowledge or stamina, all of which were acquired (unequally) in the past. Consequently, this criterion tends towards inequality. An example that springs to mind in the context of globalization is the important aspect of income distribution. This is almost a reflection of the inherently unequal distribution of,

7   H.-C. de Bettignies and F. Lépineux, *op. cit.*, p. 11.
8   For an analysis on Globalization and Marxism, see the contribution of R. Devos in H. Opdebeeck, *Building Towers* (2002).

for example, intelligence among the population. As the globalization logic attributes such a central role to earnings, one obviously aims at increasing economic output quantitatively and qualitatively by stimulating performance with a view to realizing the greatest possible utility.

As regards the second important principle, i.e. distributive justice by "granting everyone their share in accordance with their needs", this refers to the most essential needs of human beings. These needs are inherent in "being human", and besides the need for food, clothing, housing etc. human needs have been transformed to the point where, in the marketplace, consumers focus on knowledge-representations as much as they do on physical entities. If one interprets justice in the sense of granting to the other whatever the other is entitled to, then this second principle may offer a guarantee for realizing more social justice. On condition, that is, that one considers intrinsic basic needs that are a genuine prerequisite for a dignified human existence.

6. Limits of the Market Economy

Certainly in business circles where people are sensitive to criticism of globalization, it is usually claimed that it is impossible to realize both principles of justice in the economy. The application of both the principle "grant everyone their share on account of merit" and that of "grant everyone their share on the basis of their needs" would result in a short circuit, if only because the merit principle creates inequality while the needs principle does the opposite. The anti-globalist movement tends to argue in favor of the needs criterion. This in itself is no problem according to proponents of globalization, but the latter also claim that those same anti-globalists wrongfully accuse the free market of not applying the needs principle and overemphasizing merit and pay according to work. They argue that anti-globalists tend to lose sight of the fact that the market economy is based on the performance criterion rather than the needs criterion. Consequently, they denounce familiar economic power mechanisms: they reject excessive economic competition, propose rather drastic redistributive measures, criticize multinationals, disapprove of the stimulation of consumerism (through advertising), deplore the substitution of capital for labor, and suspect the market of wanting to reduce humans to the status of slaves of commodities. Therefore, in the eyes of the anti-globalists at least, it is justified to give the state more of a carte blanche.

The traditional proponents of globalization argue that, if one does want to take into account both the merit and the needs principles, without imposing these criteria on either the economy or globalization, then it is essential that the economy and politics should be made to function as efficiently as possible. For this reason, they defend free competition and true democracy, claiming that they serve the general interest. The merit issue is resolved on the basis of the free (i.e. economic) market mechanism, while the needs problem is approached from the perspective of democratic (i.e. political) decision-making. The general interest objective realized in this manner brings forth the greatest possible degree of justice. But is this so called "general interest" really the foundation of the common good?

According to the champions of globalization, this at once shows that human self-interest, to which the profit principle is so often equated, is not entirely negative; on the contrary, self-interest may be the very foundation of the general interest. However, if this mechanism is to be sustainable and not lead to collective self-destruction, then moral characteristics such as sympathy and collaboration, mutual trust and justice are required. Self-interest and the general interest would then complement each other in much the same way as two buttresses carry the vaulting in a cathedral. Globalization and justice, self-interest and general interest, the merit principle and the needs principle, free competition and true democracy: according to the proponents of globalization, each of these pairs can be combined most effectively in a mixed market economy. This system allows one to reconcile the production issue (cf. efficiency) with the distributive issue, where satisfying basic needs is of primary importance. Indeed, a public authority is necessary in order to guarantee that the degree of private power within a national community remains within the general interest, as a guaranty of the common good.

7. The Ethical Dimension

While a mixed market economy would appear to offer a logical solution to the tension between the globalization process and justice, the question remains whether this partition between (economic) efficiency and (democratic) justice, or between globalization and ethics, is justifiable in this day and age. After all, the merit principle that is central to the economy not only causes inequality, it also stimulates economic growth and progress, unlike the needs principle, which tends to restrict growth. However, in recent years serious side effects have been occurring in relation to economic progress. It is apparent from the emergence of the anti-globalist movement that there is growing awareness of the end to growth and progress. It has become very clear that, if the industrialized Western countries want to avoid undermining themselves, the emphasis in economic growth needs to shift from quantitative to qualitative growth. One needs to abandon the traditional concept of growth, as it results not only in a disproportionate appropriation of scarce resources but also in irreversible damage to the environment.

This conception is contrary to the policies pursued in many Western countries. All too often, growth of GDP is seen as the prime objective, to be achieved by a market that is unimpeded by government. Thus the most pressing problems facing the world today are transferred unscrupulously to the environment, to the third and fourth worlds, and to the quality of inter-human relationships. The question "What is the sense of it all?" resounds loudly in Seattle, Genoa and Laken. Indeed, in this manner, economic power enters the triangle of profit, progress and needs, rather than merely confronting the issue of justice. Goudzwaard and De Lange[9] have long asserted that, in the iron law of so-called economic and technological progress, which forces everything and everyone to constantly adapt, we have discovered the secret we were searching for.

9   B. Goudzwaard and H. de Lange, *Beyond Poverty and Affluence. Toward an Economy of Care*, Geneva: WCC Publications, 1995, p. 92.

In an economic order where progress occupies a central place, wielding of power can indeed develop in only one direction: that of ever-greater productivity increase and a matching standard of living. This compelling force can apparently afford to neglect the negative power effects of globalization (third world, unemployment, environmental degradation ...). In view of the negative effects of growth, as articulated in the dynamics of globalization, striking a balance between democracy and market economy (i.e. the mixed market economy) is no longer guaranteeing the Common Good. Due to the intrinsic logic of the merit principle, which not only induces inequality and economic growth, but also impermissible power effects, the boundaries of globalization call into question whether this exclusive principle is sufficient in the economic field, let alone acceptable.

Consequently, more and more people are calling for a broader ethical dimension in the globalization process (rather than ethical decay). This way, one can prevent that the one-sided merit principle continues to occupy a central position in the globalization process. It is striking that these calls are now heard right up to the highest levels. Participatory justice is considered to be of the utmost importance. One goes beyond the two principles of distributive justice and abandons the (dualistic) opposition between the individual and the community in order to arrive at a shared responsibility for the common good at national and international level.

8. The Common Good as Global Wealth

The concept of a global social contract is thus an important elaboration of the concern with institutionalizing more equality besides efficiency as a Common Good. Petrella rightly asserts that the essential challenge for the global economy lies not so much in the integration and adaptation of the national economies to the world economy. It lies in adequately determining the principles and rules within the institutions that are required to provide the world's population with its basic needs in terms of food, housing, energy, health, education, transport and employment. The central question is, in other words, how can one achieve the Common Good as global wealth rather than predominantly private wealth at a global level? Or how can one assume responsibility in true collaboration instead of developing one-sided competition?[10] The main difficulty in realizing a global social contract is, however, the virtual lack of a global political system that can shoulder the responsibility of protecting the Common Good.

Conclusion

Clearly, politics needs to assure the survival of the community, all the more so if its future is under considerable threat. This acceptance of responsibility however implies caring for the most brittle, the most threatened. With this we have arrived at the philosophy of E. Levinas: we are ultimately responsible for the other(s), without thoughts of reciprocity and without room for calculus. The purely reciprocal recognition between people is however transcended in order that everyone would assert himself in individuality, which is in fact the starting point for Ricœur's ethical genesis. According to Levinas the egocentric longing for being of the self is only transcended when the "I" is obliged to do so, and, in particular, when it responds positively to the appeal of the Face of the Other.[11] When Ricœur discusses the recognition of the other, there would appear to be a certain ambiguity. Indeed, one can restrict oneself without questioning oneself, without insight into the arbitrariness of the own (despotic) longing for being.

---

10   It is clear that R. Petrella is one the same wavelength here as J. Rawls in his *Theory of Justice* (1971).
11   E.g. E. Levinas, *Autrement qu'être ou au-delà de l'essence*, La Haye: Martinus Nijhoff, 1974.

The auto-limitation is founded upon the narrow base of the war of all against all or the threat that the other poses to one's own freedom. The self does not (yet) perceive its own egocentrism as unworthy of a human being. Thus, it would appear that Ricœur runs the risk of reaching a dead end at the level of well-understood reciprocal interest. This is probably due to his perception of the other as an alter ego: alter certainly, but still an ego. But meanwhile an ego-centric globalized society has been established, which in contradiction with the common good, takes the shape of egocentrically organized structures at national, international and global level. It appears that precisely these structures are called into question today. As an open question to conclude one could ask if this phenomenon of an ego-centric globalized society could not be linked with that other remarkable phenomenon of this era: the longing for spirituality in our society, for as H.-C. de Bettignies and F. Lépineux suggest: "the common good is at once material and spiritual".[12]

References

Aristotle, 2004, *The Nichomachean Ethics*, London.

De Bettignies, H.-C. and F. Lépineux, 2005, "Should Multinational Corporations Be Concerned with the Global Common Good? An Interdisciplinary Exploration", Fontainebleau: INSEAD Working Paper Series.

Goudzwaard, B. and H. De Lange, 1995, *Beyond Poverty and Affluence. Toward an Economy of Care*, Geneva: WCC Publications.

Hume, D., 1978, *A Treatise of Human Nature*, Oxford: Clarendon Press.

Levinas, E., 1974, *Autrement qu'être ou au-delà de l'essence*, La Haye: Martinus Nijhoff.

12   H.-C. de Bettignies and F. Lépineux, *op. cit.*, p. 11.

Opdebeeck, H., 2002, *Building Towers, Perspectives on Globalization*, Ethical Perspectives Monographs Series, Leuven: Peeters.

——2000, *The Foundation and Application of Moral Philosophy*, Leuven: Peeters.

Petrella, R., 1997, *Écueils de la mondialisation. Urgence d'un nouveau contrat social*, Montréal: Editions Fides.

Rawls, J., 1971, *A Theory of Justice*, Oxford: Oxford University Press.

Ricœur, P., 1990, *Soi-même comme un autre*, Paris: Editions du Seuil.

Velasquez, M., C. Andre, T. Shanks and M. Meyer, *The Common Good*, http://www.scu.edu/ethics/practicing/decision/commongood.html.

Weil, E., 1956, *Philosophie politique*, Paris: Librairie Vrin.

CHAPTER 4

Stakeholders and the Common Good: A Polarity within Corporate Conscience[1]

KENNETH E. GOODPASTER

> In the society of organizations, each of the new institutions is concerned only with its own purpose and mission. It does not claim power over anything else. But it also does not assume responsibility for anything else. Who, then, is concerned with the common good?
>
> — PETER DRUCKER[2]

Introduction

It is common in the literature of business ethics to interpret the idea of corporate conscience using some version of "stakeholder thinking" as a conceptual guide – even as a synonym for "ethical thinking in business". Commentators often point out that publicly-held business organizations need to move beyond a preoccupation with stockholders and guide their behavior with attention to all *stakeholders*, parties whose interests and/ or rights are affected by corporate decisions.[3] I wish to question not the

---

1   This essay was originally presented to the *6th International Conference on Catholic Social Thought and Management Education*, Rome, Italy (5–7 October 2006).
2   Peter Drucker, "The Age of Social Transformation," *The Atlantic Monthly*, November 1994, p. 78.
3   Typically these parties include – in addition to owner/investors – employees, customers, suppliers, competitors, local communities, and "the environment".

necessity, but the *sufficiency* of translating corporate conscience exclusively in stakeholder categories. Moving beyond stockholder thinking to stakeholders seems to be a step in the right direction, but is it *enough*? Might there be more to institutionalizing ethical values in the marketplace? Do we risk losing something important if we settle for stakeholder thinking as a complete account of corporate conscience? Invoking the opening quotation, we can ask whether "stakeholder thinking" provides an adequate answer to Peter Drucker's question: "Who, then, is concerned with the common good?" Let us begin with the idea of *conscience* as it applies to individuals. Later we shall consider the idea as it applies to organized groups.

I. Conscience and the Individual

Royce and the Moral Insight

As an initial meditation on the idea of conscience in its more modern meaning, let us turn to Harvard philosopher Josiah Royce. Royce, a friend of William James who wrote at the end of the 19th century, believed that all of ethics was grounded in something he called the *moral insight* (a gateway to what philosophers today call the "moral point of view"). Royce described the *moral insight* in his book *The Religious Aspect of Philosophy* (Royce, 1865):

> The moral insight is *the realization of one's neighbor*, in the full sense of the word realization; the resolution to treat him unselfishly. But this resolution expresses and belongs to the moment of insight. Passion may cloud the insight after no very long time. It is as impossible for us to avoid the illusion of selfishness in our daily lives, as to escape seeing through the illusion at the moment of insight. We see the reality of our neighbor, that is, we determine to treat him as we do ourselves. But then we go back to daily action, and we feel the heat of hereditary passions, and *we straightway forget what we have seen*. Our neighbor becomes obscured. He is once more a foreign power. He is unreal. We are again deluded and selfish. This

conflict goes on and will go on as long as we live after the manner of men. Moments of insight, with their accompanying resolutions; long stretches of delusion and selfishness: That is our life.[4]

The moral insight is about the relationship between love of self and love of one's "neighbor" – and ultimately of one's community. And it is central to understanding and appreciating *conscience* in individuals. Note that Royce describes the moral life in an active, not a passive, way. He speaks of the "illusion of selfishness" from which we are rescued by the moral insight and to which we nevertheless regularly *return*: "Moments of insight, with their accompanying resolutions; long stretches of delusion and selfishness". The first moment in the "unfolding" of the moral insight is our (apparently natural) self-centeredness – which Royce calls an *illusion*.[5] The second moment is the "realization" of our neighbor, which carries with it a "resolution to treat him unselfishly". But the third moment is that we "straightway *forget* what we have seen". And then we repeat the process: "That is our life."[6] This inner movement (from illusion to insight to forgetting) portrays conscience as a living *process* that must be *managed* – not simply as a static criterion for right and wrong. The moral insight must be cultivated, renewed, challenged – as much (I will argue) for organizations as for individuals.

Piaget and Conscience: A Second Insight

If we join Royce's reflection on the moral insight to the work of Swiss psychologist Jean Piaget, we discover a second aspect of conscience. Not only does the moral insight mean reaching beyond what Royce calls the

4   Josiah Royce, *The Religious Aspect of Philosophy*, originally published in 1865; reprinted in 1965 by permission of Harper and Row, by Peter Smith Gloucester, MA, pp. 155–6. Emphasis added.
5   Echoes of Piaget's first stage of moral development, "egocentrism" (see below).
6   Plato's writings emphasize the importance of "recollection" in acquiring knowledge, and in the present context, recollection is the only antidote to a kind of "moral forgetting".

"illusion of selfishness," it also means reaching beyond another illusion, what we might call the "illusion of social authority." Moral maturity requires, according to Piaget, first overcoming *egocentrism* (through what Royce calls the "realization of one's neighbor") and then overcoming *heteronomy* (by rejecting social norms as *surrogates* for right and wrong). Only after one passes through these two illusions does conscience – what Piaget calls *autonomy* – become possible.

The two moral insights noticed by Royce and Piaget serve as *precursors* to an understanding of conscience. They remind us that whatever else conscience is, it is a form of *awareness without illusion*. And on the subject of *awareness*, Jesuit priest-psychologist Anthony DeMello is quite eloquent. He tells a Zen story about an impatient young disciple who went to the master and said:

> "Could you give me a word of wisdom? Could you tell me something that would guide me through my days?" Since it was the master's day of silence, he picked up a pad and wrote on it. He wrote, "Awareness". When the disciple saw it, he said, "This is too brief. Can you expand on it a bit?" So the master took back the pad and wrote, "Awareness, awareness, awareness". The disciple said, "Yes, but what does it mean?" The master took back the pad and wrote, "Awareness, awareness, awareness means – awareness".[7]

The point of DeMello's story, and the source of its humor, is that we sometimes look for complex solutions when much simpler ones are available. But *simple* does not necessarily mean *easy*.[8]

---

7   Anthony DeMello, S.J., *Awareness*, NY: Doubleday, 1990, p. 56.

8   DeMello would have agreed wholeheartedly with philosopher Hannah Arendt's observation that "A life without thinking is quite possible – but it is not fully alive. Unthinking men are like sleepwalkers". Hannah Arendt, "Thinking," *The New Yorker*, 5 December 1977, p. 195. Indeed, DeMello's view is reminiscent of the views of the intuitionists in ethical theory at the beginning of the 20th century. *Awareness* is an active, engaged, perspective on decision making that resists "definition" – replacement by surrogates that claim to "automate" our moral judgment.

An Inner Polarity of Conscience –
Thomas Nagel and Joseph Cardinal Ratzinger

Appreciating that the inner life of conscience begins with overcoming two persistent *illusions* is important. And understanding that it involves a special kind of *awareness* is also important. But what can we say – if anything – about the *kind* of awareness that conscience provides in human life? Philosopher Thomas Nagel wrote 30 years ago about conscience that:

> [t]he real issue is the relative priority, in regard to action, of two ways of looking at the world. On the one hand there is the position that one's decisions should be tested ultimately from an external point of view, to which one appears as just one person among others [...] This point of view claims priority by virtue of greater comprehensiveness [...] On the other hand there is the position that since an agent lives his life from where he is, even if he manages to achieve an impersonal view of his situation, whatever insights result from this detachment need to be made part of a personal view before they can influence decision and action.[9]

Nagel's phenomenology of conscience is perceptive. He reminds us of our human capacity for alternative perspectives in the moral life – specifically an *agent-centered perspective* that contextualizes our decision making in the "here and now" and a more detached or *impartial perspective* that deliberately steps back from the "here and now" to assess more comprehensively the promptings of conscience. When Nagel refers to an "agent-centered perspective," he is clearly *not* referring to Royce's "illusion of selfishness." On the contrary, he means a perspective that acknowledges obligations to others as well as to oneself – but which derive their authority from the point of view of an embedded agent in a concrete decision-making situation. It is in the nature of agent-centered thinking that decision makers make their choices using a *situational framework* – rather than general principles alone.

The "choice" to which Nagel refers is, of course, a *dilemma* or a paradox only if the two alternatives are somehow contradictory, incapable

---

9   Thomas Nagel, "Subjective and Objective", in *Moral Questions*, Cambridge: Cambridge University Press, 1979, p. 205.

of being united in the same moral life. But sometimes the *dilemmas* of philosophers are the *mysteries* of theologians. We may be able to join the motivational intimacy of the subjective point of view with the transcendence of the impartial point of view if we understand these two dimensions of conscience as potentially aligned through communication with a Creator – one who has "written in our hearts" a natural law with higher authority than the authority of subjective will.

Our conviction that these two viewpoints are jointly necessary and that we cannot escape the polarity simply by eliminating one of the poles comes, I believe, from the fact that each pole represents one of the pillars of moral thought: (a) the *dignity* of the human person or subject, and (b) the importance of the *common* good. The dignity of the person creates a zone of respect around each of us which we frequently call autonomy or freedom of conscience. But the importance of the common good reminds us that reason or a higher law must discipline the freedom of conscience.[10]

Nagel's philosophical observations seem congruent with the theological perspective articulated in 1991 by Joseph Cardinal Ratzinger (Pope Benedict XVI since April 2005) in a workshop for bishops:

> The medieval tradition was right, I believe, in according two levels to the concept of conscience. These levels, though they can be well distinguished, must be continually referred to each other. It seems to me that many unacceptable theses regarding conscience are the result of neglecting either the difference or the connection between the two.[11]

---

10 Philosopher Richard M. Hare, in the title of his classic, *Freedom and Reason* (1960), emphasized the centrality of autonomy or freedom in normative ethics. At the same time, however, his title suggested a second central aspect of moral thinking (*reason*).

11 Joseph Cardinal Ratzinger, "Conscience and Truth", Workshop for Bishops, Dallas, TX (February 1991).

Ratzinger goes on to explain:

> [T]he fact that the conviction a person has come to certainly binds in the moment of acting, *does not signify a canonization of subjectivity*. It is never wrong to follow the convictions one has arrived at – in fact, one must do so. But it can very well be wrong to have come to such askew convictions in the first place, *by having stifled the protest of the anamnesis of being*. The guilt lies then in a different place, much deeper – not in the present act, not in the present judgment of conscience *but in the neglect of my being which made me deaf to the internal promptings of truth*.[12]

The "anamnesis of being" is an allusion to Plato's doctrine of knowledge as a kind of "memory" or "recollection" rooted not in the world of appearances, but in what is "really real." But we are also reminded of Royce's observation about "forgetting" as part of the life of conscience.

Both Nagel the philosopher and Ratzinger the theologian are drawing our attention to a *polarity* at the core of conscience between subjective and objective; between the perspective of the decision maker who must act embedded in a context using a "framework," and a perspective that is anchored in a more holistic awareness of moral truth. And neither author is suggesting that the polarity be *eliminated*. On the contrary, both see the polarity as part of the inner dynamism of conscience itself. We must *follow* our convictions; but we must also *examine* and *discipline* our convictions, seeking their justification in a larger vision of human good[13] (see Figure 1).

Another way to think about the polarity to which Nagel and Ratzinger allude is to see it as a reflection of two aspects of every human action: an *expressive* aspect and an *effective* aspect. On the one hand, our actions express or manifest our inner lives, our personal moral prefer-

---

12 Ratzinger, *ibid*. Emphasis added. He continues: "For this reason, criminals of conviction like Hitler and Stalin are guilty. These crass examples should not serve to put us at ease but should rouse us to take seriously the earnestness of the plea: 'Free me from my unknown guilt' (Ps 19:13)."

13 With the eyes of faith, of course, the transcendent vision of the Creator can be seen as joined to the (immanent) subjectivity of the decision maker through a personal relationship.

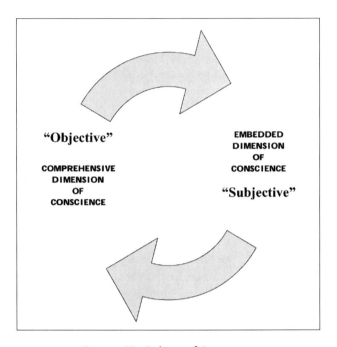

Figure 1: The Polarity of Conscience.

ences among the options available to us. When we act, we inevitably *say something about ourselves*. Action is, in part, autobiography. On the other hand, our actions also have effects on the world around us, they have consequences for the freedom and well-being of others; they are "trans-actions." When we act, we inevitably *make a difference in the world around us*. These two aspects of human action invite two ways of *assessing* human action, one subjective and the other objective; one "embedded" in the flow of daily decision making and the other more "comprehensive" in its (less partial) awareness. Both ways of assessing human action are essential: (1) the subjective exercise of conscience affirms the dignity of the human person, and (2) the objective or impartial exercise of conscience affirms the common good.

As Royce might say, left to our subjectivity alone, we inevitably return to the illusion of selfishness, "forgetting what we have seen". And Piaget might add a similar observation about the illusion of compliance with social norms. Finding a reliable (non-illusory) perspective for moral judgment calls for remembering (*anamnesis*) – a task that is assisted by both nature and nurture.

Summary of Part I

Conscience seeks to discern in human nature a platform for non-arbitrarily resolving competing ethical loyalties. Perhaps the "postmodern" fear is that this kind of discernment might involve the sacrifice of freedom or autonomy. But on this point, we would do well to consider the wisdom in philosopher Richard Norman's observation that:

> [t]he sacrificing of one's own interests need not be a sacrificing of oneself to something *external*. My commitment to my friends or my children, to a person whom I love or a social movement in which I believe, may be a part of my own deepest being, so that when I devote myself to them, my overriding experience is not that of *sacrificing* myself but of *fulfilling* myself.[14]

Norman seems to be suggesting – echoing Ratzinger – that each of us ultimately finds the same basis for conscience in his/her own "deepest being". The idea of conscience carries with it the idea of a *shared moral consciousness*, which we can approach in a disciplined way rather than fleeing it as if it were fragile and fragmentary. An adequate account of the inner dynamics of conscience appears to call for supplementing our embedded decision making with a more comprehensive view of the "big picture" – the patterns and directions that multiple decision makers (acting independently) display over time. "Conscience itself" seems to be the answer to Drucker's question as it is directed to organizations: "Who, then, is concerned with the common good?"

---

14   *The Moral Philosophers*, Oxford: Oxford University Press, 1983, p. 249. Emphasis added.

II. Conscience and the Corporation

Let us now reflect on the analogy between the polarity within personal conscience and a polarity within conscience as it applies to organizations – especially business corporations.

Moral Projection and the Polarity of Conscience

Often the leaders of organizations can profit from what we understand about ourselves as individuals. In the case of conscience, I believe this is especially true. Ethical values are present in both individual and organizational decision making and our understanding can be enriched in both directions. In the *Encyclopedic Dictionary of Business Ethics*, I formulated this analogical approach as follows:

> *Moral Projection Principle.* It is appropriate not only to describe organizations and their characteristics by analogy with individuals, it is also appropriate normatively to look for and to foster moral attributes in organizations by analogy with those we look for and foster in individuals.[15]

We have seen that the consciences of individuals in their subjectivity – however "awakened" they might be from the slumber of selfishness or compliance – need to seek validation in a more comprehensive perspective, lest they become "deaf to the internal promptings of truth" or – at the extreme – "criminals of conviction". Can we connect this observation to our understanding of *corporations* as moral actors? Does it apply to the idea of corporate conscience? What does it say about stakeholder thinking?

---

15   See "moral projection, principle of", in *Encyclopedic Dictionary of Business Ethics*, Werhane and Freeman, eds, Blackwell Publishers, 1997, p. 432. The idea is at least as old as Plato – that organizations are in many ways macro-versions (projections) of ourselves as individuals – human beings writ large.

What is Stakeholder Thinking?

It behooves us to clarify the normal meaning of the phrase "stakeholder thinking" for purposes of analysis in what follows. The phrase usually refers to a decision process used by corporate management, a decision process that highlights the implications of various available courses of action for different groups of affected parties (the stakeholders). As a process, stakeholder thinking might be orchestrated in different ways, but whatever the orchestration, it involves an analysis of specific impacts on specific groups within an assumed economic and political system. In other words, stakeholder thinking is intended to function within the context of the decision making that corporations already do in other (non-ethical) arenas.[16] For different corporate decisions, the concrete set of stakeholders can vary along many dimensions, including time and place, *which* parties are affected, the *magnitude* of the effects upon persons within each class of stakeholders, and the *significance* of the effects upon those in each class of stakeholders. For example, are these stakeholders affected strictly in economic terms, or are the effects psychological or spiritual – involving rights or levels of well-being more significant than, say, material disappointment?

Stakeholder thinking "operationalizes" corporate conscience within its specific circumstances. In this respect, stakeholder thinking is the corporate analogue to *subjective* thinking on the part of individual conscience. A more *comprehensive* perspective would involve stepping outside of the limitations of time and place, searching for impartiality with attention to the ways in which markets, laws, and social norms may actually undermine their assumed and intended directions. The phrase "stakeholder thinking" in its normal use *presupposes* a context that is politically and economically

---

16 Frameworks allow us to organize, and ultimately to *manage*, the decision-making process. In other contexts, the word "ideology" is used with a similar connotation: "a body of doctrine or belief that guides an individual, social movement, institution, class, or large group [...] along with the devices for putting it into operation." (Random House *Webster's Unabridged Dictionary*). And in some ways, what we call the "culture" of a social group has a similar function.

given. A company that does stakeholder thinking is typically thinking "inside its box" we might say, with specific customers, employees, suppliers, capital markets, laws, and regulations. The ethical value of stakeholder thinking is (i) that it enlarges moral consideration from a narrow group of parties (stockholders) to a broader group of parties; and (ii) that it makes ethical decisions systematic and to some degree open to measurement ("triple bottom line reporting", "balanced scorecard", etc.).

Stakeholder thinking therefore corresponds on an organizational level to what Nagel called agent-centered thinking, *not* in the sense of self-interested thinking, of course, but in the sense of thinking that departs from the agent's perspective (location) in the here and now. It is the thinking of a corporate actor that is *embedded* in a network of transactions with parties whose conceptions of their own goods, their own interests, their own rights – may or may not survive scrutiny from a more objective point of view.

Reflections about the larger social implications of corporate decision making (e.g., regarding the family, the moral and spiritual development of children, public health, civic virtue, and the natural environment) are typically *not* framed in stakeholder terms. This is mostly because they involve stepping "outside of the box" and turning a critical eye toward the influence of business behavior within the social system as a whole, what some would call "the common good."[17] Perhaps this is a useful way to distinguish the contributions of CSR and the Catholic Social Tradition (CST) from conventional approaches to business ethics.

17   Philosopher Immanuel Kant invoked ideas like a "kingdom or community of ends" and "universalizability" in relation to objective ("categorical") moral imperatives and Rousseau invoked "the General Will". Today the concept of "sustainability" is used by those who seek to remind us of a "macro" point of view. These ideas recall the comprehensive perspective to which both Nagel and Ratzinger referred. They go beyond compartmentalizing affected parties, politically segmenting, as it were, the moral community.

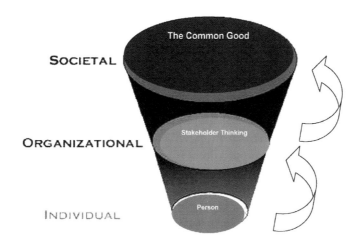

Figure 2: Levels of Moral Awareness.

Three Levels of Reflection in Business Ethics

It has been standard over the past three decades to think of the field of business ethics as involving three levels of analysis: 1) the level of individual responsibility and decision making; 2) the level of corporate responsibility and decision making; and 3) the level of the social system as a whole. Conscience is present at each level (see Figure 2), and at each level there are questions about the sufficiency of market-based and law-based reasoning. The challenge before us relates to the relationships between and among these three levels.

What is often overlooked is that these levels of analysis are not morally independent or autonomous. That is, the pursuit of *conscientiousness* at one level may require reflection on an adjacent level. Just as conscience at the level of the individual seems to call for supplementation from a less *partial* perspective – inviting more comprehensive moral reflection – so too conscience at the level of the organization seems to call for supplementation from a less *partial* perspective.[18] Conscience involves *polarities*.

Whether human beings can ever be *completely impartial* is doubtful, of course, but it seems clear that we can be *more or less partial*. So perhaps a better way to describe the polarity of conscience is in terms of a *relatively partial* and a *relatively impartial* perspective on a given decision-making situation.

In the case of an organization, *stakeholder thinking* represents the more embedded, less comprehensive outlook, the more "subjective" point of view (recalling Nagel and Ratzinger). Corporate conscience calls for stakeholder reflection, to be sure, but it also calls for a shift to the societal or social system perspective, asking of corporate leadership more than simply stakeholder satisfaction. The "common good" offers a new challenge to business leaders – a challenge that reaches beyond stakeholder thinking. Some examples may help to clarify the point:

– Some cigarette companies appear to pay regular attention to their stakeholders with focus groups, warnings about health effects, and philanthropy. Yet a more comprehensive (less "embedded") look at the common good (through the lens of public health) might well lead to decision making that would diversify away from tobacco products entirely. Such a corporate reorientation need not be forced by making tobacco products illegal. Indeed, "prohibition" in its many forms can be ineffective, as Americans know well from their experience with the 18th and 21st amendments to the US Constitution. Conscience in this context is about corporate *choices*, not simply or necessarily about corporate *compliance*.

– Producers of certain interactive video games market them to adolescents even though there is significant evidence that explicit sex and violence in these games actually does affect behavior. Does "stakeholder thinking" reach this level of social awareness – or does it

18   An individual can seek a more impartial perspective from any number of social contexts, including – but not limited to – his or her family, neighborhood, church, professional association, or organizational workplace.

remain in the realm of organizational market competition, legal compliance, rights of free speech and "giving the customer what he/she wants"?[19] When an industry appears to have a "vested interest" in certain rights protections – whether the industry be video games or news media – *insisting* on those rights can be dysfunctional for the society as a whole.

– In a related area, television networks and movie studios frequently look at stakeholders such as employees, viewers, investors, etc. in deciding what programs and films to produce. Yet there is no doubt that sex and violence in these media has escalated to a point where families have difficulty finding appropriate entertainment within the home. The common good seems to call for as much attention to the *informational* and *entertainment* environments as to the *natural* environment.

– Concern about "global warming" is a concern about the common good of humankind. Indifference to this concern (assuming it is not based on scientific counter-evidence) seems to be due to conventional stakeholder logic which is *partial* to stakeholders in a short-term time horizon. "Future generations" are typically not listed as stakeholders in conventional stakeholder thinking.[20]

What these four examples seem to share is a call for a "larger" social awareness that steps outside of the embedded stakeholder framework in an effort to see whether (or not) the implications for the *common good* of the identified decision-making patterns are dysfunctional. Stakeholder thinking needs to be balanced by a more comprehensive concern.[21]

19   Shannon Prather, "US Judge Throws Out Minnesota Video Game Law", *Pioneer Press*, 1 August 2006. The Minnesota Attorney General said he would consider appealing the ruling.

20   For an example of a company that thinks "outside the box" on matters ecological, see Ray C. Anderson, *Mid-Course Correction: Toward a Sustainable Enterprise*, White River Junction, VT: Chelsea Green Publishing Company, 1998.

21   Charles Handy, "What's a Business For?" *Harvard Business Review*, December 2002, wrote: "*We need to associate with a cause in order to give purpose to our lives.*

Whose Responsibility is the Common Good?

The common good cannot, of course, be the exclusive concern of any single *organization* – or indeed of any *sector* of a socio-economic system. The more comprehensive perspective invited by the examples above calls for solutions that might be *beyond the control* of any given stakeholder-atten-tive entity; solutions beyond the capacities of corporations, government agencies, NGOs, and others *acting separately*. Multi-sector challenges call for collaborations that surpass (almost by definition) the more narrowly-focused stakeholder thinking that we ask of individual organizations. One might say that there are multiple responsibilities attaching to any company's *place* in the community (stakeholder responsibilities) and there is also a responsibility of a different *kind* (or of a different *order*), namely, the responsibility (deriving from membership in the human com-munity) to *contribute* to solutions, to *collaborate* ethically – in contrast to a company's transactions with its own set of stakeholders.

Adjustments to the social system itself may need to be made in order to avoid tragic trends emerging from stakeholder thinking by each corpo-ration operating independently. Such adjustments may come in the form of interventions by the public sector, but they may not. Other influences on corporate decision making over many decades have also been effec-tive, such as appeals to corporate consciences and industry associations by NGOs, education at home and in schools, consumer boycotts, social investment screens, community-sponsored ethics awards, etc. Perhaps most importantly, public – private – nonprofit partnerships may be the only match for common good challenges like those illustrated above in the areas of public health, the natural environment, and the moral climate of entertainment.

So we see that the three-level analysis of business ethics not only carries with it taxonomic utility for mapping the subject matter of the field, it *also* speaks to the normative demands of moral insight in business

The pursuit of a cause does not have to be the prerogative of charities and the not-for-profit sector. Nor does a mission to improve the world make business into a social agency." (Emphasis added).

decision making. Individuals are called to get outside of themselves in assessing the deliverances of their subjective consciences. And organizations, similarly, are called to get "outside of themselves" in assessing the deliverances of their stakeholder analyses. John Paul II seems to have appreciated this point when he wrote in 1991:

> In singling out new needs and new means to meet them, one must be guided by *a comprehensive picture of man* which respects all the dimensions of his being and which subordinates his material and instinctive dimensions to his interior and spiritual ones. If, on the contrary, a direct appeal is made to his instincts – while ignoring in various ways the reality of the person as intelligent and free – then *consumer attitudes* and *life-styles* can be created which are objectively improper and often damaging to his physical and spiritual health.[22]

John Paul II is saying that any market system, even a regulated and stakeholder-driven market system, depends profoundly on a view of human nature (a "comprehensive picture of man") and on a view of the common good that guides its business leaders and corporate practitioners.[23] Stakeholder thinking may be necessary, but other kinds of thinking – more holistic in nature – are also necessary.

---

22   *Centesimus Annus*, 36. Emphasis mine.
23   Recall Ratzinger's warning (alluded to earlier) for us not to neglect "the internal promptings of truth".

Summary and Conclusion

We have puzzled over a question asked by Peter Drucker over a dozen years ago: "In the society of organizations [...] Who is concerned with the common good?" In responding to this question with the help of both philosophical and theological reflections on conscience, we have found that the answer lies beyond conventional stakeholder thinking.[24]

The consciences of corporations involve a kind of partiality or subjectivity, even when they appreciate the importance of stakeholders and go beyond profitability and legal compliance. Like individual consciences, corporate consciences must seek validation lest they become unduly committed to stakeholder demands that are not sustainable from a more impartial perspective.

Business ethics can be seen in terms of relationships to various constituencies or stakeholders in a spider web diagram, and the morality of those relationships is certainly an important part of business ethics. But there is another dimension to the moral point of view than current relationships to discrete groups of affected parties. There is a whole which is greater than the parts but this whole does not show up in "constituency reasoning". Perhaps we should reserve the phrase "the common good" (a central theme of CST) for this dimension of moral awareness. Without attention to the whole, corporate leaders are in danger of missing their moral responsibilities for collective action, for action as participants in a human community when they see that community tilting in a tragic direction.

I observed earlier in this essay that the inner life of conscience begins with a kind of *awareness* that overcomes two persistent *illusions* – the

24   It lies in the direction of a further comment by Drucker: "The emergence of a strong, independent, capable social sector – neither public nor private sector – is thus a central need of the society of organizations. But by itself it is not enough – the organizations of both the public and the private sector must share the work." Peter Drucker, "The Age of Social Transformation," *The Atlantic Monthly*, November 1994, pp. 53–80.

illusion of selfishness and the illusion of social authority. Perhaps we can now discern the need for another kind of awareness that helps to overcome a third persistent illusion – an illusion of stakeholder sufficiency. It is the awareness of a shared or common good that all institutions, economic, political, and civil must join in supporting.

T.S. Eliot, in one of his *Choruses from the Rock* (1934), observes that humankind spends a great deal of time "dreaming of systems so perfect that no one will need to be good."[25] The power of this poetic phrase can be appreciated in the present context because the "systems so perfect" include the external systems of the market, the law and regulatory machinery of government. But perhaps to the surprise of some, they also seem to include the venerated apparatus of "stakeholder thinking".

25 T.S. Eliot, *Choruses from The Rock*, VI (1934).

CHAPTER 5

Business Ethics and Inter-Religious Contribution in the Age of Globalization

NOEL KEIZO YAMADA

Introduction: Religious Contribution to Business Ethics

The World Conference on Religion and Peace (WCRP) held its Seventh Assembly in Amman, Jordan in November 1999, and had as its theme: *Global Action for Common Living*. The Assembly brought together 1,400 delegates and participants from fifteen religious traditions drawn from seventy countries, carrying on a tradition begun by the WCRP in Kyoto, Japan in 1970. The Amman Declaration was as follows: "Economic systems must enable the elimination of the poverty and powerlessness that characterizes the lives of a major portion of the human family. Eradicating poverty in the first decades of the 21st century is feasible, affordable and a moral imperative for humanity. Developmental and environmental challenges cannot be separated because of the depletion of non-renewable resources, global warming and all forms of pollution and degradation."

The eighth Assembly of the World Conference on Religion and Peace took place in Kyoto, Japan, in August 2006. It brought together 2,000 delegates and participants from 100 countries and regions. As a staff member of the Peace Research Center of the Japanese Committee of the WCRP, I joined the Assembly as one of the representatives from Japan. I would like to present the Assembly's main points regarding business ethics. The rights embodied in the International Bill of Rights, with its inclusion of civil, political, economic, social, and cultural rights can never be realized apart from the actualization of the common ethical concerns embodied in all religious traditions. These call us to be individually and socially responsible for our neighbors and those in need. They help us draw on the sources of love, duty, and responsibility as the foundations for the establishment of justice. WCRP recognizes that the peoples of the world are interdependent, existing within a web of economic and environmental realities which is made more urgent by the dynamics of globalization with both its positive and negative impact.

A concept of just and sustainable human development, holistic in its nature, depends on the development of equitable and fair systems of production and distribution capable of providing for the material survival and needs of all persons and accessible to all. Such systems must enable the elimination of the poverty and powerlessness that characterize the lives of a major portion of the human family. Eradicating poverty in the first decades of the 21st century is feasible, affordable, and a moral imperative for humanity. Developmental and environmental challenges cannot be separated because of the depletion of non-renewable resources, global warming, and all forms of environmental pollution and degradation. These weaken the capacity of the ecosystem to produce and regenerate, particularly as population growth multiplies the demands. Exploitative patterns threaten not only the eco-system, but also increase the hardships and suffering of the marginalized and portend a damaged if not destroyed planet for future generations.

WCRP's vision and hope are for common living in the 21st century. Hope because the vision of a just and peaceful world is attainable. Hope because we know both the challenges of the world and the possibilities for their solutions. Hope because the resources for meeting humanity's basic needs are available if only we have the will to use them appropriately. Hope because all our religious traditions claim commitment to peace and the achievement of the common good.

I. The Role of Business Ethics in the Age of Globalization

Lights and Shadows of Globalization

Especially in economic life, the peoples of the world are linked together as never before. This is a source of hope for the deepening of a truly world-wide sense that all men and women on this earth are brothers and sisters in one global family, created by one God, having one common destiny. The paradox of the moment, however, is that the process of globalization is simultaneously leading to an increasingly ruptured and unjust world. Cultural traditions that have meaning to the lives of whole peoples are under threat. The global market enriches some while impoverishing others. Many communities – both in the developed and developing worlds – are fragmented by the dynamics of the market. The result is growing inequity, declining quality of life, and even life expectancy for many, and increasing powerlessness of the most vulnerable. The paradox of globalization thus confronts the human race with a challenge different from any it has had to address in past history: how to be one world-wide community while respecting the dignity of all the sub-communities that make up the human family around the globe.

The Challenge of Globalization

A key aspect of the paradox of globalization is that different persons make such divergent assessments of its positive and negative consequences. These disagreements are in part due to the differing social standpoints from which the emerging global realities are considered. It is important to highlight some of the key signs of the times that call for deeper reflection if the challenges of globalization are to be addressed.

- Globalization brings enhanced economic growth in many parts of the world to the benefit of some people, yet the gap between rich and poor continues to widen everywhere.

– Globalization enhances international trade and communication, but it also intensifies the destruction of local and even national communities. All the data indicate that inequality is significantly increasing throughout the world; this inequality itself leads to reduced social solidarity and weakened community.

– With globalization, downsizing and outsourcing enhance the competitiveness of many enterprises and help sustain their productivity and competitiveness. But in the process many workers see their once secure jobs eliminated and few replacements in sight.

– Global trade serves the needs of many people by providing numerous products they want at decreased prices, but the global arms trade and traffic in drugs has enormously destructive effects on the security and health of many communities.

– Many in the business community and in other sectors of civil society have worked to promote socially responsible investment, to create codes of global business conduct, and to form partnerships with local groups seeking the well-being of those affected by global trends. Yet the World Trade Organization's strategy and ideology that see unimpeded markets as essential, suggest that such measures could be challenged as unfair restraints on trade.

– International financial institutions seek to regulate flows of credit and terms of trade in ways that will enhance the efficiency and productivity of developing countries. The burden of conditions these institutions set for credit and debt reduction is most often borne disproportionately by the poorest and most vulnerable members of the communities involved.

– Global technology transfers increase productive capacity, generate new jobs, and enhance important dimensions of human well-being. However, unequal access to this technology leads to the growing inequality of power, political influence, and ability to shape the economic decisions that affect the common good, especially the well-being of the poor.

– Awareness of the need to protect the natural environment is growing throughout the world, but this awareness is not accompanied by willingness to address the ways the natural world is increasingly treated as a commodity. There are limits to the use of finite natural resources and to the levels of consumption the biosphere can sustain.

– While an increasing number of women have moved into the paid labor market, they remain highly vulnerable to dangerous labor conditions and still bear compounding burdens of unpaid housework.

All of these signs of our times call for decision and action. Looking forward to the future, confidence must be sustained that human decisions of today can encourage the positive, and can reduce the negative aspects of globalization.

The Challenge of the Spirit of God, i.e. Business Ethics

Responding to these challenges requires innovative thinking, courageous experimentation, and moral commitment to the justice due to all inhabitants of this globe. We stand at a crossroad which is above all a crossroad of the spirit; therefore, it requires a response which is rooted in spirituality and imaginative vision. The Spirit of God is active in a world seeking fullness of life for all of God's people. The task before people of faith is to discern where God's Spirit is laboring to bring a new creation into being and to join their efforts to that work of God. Such discernment calls for a conversion of heart and transformation of society, a reclamation of values, and a renewed spirituality. Deep attention to the presence of the unifying Spirit of God can draw people of diverse religious traditions together in ways that foreshadow the truly humane global community God wills for all of humanity. It will lead to mutually sustaining relationships with one another and with all creation, encountering a God who lives among us and honoring that Presence by our treatment of the other with justice and compassion – with love. This renewed spirituality will feed our hunger for meaning and temper culturally cultivated temptations to excessive individualism, to consumerism, to control, and to greed.

The Vision of Catholic Social Thought: A Basis for Business Ethics

The tradition of Catholic social teaching can help sustain this spirituality and shape the social structures it suggests by the ethical principles it draws from the gospel and from the wisdom forged by reasoned reflection on human experience.

First, the dignity of the human person, created in the image and likeness of God, is the central goal and governing norm for all economic and political structures, policies, and activities.

Second, this dignity can be realized only in community and solidarity with others in sustainable development that cares for the natural environment.

Third, this implies that participation by all is an essential touchstone for assessing the justice of the emergent patterns of the global marketplace.

Fourth, where such injustice is in fact occurring, those who are poor, marginalized, or powerless have the single most urgent claim on our concern and practical action.

Fifth, the practical realization of this vision calls for the development of global institutions that are respectful of small and intermediate sized communities following the principle of subsidiarity.[1]

II. Generating the Dynamism for a Value Shift

The global problems spawned by highly industrialized societies in the second half of the twentieth century can be divided into at least five major categories: the proliferation of nuclear weapons and arms buildups, environmental problems, the North-South problem, the structural injustice and violence associated with human-rights violations, and discrimination

---

1   I partly quote from "Social Responsibility in the Age of Globalization", 1999.

against and abuse of ethnic minorities. Most of these problems cannot be resolved through technological measures alone; a radical change in the value system of the world's leading nations is required.

What factors might encourage a shift in the values that are now dominant? The commentator, Shuichi Kato, has written: "I think we can learn a great deal from such traditional religions as Buddhism and Christianity." He explains his conclusion as follows:

> Buddhism has the concept of the bodhisattva, who aspires to altruistic action. The bodhisattva's mission is not just to attain personal enlightenment but also to lead all people to enlightenment. This represents a qualitative shift away from such egocentric values as the wish for worldly benefits or fatalistic resignation. Christianity has the concept of neighborly love. Altruism is an ideal shared by many religions. It constitutes one paradigm for a basic value shift.[2]

The Gospels set forth the dichotomies of rich versus poor, Solomon's glory versus the lilies of the valley, and worldly power versus the kingdom of heaven. In the Buddhist world too, just as the Buddha gave up his kingdom to devote himself to austerities, spiritual practice begins with renunciation of the world. Poverty and powerlessness are elected over wealth and power. It is not only a matter of religious good works based on altruism. Good works may provide symptomatic relief to an ailing society, but they do not lead to a lasting cure. Nor is it only a matter of individual conversion. Society is not just a collection of individuals; it moves in accordance with its own mechanisms, which transcend the individual. If society as a whole is to change its direction, it must alter its dominant values (wealth, power, efficiency). The value-shift dynamism with which traditional religions were originally equipped can make some kind of contribution to this change. The question is whether society can learn from them.

The dynamism for the value shift needed to cope with the challenges of the world today is beyond the resources of any one religion. It calls for inter-religious cooperation. Solving the global structural problems that give rise to human-rights violations and discrimination demands active cooperation, surmounting the barriers that separate religions, by means of initiatives for world peace, the protection of human rights, and the promotion of justice. For the past 30 years I have been involved in joint activities with local residents in Chiba Prefecture, Japan, and on the Philippine island of Mindanao, whose human rights have been infringed and environment ruined by Japanese firms' pollution. The Chiba residents finally won their court case against a Japanese corporation. This grassroots movement was made possible by the cooperation of various religious groups and non-governmental organizations.

III. Inter-Religious Cooperation to Promote Tolerance and Ethical Business

Since the end of the Cold War, triggered by the fall of the Berlin Wall in 1989, ethnic and tribal conflict has flared up around the world. In these circumstances, the United Nations' decision to emphasize the importance of reconciliation and coexistence by designating 1995 the United Nations Year for Tolerance has deep significance. A new world order based on respect for each person's dignity, and indeed, reverence for all life, is now being sought. Today, 63 years after the end of World War II, it is time for Japan, too, to make a new start toward contributing to world peace. I believe inter-religious cooperation is the best way to generate the dynamism for the necessary value shift.

The Conference on "Ethics and Economics" was held at Columbus, Ohio in November 1995. I summarize the work of one of the Dialogue groups dealing with "The impacts of Religious Faith on the Ethics of Business". The group members were more than thirty, including Jewish, Hindu, Muslim and Christian panelists.

1) The main questions which focused the presentations and group discussions were as follows: how does religious faith impact one's business

practices? How are people related to their ultimate destiny, and what is the principle that lies at the heart of this destiny?

a) From a Jewish point of view, moral obligation to society grows out of religious commitments. Jewish literature is replete with references to business and earning a livelihood in honesty. The Jew is very centered on the ordinary and mundane of daily living and work. Through this commitment to the ordinary the Jew fulfills his or her duties to others and to God. We must ask how one's actions affect others. The philosophy of egoism is not acceptable in the realm of commerce wherein one's actions have consequences upon the dignity of others.

b) From a Christian point of view, the Brethren tradition puts emphasis on putting faith to work. Business practices must be embedded in moral behavior and dispositions which in turn are embedded within religious commitment and practices. Usually religion and business are not freely discussed together. This reticence might be changing within the current Western culture. For Christians the teaching of the incarnation is central for an ethical orientation. If God became human in Christ this sets up a high standard for the business person regarding the manner in which he or she treats others. Also, Jesus' behavior gives clues for the business person. Jesus came to serve and not seek authoritarian power, for example, Christians' goal is to imitate Jesus in humble service. Christian commitment allows one to engage in the type of business which serves a legitimate purpose in society. Quality is moral value in the product one makes; it is not simply a business approach. A Christian sees all of life as sacred, and brings his whole self to work including his faith. Some have commented that the company reflects his personality which is imbues with faith.

c) In finding Hinduism through its scriptures, a Hindu comes to respect all religions and their scriptures. Can we relate an intense inner life to business? Believers of Hinduism see Hinduism as complementary with other religions and their codes of living. All ethical codes echo the other major world religions. The important thing is to struggle to reconcile the life of faith within the world of business. Sometimes

the simplicity and clarity of the world's religious codes challenge the
individual not to compromise or rationalize ethical duties into complex claims. But it is difficult to live out these codes. If ethics could
be in the open, work could become uplifting and noble.

d) Islam means to submit to the will of God. All the prophets of Judaism
and Christianity are respected in Islam. It is a religion which emphasizes peace, equality and social justice. All trade in Islam must be
honest and not entail exorbitant profits. The product of trade must
be moral and in accord with Islam's doctrines. Business cannot be
run at any cost. Greed and ego are condemned in the Koran. Care
for the poor and needy is extolled. A Muslim's character is dictated
by the Koran and the holy practices and sayings of Mohammed. In
Islam the believer is conscious of the fact that one is never alone.
He or she is always with the Creator and must answer to Him at
the time of judgment. This is a consciousness that should fill the
business day.

2) The highlights of the Dialogue group were as follows:

a) Religious faith and the surrender of oneself to God's keeping, which
faith includes, gives one the freedom and the courage to do the ethical thing despite the risk of loss.

b) Central to religious faith is the "divine" dimension of our fellow
humans to whom we are drawn, therefore, to relate with respect,
compassion, caring, justice, and equality. Faith vividly grounds in
living consciously the "Golden Rule" in its various expressions: "Love
thy neighbor as thyself", or "Do unto others as you would have them
do unto you".

c) Our religious faith tells us and others who we are, i.e. our deepest
identity. Ethical behavior rooted in a person's faith is, therefore, not
a compliance with some principle "out there", but an expression from
within of "who I am". So rooted, ethical behavior is consistent, per-
severing, and almost predictable.

d) Doing work well as an expression of faith makes it a joy. It brings
peace, consolation. It is fun even in the midst of challenge and
ambiguity.

e) There have been very helpful exercises of leading people of different faiths or belief systems to give common expression to their faiths through the process of inter-religious dialogue. At the heart of most religious and belief systems are core common meanings and values which, therefore, bond all believers together somehow. Out of such commonly experienced faith, ethical codes or statements of value can emerge. Such grounding gives conviction and elicits commitment.

IV. Putting the Spirit of Tolerance into Action

At the Conference on Human Rights in Asia, organized by the Society of Jesus and held at Ateneo de Manila University in the Philippines in October 1994, I learned a great deal about the spirit of tolerance from Buddhist priests from Cambodia, Thailand and South Korea, and Muslims from Indonesia. I have been trying to put the insights gained there into practice in my own way. Building on more than 30 years of joint activities with people in other Asian countries, including the above-mentioned movements to oppose Japanese companies' export of pollution, I am now engaged in activities and studies aimed at making Japanese corporate managers more aware of business ethics. I am also participating in joint research on the theme "Religion and the Promotion of Human Rights, Justice and Tolerance in Japanese Society and the International Community". Cooperation with various religious organizations is indispensable to the development of these activities and research.

The legacy of Asian religious traditions provides essential motive power. In particular, I am deeply impressed by the basic philosophy of Cambodian Buddhism, tested in the crucible of a quarter century of war that caused untold suffering and transformed Cambodia into tragic wasteland. During the brutal Cambodian civil war the great Buddhist priest, Maha Ghosananda, left his temple and devoted himself to working for peace alongside people suffering on battlefields and in refugee camps. He has written: "Human rights begin when each man becomes a brother and each woman becomes a sister; when we honestly care for each other, we will all become servants for each others' rights. When we accept that we are part of a great human family – that every man and every woman has the nature of Buddha, Allah, and Christ – then we will sit, talk, make peace, and bring humankind to its fullest flowering."[3] Peacemaking is at the heart of life. We peacemakers must meet as often as possible to make peace in ourselves, our countries, and the whole world.

Any real peace will not favor East, West, North or South. Peace is nonviolent. Peace is based on justice and freedom. Our journey for peace begins today and everyday. Making peace is our life. We must invite people from around the world to join in our journey. As we make peace for ourselves and our country, we make peace for the whole world. The suffering in Maha Ghosananda's homeland continues. Great suffering generates great compassion. Compassion creates peace. Peaceful hearts create peaceful individuals, families, communities and nations, and ultimately a peaceful world. What can religions do to heal this suffering world? What did the Buddha and the Christ teach? According to Maha Ghosananda, "one of the Buddha's most courageous acts was to walk onto a battlefield to stop a conflict. He did not sit in his temple waiting for the opponents to approach him. He walked right onto the battlefield to stop the conflict ..." How do we resolve a conflict, a battle, a power struggle? What does reconciliation really mean? Gandhi said that the essence of nonviolent action is that it seeks to put an end to antagonism, not the antagonists. This is important. The opponent has our respect. We implicitly trust his or her human nature and understand that ill-will is caused by ignorance. By appealing to the best in each other, both of us achieve the satisfaction of peace. We both become peacemakers. Gandhi called this a "bilateral victory".

Maha Ghosananda exhorts Buddhists:

> Many Buddhists are suffering in Tibet, Cambodia, Laos, Burma, Vietnam, and elsewhere. The most important thing we Buddhists can do is to foster the liberation of the human spirit in every nation of the human family. We must use our

3   Maha Ghosananda, *Step by Step*, Parcuax Press, 1992.

religious heritage as a living resource. We Buddhists must find the courage to leave our temples and enter the temples of human experience, temples that are filled with suffering. If we listen to the Buddha, Christ or Gandhi, we can do nothing else. The refugee camps, the prisons, the ghettos and the battlefields will then become our temples. We have much work to do.

These words apply equally to Christians and followers of other religions. They exemplify the spirit of tolerance, the essence of inter-religious cooperation.

In Asia, human rights are rooted in the community and lead to a sense of social responsibility. If human rights and tolerance are to be respected, local communities must be respected, supported and utilized. If communities are to promote human rights on the basis of love, justice and wisdom, they must be linked in a strong network transcending national borders. Inter-religious cooperation is the key. While respecting one another's differences, religions should set aside their petty quarrels and work together whole-heartedly to accomplish humanity's major goals. This is the significance of community in the world today, and this is what can provide the dynamism for a value shift. Only on this basis will the word "Japan" become an acronym for "Justice for All, Peace for All Nations."

Let me conclude this part with the final words of Cardinal Arns' 1994 commemorative address: "There will never be peace in Latin America, in Japan, or in the world, if we do not build step by step, day by day, the conditions for peace. The way of peace is the object of our faith. It is the meaning of our lives in this suffering world."[4]

---

4   Paulp Evaristo Arns, "The Way of Peace", *Echoes of Peace*, 1994.

Conclusion: Global Leadership through the 21st Century

I would like to introduce the concept of "Kyosei" which means "living together and working together for the common good." A more detailed definition: "all people, regardless of race, religion, or culture, harmoniously living and working together, accepting, recognizing, and respecting each others' differences, and having confidence in their mutual support for one another." I introduced this concept at the first International Business, Economics, and Ethics World Conference (ISBEE) in Chiba, Japan from the side of business, but I would like to develop this idea of "common living" from the viewpoint of religious tradition in our day.

Kyôsei is originally from Indian Buddhism in the 4th century. In order to implement common living, four elements are necessary:

1. Understanding: "stand under" others, only then can we *understand* others.
2. Relationships: with who are we related?
   a. God   b. self   c. other people   d. other countries   e. all creation
3. Responsibility: "response-ability" – to whom do we respond?
   a. God   b. self   c. other people   d. other countries   e. all creation
4. Compassion: this is the most important condition for implementing *common living (Kyôsei)*.

Love your neighbors as you love yourself. Compassion and love is to bear the burdens and sufferings of your neighbors as your own burdens and sufferings. Love according to the Gospels is the same as the mindfulness of Buddhism, i.e. to bear the burdens and sufferings together.

This *togetherness* is the treasure of Asian culture. We Asians can share this treasure of *common living* with the rest of the world through the abundant treasure of inter-religious cooperation to promote business ethics. As mentioned previously. Christians, Buddhists, Shintoists and many other religious peoples have a wonderful ecumenical spirit, cooperating together for world peace and global ethics. In Japan, I am happy to be committed to the WCRP. In the spirit of *kyôsei*, we established the Japanese Society for Business Ethics in 1993 and the Japanese Business

Ethics Research Center in 1997. I have a dream through these activities that "JAPAN" will truly come to stand for "Justice for All, Peace for All Nations." I hope Japan may become a nation that truly contributes to the justice and peace of the world.

PART II

Achieving the Common Good in the Globalization Context:
A Variety of Initiatives Involving Business at Different Levels

CHAPTER 6

Nature, Society and Future Generations

LÁSZLÓ ZSOLNAI

Today's business has a major impact on society and the natural environment. It considerably affects the fate and survival of natural ecosystems and the life conditions of present and future generations. Applying the imperative of responsibility developed by Hans Jonas, we can say that business has a one way, non-reciprocal duty: to care for the beings which are under the impacts of its functioning.

1. The Imperative of Responsibility

To catalyze a responsible management ethos is needed to study moral responsibility in the context of the ecological, technological and social reality of our age. The most comprehensive theory of moral responsibility was presented by the German-American philosopher Hans Jonas in his opus magnum *The Imperative of Responsibility* (Jonas, 1979, 1984).

Jonas was born in Germany in 1903. He was tutored under the guidance of Edmund Husserl, Martin Heidegger, and Rudolf Bultman. Jonas began his philosophical work on Gnosticism and its role in the late Antiquity. In the post-war period Jonas was teaching philosophy at *The New School for Social Research* for decades. He published the German version of his theory of responsibility in 1979 under the title: *Das Prinzip Verantwortung. Versuch einer Ethic fur die Technologische Zivilization* (Jonas, 1979). The re-written and enlarged English edition was published in 1984 under the title: *The Imperative of Responsibility – In Search of an Ethics for the Technological Age* (Jonas, 1984).

In his book Jonas' basic preoccupation is the *impact* of *modern technology* on the *human condition*. The major theses on which his theory of responsibility is based are the following:

(i) The altered, always enlarged nature of human action, with the magnitude and novelty of its works and their impact on man's global future;

(ii) Responsibility is a correlate of power and must be commensurate with the latter's scope and that of its exercise;

(iii) An imaginative "heuristics of fear", replacing the former projections of hope, must tell us what is possibly at stake and what we must beware of;

(iv) Metaphysics must underpin ethics. Hence, a speculative attempt is made at such an underpinning of man's duties toward himself, his distant posterity, and the plenitude of life under his dominion;

(v) Objective imperatives for man in the scheme of things enable us to discriminate between legitimate and illegitimate goal-settings to our Promethean power.

Jonas argues that human action has changed so dramatically in our times that this changed nature of human action calls for a radical change in ethics as well. He stresses that in previous ethics

all dealing with the nonhuman world, that is, the whole realm of techne [...] was ethically neutral. [...] Ethical significance belonged to the direct dealing of man with man, including man dealing with himself: all traditional ethics is anthropocentric. [...] The entity of "man" and his basic condition was considered constant in essence and not itself an object of reshaping techne. [...] The effective range of action was small, the time span of foresight, goal-setting, and accountability was short, control of circumstances limited (Jonas, 1984, pp. 4–5).

According to Jonas new dimensions of responsibility emerged because *nature* became a *subject* of *human responsibility*. This is underlined by the fact of the irreversibility and cumulative character of man's impact on the living world. *Knowledge*, under these circumstances, is a prime duty of man, and must be commensurate with the causal scale of human action. Man should seek "not only the human good but also the good of things extra human, that is, to extend the recognition of 'ends in themselves' beyond the sphere of man and make the human good include the care of them" (Jonas, 1984, pp. 7–8.)

For Jonas an *imperative* that is responding to the new type of human action might run like this: "Act so that the effects of your action are compatible with the permanence of genuine human life". Or expressed negatively: "Act so that the effects of your action are not destructive of the future possibility of such life" (Jonas, 1984, p. 11). Since future human beings and non-human beings do not have rights, our duties to the future generations and to nature are independent of any idea of a right or reciprocity. Human responsibility is a *non-reciprocal duty* to *guarding beings* (Jonas, 1984, pp. 38–9).

Jonas states that the necessary conditions of moral responsibility are as follows: "The first and most general condition of responsibility is causal power, that is, that acting makes an impact on the world; the second, that such acting is under the agent's control; and the third, that he can foresee its consequences to some extent." (Jonas, 1984, p. 90). Jonas underlines that prospective responsibility is never formal but always *substantive*: "I feel responsible, not in the first place for my conduct and its consequences but for the matter that has a claim on my acting." For example "the well-being, the interest, the fate of others has, by circumstance or by agreement, come to my care, which means that my control over it involves at the same time my obligation for it." (Jonas, 1984, pp. 92–3).

The common features in responsibility are totality, continuity, and future-orientation. "Responsibilities encompass the total being of their object. [...] The pure being as such, and then the best being of the child, is what parental care is about." The statesman's responsibility is

for duration of his office or his power, is for the total life of community, the "public weal". [...] Neither parental nor governmental care can allow itself a vacation or pause, for the life of the object continues without intermission, making its demands anew, time after time. More important still is the continuity of the cared-for *existence* itself as a *concern*. [...] It is the future with which responsibility for a life, be it individual or communal, is concerned beyond its immediate present. [...] An agent's *concrete* moral *responsibility* at the time of action does extend further than to its proximate effects (Jonas, 1984, p. 102 sq).

Jonas summarizes the *imperative* of *responsibility* as follows. "The concept of responsibility implies that of an ought – first of an ought-to-be of something, then of an ought-to-do of someone in response to the first." This is the most evident in the case of a *new-born baby* "whose mere breathing uncontradictably addresses an ought to the world around, namely, to take care of him." Not only does the new-born call us in this way but "the unconditional end-in-itself of everything alive and the still-have-to-come of the faculties for securing this end" (Jonas, 1984, p. 130, 134).

2. Primordial Stakeholders of Business

Business activities considerably affect nature, society and future generations. These three entities are primordial stakeholders of business, with whom business has a non-contractual responsibility relationship. We should evaluate business activities from the perspective of nature, from the perspective of society, and from the perspective of future generations (Zsolnai, 2003).

From the perspective of nature, *integrity* is a central value. The notion of ecological integrity was first introduced by the American naturalist Aldo Leopold in his environmental classic *A Sand County Almanac*. He wrote: "a thing is right when it tends to preserve the integrity, stability, and beauty of the biotic community. It is wrong when it tends otherwise" (Leopold, 1948).

Business activities might be evaluated against sustainability indicators that operationalize the notion of ecological integrity (Azar, et al., 1996).

Let A be a business activity. Let E_1, ..., E_i, ..., E_m be sustainability indicators ($m > 1$).

E_i ( ) is an ecological value function defined as follows:

$$(1) \quad E_i(A) = \begin{cases} 1 & \text{if business activity A is good regarding sustainability indicator } E_i; \\ 0 & \text{if business activity A is neutral regarding sustainability indicator } E_i; \\ -2 & \text{if business activity A is bad regarding sustainability indicator } E_i. \end{cases}$$

$E_i(A)$ reflects the ecological value of A regarding sustainability indicator E_i.

The following vector represents the ecological value of business activity A regarding all the sustainability indicators E_1, ..., E_i, ..., E_m:

$$(2) \quad \underline{E}(A) = [E_1(A), ..., E_i(A), ..., E_m(A)]$$

To get an aggregate picture about the ecological value of a business activity system, we should define weights that show the importance of the sustainability indicators. Let w_1, ..., w_i, ..., w_m be such importance weights.

It is required that:

$$(3) \quad \sum w_i = 1$$

The aggregate ecological value of business activity A can be calculated as follows:

$$(4) \quad E(A) = \sum w_i E_i(A)$$

$E(A)$ shows the aggregate ecological value of business activity A ($1 \geq E(A) \geq -2$).

A business activity is considered *sustainable* if and only if its aggregate ecological value is positive. That is:

$$(5) \quad E(A) > 0$$

Evaluating business activity systems from a social perspective has been a long-lasting enterprise of welfare economics. Here *human well-being* is the central value. Amartya Sen proposed to understand human well-being in the terms of *capabilities*. Capability is a reflection on the freedom of a person to achieve valuable functioning. Therefore capabilities can be interpreted as substantive freedom that people enjoy (Sen, 1992).

Let C_1, ..., C_j, ..., C_n be capability indicators against which business activity systems can be evaluated $(j > 1)$.

Let the social value function C_j ( ) be defined as follows:

$$(6) \quad C_j(A) = \begin{cases} 1 & \text{if business activity } A \text{ is good regarding capability indicator } C_j; \\ 0 & \text{if business activity } A \text{ is neutral regarding capability indicator } C_j; \\ -2 & \text{if business activity } A \text{ is bad regarding capability indicator } C_j. \end{cases}$$

$C_j(A)$ shows the social value of business activity A regarding capability indicator C_j.

The following vector represents the social value of business activity A regarding all the capability indicators C_1, ..., C_j, ..., C_n.

$$(7) \quad \underline{C}(A) = [C_1(A), ..., C_j(A), ..., C_n(A)]$$

To get an aggregate picture about the social value of business activity system A we should introduce weights that show the importance of the capability indicators. Let u_1, ..., u_j, ..., u_n be such importance weights.

It is required that:

$$(8) \quad \sum u_j = 1$$

The aggregate social value of business activity A can be calculated as follows:

$$(9) \quad C(A) = \sum u_j C_j(A)$$

C (A) shows the aggregate social value of business activity A ($1 \geq$ C (A) $\geq$ -2).

A business activity is considered *pro-social* if its aggregate social value is positive. That is:

(10) C (A) > 0

How can we evaluate a business activity from the perspective of *future generations*? We cannot know too much about future generations but *freedom* is a central value here. According to Edith Brown Weiss the freedom of future generations is insured by satisfying the following principles (Brown Weiss, 1989):

(i) conservation of options;
(ii) conservation of quality;
(iii) conservation of access.

Considering principles (i), (ii) and (iii), future generations indicators can be generated. Let F_1, ..., F_k, ..., F_p be such indicators against which business activity systems can be evaluated ($p > 1$).

Future generations value function F_k ( ) is defined as follows:

$$(11) \quad F_k (A) = \begin{cases} 1 & \text{if business activity A is good regarding future generations indicator } F_k; \\ 0 & \text{if business activity A is neutral regarding indicator } F_k; \\ -2 & \text{if business activity A is bad regarding future generations indicator } F_k. \end{cases}$$

F_k (A) reflects the future generations value of business activity A regarding indicator F_k.

The following vector represents the future generations value of business activity system A regarding future generations indicators F_1, ..., F_k, ..., F_n.

(12) $\underline{F}$ (A) = [F_1 (A), ..., F_k (A), ..., F_p (A)]

To get an aggregate picture about the future generations value of business activity **A** we should introduce weights that show the importance of indicators **F1**, ..., **Fk**, ..., **Fp**. Let **v1**, ..., **vk**, ..., **vp** be such importance weights.

It is required that:

(13) $\sum vk = 1$

The aggregate future generations value of business activity **A** can be calculated as follows:

(14) $\sum vk\, Fk\, (A)$

F (**A**) shows the aggregate future generations value of business activity **A** ($1 \geq F(A) \geq -2$).

A business activity can be considered *future respecting* if its aggregate future generations value is positive. That is:

(15) **F** (**A**) > 0

3. Responsibility for the Common Good

The *common good* is a notion that originated over two thousand years ago in the writings of Plato, Aristotle, and Cicero. More recently, John Rawls defined the common good as "certain general conditions that are [...] equally to everyone's advantage". The Catholic religious tradition, which has a long history to promote the common good, defines it as "the sum of those conditions of social life which allow social groups and their individual members relatively thorough and ready access to their own fulfillment." The common good, then, consists mainly of having the social systems, institutions, and environments on which we all depend in order to work in a manner that benefits all people (Velasquez, Andre, Shanks and Meyer, 2004).

Sustainability, pro-socialness and respect for the future are important components of the common good. In their paper "Should Multinational Corporations Be Concerned with the Global Common Good? An Interdisciplinary Exploration", Henri-Claude de Bettignies and François Lépineux argue that multinational corporations, because of their huge economic power, their influence capacity and the multiple consequences of their activities, have to serve the global common good (de Bettignies and Lépineux, 2005). Therefore business activities should be judged on the basis of serving the common good. I want to develop the argument of de Bettignies and Lépineux further. I claim that in today's world characterized by climate change, ecological degradation, human deprivation, global interdependence, and high scale technological uncertainties, not only multinational corporations but *every business organization* has responsibility for the common good. Today the legitimacy and viability of a business depends on its contribution to nature, society and future generations.

The "invisible hand" of the market advocated by Adam Smith, Milton Friedman and others does not transform individual, profit-seeking behavior into the common good any more. Just the opposite, with its exclusive focus on profit-making, today's business destroys the integrity and diversity of ecosystems, the autonomy of local communities, and the chances of future generations for a decent life. In today's world, profit is inadequate as a sole measure of economic activities and dangerous as the main motivation for business activities (Zsolnai, 2006). The problem with profit as a measure is that in the market there are *non-represented stakeholders* (natural beings, future generations), *underrepresented stakeholders* (the poor and marginalized people), and *myopic stakeholders* (who discount things in space and time). Therefore profit cannot give a complete, unbiased evaluation of business activities. Profit always reflects the values of the strongest stakeholders and favors preferences here and now. The problem with profit as a motivation is that it destroys intrinsic motivation and decreases quality and leads to manipulation of others and oneself. Business should serve something bigger than itself to become a meaningful and productive activity.

Progressive companies like outdoor clothing company *Patagonia*, retail business firm *Ishka*, natural health care company *Blackmores*, skin care specialist *Jurlique*, and organic food company *Whole Foods* are good illustrations of doing successful business by serving the common good (Pozzi, 2006; Nocera, 2006). *Patagonia* is an outdoor clothing company started by a group of climbers and surfers in the sixties. The company branched, from selling climbing equipment into clothing in the 1970s. Company founder Yvon Chouinard's vision of long-term sustainability and minimum impact on the environment has become a reality for Patagonia and its customers. This has been realized through producing quality clothing that outlasts fashion, and a business ethic which values the environment and its employees over rapid growth and the bottom line. Patagonia shows a strong commitment to the environment, donating a large percentage of the company's profits to environmental campaigns and an ongoing accountability to the environment, demonstrated by constant monitoring of the effects of its manufacturing. In 1996 the company shifted its entire cotton line to organically grown cotton: grown without the use of chemical pesticides, herbicides or defoliants. They say: "Given what we now know about conventional cotton, there is no going back regardless of the decision's impact on the company's sales or profit. It's an ethical choice we have made and hope other companies will follow."

Acknowledging the impossibility of zero environmental impact, Patagonia also has a strong commitment to research into producing durable fabrics. This company is at the forefront of technology, having been the first to introduce such fabrics as Capilene in 1985, Polyester fleece in 1977 and Post Consumer Recycled Polyester fleece in 1993. Durable fabrics, coupled with durable and versatile designs, ensure that Patagonia's customers mirror the company's own philosophy of reduced consumption. Nor does the company compromise on the care for its employees. Heavily subsidized in-house and external child-care programs, available to women and men, a commitment to employee training and pleasant working facilities are deemed important to simultaneously provide for the employees and to retain valuable people for the business. Patagonia's broad vision considers how the company impacts on the environment, its employees and the community at large. Simplicity is its philosophy. Patagonia believes that "Going back to a simpler life based on living by sufficiency rather than excess is not a step backward. Rather, returning to a simpler way allows us to regain our dignity, puts us in touch with the land, and makes us value human contact again".

A retail business that takes its business ethics seriously is *Ishka*: the chain of handcraft shops founded by Michael Sklovsky and which has been operating successfully for 25 years. This business follows Buddhist philosophy in which ethics play an important part. Most of Ishka's products are manufactured in villages across 48 countries, including India, Thailand, Nepal and Indonesia. In villages greatly needed income is generated through Ishka buying locally crafted products. The purchasing of local handcrafts provides work for people in their own village. Exporting arts and crafts is a way through which families can break out of the poverty cycle. To become a crafts-person or artist can mean a well-paid profession for life. Ishka has direct dealings with most of the artisans from whom it purchases handcrafts. The company investigates the workshops of suppliers and examines the working conditions of the artisans. Moreover, Ishka makes sure not to deal with products of exploitation such as the popular "Persian" rugs copied in Pakistan by children in slavery. Another important ethical issue considered by Ishka is the use of environmental resources. Wherever possible, the company makes use of recycled products; and it is always aware of the need to preserve natural habitats. Ishka is also regularly involved with Amnesty International and Unicef, and has been acknowledged as Unicef's biggest Victorian fundraiser.

Natural health care company *Blackmores* extends its vision of drug free health care to encompass a more widespread respect for nature and the environment. Environmentalism has been a distinctive feature of Blackmores' corporate philosophy, as evidenced by its environmental committee. This committee enforces Blackmores' environmental policy, which is about "more than just recycling and pollution control; it means integrity, quality and pride, not only in the way the company's products are manufactured, but with everything with which the company is associated". Blackmores is proud that its products are manufactured without causing suffering to animals, and that it features among the "cruelty-free" list of beauty products promoted by animal welfare groups, proving that cosmetic safety can be achieved without the use of testing on animals.

Adelaide-based skin care specialist, *Jurlique*, has successfully integrated spirituality into its corporate philosophy. Built around the three principles of "purity, care and integrity", the organization believes that incorporating these values into all aspects of the production process enhances the final product, and the well-being of the company and its staff. "Purity" is observed in Jurlique's practice of organically growing, at the Jurlique Herb Farm, 85% of the herbs the company requires. The company ensures that only natural, non-chemical, unpolluted, organically and bio-dynamically grown raw materials are used in its products. Care for the environment, for oneself and for others, form the Jurlique philosophy. Its staff is encouraged to embrace change, energize others, break down barriers, to be customer-focused, responsible and accountable, to strive for excellence and face reality. Co-founder of Jurlique, Dr Jürgen Klein considers consumer education vital in helping the public to be aware of the processes involved in "natural cosmetics". In line with this view, Jurlique offers open days at the farm and factory, cosmetic ingredient listings, education and seminars covering skin and health care, aromatherapy and herbal medicines.

American organic food company *Whole Foods* is characterized by rapid expansion, double-digit growth and a business model that no competitor seems able to touch. Its stock has returned more than 2,700 percent since it went public in 1992. Wall Street analysts could not speak enough good things about Whole Foods. John Mackey, the co-founder of Whole Foods and the executive team make no bones about the fact that shareholders rank low on their list of priorities. They speak instead about the importance of keeping customers happy and employees engaged and sticking to the company's core values. Mackey says that they consciously work for the *common good* rather than depending solely on the "invisible hand" of the market to generate positive results for the society.

Responsibility for the common good calls for a transformation of business. As we stated earlier:

(1) Business should be *sustainable*, i.e. should contribute to the conservation and restoration of the natural world;

(2) Business should be *pro-social*, i.e. should contribute to development of capabilities of the members of society;

(3) Business should be *future respecting*, i.e. should contribute to the enhancement of the freedom of future generations.

In their present forms not all business organizations might be able to make considerable steps in the direction of serving the common good. It is a demanding job for business leaders, academics and NGO people to investigate how the prevailing conflicts between conventional stakeholder groups (especially shareholders) and primordial stakeholders (nature, society and future generations) can be reconciled.

References

Azar, Christian et al., 1996, "Socio-Ecological Indicators for Sustainability", *Ecological Economics*, pp. 89–112.

Brown Weiss, Edith, 1989, *In Fairness to Future Generations: International Law, Common Patrimony, and Intergeneration Equity*, New York: The United Nations University, Tokyo and Transnational Publishers.

De Bettignies, H.-C. and Lépineux, F., 2005, "Should Multinational Corporations Be Concerned with the Global Common Good? An Interdisciplinary Exploration", Fontainebleau: *INSEAD Working Paper Series*.

Jonas, H., 1979, *Das Prinzip Verantwortung. Versuch einer Ethic fur die Technologische Zivilization*, Frankfurt am Main: Insel Verlag.

—— 1984, *The Imperative of Responsibility: In Search of an Ethics for the Technological Age*, Chicago and London: University of Chicago Press.

Leopold, Aldo, 1948, *A Sand County Almanac*, Oxford: Oxford University Press.

Nocera, John, 2006, "The Whole Truth", *International Herald Tribune*, 15–16 July, p. 17.

Pozzi, D., 2006, *Business Can Have Soul*, see: http://www.livingnow. com.au/soul/s1soulstories3.htm.

Sen, Amartya, 1992, *Inequality Reexamined*, New York: Russell Sage Foundation and Oxford: Clarendon Press.

Velasquez, Manuel, Claire Andre, Thomas Shanks, S.J., and Michael J. Meyer, 2004, *The Common Good*, Markkula Center for Applied Ethics, Santa Clara University. www.scu.edu/ethics/practicing/deci-sion/commongood.html.

Zsolnai, L., 2003, "Global Impact – Global Responsibility: Why a Global Management Ethos is Necessary?" *Corporate Governance*, 2003, n°3, pp. 95–100.

——2006, "Redefining Economic Reason", Lecture at the *Green Economics Conference* in Mansfield College, Oxford, 8 April.

CHAPTER 7

¡Ay mi Nicaragüita!
The Construction of the Common Good in Nicaragua as a "Work of Translation"

JOSEP F. MÀRIA

1. ¡Ay, mi Nicaragüita!

An intelligent and dedicated law student from the *Universidad Centro-americana de Managua* often repeated the title phrase of this paper, *¡Ay, mi Nicaragüita!* (Oh, my poor, little Nicaragua!) to a Catalonian intern from ESADE in July 2005. With this phrase, she summarized her love for her country and the difficult situation the country was traversing. Nicaragua is one of the poorest countries in Latin America, though in 1979 it became a mythical country for the Left in the West when the Sandinista Revolution succeeded in overthrowing the Somoza dynasty's terrible dictatorship. A civil war soon erupted, lasting from 1980 to 1990, between the socialist *Frente Sandinista de Liberación Nacional* (FSLN) and its opponents, the latter financed by the United States and Ronald Reagan. Peace came about when the opposition coalition led by Violeta Barrios de Chamorro defeated Daniel Ortega, the Sandinista President, in 1990.

Since 1990, the country's economic, political, and cultural situation has not improved with the neo-liberal policies promoted by the ruling *Partido Liberal Constitucionalista* (PLC). The economic indicators have not improved; the political debate is blocked by a perverse pact between Daniel Ortega (FSLN) and the PLC's powerful leader, Arnoldo Alemán; and, culturally, the country seems to have renewed its adherence to a fatalistic culture which has instilled in Nicaraguans the sense that their future is not in their own hands, but rather, that Nicaragua will be saved by foreign investment, by international cooperation, or, perhaps, by Hugo Chávez, the Venezuelan President and Daniel Ortega's friend and ally. However, there are people and organizations within Nicaragua working to establish positive agreements among the diverse political groups, NGOs, and economic organizations. These agreements may in turn lead to:

– modify the secular, fatalistic culture;
– develop a consciousness of active citizenry among the population;
– and stimulate dialogue among the different sectors of society aimed at fostering the common good.

The aim of this paper is to contrast this vision and strategy with Boaventura de Sousa Santos' sociological work. The Portuguese sociologist criticizes hegemonic globalization as an epistemic approach to social reality which occludes seeing emerging ideas and organizations working for the common good at the local level. For the construction of the common good, he proposes a "work of translation", i.e., a dialogue among the different cultural focuses or organizational praxis (beginning with grassroots organizations) for the Human Development of all citizens. As such, this paper will explore:

– the current situation in Nicaragua;
– Boaventura de Sousa Santos' position regarding the "work of translation";
– the work carried out by 4 Nicaraguan organizations in terms of the relationships they have established with other organizations for the construction of the common good;
– and lastly, the author's conclusions which point to a balance between Santos' theory and Nicaraguan reality.

The author would like to thank the Nicaraguans he interviewed in July 2006 for the purpose of this paper: María López Vigil, Chief Correspondent for the magazine *Envío*; Martha Lorena Mora, Director of *Intermon Oxfam Nicaragua*; Mario Quintana, executive of the *Coordinadora Civil de Emergencias y Reconstrucción* (CCER); Sinforiano Cáceres, Director of FENACOOP (*Federación Nacional de Cooperativas*); and Julio Flores, Director of the micro-financer, *Fondo de Desarrollo Local* (FDL). The author would also like to express special recognition to Pilar Crespo RSCJ, Kathe Welles, Marisa Olivares, and Donald Méndez from the *Universidad Centroamericana de Managua* who supported and encouraged the development of this paper. And, lastly, the author would like to thank his colleagues within the Jesuit community, Villa Carmen, who accompanied him with their patience, spirit of service, and good humor during the author's stay in Nicaragua. All these people, with the author's gratitude, are working for Nicaragua's development and share a special fondness for this beautiful country and its people. They all transmit the hope expressed by *¡Ay, mi Nicaragüita!*, a hope capable of fostering working towards justice and the common good.

2. Nicaragua Today

2.1. Economy

Nicaragua is ranked 112 out of a total of 177 countries surveyed in the Index of Human Development. Life expectancy at birth is 69.7 years. GDP per inhabitant (in PPA) is at $3,262, while 3 of every 4 adult Nicaraguans know how to read.[1] There are 5.6 million inhabitants in Nicaragua, growing at 2.4% annually, which means that by 2050 there will be 10.9 million inhabitants.[2] The food situation is beginning to be a concern: "At the beginning of February [2006] the so-called 'basic food basket' (39 products) was introduced and, according to a study coordinated between the FAO and the government, it would meet the daily caloric intake require-

---

1   www.undp.org consulted on 22 September 2005.
2   www.unfpa.org consulted on 22 September 2005.

ments for an adequate diet. The basket costs more than 2,000 Cordobas ($110 approximately), while the minimum salary varies from 800 to 1,800 Cordobas. Unemployment or under-employment affects a third of the active population."[3] In 1990 (the year the *Frente Sandinista de Liberación Nacional* FSLN left office) neo-liberal economic reforms where established in accordance with the directives of the IMF and the guiding ideology of the Washington Consensus. The result of these reforms has been that, as a whole, the economic situation has worsened for the majority of the population: from 1990 to 1999, Nicaragua went from being ranked 85 to 126 in the United Nations' Index of Human Development.[4]

With the new millennium, the US strategy and that of Nicaraguan Liberals was expressed by CAFTA (the Central American Free Trade Association): a customs union between the US, Central American countries and the Dominican Republic. CAFTA's negotiations and ratification have already finalized, but a new and broad field is opening in terms of its application. Liberals blindly believe in CAFTA as a mechanism to attract foreign investment – the only thing that can "save" Nicaragua. Daniel Ortega's hegemonic *Sandinismo* publicly rejects CAFTA while supporting alignment with Hugo Chávez, Fidel Castro, Evo Morales and ALBA (*Alternativa Bolivariana de las Américas*, an alternative Trade Association), though the party has, in fact, ratified CAFTA and seems to be taking positions to take advantage of it. However, Nicaragua's problems are not only explained by the failure of the Washington Consensus' neo-liberalism or the threats presented by CAFTA.[5] Specifically, corruption and the changes in the government since 1979 have strongly compromised *public budgets*.

As such, in the 2006 Budget, paying off public debt will account for 20% of expenses. This is especially due to the high degree of internal debt

3   Equipo Nitlapan-Envio, UCA, Managua, 2006, Mirando a noviembre, mirando al sur, *Envío*, January–February (286–7): 5.
4   Belli, G., 2001, *El país bajo mi piel. Memorias de amor y guerra*, Barcelona: Plaza y Janés, p. 421.
5   Equipo Nitlapan-Envio, UCA, Managua, 2006, Mirando a noviembre, mirando al sur, *Envío*, January–February (286–7): 9.

in the hands of domestic private bankers.[6] This debt stems from indemnity payments for the property confiscated by the Sandinista government in the 1980s and the CENI bonds issued after the fraudulent and corrupt bank failures of 1999 and 2000 in which the main political parties participated: Liberals, Sandinistas and Conservatives.[7] In addition, the Law of Fiscal Equality (*Ley de Equidad Fiscal*) approved at the end of April 2003, in theory established to correct the fiscal inequalities in Nicaragua, grants scandalous *fiscal privileges* to domestic private banks which are already decimating the public budget by means of internal debt payments.[8] The public budget is seriously hampered by debt servicing and fiscal exemptions. This has repercussions on the salaries of *civil servants*. Concretely, doctors and teachers have insufficient salaries and are low in comparison to their counterparts in the rest of Central America.[9] Administration officials attribute the inability to raise these salaries for doctors and teachers to IMF restrictions, but they have not instigated reforms because they

6   Equipo Nitlapan-Envio, 2005, ¿Tiempos nuevos? Tiempos de Güegüenses, *Envío*, December (285): 9.

7   Equipo Nitlapan-Envio, 2005, ¿Tiempos nuevos? Tiempos de Güegüenses, *Envío*, December (285): 9. "CENI bonds were negotiated at very high interest rates, reaching up to 21%. The principal on internal debt reaches approximately $500 million. From 2001 to October 2005 the State has already paid those three banks $285.1 million. And over the next seven years it will have to pay them $326 million more. The proof leads to the evidence that the portfolio of bankrupt banks did not excede $100 million ..." Equipo Nitlapan-Envio. 2005. ¿Entre Trivelli y Chávez? *Envío*. December (290): 4.

8   Equipo Nitlapan-Envio, UCA, Managua, 2003, Nuestro lugar en el mundo, *Envío*, May (254): 9.

9   "According to OXFAM International data, the salary of Nicaraguan doctors (between 200 and 500 dollars depending on the area of specialty) barely excedes that of these same professionals in Malawi, an African country with 80% lower income per capita than that of Nicaragua. In Honduras, which has a comparable per capita income to our own, doctors earn nearly three times more than their Nicaraguan colleagues. Nicaraguan nurses do not earn more than 100 dollars." Equipo Nitlapan-Envio, UCA, Managua, 2006, 75 días rizando el rizo, *Envío*, April (289): 4.

themselves are very well paid: 0.7% of civil servants account for 25% of the entire staffing budget for the State.[10]

The *informal economy* is the largest sector in Nicaragua and poverty is more frequent than in the formal sector.[11] The perspectives of commercial integration with Central America and the US are not positive for the Nicaraguan agricultural industry. In effect, *agrarian productivity* in Nicaragua is one of the lowest in Central America in terms of the country's main agricultural products. CAFTA could imply ruin for thousands of farm-workers which use their surplus crops to pay for their families' school and healthcare (not publicly financed).[12] The *emigrants' remittances* do represent good news on the economic front: this money offers relief for the Nicaraguan balance of payments and is a possible source of funds for productive investment. The risk is that this "manna" will become a new form of dependency on the exterior: a reincarnation of Nicaraguans' cultural fatalism. On the other hand, *drug trafficking* is becoming a source of unrivalled wealth, especially along the Caribbean Coast, but also something which generates violence and bends the will of judges, thereby weakening the State of Law.[13] It was estimated that in July 2006 there were some 200 landing strips for small planes carrying drugs in Nicaragua, a part of the drugs destined for the US and another

10   Equipo Nitlapan-Envio, UCA, Managua, 2006, Mirando a noviembre, mirando al sur, *Envío*, January–February (286–7): 6.

11   Cf. Gutierrez, M., 2006, Crecimiento, desarrollo y estilos de desarrollo en Centroamérica, *Revista Virtual Centroamérica en la economía mundial del siglo XXI,* Asociación de Investigación y Estudios Sociales, Ciudad de Guatemala, February (2): 1–2. www.ca-asies.org.gt.

12   Caceres, S., 2003, El el TLC definimos si nos suicidamos o si morimos de muerte natural, *Envío*, October (259): 14–21.

13   "The impact of drugs is very evident on the Coast, not only in specific construction projects ... but also on how the judicial system functions. Despite the undeniable presence of drug traficking, no one on the Coast has a firm sentence against them for any drug trafficking-related crime." Gonzalez, M., 2005, En la Costa hemos demostrado que sabemos vivir la autonomía, *Envío*, September (282): 26. See also Naim, M., 2005, El continente ilícito, *El País*, 18 November.

part to be consumed within Nicaragua itself.[14] Another especially relevant chapter in Nicaragua's illegal economy is the *exploitation of natural resources*. According to the *Procuraduría Ambiental* (Environmental Legal Agency), 80% of the wood extracted in Nicaragua is done so illegally and is untreated after being felled. Legislation to cut fraud is rejected by part of the political class which has economic interests in this million-dollar business.[15]

2.2. Politics

2.2.1. From the Somoza Dynasty to the Sandinista Decade (1980–1990)

Nicaragua awoke passions and adherence from the Left in the West when the Somoza dynasty, which had imposed a terrible and bloody dictatorship from 1936 on, was removed from power by a principally socialist and nationalist revolution in July 1979. In short time, a democratic socialist regime was installed, headed up by the *Frente Sandinista de Liberación Nacional* (FSLN). It strove to promote the people though it faced pressure from an armed opposition financed by the US, the latter having considered Central America its "backyard" for a long time. The decade spanning from 1980 to 1990 was a time of hope and war, of things done right and others, wrong. It also led to the electoral defeat of the FSLN in 1990 and the rise of Violeta Barrios de Chamorro, the widow of Pedro Joaquín Chamorro, a media businessman assassinated by Somoza in 1978.

14   Radio programme: "La primerísima", heard on 22 July 2006, 6.30 am. In July 2006, there were constant news items in the written press about planes used for drug trafficking crashing onto the runways and their crews (or cadavers) disappearing. The plane is quickly set on fire and they try to bury it.

15   Equipo Nitlapan-Envio, 2005, ¿Entre Trivelli y Chávez? *Envío*, December (290): 7.

2.2.2. 1990–2000: The New Bourgeoisies

Violeta Chamorro presided over a government whose aim was to foment internal reconciliation in the country and position Nicaragua in a new era marked by the fall of the Berlin Wall and the end of the Cold War. From 1996 on, Chamorro was succeeded in office by other members of the *Partido Liberal Constitucionalista* (PLC). But the former president, Daniel Ortega (FSLN) continued to wield great power in the country's political and economic life. In effect, in 1990 the majority of FSLN ministers and top officials appropriated public assets when leaving the Nicaraguan government, an operation known as the *Piñata*.[16] With this act, these corrupt Sandinistas formed a "second bourgeoisie" (owning companies) alongside the "traditional bourgeoisie" (longstanding rich and influential families) among the present day Nicaraguan elite. In 1996, Chamorro was succeeded in office by Doctor Arnoldo Alemán, a PLC politician who turned out to be extremely corrupt. Taking advantage of the privatizations dictated by the IMF and the World Bank, Alemán appropriated new State assets and became the nucleus of a "third bourgeoisie".

2.2.3. Bolaños, the Engineer, and the Pact (2001–2006)

Alemán's corruption soon became public and shameless. In 2001, Alemán was substituted in office by the engineer, Enrique Bolaños, also from the PLC. Bolaños, faithful to the dictates of the US, attempted to fight Alemán's corruption and try him in court. However, Alemán continued to control the PLC apparatus and retained strong influence in Nicaragua's collective political life. In 1998, Alemán had signed a "Pact" with Daniel Ortega which subsequently significantly reduced the ability of President Bolaños to act. The agreement between Alemán and Ortega is known today in Nicaragua as *el Pacto* (the Pact). Its aims are to:

16   The "piñata" is a popular children's game in Central America. It consists of a pot full of candy dangling from a rope which blindfolded children try to break open with a large stick.

– control the State apparatus among the leaders: controlling the Legislature also implies controlling the judicial, electoral and constitutional powers;
– stop the legal proceedings against Ortega and Alemán underway for corruption and other crimes;
– form an alliance between the second and third bourgeoisie to maintain and increase their economic power in Nicaragua.

In this political game, the US continues to support a non-corrupt rightwing and the continuation of the proceedings against Alemán who has been condemned but is serving his sentence from the comfort of his luxurious residence, "El Chile". The US economic wager in the region is CAFTA. But when it comes to choosing between punishing the corrupt Liberal, Alemán, or blocking the progress of the Sandinista, Daniel Ortega, the US Embassy favors the latter: it prefers a unified Right, albeit corrupt, to an FSLN victory with its sympathies for Hugo Chávez.

2.2.4. The November 2006 Elections in Perspective

Reactions to the corrupt political praxis of the *Pacto* are beginning to take shape with the upcoming presidential elections scheduled for 5 November 2006. A new leader has arisen among the liberals, the banker Eduardo Montealegre, who has broken the unity of the Right and has just launched his new party, the *Alianza Liberal Nicaragüense* (ALN). The PLC's candidate (designated by Alemán) is José Rizo.

The Left is also disunited for the November 2006 elections. In effect, a charismatic leader arose among the Sandinistas, Herty Lewites, the former Sandinista Minister of Tourism who also garnered popularity as the Mayor of Managua from 2000 to 2004. Lewites managed the capital with a progressive spirit, with little corruption and in a non-partisan fashion. In 2004, he was the highest-rated politician in Nicaragua and he wanted the FSLN to designate him the party's presidential candidate for the upcoming elections, but Daniel Ortega expelled him from the party at the beginning of 2005.[17] Lewites, who successfully united former Sandinistas disenchanted by the *Piñata* and the *Pacto* scandals, opted to present his own candidature alongside the FSLN as a coalition of Sandinista reformers, calling his party the *Alianza MRS* (*Movimiento de Renovación Sandinista*). But on 2 July 2006, Herty Lewites died of a heart attack and was substituted by the tandem, Jarquín-Mejía Godoy. Eduardo Jarquín, the presidential candidate, is a former technician with the Inter-American Development Bank (IADB) and was Lewites' vice-presidential candidate. Carlos Mejía Godoy is a famous nationalistic and progressive singer who is very popular in the rural sector. He is the present party's vice presidential candidate. In Section 4 we will further explore and elaborate on *Alianza MRS*' style and program as a political party striving for the common good in Nicaragua.

2.3. Culture

2.3.1. Nature and Providentialism

The ground frequently trembles in Nicaragua and fire often erupts from one of its many volcanoes. The Atlantic Coast is also beset by periodic hurricanes. The impotence that overcomes a European faced by these events allows one to see the fatalism which, according to the Nicaraguan political analyst, Andrés Pérez Baltodano, has consumed Nicaraguans for a long time. It is a fatalism which isn't expressed as a discourse from the elite to the masses (an ideology in the Marxist sense) but rather, it is pervasive in the *internal discourse of the elite*.[18] During the Colonial period, the combination of a Nature which "became angry" and the Catholic Church's teaching about a providential God became the first cocktail

---

17   Tellez, D.M., 2005, La alianza en torno a Herty Lewites es una oportunidad única, un capital que no podemos desperdiciar, *Envío*, December (285): 15.

18   See Perez Baltodano, A., 2004, No hay tarea más urgente hoy en Nicaragua que la de transformar la idea de Dios, *Envío*, August: 12.

fostering this fatalism in Nicaragua.[19] Later on, this fatalism (*resigned pragmatism* according to Pérez Baltodano) was reinforced by the US continued intervention in Nicaraguan history. The constant, external source of salvation for the country has been reincarnated in ideas such as globalization, free trade, foreign investment, external cooperation, money sent by emigrants, or the support of Venezuelan President, Hugo Chávez.[20] In any of these reincarnations, the practical consequences are always the same: the future is not in the Nicaraguans' own hands; others are always responsible for Nicaragua's plight or are its benefactors.[21] This fatalism ends up translating into indifference among the dominant groups when faced by the reality of poverty and into acceptance of marginalization among the masses.[22]

2.3.2. 1990: Subversion of Ethos and Conflict Consequences[23]

Any foreigner arriving in Nicaragua and conversing with social leaders will slowly discover that 1990 was a very important year for Nicaraguans' culture and values. In effect, in 1990 the FSLN was elected out of office and the *Piñata* scandal took place in which the majority of "revolutionary" leaders were involved. This was a big blow for a large part of Nicaragua's Left. Some abandoned the country, while others continued to be politically active; some were depressed and turned to drink; others even committed suicide. As of 1990, there is a subversion of values in the Nicaraguan *ethos*: what were considered anti-values in the 1980s (individualism, com-

19   See Perez Baltodano, A., 2003, Entre el Estado Conquistador y el Estado Nación, IHNCA/UCA Managua: 25.
20   Perez Baltodano, A., 2004, No hay tarea más urgente hoy en Nicaragua que la de transformar la idea de Dios, *Envío*, August: 12, 15–16.
21   See Perez Baltodano, A., 2004, *op. cit.*; and Perez Baltodano, A., 2002, *El pensamiento político nicaragüense*. Paper presented at American University, Managua, 4 September: 8–9.
22   See Perez Baltodano, A., 2004, No hay tarea más urgente hoy en Nicaragua que la de transformar la idea de Dios, *Envío*, August: 13.
23   Oral testimony of Martha Lorena Mora, General Director, Intermon Oxfam Nicaragua, on 12 July 2006, in Villa Carmen, UCA, Managua.

petition, "pull yourself up by your own bootstraps", or corruption) became dominant values which conformed to the country's political culture: "you're dumb if you don't steal." This subversion was complicated by the problems of the post-war period. From 1981 to 1990 the country was divided between *Compas* (loyal to the Sandinista Government) and the *Contras* (loyal to the counterrevolution financed by Reagan). Despite the reconciliation efforts made by Violeta Chamorro from 1990 on, the mistrust between one and another group were not easily overcome and worsened the country's social climate.

2.3.3. Tutelary Order and Corruption

The reincarnations of providentialism and the subversion of 1990 were made manifest in a political culture not centered on the citizenry but on tutelary order. Tutelary order consists of handing over one's will to a leader so that he may help you, do you favors: You do not have rights and obligations within the framework of a (democratic) State of Law.[24] There is just a fine line separating tutelary order and corruption and, in effect, corruption in Nicaragua is an important problem from a political and economic point of view as well as from a cultural perspective. Party politics and the logic behind the *Pacto* are sustained in cultural forms of tutelage which feed corruption and alienate individuals from the exercise of citizenry as a pact of rights and obligations with respect to a truly democratic State. In this sense, a former Sandinista commander who remains politically active declared in 2005: "The core of our program has to be the moral restoration of the country, re-establish the values of solidarity, work, honour, transparency, responsibility, public service, the basic values of citizenry. Without these, Nicaragua cannot move forward."[25]

---

24   Nugent, G., 2005, El orden tutelar: una clave para entender y para entendernos, *Envío*, September (282): 38–51.
25   Téllez, D.M., 2005, La alianza en torno a Herty Lewites es una oportunidad única, un capital que no podemos desperdiciar, *Envío*, December (285): 17.

3. Boaventura de Sousa Santos.
A Critical View of Globalization

After the previous, general presentation of the current situation in Nicaragua, we will now analyze Boaventura de Sousa Santos' writings. Though this Portuguese sociologist does not write specifically about Nicaragua, his theoretical models have come about specifically from his social analyzes of developing countries.[26] The author feels, as such, that they are a valid starting point to better understand the current reality in Nicaragua. In this section, we will summarize Santos' thought and especially describe the "work of translation" concept, a concept considered key to delve into the positions and praxis of the Nicaraguan organizations we will introduce in the following section.

3.1. West, Metonomic Reason and Proleptic Reason

For Santos, present-day society is deeply marked by capitalism which, in its ideological manifestation, constructed the concept of the "West" with which it has modified the vision of the world and has installed globalization. In fact, the West and capitalism have opted to abandon its founding matrix, the East, adopting a double approximation to reality that Santos defines with the terms *metonomic reason* and *proleptic reason*. The Orient as a founding matrix is, for Santos, a truly totalizing matrix because:

> [...] it includes a multiplicity of worlds (earthly and ultra-earthly) and a multiplic-
> ity of times (past, present, future, cyclical, linear, simultaneous). As such, it does
> not vindicate the totality nor subordinate itself to the parts that make it up. It is
> an anti-dichotomic matrix since it does not tend to control nor watch its limits by
> means of a police force. On the contrary, the West, aware of its eccentricity with
> respect to the matrix, barely takes from the matrix what can favor the expansion
> of capitalism. In so doing, the multiplicity of worlds is reduced to the earthly

26   See Santos, B. de S., 2005, *El milenio huérfano*, Madrid: Trotta, p. 151.

world, and the multiplicity of times to linear time. Two processes preside over this reduction. The reduction from the multiplicity of worlds to the earthly world is done by means of a process of secularisation and laity [...] The reduction from the multiplicity of times to linear time is achieved by means of the concepts, in particular, the concept of progress and the concept of revolution that substituted the idea of salvation which linked it to the multiplicity of worlds [...].[27]

The reduction the West and capitalism operate with is made manifest by the imposition of two logical systems, two ways of thinking, two reasoning styles which invade the analysis of societies. Santos defines these as *metonomic reason* and *proleptic reason*:

> *Metonomic reason* is stubbornly focused on the idea of totality under the form of order. There is no understanding or action that does not refer to a whole which has absolute primacy over every single one of the parts which make it up. For this reason, there is only one logic which governs both the behavior of the whole and each of its parts [...] The most complete form of totality in *metonomic reason* is the dichotomy since it combines symmetry more elegantly with the hierarchy. Symmetry between the parts is always a horizontal relationship which hides a vertical relationship. This is so because, contrary to what *metonomic reason* proclaims, the whole is less and no more than the set of its parts. In truth, the whole is one of the transformed parts as a reference for the other parts. For this reason, all dichotomies defrayed by *metonomic reason* contain a hierarchy: scientific culture / literary culture; scientific knowledge / traditional knowledge; man / woman; culture / nature; civilized / primitive; capital / work; black / white; North / South; West / East; and so on.[28]

One of the dichotomies presented by Santos which is especially relevant for our paper is the global / local dichotomy. The entities or realities which extend their ambit around the globe acquire a superior status to the local realities with this dichotomy. Local realities are trapped on a scale which makes them unable to be credible alternatives to what exists globally.[29] If metonomic reason subordinates one reality to another, *proleptic reason* enables the reduction of time to linear time. As a result

27   Santos, B. de S., 2005, *op. cit.*, pp. 156–7.
28   Santos, B. de S., 2005, *op. cit.*, pp. 155–6.
29   Santos, B. de S., 2005, *op. cit.*, pp. 161–2.

of this logic, the future only has the sense and direction that progress gives it, and since progress has no limits, the future is, therefore, infinite. The future has only one direction and it is infinite. Infinitely equal and abundant, it only exists to become homogenous and empty, to become the past.[30] Since there are no options with which to assess the future and "in the end, everything will be for the better", the future ends up being a repetition of the past.

3.2. Celebratory Postmodernism or Oppositional Postmodernism

Santos notes that modernity, guided by proleptic and metonomic reasons, has not fulfilled the promises it was inspired by: equality, liberty, peace, progress, and dominion over nature.[31] With modernity's failure, Santos distinguishes two postmodern positions: celebratory postmodernism and oppositional postmodernism. *Celebratory postmodernism* is linked, according to proleptic reason, with the goal of the idea of progress, the end of history, the celebration of the present. Proleptic reason, which has extended the future by homogenizing time and eliminating its options, now proclaims the end of history, the end of the idea of progress, to repeat the dominion of the bourgeoisie automatically and infinitely.

> The degree of truth to the theory regarding the end of history is grounded in the latter; it is the maximum possible in an international bourgeoisie's conscience which finally observes time transformed into the automatic and infinite repetition of its dominion. As such, the long term is paralysed into the short term, and the latter, which was always the temporal framework for capitalism, allows the bourgeoisie to produce the only truly bourgeois theory of history: the theory of the end of history. This theory's complete lack of credibility does not interfere at all with the fact that it is in itself a spontaneous ideology of victors. The other side to the end

30   Santos, B. de S., 2005, *op. cit.*, p. 167.
31   Cf. Santos, B. de S., "Sobre el posmodernismo de oposición" in *El milenio huérfano. Ensayos para una nueva cultura política*, Madrid: Trotta, pp. 97–9.

of history is the slogan celebrating the present, which the apocalyptic versions of postmodern thought are so enamored of.[32]

The end of history, the triumph of capitalism, and its pacific extension around the world constitute the ideology of the winners of the Cold War. For Santos, postmodern discourse is, in reality, the other side of the end of history: the ideology of neo-liberal globalization[33] or, in Santos' own words, hegemonic globalization.[34] Santos advocates, instead, an *oppositional postmodernism* characterized by the following traits:

a) the criticism of modernity is taken as the starting point for the construction of epistemological and political alternatives to the current situation;[35]

b) the construction of these alternatives must begin from below, in a participatory and multicultural manner;[36]

c) in particular, these alternatives will only be possible if the dichotomous thought behind proleptic reason is ruptured as it considers inferior all that is local while exalting the political and epistemic schemes linked to "the global". All this is understood as hegemonic globalization because hegemonic globalization is nothing more than a globalized localism belonging to the new cultural imperialisms;[37]

d) and lastly, the articulation of these alternatives cannot be carried out by a single principle of social transformation or by only one collective actor as modern sociological thought exalting the role of the State proposes, but rather, by the diverse principles and actors.[38]

---

32   Santos, B. de S., 2005, *El milenio huérfano, op. cit.*, p. 115.
33   Mària I Serrano, J.F., *Globalization. A marvellous excuse for many things*, Barcelona: Cristianisme i Justícia Booklets.
34   Santos, B. de S., 2005, *El milenio huérfano, op. cit.*, p. 134.
35   See editor's note in Santos, B. de S., 2005, *El milenio huérfano, op. cit.*, pp. 111–12, footnote by the editor.
36   Santos, B. de S., 2005, *op. cit.*, p. 112.
37   Santos, B. de S., 2005, *op. cit.*, p. 134.
38   Santos, B. de S., 2005, *op. cit.*, p. 101.

3.3. Sociology of Absences and Emergencies

According to Santos, oppositional postmodernism's program develops based on three logical moments or approximations to reality: the sociology of absences, the sociology of emergencies, and the work of translation. Below is a description of these first two moments.

3.3.1. Sociology of Absences

As seen above, metonomic reason configures the complexity of reality – and in particular, social realities – along dichotomies which create a hierarchy and subordinate one to the other within that dichotomy: the South to the North, woman to man, local to global, work to capital, literary culture to scientific culture, etc. The creation of a hierarchy converts social experiences or organizations which aren't at the hierarchical top of their dichotomies into socially irrelevant or marginal elements, though they, in fact, promote the common good in diverse societies. Santos believes that oppositional postmodernism must begin by investigating social experiences, or the actions of those organizations beyond the logic of occidental totality, which offer benefits for the common good: the sociology of absences program.

> Imagine the South as if there were no North; imagine the woman as if there were no man; imagine the slave as if there were no master. The budget of this procedure is that metonomic reason, when dragging these entities into the dichotomies, was not completely successful because components or fragments not socialised by the order of the whole were left out. Those components of fragments have wandered beyond that totality like meteorites lost in that order's space, without being perceived or controlled by that order. In the transitional phase we now find ourselves, metonomic reason is still dominant despite having been discredited. The broadening of the world and the prolongation of the present have to begin by a procedure I call the sociology of absences. This is a type of research which attempts to demonstrate that what doesn't exist is, in reality, actively produced as non-existent, that is, as a non-credible alternative to what exists. Its empirical objective is considered to be impossible in the eyes of conventional social sciences and, as a result, its mere formulation represents a break from these sciences. The aim of the sociology of absences is to transform impossible objects into possible ones and, based on these,

transform absences into presences, focusing on the fragments of social experience not socialised by the metonomic whole. What is there in the South beyond the North / South dichotomy? What is there in traditional medicine that escapes the modern medicine / traditional medicine dichotomy? What is there in the woman which is independent of her relationship with man? Can we see what is inferior without taking into account its subordinate relationship?[39]

3.3.2. Sociology of Emergencies

Proleptic reason has reduced multidimensional time into linear time guided forward by the idea of progress. This linear time subject to progress has practically eliminated many of the alternatives for the future when considering the possibility of constructing the common good. For this reason, Santos proposes the program of sociology of emergencies which allows for exploring the future based on plural, concrete, and both realistic and utopian possibilities which are already being built in diverse societies.

> While the prolongation of the present is achieved by means of the sociology of absences, the contraction of the future is achieved by the sociology of emergencies. The sociology of emergencies consists of substituting the void of the future according to linear time (a void which, as such, is like nothing) with a future of plural and concrete, and both utopian and realistic possibilities currently being constructed based on activities designed to offer care. The concept dominating the sociology of emergencies is the concept of "not yet" (Noch nicht) as proposed by Ernst Bloch [...] The "not" is the lack of something and the expression of the will to overcome that lack. As such, "not" is distinguishable from "nothing". Saying "no" is saying "yes" to something different. That which is "not yet" is how the future is inscribed in the present and dilates it. It is neither an undetermined or infinite future. It is a concrete possibility and ability which do not exist in a void nor are they completely determined. In fact, they actively re-determine all that they touch and, in so doing, they question the determinations which exist at any given moment.[40]

39   Santos, B. de S., 2005, *op. cit.*, pp. 159–60.
40   Santos, B. de S., 2005, *op. cit.*, pp. 167–8.

3.4. Work of Translation

After the sociology of absences and the sociology of emergencies, the third moment within the program of oppositional postmodernism is the work of translation. A more detailed view of this concept is offered because it is the most applicable part of Santos' theory to the present analysis of Nicaragua. The work of translation constitutes the immediate base for recognizing the ideas and organizations constructing the common good in Nicaragua: a recognition which is presented in Chapter 4 of this paper.

3.4.1. Alternative to a General Theory

The work of translation constitutes an alternative to the general theories that presuppose a mono-culture of a given whole and the homogeneity of its parts. The objective of the work of translation is not merely theoretical. According to Santos, it is aimed at constructing an alternative to neo-liberal globalization.[41] This duality between theory and praxis leads Santos to affirm that the work of translation can arise both within theoretical knowledge as well as within social practices and among its agents. "More than a common theory, what is needed is a theory of translation capable of making the different struggles mutually intelligible, thereby permitting the collective actors to express themselves regarding the oppression they are resisting and the aspirations which mobilize them."[42]

---

41   "The objective of the work of translation is to create constellations of knowledge and practices which are strong enough to offer credible alternatives to what is defined today as neo-liberal globalisation and which is nothing more than a new step of global capitalism to hold the never-ending totality of the world to merchantile logic." Santos, B. de S., 2005, *op. cit.*, p. 186.
42   Santos, B. de S., 2005, *op. cit.*, p. 103.

3.4.2. Translation between Knowledge and between Practices

For Santos, the work of translation can arise between knowledge or between practices. In the field of *translation between knowledge*, he distinguishes between hegemonic knowledge, non-hegemonic knowledge, and counter-hegemonic knowledge. *Hegemonic knowledge* belongs to western capitalism and occupies the top position in the dichotomies used above to explain metonomic reason: scientific culture, scientific knowledge, man, culture, civilized, capital, white, North, West, etc. *Non-hegemonic knowledge* occupies the secondary position in the respective dichotomies, namely: literary culture, traditional knowledge, woman, nature, primitive, work, black, South, Orient, etc. Santos feels that the translation between non-hegemonic knowledge may construct a *counter-hegemony*: an alternative to neo-liberal thought and *hegemonic globalization*.[43]

3.4.3. Translation between Social Practices and Agents

As regards the *translation between social practices and its agents*, Santos begins by highlighting that all practice is based on knowledge, but he defends the specificity of translation between practices due to two circumstances.

> The importance of the work of translation between practices is due to a double circumstance. On the one hand, the sociology of absences and the sociology of emergencies allow for the enormous increase in available and possible stock of social experiences. On the other, since there is no single principle of social transformation, it is impossible to determine in the abstract articulations and hierarchies among the different social experiences and their conceptions of social transformation. Only by means of reciprocal intelligibility among the practices is it possible to evaluate them and define possible alliances among them. As occurs with the work of translation of knowledge, the work of translation of practices is particularly important among non-hegemonic practices given that intelligibility among them is a condition of their reciprocal articulation. The latter is, at the same time, a condition of the conversion of non-hegemonic practices into counter-hegemonic practices. The

43   See Santos, B. de S., 2005, *op. cit.*, pp. 177–8.

anti-systemic or counter-hegemonic potential of any social movement resides in its ability to be articulated alongside other movements, with its organizational forms and its objectives. For this articulation to be possible, the movements must be reciprocally intelligible.[44]

With respect to focus of this paper, the author feels that it is important to highlight two characteristics of the translation of practices that are mentioned in the previous quote. Firstly, we have the *non-existence of a single principle* of social transformation. In effect, the next section will focus on organizations that operate with a different logic rather than remain subordinate to a State or the strict logic of the market, the respective "single principles of social transformation" of pure socialists and liberals. Secondly, it is *impossible to determine articulations and hierarchies a priori* when immersed in works of translation of practices. For example, when two organizations sit down to negotiate an agreement or alliance, the conclusion of this negotiation may be one type or its opposite depending on what elements the two parties are willing to share to establish the accords and which elements they consider non-negotiable, resulting in the limitation or rupture of the initial alliance sought.[45] In either case, the work of translation implies the possibility of aggregation from the *bottom up* within a society as an alternative to a *top down* aggregation, the latter will always be "imposed by a great theory or by a privileged social actor."[46]

3.4.4. Political and Technical Work

The work of translation does not seek a solution to a technical problem because the richness of the reality (as has been revealed by the sociology

---

44   Santos, B. de S., 2005, *op. cit.*, pp. 178–9. The example Santos uses to explain the translation of non-hegemonic practices to articulate a counter-hegemonic movement is the series of World Social Forums inaugurated in Porto Alegre in 2001.

45   "The work of translation tends to clarify what unites and separates the different movements and practices so as to determine the possibilities and the limits of the articulation or aggregation of the same." Santos, B. de S., 2005, *op. cit.*, p. 178.

46   Santos, B. de S., 2005, *op. cit.*, p. 180.

of absences), as well as the multiplicity of options (as has been revealed by the sociology of emergencies), overwhelm a purely technical solution. Technical and political questions are combined in the work of translation, and no problem can be reduced to a technical question.

> The work of translation is complementary to the sociology of absences and the sociology of emergencies. If the latter enormously increase the number and diversity of the available and possible experiences, the work of translation tends to create intelligibility, coherence, and articulation in a world enriched by that multiplicity and diversity. The translation is not reduced to the technical components it obviously has; those components and how they are applied throughout the process of translation have to be the object of democratic deliberation. Translation is, simultaneously, an intellectual and political task. And it is also an emotional one because it presupposes non-conformism to a lack which arises from the incomplete or deficient character of a given knowledge or practice. For these reasons, it is clear that conventional social sciences are not very useful for the work of translation.[47]

4. The Work of Translation in Nicaragua

The overall balance of Nicaragua's economic, political, and cultural situation as described in Section 2 of this paper is certainly somber. We could synthesize the situation as follows: neither the market – with CAFTA's neo-liberal globalization strategy – nor the State – with the Pact between Alemán and Ortega, political clientelism, and corruption – are leading Nicaragua down the road of development. However, this synthesis corresponds to a *modern* vision belonging to general sociological theories in which a single actor (the market or the State) is key to resolving a country's social ills. Santos' *oppositional postmodernism* which we have just discussed, on the other hand, invites us to focus on ideas or organizations beyond neo-liberalism and the market as well as beyond socialism and the State.

---

47   Idem.

Santos focuses our attention on organizations which, from a local but non-denigrated reality, are working to respond to concrete social needs and which are, in addition, building bridges with other organizations to share strategies for the construction of the common good and development strategies.

In effect, there are organizations and initiatives within Nicaragua to which *modern, capitalistic reasoning* gives little importance, even ignoring their existence (*absence*) and discarding them as a source of realistic, *emerging* options which, through a *work of translation*, generate common development strategies. These emerging initiatives and the works of translation they are involved in signal a different development than that of the hegemonic globalization model which continues to consecrate all that is external as Nicaragua's savior and which continues to reinforce the fatalism that impregnates Nicaraguan values. In effect, the neo-liberal discourse continuously repeats that development will come from foreign investment and that Nicaragua must change its legislation to make it more attractive for this investment. This discourse legitimizes tax relief for everything that sounds "external": tax relief for tourism enterprises;[48] tax exemption for an office building belonging to the country's most important businessman with the excuse that it is important for tourism;[49] and other tax measures serving only to deplete tax revenues rather than offer an incentive to the business class. This all serves to perpetuate a dual society and dual economy: a division between the elite connected to the outside world, taking advantage of its connections to get rich, and the middle and lower classes struggling to survive and develop the country, overcoming the obstacles implied by the elite's actions and discourse.

48 As of July 2006, the debate surrounding the tax relief for such businesses was still alive in Nicaragua. If Liberal theses were to impose themselves, they would suppose a considerable fiscal loss. See Roundtable discussion on the Tourism Law held at UCA de Managua on Friday, 14 July 2006.

49 This refers to the Pellas building in Managua, belonging to the richest and most influential family in Nicaragua. Conversation with María López Vigil, *Envío* headquarters, Managua 11 July 2006.

Santos' outline also differs from the Ortega-Alemán Pact which holds the State hostage to the three bourgeoisies and which allows the middle and lower classes to participate only as political-economic clients of these three groups or their political representatives. Among these three is the FSLN, a socialist party waving the flag of the State and opposed to the US. However, it did not block approval of CAFTA and, by means of businessmen from the second bourgeoisie, the party has positioned itself economically within the capitalist framework that it is ultimately helping to establish. Within this context, applying the work of translation to Nicaragua will allow us to analyze:

- the coordinating initiatives or joint efforts that various organizations from or centered in the lower and middle classes are using to foment development from below while not believing in external salvation as a neo-liberal excuse;
- the possible alliances between organizations in this sector or with market organizations (essentially, upper class) in order to articulate a more integrated economic and social fabric which will allow Nicaragua to face the challenges of the future with a reduced incidence of duality.

In this section, then, we will analyze various citizen, political, and economic initiatives in present day Nicaragua from the perspective of the work of translation. Specifically, we will present and analyze organizations who work in Nicaragua from the perspective of their relationships with other organizations all with the aim of constructing the common good or developing the country. The organizations analyzed are:

Intermón Oxfam, an NGO for international cooperation which is developing a program in Nicaragua (*La Nicaragua possible* – The Possible Nicaragua) with which it aims to foster and facilitate links between grassroots organizations to elaborate local, regional, and national development strategies;

Alianza MRS, a political party which, as detailed in Section 2 of this paper, splintered from the FSLN and is based around two axes: regrouping Sandinista politicians and voters disappointed with the *Piñata* scandal and the corruption implicit in the *Pacto*; and a social-democratic project critical with neo-liberalism;

FDL, the *Fondo de Desarrollo Local* (Local Development Fund), a Nicaraguan NGO offering micro-credits and seeking alliances with other organizations (financial and business organizations, NGOs, and companies) to foment micro-businesses and small and medium-sized companies;

FENACOOP, the *Federación Nacional de Cooperativas* (National Federation of Cooperatives), an important Nicaraguan federation working with a non-capitalistic logic, though frequently in touch (work of translation) with political parties and businesses to support the country's economic development.

The sources of information used to present these four "work of translation" *cases* are *written material* relative to these organizations, but are especially the *result of interviews* between the author and the leaders of the respective organizations during his stay in Nicaragua in July 2006.

4.1. Intermón Oxfam: Translation and International Cooperation

4.1.1 Intermón Oxfam and "La Nicaragua posible"

Intermón Oxfam (IO) is an NGOD founded in Barcelona in 1956 as a Missionary Service for the Catalonian Jesuits. In 1997, Intermón federated with Oxfam International giving birth to IO. IO has been in Nicaragua since 1989. After Hurricane Mitch in 1998, IO Nicaragua launched its most ambitious and complete program to date: *La Nicaragua posible* (the Possible Nicaragua).[50] IO went from managing small, local projects to coordinating all its efforts in this program with the organizations it had been collaborating with.[51] *La Nicaragua posible* is an interesting case to

---

50 http://www.intermonoxfam.org/page.asp?id=904# – Consulted on 30 June 2006.

51 http://www.intermonoxfam.org/page.asp?id=2417# – Consulted on 30 June 2006.

analyze from the *work of translation* perspective. The program's focus is
as follows:

> La Nicaragua posible provides coverage to seven provinces within the country;
> we work – shoulder to shoulder – with 23 local organizations to benefit 16,000
> families. Our objectives are to:
> – Promote citizen participation to change the situation of poverty. We support
>   the Coordinadora Civil, an entity representing approximately 500 local orga-
>   nizations in their struggle against the controversial Water Law which aims to
>   privatise the watersheds, as well as working to refinance external debt;
> – Improve food safety by means of crop diversification and the introduction of
>   vegetables destined for the local markets. We also participate in the distribu-
>   tion of food and seeds in the Región Autónoma del Atlántico Norte region to
>   stop the hunger caused by a plague of rats threatening the crops;
> – Favor and promote access to the markets. We buy, foster, and distribute coffee
>   from and for small producers according to fair trade criteria. Additionally,
>   we keep track of and denounce the CAFTA accords which clearly leave small
>   producers at a disadvantage with respect to the large food corporation;
> – Strengthen the role of *women*, especially in rural areas, as well as fight against
>   domestic violence.[52]

4.1.2. Evaluation of "La Nicaragua Posible" and the Coordinadora Civil (CCER)[53]

How *La Nicaragua posible* functions can only be understood within the
context of the last 20 years in Nicaraguan history. In 1990, the FSLN's
electoral loss and the *Piñata* scandal were a significant shock for many
Nicaraguans. Some political and social activists left the country while
others stayed to continue working; other, more desperate activists became
depressed and some even committed suicide. Eventually, other activists

---

52   http://www.intermonoxfam.org/page.asp?id=2417# – Consulted on 30 June
     2006.
53   The contents of this section stem from a conversation between the author and
     Martha Lorena Mora, Director of IO Nicaragua, at the UCA de Managua, on
     12 July 2006, and a conversation with Mario Quintana, National CCER Liaison
     at CCER headquarters in Managua, on 20 July 2006.

decided to work for their ideals by means of NGOs, albeit focused on responding to the immediate needs of the people and preserving the conquests achieved by the Revolution for the poor. This re-conversion took place within the post-war period, with many open wounds and mistrust among the previously rival sides. This resulted in the work of each organization being easily isolated from that of other organizations. With the effects of Hurricane Mitch in 1998, some NGOs organized to demand that they be granted the power to dialogue with the government: the *Coordinadora Civil para Emergencias y Reconstrucción* (CCER) – Civilian Coordinator for Emergencies and Reconstruction – was created and is still faithful to its mission of reconstruction and serves institutionally as a means of dialogue between the NGOs and the political powers. IO's *La Nicaragua posible* program helps fund CCER so it can continue to meet, participate in negotiations at diverse levels, and increase the number of organizations that participate within it: IO invites all the organizations it works with to participate in CCER.[54]

Mario Quintana, a CCER manager, insists that the tasks of public resource redistribution and fomenting public participation are aimed at negotiating *a new State model*. In effect, since 1990, the neo-liberal State is being imposed by the ideas and praxis of certain international organizations. Deep down, what is being discussed is, *from a participatory focus*, the role of NGOs with respect to the void being left by the State:

– Should that void be filled by friendly cooperation?
– Should those voids be maintained to heighten the State's contradictions?

---

54   CCER is a network of networks which includes more than 600 organizations from diverse sectors and works with 16 thematic networks and 12 territorial networks. In 2006, its main objectives were divided along two axes: *aspects related to the redistribution of public resources* (budget constraints imposed by international financial organisms; three-tier analysis of the Administration's public budgets; tax policy; internal debt and CENI bonds originating from fraudulent bank closures); and *participation by citizens* (election observers; political observation; access to public information).

– Should those voids be alleviated while working at the same time for
the State to assume its responsibility in defense of the common good
and guarantee it for all the citizens?
– And, finally: what has happened to national sovereignty when international financial organizations dictate the country's budgets?

4.1.3. A New Focus on Cooperation

This political work which IO has involved itself in represents a broad-
ening of the technical work which it had undertaken up until recently.
Concretely, IO has not stopped co-operating on technical projects, but
rather, those relationships are deeper. Its new positioning implies a *high
degree of dialogue*: "The NGOs now have to let us into their kitchens, not
just to eat but to prepare the meal together" (IO Nicaragua Director).
In effect: the project and financial aid continue to be offered and they
serve to initiate and maintain the relationship. In this sense, IO demands
the same technical requirements as always from the local organizations
receiving funds, but this only refers to *technical cooperation*. The NGO is
now more focused on *solidarity-minded cooperation* which involves local
NGOs in a political dialogue so that they talk to other organizations
and, as a result, mutually strengthen their positions with respect to the
political powers and become agents of social change. Solidarity-minded
cooperation, which implies establishing relationships with the *political
powers* (not necessarily partisan politics), is what will allow a society to
advance towards true development.

The difficulties in creating a network of NGOs to serve as inter-
mediaries with the political powers are: the lack of power of NGO; the
attempts of political parties to enter or manipulate these networks; and
the need of qualified human resources (experts to analyze the national
and international situations, campaign specialists, etc.) in each organization to effectively transform the protest into a proposal. The Director
of IO Nicaragua emphasized to the author that this dynamic of dialogue between organizations to prepare and defend collective proposals
is, in fact, replacing weapons which, up until 1990, were the tools used
to "resolve conflicts". This cooperation is also contributing to peace by

means of the construction of sector or territorial networks which foster a culture of reconciliation.

4.2. Alianza MRS: Translation and Political Parties

4.2.1. The Political Map in July 2006

Alianza MRS was created within the complicated Nicaraguan political context as a Sandinista off-shoot, without links to the Ortega-Alemán Pact and with the charismatic Herty Lewites as its presidential candidate for the upcoming elections in November 2006. Four main political parties or coalitions will participate in these elections:

> a) FSLN – *Frente Sandinista de Liberación Nacional* with Daniel Ortega as its candidate. He has received the explicit support of Hugo Chávez: not only in public declarations in the press or at joint meetings, but also with donations of petroleum for Nicaraguan municipalities controlled by the FSLN. The fact that the party controls part of the judicial system and that Sandinista judges have pardoned Nicaraguan drug traffickers leads some to question the party's financing of its spectacular campaign;
>
> b) PLC – *Partido Liberal Constitucionalista* with José Rizo as its candidate. He is Arnoldo Alemán's candidate. The party's program is generally neo-liberal, but the party is still tainted by the corruption deriving from the Pact with the FSLN;
>
> c) ALN – *Alianza Liberal Nicaragüense* with Eduardo Montealegre as its candidate. They are "non corrupt" Liberals with a liberal model unconditionally open to the US and with the outgoing President, Enrique Bolaños' clearest sympathies, but especially that of the US Embassy's;
>
> d) *Alianza MRS – Alianza Movimiento de Renovación Sandinista* with Edmundo Jarquín as its candidate. Herty Lewites' sudden death on 2 July forced the party to change the Lewites-Jarquín ballot for that of Jarquín and Mejía Godoy.

4.2.2. Alianza MRS: A Political Style

The MRS' political style is clearly reminiscent of the *work of translation* and can be described by a beautiful, Central American image used by one of the MRS leaders, Dora María Téllez: the aim of *Alianza MRS* is to rejoin the dispersed pieces of *Sandinismo* that Daniel Ortega ripped apart, sewing them back together to make a unique and multi-colored coverlet.

> How are so many dispersed pieces of Sandinismo going to be rejoined? Our challenge is to carry out a job like the Guatemalan indigenous women who sew coverlets from pieces of coloured cloth. Piece by piece has to be rejoined, with the understanding that the result will be a mosaic making the whole, unique. The first thing is to recognise, with the greatest humbleness possible, that there are pieces, and pieces, and pieces which have been scattered everywhere. We have to recognise this in order to begin to sew them together. It is no easy task, because we all went to school during Sandinismo's last years: our background includes authoritarianism, sectarianism, exclusion, caudillismo, and vices that not only were and continue to hover above us, but which we all have shared [...] I hope we have the wisdom to be able to sew the pieces together to make a unique and plural whole.[55]

In this same vein, the *Alianza MRS* describes itself with the following words in a publicity pamphlet for the November 2006 elections:

> Our Alianza (Alliance) unites political, social, union, and trade leaders. There are Sandinistas, Liberals, Christian Socialists, Conservatives, Socialists, and Ecologists in our Alianza. Women, young and old people, farm workers, big and small business executives, workers and shopkeepers, the self-employed, indigenous people, criollos and mestizos have all joined together. We want to work with any Nicaraguan woman or man interested in a change in Nicaragua. We have come together to defeat the dirty pact and win the Presidency for Herty Lewites. We also want to take honest and brave representatives who are firmly committed to serving the people to the National Assembly.[56]

---

55 Tellez, D.M., 2005, La alianza en torno a Herty Lewites es una oportunidad única, un capital que no podemos desperdiciar, *Envío*, December (285): 16.

56 *El pacto limpio es el pacto con la gente. Herty Lewites. Votá Casilla 14* (The clean pact is the pact with the people. Herty Lewites. Vote Box 14). Electoral campaign pamphlet, Managua, July 2006, p. 2.

4.2.3. Alianza MRS' Program

Alianza MRS' electoral program for the November 2006 elections is complex. There are diverse and interesting proposals in its 70 pages,[57] all in line with a development centered on the fight against poverty. The *Alianza MRS* program is summarized by "14 commitments for a clean pact":[58]

> Herty proposes a clean pact with the people:
> 1. Put an end to the dirty pact and corruption by means of profound institutional reform to rescue democracy and end the impunity of the powerful;
> 2. Put an end to the mega-salaries and mega-pensions to improve salaries among teachers and healthcare workers;
> 3. Create 500,000 new and dignified jobs, especially for the young beginning to work;
> 4. Eradicate hunger and malnutrition among children;
> 5. Guarantee free and better education to every boy and girl;
> 6. Guarantee low cost medicine;
> 7. Create a Development Bank for small producers in all economic sectors and guarantee land ownership to the rightful owners;
> 8. Provide 40,000 housing solutions for the neediest people;
> 9. Prioritise the construction of roads in the country's productive regions in the centre and north of the country and a connection with the Caribbean Coast;
> 10. Make the Autonomy of the Caribbean Coast area a reality and finalise the entitlement of communal lands;
> 11. Protect our emigrants and guarantee their right to vote;
> 12. Improve public safety in all communities around the country and stop the violence against women and children;
> 13. Protect, renew, and make sustainable use of our natural resources for the benefit of all Nicaraguans;
> 14. Develop renewable sources of energy, take electricity to the countryside, foment tourism, and develop small companies to create jobs and improve the lives of Nicaraguans. Herty Lewites.

---

57   *Alianza MRS. Propuesta de programa para las elecciones generales. Mayo, 2006.* Alianza MRS electoral program.
58   *El pacto limpio es el pacto con la gente.* Electoral campaign pamphlet, *op. cit.*, pp. 3–4.

4.2.4. Evaluation of Alianza MRS[59]

Alianza MRS cannot be understood without understanding the context of the Revolution and the disappointment felt among the Left and Nicaraguan society in general as of 1990. The Revolution changed Nicaragua. Those who had never been in power were soon empowered. In 1990, however, the Revolution's values were defeated by the pragmatism that led many to vote for Violeta Chamorro in order to end the war and by the *Piñata* scandal which corrupted the ideals of the Revolution. 1990 was not the end of a government for many people; it was the end of the world. In this context of growing corruption, a lack of reconciliation, and of rigidly partisan politics, Sergio Ramírez (former Sandinista Vice President) and Dora María Téllez founded the *Movimiento Renovador del Sandinismo* in 1995, though it received few votes in that year's elections.

Herty Lewites would truly impulse this dissident branch of *Sandinismo* later. He was an untiring financier of the guerrilla movement against Somoza, he lived life to the fullest and was close to the people. He was friendly, frank, critical, and had few formal studies but was an excellent communicator. Between 2000 and 2004 he was Managua's mayor and that is when he distanced himself from Daniel Ortega because he was now governing for all. He did not deviate funds for the FSLN nor did he expel non-Sandinistas from the city council who were efficient workers. He did not identify city hall with the party. In a Nicaragua which had not been able to reconcile, Herty captured and made the people feel that that reconciliation was possible. He was a Sandinista but everybody liked him. "The poor like him and the rich aren't afraid of him." He would silently negotiate with the rich for them to pay their municipal taxes; he had a non-confrontational leadership style.

In 2004 Lewites was the country's most popular politician and he requested primary elections within the FSLN for the elections scheduled

---

59   This section is completely based on a conversation between the author and María López Vigil, an *Alianza MRS* activist and chief correspondent for *Envío* magazine on social and political thought. The conversation was held in Managua at *Envío* headquarters on 11 July 2006.

for 2006. In early 2005 he was expelled from the FSLN and, in February of that year, Daniel Ortega proclaimed himself the party's presidential candidate. Later in 2005, Herty declared himself a Sandinista despite his expulsion and challenged Daniel. In the *caudillista* and *machista* Nicaraguan political context, he became the rival "rooster" who stood up to the country's most powerful man. Little by little, he gained the support of social and political leaders, and his popularity did not waiver. Herty went on to lead the *Alianza MRS*. Herty's death in July 2006 created an emotive backlash which catalyzed sympathy for *Alianza MRS*. Hope was rediscovered in many popular sectors of society. The business world is not afraid of the *Alianza*, and a successful and educated businessman, Manuel Ignacio Lacayo, is running for office as a representative of this party, though the majority of businessmen favor Eduardo Montealegre or José Rizo. The elections slated for 5 November 2006 will be an important test for Jarquín and Mejía Godoy. The question that arises is if they will be able to substitute Herty's style and popularity. The Alianza's political project has depended to great measure on Lewites' leadership and it does not have the resources to fend off the legal battles – a deep-rooted practice in Nicaraguan political culture – which the two parties in the *Pacto* can afford.

4.3. Fondo de Desarrollo Local (FDL): Translation and Micro-financing

The FDL is a not-for-profit foundation dedicated to micro-financing development at the local level. In addition, the FDL lends funds to entrepreneurs and offers them economic advice. This puts the FDL in a position of serving as a catalyst, with its own development horizon within the context of the work of translation. The FDL is prestigious within Nicaragua. In 2005 it was awarded the Inter American Development Bank's prize for the best micro-finance institution in Latin America. It has established relationships with other not-for-profit organizations in Nicaragua as well as other financial institutions in the country. This will allow us to examine the work of translation of this organization with other non-market organizations or otherwise within the Nicaraguan context.

4.3.1. FDL Description[60]

The FDL is a micro-financing institution which caters especially to the
rural sector, though it also offers credit in the urban sectors to guarantee
the organization's sustainability. Nicaragua is a country with 500,000
small and medium-sized companies which employ more than 50% of the
active population. The rural sector is an important one because, after the
Sandinista agrarian reform (1980–1990), thousands of farm workers now
own land though they lack the financial resources, technical assistance
and capability of focusing on the market. In 1990, financial reform liber-
ated the banking sector and the state banking institutions were nearly all
closed. Private banking abandoned the rural sector once more. That is
when the FDL came onto the scene to service the rural sector excluded
from the financial market. In 2005, more than 30,000 of the FDL's 52,000
clients received credits of less than $500. The sector is a low income one.
However, in 2005 the FDL's portfolio of credits ascended to $34.6 mil-
lion. The problem in Nicaragua with micro-financing institutions arises
from the restrictions placed on these:

– they are not subject to banking regulations;
– they cannot capture funds from their clients;
– they cannot execute debts unlike the banks;
– they have greater interest rates which make their credit more
  expensive.

Although they cannot receive funds from their clients, they can
receive money from NGOs and multilateral banks. In general, they do
not face competition from the banks since the latter do not dispose of
the technology for micro-finances. One of the methods used by the FDL
is that of solidarity-minded groups. Groups are created and the untrust-

---

60   The data from this and the following sections stems from a conversation between
     the author and Julio Flores, FDL Manager, which took place in Managua at FDL
     headquarters on 28 July 2006.

worthy clients are eliminated. Intense work is carried out to get in-depth knowledge of these groups. They then receive credit:

- for short-term loans;
- especially aimed at women;
- along a scale which begins with $60 or $70 and is broadened later in terms of amount and due date;
- services, small industry, the urban and rural sectors.

The FDL is supervised by public and private international organizations, some of these supported by the World Bank.

4.3.2. FDL and the Work of Translation

Recently, the FDL has established and renovated its relationships with other organizations. These can be grouped into three types: organizations which finance the FDL; other micro-financing institutions or banks offering micro-credits; and organizations that work in complementary sectors with respect to economic development.

a) *Financing.* The FDL receives funds from various NGOs and international financial institutions dedicated to supporting micro-credits: DANIDA (Danish Official Development Cooperation), the Inter-American Development Bank, BCIE (Central American Bank of Economic Integration), Blueorchard, Proyecto DECOPANN (European Union), etc. Lately, the private *Banco de América Central* (BAC) has lent the FDL funds, though the Pellas family, BAC's proprietors, has its own NGO to support small and medium-sized companies. In July 2006, the BAC was sold to General Electric, which offers micro-financing, and it is probable that this Bank will enter the micro-credit sector.

b) *Credit Granting Sector.* ASOMIF is the trade union of micro-financing institutions and was founded, among others, by the FDL. They manage resources and laws. It founded SINRIESGO ("without risk"): a risk-processing institution which groups together 20 micro-credit institutions and commercial companies (including Unilever which provides credit for the purchase of appliances). SINRIESGO has a web page which can be consulted by paying $1 per visit. In 2005 FDL carried out 6,000 consultations. Risk data is not shared with private banks, though SINRIESGO will be regulated and registered in the future and private banking will probably participate at that moment since the official risk-processing centre provides a less than optimal service. FDL, with its network of offices in the principal cities around the country, also holds the concession for Western Union for the payment and shipment of funds.

c) *Complementary Organizations.* FDL's 2005 yearly report presents a policy of alliances with complementary organizations related to fostering development:

> This year we increased the number of agreements signed with institutions and companies dedicated to offering technical and commercialisation assistance. The agreement with Atlantic, the coffee exporter, was renewed, and we signed with Aldea Global to commercialise "high-altitude" coffee produced by small producers. Additionally, we worked together with CLUSA to offer complementary technical assistance to small producers and women in the Chinandega province and with TECNOSERVE for technical and commercialisation assistance for onion producers in the Jinotega province. In both cases, the FDL offers credit for work and investment capital.[61]

When founded, the FDL was originally linked to the *Instituto Nitlapán*, an institution dependent on the *Universidad Centroamericana de Managua* and dedicated to offering technical assistance to small and medium-sized companies. The FDL separated itself from Nitlapán 8 years ago but the latter still has signed agreements to offer technical assistance to clients receiving credit from the FDL. However, Nitlapán does not work in the area of commercialization. In this sense, agreements were signed in 2005 with organizations that do commercialize (cooperatives such as Aldea Global or private corporations such as Atlantic) to help the producers in these areas:

---

61   FDL., 2006, *Memoria anual FDL 2005*, Managua: 4–5.

– in ranching, FDL finances the conversion of extensive ranches to semi-intensive ones as the latter are less harmful for the environment and more productive. The FDL and Nitlapán have reached an agreement with slaughterhouses (private corporations) to commercialize (and export) this higher quality meat;

– in terms of coffee, FDL and Nitlapán have reached an agreement with the cooperative Aldea Global to commercialize high-altitude coffee (grown at more than 1000 m above sea level) and another agreement with Atlantic SA, which promotes the commercialization of conventional coffee. The benefit for the producers is a higher price.

4.4. FENACOOP: Translation and a Cooperative Economy[62]

The *Federación Nacional de Cooperativas* represents 620 productive cooperatives and approximately 40,000 families out of a total of 80,000 in the cooperative sector in Nicaragua. FENACOOP is leaded by Sinforiano Cáceres, a peasant with few diplomas but very smart, honest and active – according to the opinion of the author of the present paper. FENACOOP has 32 employees in total. The member cooperatives purchase FENACOOP's services for $40,000 per year. It is not financed externally nor does it receive subventions, but rather, it is sustained by the services it offers to meet the specific needs of the cooperatives. "FENACOOP, RL, is a third-degree integration Cooperative. It was founded on the need of the Cooperative movement to strengthen its organizational structures and units within the agricultural Cooperative sector and industry based on farm workers, analysing how these should be integrated, adopted and suited to meet the idiosyncrasies of the farm workers."[63] FENACOOP was founded in April 1990, with 90% of its members having benefited from the Sandinista agrarian reform. The

---

62   The contents of this section stem from a conversation between the author and Sinforiano Cáceres, FENACCOP Director which took place at FENACOOP headquarters in Managua on 24 July 2006.

63   *Mesa Agropecuaria y Forestal. Nicaragua, Centroamérica*. Explanatory pamphlet.

organization's Sandinista origins excluded it from receiving financing in 1991 from international organizations under the influence of the US.

4.4.1. New Leadership

Despite the explicit US blockade, FENACOOP's survival and growth from 1990 to 2000 was due to a new focus on cooperativism and its leadership. In effect, FENACOOP has achieved a new style of leadership within the Cooperatives and in a non-partisan fashion. The State socialism of the Sandinista decade (1980–1990) was focused vertically, an inheritor of vertical *caciquismo*. In the 1980s, leadership was styled on protest. Now it needed to be more active because it had to be better informed. Leadership's political dimension had to turn to proposals rooted in the actions of its bases and with its own technical base, centered on in-depth analyzes of complex problems. *Land-grabbing* leaders are of no use today, with an ego so large that after seizing land they would later be "unable" to accompany the farm workers to legalize their ownership and work them efficiently, the end result being that the land would eventually be sold off. A new political relationship was necessary for those *shipwrecked* in the Nicaragua of 1990: those surviving on pieces of the wrecked ship, a new relationship so that the shipwrecked could recover mutual trust, rejoin the pieces, and rebuild the ship.

4.4.2. FENACOOP and the Political Parties

FENACOOP was founded in 1990 in the middle of the internal FSLN crisis. However, during the Cooperative's first decade, while the FSLN's identity faded and degenerated, FENACOOP's image began to take shape by meeting its objectives and cooperative values. Currently, although the majority of FENACOOP's member cooperatives and leaders are FSLN sympathizers, it is not subject to said party. Sinforiano Cáceres has turned down a seat as an FSLN representative on two occasions. And he feels that if FENACOOP is respected – and not absorbed – by the FSLN, then the social and political ideals of the cooperative movement may inspire the electoral programs of parties such as the FSLN. The latter has a clearly corrupt nucleus, but there are people with other ideas in its environment. If this environment can stand firm without submitting to the FSLN, it will be able to establish alliances with the FSLN and weave a new institutionality which will foment well-being among Nicaraguans. An example of cooperation between FENACOOP and the FSLN benefiting the member cooperatives is FENACOOP's importation of urea, a fertilizer, from Venezuela into Nicaragua, thanks to FSLN contacts with Venezuelan President, Hugo Chávez. Importing this fertilizer has broken the urea market oligopoly in Nicaragua and managed to reduce prices which were higher than the average for the region. After the operation was finalized, certain FSLN politicians, however, asked Sinforiano Cáceres to give urea to the party for the latter to distribute in rural areas that did not vote for the FSLN. Cáceres rejected the offer and maintained FENACOOP's independence with respect to the FSLN.

4.4.3. Relationships with Market Organizations

LAFISE, an important Nicaraguan private financial institution operating in 18 countries, met with Sinforiano Cáceres in early 2006. They offered FENACOOP credits for commercialization, leasing, and franchises, support to find markets, and international payment management. Cáceres turned the offer down, saying that FENACOOP worked with a cooperative's logic: FENACOOP's business is to buy cheap from the suppliers and sell the end product more expensively for its members. This logic is contrary to the capitalist logic inspiring LAFISE.

4.4.4. Fair Trade: A New Vocabulary for Development

FENACOOP has also sought commercialization channels by means of *fair trade*. In this respect, Sinforiano Cáceres believes that "fair trade" is a term defined by NGOs from the North. This is clear by a series of norms which producers in the South have to comply with for their products to be labeled "fair trade". The result is a slightly higher price though only for a small part of local producers in the South, while the final product will be sold only in certain commercial areas in northern countries. For

Cáceres, both the definition of the rules as well as the commercialized volumes and prices should be agreed upon by both parties: the process must be defined jointly and the North should not impose its rules.

5. Conclusions

5.1. General Situation in Nicaragua

The economic, political, and cultural analysis carried out began with the determination that Nicaragua is one of the poorest countries in Latin America. In the *economic field*, today, with a globalization process completely underway, CAFTA is seen as a challenge to regional integration and, with the United States, it may impoverish Nicaragua's economy. However, the geopolitical alternative is free trade as promoted by the WTO, which would not allow the preferential treatment for Nicaraguan products in the US market that CAFTA permits. In fact, the Central American products in the US are already beginning to feel the competition from Chinese products. However – and this has been an underlying thesis of this paper – neither the economic nor political situation in Nicaragua are fatalistically determined by external countries or agents. The Nicaraguan economy suffers from the obstacles resulting from recent political changes which have burdened the public budget with debts to the national and private banks; the informal economy is wide-spread; agricultural productivity is low compared to other countries in the region; the illegal trafficking of natural resources, especially along the Caribbean Coast, reduces the national value added and the taxes collected; and drug trafficking is extending itself as an economic activity which has also penetrated the mechanisms of political power.

The *political system* is debating between continuity and change with respect to the pincers represented by the Pact between Arnoldo Alemán and Daniel Ortega. These two politicians aim to wield an iron-clad control over their respective parties and monopolize the political spectrum with the dramatization of a left-right debate which in all practicality is a submission, including for the FSLN, to the economic dictates of the US and a neo-liberal vision of the role of globalization in Nicaragua. In terms of foreign policy, the US insistence on involving itself in Nicaraguan politics is aiding Daniel Ortega and is legitimating him to seek out the patronage of Hugo Chávez. But between Alemán and Ortega, and between the US and Chávez, there is room to renovate the party system and for a new style of politics and economics to emerge: more centered on consolidation and support for local economic initiatives which will generate wealth in Nicaragua, allowing for a larger part of the added value of the country's products to remain in Nicaraguan hands.

The *cultural debate* has been presented based on the fatalism that nature and Colonial evangelization solidly established in Nicaragua. This fatalism has reincarnated itself as a determining force throughout Nicaraguan history in the guise of US intervention, globalization, free trade, cooperation from abroad, or emigrants' remittances. In any of these reincarnations, the anthropological conclusion is the same: the future of Nicaragua is not in the Nicaraguans' own hands because all things good and bad come from abroad. In this sense, 1990 marked a significant cultural change: the FSLN, which had ruled the country nationalistically for 10 years, promoting the poor and freedom, lost the elections because the people wanted to end the war financed by the US. Once again, Nicaragua had to bend to the will of a foreign power. So began the post-war period whose main task was and continues to be to reconcile the *Compas* and the *Contras*, the two opposing sides in the 1980–1990 war. 1990 was also the year of the *Piñata*, which destroyed the hopes of the Nicaraguan Left and vitally and psychologically disoriented a large part of the population: "We gave our lives and those of our own for a Revolution whose leaders became corrupt the moment they left the government." A culture with a history of tutelage, not of citizenry, had just contributed to the subversion of the revolutionary ethos: the culture of thieving, corruption, and anti-solidarity became the dominant culture.

5.2. Dichotomic Thought and Analysis of Nicaragua

To delve more deeply into the analysis presented in Section 2, we used the sociological theories of the Portuguese sociologist, Boaventura de Sousa Santos regarding the development of poor countries in the context of globalization. Specifically, in terms of Santos' focus on capitalism's *dichotomic thought*, we feel that the main dichotomies in Nicaraguan reality which we have analyzed are: global / local, market / non-market, and partisan politics / non-partisan politics.

The *global / local* dichotomy. The hegemonic globalization model as described by Santos is an ideology used by the elite to maintain their privileges and reproduce the belief that Nicaragua's salvation will come from abroad: submission to CAFTA without local, national, or regional negotiations, and submission to the US ambassador. The Nicaraguan Left's visceral reaction to submission to the US has been taken advantage of by Daniel Ortega who is not working, however, on a strategy for national construction: his friendship with Chávez forewarns of another submission while the political and economic practices of those around him (the second bourgeoisie) are fundamentally in favor of CAFTA's neo-liberal logic.

The *market / non-market* dichotomy. There are capitalistic companies in the market; in the non-market, we have the informal sector, Cooperatives, and NGOs. We have seen that organizations within the non-market are creating value, avoiding poverty and thereby promoting the development of Nicaragua. And yet, the legal system grants de facto privileges to the interests of large firms. The non-market organizations must work with each other to change "the rules of the game" (the legal and political system) in order to be able to play in the system and hope to survive while serving the segments of the population on the outer edges of the market and power.

The *partisan politics / non-partisan politics* dichotomy. Political parties are central agents in the country's political life. Some of them (especially the FSLN and the PLC and their *Pacto*) wield great power and try to monopolize political action. But this action would translate into development only if other parties were to emerge (the ALN and

MRS, for example) which would translate this party system into effective democracy. For this to occur, it is equally important for the organizations analyzed (IO, *Coordinadora Civil*, FENACOOP) to maintain their independence with respect to political parties while at the same time establishing direct dialogue with these parties, thereby creating a non-partisan political space.

With respect to these dichotomies, we should not that, firstly, the market and the party system as they are today have the power to marginalize, something which is especially harmful in a country such as Nicaragua with a clearly dual society. Globalization has more negative repercussions in countries such as Nicaragua with much less integrated societies than those in Europe, for example. And so the inevitable, marginalizing component of globalization unfolds its perverse potential much more powerfully than in the European Welfare States. Secondly, we should highlight that *at least* the third dichotomy between partisan and non-partisan politics is not directly linked to globalization. If the economically or politically powerful leaders in Nicaragua call on globalization to maintain their *Pacto* or to marginalize those without power, they are using globalization as an excuse, as an ideology.[64] In either case, the analysis of Nicaragua based on the dichotomies presented leads us to underscore the importance of the work of translation to overcome social dualism and construct the common good within the context of globalization. In the next section we will present some conclusions about the experience of the examined organizations with respect to this work of translation.

5.3. Work of Translation and the Organizations' Experience

In the study above on the work carried out by various Nicaraguan organizations, we have discovered two analogous images for the *work of translation*:

---

64 Robert Solow, Nobel Prize Laureate in Economics, states that globalization is a marvellous excuse for many things. Cited in Mària, J.F., 2000, La globalización: una maravillosa excusa para muchas cosas, *Cristianisme i Justícia Quaderns*, Barcelona, December (103).

the multi-colored coverlet and the shipwreck. According to Dora María
Téllez, the *Alianza MRS* sees itself as the *coverlet* Guatemalan women
make by sewing together multi-colored pieces of cloth. According to
Sinforiano Cáceres, 1990 was a year Nicaragua's boat was *shipwrecked*.
The remains of the shipwreck have to be brought together and rejoined
in order to rebuild the country and avoid anyone remaining at the mercy
of the waves or the sharks. However, the colored pieces of the coverlet or
the remains of the 1990 shipwreck, which are generally left to the side,
are valuable in two senses: because they are inhabited by people and
because the organizations these people belong to are generating economic,
social, and cultural value for Nicaraguan society as a whole. The work of
translation may increase the efficiency of these organizations in fostering
development and in constructing the common good.

Specifically, the management and strategy experiences of the
Nicaraguan organizations analyzed signal the following conclusions with
respect to the work of translation.

a) *The work of translation opens the debate on a neo-liberal model of
the State in power since 1990*. The defeat of the Sandinistas in 1990 and
the IMF and World Bank's neo-liberal policies have led to the retreat of
the State from Nicaraguan social reality. According to Mario Quintana
(*Coordinadora Civil*), this retreat opens a debate on whether the NGOs
should fill the void left by the State or if they should alternatively pressure
the State to assume its responsibility for guaranteeing effective citizenry
for all Nicaraguans.

b) *The work of translation is necessary for complete and long-lasting
development*. As described when presenting the program *La Nicaragua
posible*, Intermón Oxfam is working to broaden the meaning of development by means of a new vision of cooperation. In effect, going from
technical cooperation to solidarity-minded cooperation supposes changing from temporarily solving concrete social problems to continuously
solving concrete problems while, at the same time, trying to change the
economic and political structures so that these problems do no reoccur or
worsen in the future. Changing the laws or how the political system acts
may guarantee social cohesion and equality in the creation and distribution of present and future wealth. For this to occur, local organizations

have to be involved in political work (not necessarily partisan) and at the different political levels affecting them (local, provincial, national, regional, global).[65] The development of this political facet is essential for the long-term survival of these organizations and their contribution to the common good. Confrontation or collaboration between organizations without power and those with power are not options which can be prescribed a priori, nor can they be generalized as strategies for action.

c) *The work of translation is an instrument for cultural change among Nicaraguans.* Cultural change is a necessary condition for development. In the historical context of the post-war period, with corruption and submission to neo-liberal globalization after 1990, the traditional fatalistic Nicaraguan culture was reinforced. The ethos subverted in 1990 can be changed, allowing for the reinforcement of a culture of peace and development. As such, *La Nicaragua posible* implies contact between NGOs whose members carry with them mistrust or hate derived from the decade-long civil war (1980–1990). Sitting them down to dialogue, offering them instruments for peaceful protests, or helping them prepare proposals for solutions to their problems implies changing a culture of violence for one of peace. And this task implies fomenting the construction of the common good versus the culture of corruption or fatalism derived from the neo-liberal vision of globalization.

d) *The work of translation in Nicaragua requires leaders but it should require programs.* This is the sad lesson to be learnt from Herty Lewites' death. Changing from a focus on the leader to the program also implies a cultural change with respect to the values of loyalty to a leader and

---

65 This "bottom up" work will lead to another required work of translation, the one the local social actors will have to carry out in relation to the diverse development focuses proposed by the NGOs from the North working in Nicaragua: what is cooperation, what is development, how are "fair trade" and "ecological sustainability" defined in a certain country and for a certain development project? These are problems which cannot be exclusively resolved by the conceptual frameworks of the northern NGOs' country of origin or the country receiving funds. Once again, dialogue and agreement bring us back to the work of translation and its theoretical component, the *translation between knowledge.*

tutelage. In European political science terms, this change implies converting the subject-client into a citizen, a prerequisite being eliminating corruption understood as clientelism. The Alianza MRS' dependency on Herty Lewites may be considered a trait of Nicaraguan political culture, accustomed to battles between *machos* challenging each other to brawls. But the work cut out for the Alianza is a slow work of translation with respect to the social reality and the organizations working for the development of the country in all the different aspects. On the other hand, Sinforiano Cáceres' leadership in FENACOOP shows us that social leaders in Nicaragua today cannot pursue confrontational dynamics out of principle, but rather, they should be able to articulate and execute complex proposals, proposals with political and technical content and managed by teams or networks of leaders who follow complex norms. From Cáceres' discourse we can see that those networks of leaders trust one another; they know how to consult competent experts; and in their work of translation between organizations, they do not disconnect from the bases of their respective organizations.

e) *The work of translation between organizations without power and those with power is very delicate.* The *Coordinadora Civil*'s proximity to political parties (PLC or FSLN) implies the risk of being absorbed. The FDL's partial financial dependence on BAC and General Electric's interest in micro-financing may imply BAC's entrance in the micro-credit field and the displacement of NGOs, including the FDL, with all the possible consequences on credit aimed at the middle and lower economic classes. FENACOOP, with its Cooperative logic, has had contact with large firms but has not formed an alliance with them given the different visions between a market organization and a Cooperative. However, the FDL has formed and alliance with Atlantic, SA (and Nitlapán, an NGO) to commercialize conventional coffee; and FENACOOP has taken advantage of the FSLN's friendship with Hugo Chávez to lower the price of urea in Nicaragua. We have also seen how relationships between NGOs and political parties can vary from one of dialogue to an attempt to absorb the NGO. The debates on possible alliances between organizations with and without power are delicate exercises of the work of translation.

f) *Translation between Organizations with Power*. There is also work of translation between organizations with economic power and with political power. The economic elite have their connections in political parties, especially the Liberal ones. One clear example of this translation between parties with power is the Pact between Arnoldo Alemán and Daniel Ortega. The balance in terms of the Pact's effect on the country's development is nefarious, at least in the short-term. However, we cannot discard that other works of translation between market organizations or between political parties may have positive repercussions on Nicaragua's development. All in all, these types of relationships are beyond the scope of this paper.

5.4. Hope

¡Ay, mi Nicaragüita! is the sorrowful yet immensely tender and patriotic exclamation of a young Nicaraguan university student which has served as title to the paper we now close. The expression is also a shout for hope signaling a paradox: Nicaragua, can be "the mother" who gives birth to its citizens, or, at the same time, a daughter, "*mi Nicaragüita*" (from the diminutive form in Spanish). If the country is in fact a daughter, then it is up to Nicaraguans to successfully have their country grow and promote the common good for all its citizens. Like a child, we have to take care of her, love her, help her grow ... because she is ours – as a mother or as a daughter. We were given life through her and by constructing her as a positive place for relationships, life for all Nicaraguans will improve. To conclude and as Santos declares: "... human initiative, and not just an abstract idea about progress, may be the basis for the principle of hope."[66] We wish that this paper has accurately reflected the efforts made by Nicaraguans to construct the common good and thereby foster this hope.

66　Santos, B., 2005, *El milenio huérfano, op. cit.*, p. 131.

CHAPTER 8

The Common Good as a Criterion for a Globalization in the Service of Mankind

JEAN-MARIE FÈVRE

Introduction

The "Unanimous Declaration" [of Independence] of the thirteen States of North America by their Congress met on 4 July 1776 is a remarkable document not only since it marked the birth of the USA but also because it is *sui generis* for it proclaimed "that all men are created equal, that they are endowed by their Creator with certain unalienable Rights, that among these are Life, Liberty and the pursuit of Happiness."[1] It mentioned further that "Whenever any Form of Government becomes destructive of these ends, it is the Right of the People to alter or to abolish it, and to institute new Government, laying its foundation on such principles and organizing its powers in such form, as to them shall seem most likely to effect their Safety and Happiness." *Prudence* and *Justice* are required for good governance and so the text states that "The history of the present King of Great Britain [George III] is a history of repeated injuries and usurpations, all having in direct object the establishment of an absolute Tyranny over these States. To prove this, let Facts be submitted to a candid world. He has refused his Assent to Laws, the most wholesome and necessary for the public good."

---

1   Cf. annexed document: "The Unanimous Declaration of the thirteen States of America", fac-simile of the original document and then easy-to-read transcription, first sentence.

I refer to this Declaration for two reasons. In the first place it provides a fine example of collaboration and union of a great number of different States with different concerns and geographically far apart, in view of an overriding good, that is their political freedom and independence. In this respect it sets an example and suggests that in our time the different countries of Europe and of the world at large should seek new forms of cooperation and overcome petty egoisms and partisan interests in view of the greater good – one might call it the common good – of mankind. In the second place, behind the lines of the text of this Declaration, we see a very positive view of man, a creature endowed with rights who voluntarily enters into an alliance and union with his like, in order to obtain a greater good. This means that the so-called cardinal virtues (of which I shall speak further on), that is to say prudence, justice, courage and moderation or self-restraint, are presupposed as the basis of the new civic and political life the Founding Fathers of the United States were at that time constructing.

One notices here the notion of the Common Good, developed over centuries within the framework of Christian Social Teaching. One may wonder whether this notion is vague or outdated. This paper aims to formulate accurately its assumptions, limits and aims. A clear presentation of the Common Good with a resolute reference to St Thomas Aquinas and the contributions of scholars of the 20th century, of Arthur-Fridolin Utz and Leo Elders especially, is of critical importance to avoid hollow verbiage or maybe fashionable but superficial and useless commonplaces.

Globalization is not a specter haunting the world as is shown by the examples of globally active and successful firms as well as of some remarkable public policies. But the world needs more harmony and coordination of efforts to reach a global positive and sustainable synergy rather than a chaotic and potentially lethal struggle for short-term wealth and power. Should the world develop the idea of a Common Good of all countries, which reminds *mutatis muntandis*, some aims of the *Pax Romana*, the *Commonwealth*, the *Dai Nippon* or the *Francophonie*? Or is this a misleading option as one considers the limits on many issues of multilateral institutional actors?

Anyway, some firms already show that it is possible – for instance in logistics – to make profit and get a positive image by contributing to a sustainable development respecting the environment and promoting people within the framework of the Common Good. One may therefore consider them as a useful criterion of knowledge, judgment and action for a globalization in the service of mankind according to the Declaration of Human Rights of Dec. 10th 1948.

1. The Common Good According to Christian Social Teaching

The great medieval philosopher St Thomas Aquinas, "looking unreservedly to truth,"[2] has given us a magnificent outline of the Common Good which – even when one would leave out the reference to Divine grace as a source of human virtues – preserves its value.[3] Indeed, in the footsteps of the church fathers, St Thomas Aquinas used both Faith and reason to increase his understanding; Christianity doesn't assert the superiority of the past but is oriented to the future.[4]

Indeed, the steadily growing globalization and frequent offshoring of factories and main offices cause problems at the local, and sometimes even at the national level. While the board of directors may not see a way

2   John Paul II, *Fides et Ratio*, § 44, Libreria Editrice Vaticana, 14 September 1998.
3   N.B. St Thomas Aquinas uses the term "*Bonum Commune*" [Common Good] 370 times in his works.
4   Stark, Rodney, *The Victory of Reason*, New York: Random House, 2005, pp.x–xi: "Encouraged by the Scholastics and embodied in the great medieval universities founded by the church, faith in the power of reason infused Western culture, stimulating the pursuit of science and the evolution of democratic theory and practice. The rise of capitalism was also a victory for church-inspired reason, since capitalism is in essence the systematic and sustained application of reason to commerce – something that first took place within the great monastic estates".

out to keep their enterprise afloat, the employees and the local population will often protest and assert that their interests are sacrificed for the sake of more profits for the shareholders. Sometimes these protests may be justified, if management has been sloppy and innovations were not introduced on time, and valuable money was wasted on excessive salaries, stock-options and other remunerations for the direction. However, it also happens that a certain short-sightedness and narrow-minded attention to particular interests influence behavior. It is also a fact that shorter working hours, long vacations and relatively high salaries put our companies in an unfavorable position in respect of the competition in countries with cheaper labor. It is also possible that the work ethos of some employees in Western countries is not as good as it used to be 50 years ago. Sometimes the direction is considered by a number of employees, who think that they are exploited, as the enemy, while the direction is dissatisfied with the productivity and behavior of some of its personnel.

It is here that we see the need for a broader perspective, which tries to reconcile the interests of the company and management with those of all the employees. In this connection it is helpful to recall the doctrine of the common good. It is generally recognized that the political society, let us say the State, must pursue the good of all the different citizens and the various groups within its borders. Since all citizens, as men, are social beings, they need the State in order to develop their faculties and to reach their private well-being. The good of the individual citizen can only be reached within the political community. Pursuing their particular interests, the citizens will normally promote the public good too, but a community can only develop and be prosperous when its members also keep in view the interest of the whole. Unfortunately contemporary individualism is the cause of the fact that some experience an opposition between their own good and that of the State. The common good is a difficult concept, for it seems to refer to something which often is not palpable. Modern States, even greater comprehensive commonwealth of States such as the European Union, have developed so numerous complex rules and laws that they alienate the citizens. Nowadays, some people wonder to which point they are social beings.

At this point it is imperative to underline the principle of *subsidiarity*, so often forgotten, according to which an administration at a higher level should not attempt to regulate what can easily and correctly be done at a lower and more local level. But much more important is the education to the main virtues. In recent years leading authors in the field of ethics have drawn attention to the need of returning to an education to the virtues, following the lead of such geniuses as Aristotle, the Stoics and St Thomas Aquinas. In this connection we mean the virtues of prudent deliberation, taking into consideration all the aspects of a question, and also what hap-pened in the past and what can be foreseen for the future, both on the private and public levels. Secondly, education to virtuous behavior in the field of justice is also important. It is here that I recall the doctrine of St Thomas Aquinas who explains that there is a type of justice we all know and practice, viz. the so-called commutative justice between people, like being just in selling and buying, but there is also a form of justice which makes us carry out our duties toward the community and our country, while a third class of justice is that of persons in command, who govern a country, or a company, and must give everyone his due.

What I am saying seems so simple, to the point of being naïve. Everyone sees the importance of these virtues, but will think: in every-day life people cut corners, try to get away with what seems difficult for them. Now this is precisely the point I am making: just like we practice in our youth a musical instrument to become proficient and to enjoy playing, we must in the same way learn these virtues by being educated to them and practicing them. Virtuous acts are beautiful, give us joy, fulfill our human being, and ennoble us. In the past, much of this education was dispensed in our families, at our schools, by the Church. Nowadays that has become far more difficult, and one can only obtain some result by collaboration and consistent efforts at different levels.

You may want to have a look at the schematic representation (Figure 1) which I have developed as an illustration of the Common Good in the modern and very precise interpretation of my two remarkable masters on this matter: the Swiss scholar Arthur-Fridolin Utz[5] and the Dutch scholar Leo Elders.[6] This figure shows how the cardinal virtues cooperate to promote the common good, how through cooperation the human being may realize the Common Good and reach happiness. The human person as *"rationalis naturae individua substantia"*[7] is in the center of the Common Good and owns in this respect a sort of Janus face:[8]

– as an individual, the human being owns liberty and responsibility outside the causality of Nature;
– as a social being, he/she needs the community for his/her personal fulfillment.

One may not interrupt or suppress the link between both poles of this field of tension. The own good of the individual is not its own end but the Common Good is of superior importance. The authority of a State depends on its respect of what is socially righteous and of its respect of the dignity of every person individually. If this is not the case, the State only represents the sum of particular and contradictory interests, its power (*Imperium*) gives it no authority (*Auctoritas*). This State must impose itself by force and oppression; legal justice is therefore not the same as general justice and is not righteous.[9]

Or, "if justice fails, are the rich anything else but a gang of brigands?"[10]

5   Cf. Utz, Athur-Fridolin, OP: *Sozialethik*, I: "Die Prinzipien der Gesellschaftslehre", 2nd edition, Heidelberg: Kerle, 1964, Chapters 6 and 7, pp. 127–234.
6   Cf. e.g. Elders, Leo and E. De Jonghe (eds), *De beginselen van de sociale leer van de Kerk*, Leuven: Acco, 1994; *De ethiek van Thomas van Aquino*, Oegstgeest, 2001, French translation: *L'éthique de Saint Thomas d'Aquin*, Paris: Presses de l'IPC – L'Harmattan, 2005, pp. 263–6.
7   St Thomas Aquinas, *Summa Theologica*, Ia, Quaest. XXIX, Art. I, Latin edition, Turin, 1922, p. 203.
8   Cf. Utz, Arthur-Fridolin, *Sozialethik*, Heidelberg: F.H. Kerle, 1964, p. 311 sq.
9   Fèvre, Jean-Marie, *Der Indirekte Arbeitgeber*, Frankfurt am Main / Bern: Peter Lang, 1990, p. 75.
10   Augustinus, *De Civitate Dei*, IV, 4.

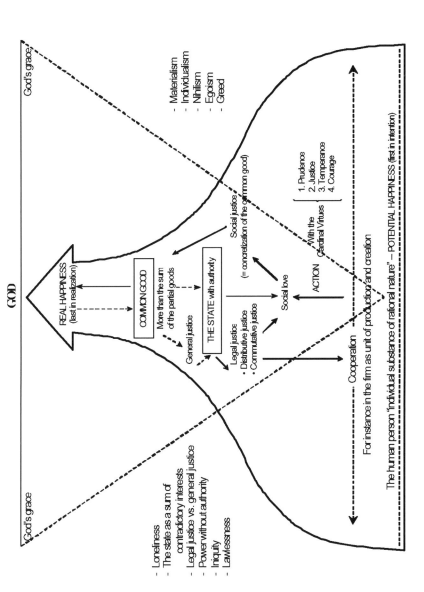

Figure 1: The Common Good – A Schematic View

Furthermore, the Common Good is a spiritual and temporal unity. The Christian must contribute to it and be conscious of perennial requirements:[11]

- *Mutatis mutandis*, the Common Good stands for political thinking as the Natural Law for the theory of Law;
- Within the perspective of the Common Good, one has to promote by individuals what is good for the human being;
- One should also realize that the Common Good is not a ready made value, but a goal which the citizens must actively pursue and develop together. In dictatorial regimes, on the other hand, goals are defined *a priori*.[12] There are further no clear conclusions a priori but one has to observe the social structures resulting from experience and History in order to determine which of them are promoting the human well-being;
- The State has to care for the prosperity of everyone and above all for Justice: the first encyclical of Benedict XVI, *Deus Caritas Est*[13] reminds in its second part, bearing the title "The practice of love by the Church as a community of Love", that the Church has to plea for Justice and to practice charity in its own original and independent way as the third of its tasks.[14] But the encyclical emphasizes further that Justice is the main duty of the State.[15] It recalls that the political and the religious areas are of different nature, distinguishing "what

11   Cf. Dougherty, Jude P., "Keeping the Common Good in Mind", in Autori Vari, *The Ethics of St Thomas Aquinas*, Studi Tomistici, Pontificia Accademia di S. Tommaso, Libreria Editrice Vaticana, 1984, pp. 188–201.

12   Fraenkel, Ernst, *Deutschland und die westlichen Demokratien*, 3rd edition, Stuttgart: Kohlhammer, 1968, pp. 64, 167, 171 and 176.

13   Benedict XVI, *Deus Caritas Est*, English edition, Libreria Editrice Vaticana, 25 December 2005 – this document reminds Joseph Ratzinger's talent to link science to clarity, depth to accuracy, theology to reality.

14   Ibid., § 25, a): "The Church's deepest nature is expressed in her three-fold responsibility: of proclaiming the word of God (kerygma-martyria), celebrating the sacraments (leitourgia) and exercising the mystery of charity (diakomia)."

15   Ibid., § 26.

belongs to Caesar and what belongs to God (Cf. Mt 22,21)" so that the Church is different from the State but that "the two spheres are distinct yet always interrelated" and that "justice is both the aim and the intrinsic criterion of all politics [...] A just society must be the achievement of politics, not of the Church. Yet the promotion of justice through efforts to bring about openness of mind and will to the demands of the common good is something which concerns the Church deeply";[16]

– The same encyclical insists then that "Love – caritas – will always prove necessary".[17] This underlines the importance of solidarity: the Christians have to act for the Common Good "for as the body without the spirit is dead, so Faith without works is dead also";[18]

– Private property, of secondary Natural Law, best promotes independence, the sense of the value of the human being, conscientious work (Parable of the Good Shepard), favors prosperity but implies reciprocal obligations (Parable of the talents);

– The Common Good as a goal ensures a balanced compatibility between the interests of the individual and those of the community;

– The objective of the Common Good underlines the link and thus the obligations between generations: one doesn't act only here and now but for coming generations too (sustainable action);

– The Common Good is no sum wherein the suffering of some may be counterbalanced by the well-being of others: "The Common Good [*Bonum Commune*] is a category that has been playing a central role in the Social Teaching of the Church. It essentially expresses what is intended by the call for solidarity [...] Common Good is a good that can be achieved only in cooperation thus with the help of all social elements. It describes the qualitative state of society and may be interpreted as the epitome of the means and opportunities at the

16 Ibid., § 28, a).
17 Ibid., § 28, b).
18 James Epitle, 2, 26.

disposal of the society which are necessary in order that all people can achieve the complete fulfillment of their persons";[19]
- The notion of Common Good goes beyond economics.[20] One notices the harmony of the *Thomistic* system as a whole of reciprocal subordinations.

One may evoke historical concepts: The *Pax Romana* made the longest era of prosperity and peace in History. But it relied on the rule of an absolute power "with a hard voice and a big stick". The British *Commonwealth* on its part has clear roots in the medieval notion of Common Good: this notion was used to define the political organization.[21] But in 1931,[22] this defined a federation of sovereign States and colonies (which would become politically independent within the following 30 years) pledging freely allegiance to the British Crown. Some did quit it later. This Commonwealth is more a moral than a legal alliance of countries which have been colonies of the British Crown and still have strong cultural and economic links with the UK. This expression is still used in the UK and overseas. The link to the Common Good is nevertheless rather vague. The *Dai Nippon* of the first half of the 20th century has really almost nothing to do with the Common Good because it is more the organization of territories procuring cheap raw materials and energy to an authoritarian central power pursuing the goal of autarchy. The *Francophonie* is more a loose rally of heterogeneous countries "sharing the French language" which plays a small role on the world political stage in the beginning of the 21st century – besides at some occasions for the constitution of topic majorities within the General Assembly of the United Nations under the auspices of the French Republic. These examples may remember the

19   Marx, Reinhard and Wulsdorf, Helge, *Christliche Sozialethik; Konturen Prinzipien – Handlungsfelder*, Paderborn: Bonifatius Verlag, 2002, p. 178.
20   Cf. Maritain, Jacques, The *"Spiritual Common Good"*.
21   And still today, this expression is used in the UK and in the USA for certain public bodies.
22   Typically in a time of economic hardship, of monetary weakness of the UK and of difficulties in the British Empire.

notion of Common Good but only up to a point and in a very limited extent. This would anyway be a misleading option as one considers the limits on many issues of multilateral institutional actors.

After these considerations which may seem somewhat abstract and general, I would like to give two practical examples of how the approach of the Common Good as a criterion may be applied to the advantage of all:

- that of a company founded in 1748 which tries to remain perennial and to keep social justice in mind in its struggle to survive within the framework of globalization, and whose board of directors practices – *mutatis mutandis* – the virtues of moderation and simplicity: Villeroy & Boch AG Mettlach (Germany);
- a second illustration is an international organization – which at first glance may seem only concerned with technical matters but plays a growing and positive role in our contemporary world: ISO.

2. Common Good and a Globally Active Firm: Villeroy & Boch

This paper began with a text of 1776. It now considers a Franco-German firm founded in 1748 (thus older than the USA) which survived wars, industrial and political turmoil and is still mainly owned and directed by members of the founding family: Villeroy & Boch. This firm is strongly anchored in the local core of what is called these days the Region "Saar-Lor-Lux" but is one of the world's major brands in the tableware and sanitary-ware sectors with production sites on different continents. The HQ of Villeroy & Boch are still in the historic buildings of the former abbey in the small town of Mettlach, Germany, ca. 40 km downstream Saarbrücken, about 60 km from Frauenberg (near Sarreguemines, France) where it began. In the beginning of the 19th century, its main workshop was at Vaudrevanges near Sarrelouis and the former abbey was bought in Mettlach. This area fell to Prussia in 1815. The families Villeroy and Boch cooperated and the Villeroy branch is still French. Their mansion is in Vaudrevanges (in German: Wallerfangen) while a new mansion has been built in Mettlach, on the left bank of the river Saar, just opposite the HQ and is still used for special events.[23] The really modern warehouses in the neighbouring Merzig carry a strong slogan: "You, your world, your house and Villeroy & Boch".

Corporate Governance and Villeroy & Boch

Contrary to widespread prejudices against globalization and numerous sweeping statements about the strategy of globally active enterprises, there exists also a movement for a more responsible way of doing business. In Germany, the Corporate Governance Codex has been updated in June 2005, endorsing the majority of the recommendations proposed by the ad hoc Government commission. The principle of corporate governance

> stands for sound and responsible corporate management and supervision aimed at long-term real net output. It essentially includes protection of shareholder interests, the system of the decision-making, management and supervision mechanisms, as well as transparency and openness in corporate communication.

The conformity of the firm Villeroy & Boch AG to the German corporate principles has been examined by KPMG and recognized on 3 April 2004.[24] In the 2005 business year, "Villeroy & Boch AG once again followed the recommendations put forward by the Codex with the exception of an itemized report on Management Board remuneration".[25] During the annual assembly of 2006, Prince Peter Wittgenstein, Chairman of

---

23   As for instance for a Franco-German-Polish Summit between President Chirac, Chancellor Merkl and President Kacziński.
24   For the text of the declaration of conformity: http://www.villeroy-boch.com/fileadmin/use/ir/Entsprechendserklaerung20041214.pdf.
25   Villeroy & Boch 1748 – Annual Report 2005, p. 13.

the Supervisory Board, explained this exception by the need of discretion vis-à-vis head-hunters and also by the fact that most Board members (as for instance Wendelin von Boch-Galhau, Chairman of the Management Board) are living in a rural area, meet regularly unsophisticated people, buy in local shops and have common activities. Some figures of remuneration may be confusing and harmful for social life.

An Unusual Annual Assembly for a Global Player

Indeed, the annual assembly of Villeroy & Boch is rather unusual for a global player: it does not take place in a prestigious location but in the modest celebration hall of the small town of Merzig, which is simply adapted for this event: everything is well organized but with no frills.[26] The local volunteers of the fire-brigade regulate the traffic and the parking. One notices the serious, polite but unsophisticated attitude of the attendants: there are leaders of the industrial, banking and political sector, wealthy shareholders, journalists, but also clearly retired employees who have a couple of shares, and small shareholders. The courtesy coffee with cake or sandwiches is served generously but simply. There is a simultaneous French-German translation due to the particular structure of the ownership and firm. The ambiance is relaxed but full of dignity. One may talk to anyone and the frugal buffet at the end of the meeting displays typical rural food of the area, with local sausages, beer, wine and mineral water, French cheese and mozzarella. No food or drink is exotic or sophisticated. Everyone should feel comfortable. This is of course no coincidence but a resolute self presentation of Villeroy & Boch: premium style through simplicity, *grandeur* through modesty. The Villeroy & Boch Group is registered under German Law and in a German small town (Mettlach / Saarland). Most members of the Board live in small towns. One may mention a significant detail: according to the rules of the firm, any senior manager should leave at 65. Wendelin von Boch Galhau is becoming 65

26   Cf. copy of the Invitation in annex.

so he will respect this rule and resign. One person present asked for an exception for him but he himself denied and announced that he would respect this rule.

How Villeroy & Boch Meets Today's Challenges

Items	Figures	%
Sales	893.2 M€	—
EBIT	24.3 M€	—
Employees	9,521	—
ROS	—	1.5
Equity Ratio	—	44.8
ROE	—	3.8
Cash Flow Profitability	—	6.4

Table 1: The Villeroy & Boch Group at a Glance (2005)[27]

These basic figures give of course just a small indication of reality. Villeroy & Boch faces hard challenges. On the world markets, demand is growing for both cheap products offered by hard discounters and on the other hand for premium products (for instance in China). This means that V & B must remain a leading premium brand because the price segment of the middle is shrinking. The competition is aggressive. For chinaware, the number of jobs has been reduced drastically over the last 10 years. Product piracy is a real plague and neither contingents nor complaints make sense because some governments are accomplices of imitators who show a real criminal energy: in 2004, a complete new shower display at an exhibition (ISA in Paris) has been dismantled and photographed. But still, V & B is the world leader in the premium segment.

27   Villeroy & Boch 1748 – Annual Report, 2005, p. 1.

	1996	2005
Share of Turnover abroad	46 %	69 %

	Tiles	Bath & Wellness	Tableware
Turnover 2005	- 11.2 %	+ 1.8 %	+ 0.6 %
EBIT 2005	- 6.7 M€	+ 20.3 M€	+ 10.7 M€

Table 2: Evolution of the Turnover of Villeroy & Boch

– 30 years ago, tiles represented 70 % of the turnover;
– The sum of EBIT (+24.3 M€) represents 2.7 % of the turnover
[vs. 33.8 M€ in 2004].

In his report to the assembly, the Chairman of the Management Board, Wendelin von Boch-Galhau, admits that errors have been committed in the wellness sector. The management is completely new, deficits have been recognized and a program of cost-reduction is implemented. The firm has in fact almost no bank debts. Production is concentrated on a few sites and logistics on one site: Merzig (Saarland). Logistics is now functioning splendidly (thanks to so-called "K-shops").[28] Because of the Olympics in Beijing in 2008 and of the International Exhibition in Shanghai in 2010, the production of hotel china will be concentrated in China because the prospects of profitability are good in spite of imitations. From the point of view of Villeroy & Boch, the markets within the coming decades will be:

28   K stands for *Konzession*; it is an internally developed system which makes logistics easier and more efficient and supports the commercial strategy of the firm: in big shops, V & B pays the storage and the salespersons. The advantage for the firm is that the customer buys at Villeroy & Boch.

Rank	Country
1	China
2	USA
3	India
4	Japan
5	Germany

Table 3: The Future Markets of Villeroy & Boch

The Human Dimension at Villeroy & Boch

Villeroy & Boch had to give up some production sites in Europe. In total, the personnel in the branch have been reduced by 2/3 in Germany. At Villeroy & Boch in Luxemburg, this unavoidable process has been harmful because china designers and painters could not be employed in such numbers anymore. For Villeroy & Boch, the following figures about labor cost underline the challenge.[29]

V & B site	Cost (€ per hour in 2004)
Germany	21.50
Gustavsberg (S)	21.50
Valence d'Agen (F)	19.25
Aföld (H)	4.50
World average (some V & B sites)	2.-
China (V & B not yet present)	1.20

Table 4: Labor Cost at Selected V & B Production Sites

29   Von Boch-Galhau, Wendelin, Press Conference at the Chamber of Commerce of Saarbrücken on 30 May 2005.

All in all, labor costs at Villeroy & Boch are 18% higher in Germany than in the USA. This means that labor-intensive production sites have to be transplanted while automatized productions can remain in Germany. In other words, Villeroy & Boch lets expensive, labor-intensive products (requiring for instance high-qualified designers and china-painters or decoration specialists) be produced in Asia and cheap ones in Europe. Through intensive input of technology, V & B succeeded in a unique process: the production of a cup with its handle in one operation. All this means that the firm has to anticipate with the words of Wayne Gretzky for ice-hockey: "I don't run where the puck is but where it will be next".[30] Thus, the enterprise supports intensive training programs for the employees, develops social schemes with the trade unions, and transforms the production sites. In this respect, the huge development of the logistical platform in Merzig has permitted to keep many local employees within the firm in spite of the technological evolution destroying production jobs.

One notices the real commitment of the managers of Villeroy & Boch to profitability and to social responsibility. This approach of sustainable development is remarkable and has permitted to this unique firm to flourish in spite of centuries of hard challenges: it celebrated its 250th anniversary in 1998. And this is a real performance for the Common Good through responsible and solid entrepreneurship. The second example is pregnant for almost the whole world: the work and influence of the International Organization for Standardization in Geneva.

3. ISO as a NGO Serving the Common Good

Many critics may consider that the notion of Common Good is far from reality. One could object that there are indeed real elements serving the Common Good. The best example is the International Organization

---

30   Quoted by Wendelin von Boch-Galhau during the same Press Conference.

for Standardization, better known under its acronym ISO.[31] When the
organization began officially its operation on 23 February 1947, it was
decided to use a word derived from the Greek "*isos*", meaning "equal", in
order to avoid the difficulties of abbreviations in different languages.[32]
ISO as a network of the national standards institutes of 157 countries is
a NGO with its Central Secretariat in Geneva, Switzerland. It has links
to the private and public sector and develops standards which contribute
to promote quality, safety, reliability, efficiency and interchangeability
in a spirit of coordination and unification of industrial standards in the
world. Most people are unaware of its positive role for business, customers, governments, etc.

Especially from the point of view of the Common Good, it is fasci-
nating to consider the hallmarks of the ISO brand being equal footing,
voluntary, market-driven in a worldwide consensus. No law enforces its
standards but the market confirms them everyday. ISO's Strategic Plan
2005–2010 and its specially designed scheme for developing countries
(DEVCO) are really pregnant for a more efficient world economy. ISO is
managed and financed by its members and the achieved standards allow
for instance economies of scale, rationalization and positive transfer of
technology. In today's globalization, wise managers try to adapt their
firms to ISO standards in order to compete better: ISO certification is a
clear commercial bonus and in fact a must. Even modest operators work
and live with ISO. One may naturally argue that in some fields, there is
a risk for firms to try to reach ISO standards by investing a lot of money
and resources and become too expensive. But this is only a side-effect:
the main trend is proving the global positive effect of ISO standards. In
this sense, ISO is objectively serving the Common Good by promoting
standards not only for a better production and distribution but for society
as a whole and for the world at large.

31   Source for this point: overview of the ISO system, site of ISO, version of 5 July
      2006.
32   IOS in English, OIN in French.

Conclusion

This paper has presented and discussed the notion of Common Good within the framework of the development of Christian Social Teaching and tried to emphasize its comprehensiveness in a broader perspective. This was sustained especially by the scholarly studies of Arthur-Fridolin Utz and Leo Elders. The author proposed an illustration for an easier synoptic view of the concept of Common Good. Furthermore, two examples of realities in today's globalized world underlined the possibility of using the concept of Common Good as a useful tool to describe, to analyze and to appraise different aspects of the socio-economic evolution. This enables the scholar as well as the manager to consider globally active private firms and institutions with other eyes and perceive dynamic incentives for his or her work. In this sense especially, the notion of Common Good represents a serious criterion to estimate in how far globalization is serving Mankind according to the Universal Declaration of Human Rights of 10 December 1948.

References

Augustinus, *De Civitate Dei*, IV, 4.

Benedict XVI, Encyclical *Deus Caritas Est*, English edition, Libreria Editrice Vaticana, 25 December 2005.

The Holy Bible.

Dougherty, Jude P., 1984, "Keeping the Common Good in Mind", in Autori Vari, *The Ethics of St Thomas Aquinas*, Studi Tomistici, Pontificia Accademia di S. Tommaso, Libreria Editrice Vaticana.

Elders, Leo and E. De Jonghe (eds), 1994, *De beginselen van de sociale leer van de Kerk*, Leuven: Acco.

Elders, Leo, SVD, *De ethiek van Thomas van Aquino*, Oegstgeest 2001, French translation: *L'éthique de Saint Thomas d'Aquin*, Paris: Presses de l'IPC / L'Harmattan, 2005.

Fèvre, Jean-Marie, 1990, *Der Indirekte Arbeitgeber*, Frankfurt am Main / Bern: Peter Lang.

Fraenkel, Ernst, 1968, *Deutschland und die westlichen Demokratien*, 3rd edition, Stuttgart: Kohlhammer.

ISO site, version of 5 July 2006.

John Paul II, Encyclical *Fides et Ratio*, English edition, Libreria Editrice Vaticana, 14 September 1998.

Marx, Reinhard and Helge Wulsdorf, 2002, *Christliche Sozialethik; Konturen Prinzipien – Handlungsfelder*, Paderborn: Bonifatius Verlag, p. 178.

St Thomas Aquinas, 1992, *Summa Theologica*, Latin edition, Turin.

Stark, Rodney, 2005, *The Victory of Reason*, New York: Random House.

Utz, Athur-Fridolin, OP, *Sozialethik*, I: "Die Prinzipien der Gesellschaftslehre", 2nd edition, Heidelberg: Kerle, 1964. Villeroy & Boch 1748 AG, Mettlach (Germany), Annual Report 2005. http://www.villeroy-boch.com/fileadmin/use/ir/Entsprechend serklaerung20041214.pdf.

Von Boch-Galhau, Wendelin, Press Conference at the Chamber of Commerce, Saarbrücken, Germany, 30 May 2005.

Annex 1

Annex 2

Transcription of the Declaration of Independence.

In CONGRESS, July 4, 1776

The unanimous Declaration of the thirteen united States of America

When in the Course of human events, it becomes necessary for one people to dissolve the political bands which have connected them with another, and to assume among the powers of the earth, the separate and equal station to which the Laws of Nature and of Nature's God entitle them, a decent respect to the opinions of mankind requires that they should declare the causes which impel them to the separation.

We hold these truths to be self-evident, that all men are created equal, that they are endowed by their Creator with certain unalienable Rights, that among these are Life, Liberty and the pursuit of Happiness. – That to secure these rights, Governments are instituted among Men, deriving their just powers from the consent of the governed, – That whenever any Form of Government becomes destructive of these ends, it is the Right of the People to alter or to abolish it, and to institute new Government, laying its foundation on such principles and organizing its powers in such form, as to them shall seem most likely to effect their Safety and Happiness. Prudence, indeed, will dictate that Governments long established should not be changed for light and transient causes; and accordingly all experience hath shewn, that mankind are more disposed to suffer, while evils are sufferable, than to right themselves by abolishing the forms to which they are accustomed. But when a long train of abuses and usurpations, pursuing invariably the same Object evinces a design to reduce them under absolute Despotism, it is their right, it is their duty, to throw off such Government, and to provide new Guards for their future security. – Such has been the patient sufferance of these Colonies; and such is now the necessity which constrains them to alter their former Systems of Government. The history of the present King of Great Britain

[George III] is a history of repeated injuries and usurpations, all having in direct object the establishment of an absolute Tyranny over these States. To prove this, let Facts be submitted to a candid world.

He has refused his Assent to Laws, the most wholesome and necessary for the public good.

He has forbidden his Governors to pass Laws of immediate and pressing importance, unless suspended in their operation till his Assent should be obtained; and when so suspended, he has utterly neglected to attend to them.

He has refused to pass other Laws for the accommodation of large districts of people, unless those people would relinquish the right of Representation in the Legislature, a right inestimable to them and formidable to tyrants only.

He has called together legislative bodies at places unusual, uncomfortable, and distant from the depository of their public Records, for the sole purpose of fatiguing them into compliance with his measures.

He has dissolved Representative Houses repeatedly, for opposing with manly firmness his invasions on the rights of the people.

He has refused for a long time, after such dissolutions, to cause others to be elected; whereby the Legislative powers, incapable of Annihilation, have returned to the People at large for their exercise; the State remaining in the mean time exposed to all the dangers of invasion from without, and convulsions within.

He has endeavoured to prevent the population of these States; for that purpose obstructing the Laws for Naturalization of Foreigners; refusing to pass others to encourage their migrations hither, and raising the conditions of new Appropriations of Lands.

He has obstructed the Administration of Justice, by refusing his Assent to Laws for establishing Judiciary powers.

He has made Judges dependent on his Will alone, for the tenure of their offices, and the amount and payment of their salaries.

He has erected a multitude of New Offices, and sent hither swarms of Officers to harass our people, and eat out their substance.

He has kept among us, in times of peace, Standing Armies without the consent of our legislatures.

He has affected to render the Military independent of and superior to the Civil power.

He has combined with others to subject us to a jurisdiction foreign to our constitution and unacknowledged by our laws; giving his Assent to their Acts of pretended Legislation:

For Quartering large bodies of armed troops among us:

For protecting them, by a mock Trial, from punishment for any Murders which they should commit on the Inhabitants of these States:

For cutting off our Trade with all parts of the world:

For imposing Taxes on us without our Consent:

For depriving us, in many cases, of the benefits of Trial by Jury:

For transporting us beyond Seas to be tried for pretended offences:

For abolishing the free System of English Laws in a neighbouring Province, establishing therein an Arbitrary government, and enlarging its Boundaries so as to render it at once an example and fit instrument for introducing the same absolute rule into these Colonies:

For taking away our Charters, abolishing our most valuable Laws, and altering fundamentally the Forms of our Governments:

For suspending our own Legislatures, and declaring themselves invested with power to legislate for us in all cases whatsoever.

He has abdicated Government here, by declaring us out of his Protection and waging War against us.

He has plundered our seas, ravaged our Coasts, burnt our towns, and destroyed the lives of our people.

He is at this time transporting large Armies of foreign Mercenaries to compleat the works of death, desolation and tyranny, already begun with circumstances of Cruelty and perfidy scarcely paralleled in the most barbarous ages, and totally unworthy the Head of a civilized nation.

He has constrained our fellow Citizens taken Captive on the high Seas to bear Arms against their Country, to become the executioners of their friends and Brethren, or to fall themselves by their Hands.

He has excited domestic insurrections amongst us, and has endeavoured to bring on the inhabitants of our frontiers, the merciless Indian Savages, whose known rule of warfare, is an undistinguished destruction of all ages, sexes and conditions.

In every stage of these Oppressions We have Petitioned for Redress in the most humble terms: Our repeated Petitions have been answered only by repeated injury. A Prince whose character is thus marked by every act which may define a Tyrant, is unfit to be the ruler of a free people.

Nor have We been wanting in attentions to our British brethren. We have warned them from time to time of attempts by their legislature to extend an unwarrantable jurisdiction over us. We have reminded them of the circumstances of our emigration and settlement here. We have appealed to their native justice and magnanimity, and we have conjured them by the ties of our common kindred to disavow these usurpations, which, would inevitably interrupt our connections and correspondence. They too have been deaf to the voice of justice and of consanguinity. We must, therefore, acquiesce in the necessity, which denounces our Separation, and hold them, as we hold the rest of mankind, Enemies in War, in Peace Friends.

We, therefore, the Representatives of the united States of America, in General Congress, Assembled, appealing to the Supreme Judge of the world for the rectitude of our intentions, do, in the Name, and by the Authority of the good People of these Colonies, solemnly publish and declare, That these United Colonies are, and of Right ought to be Free and Independent States; that they are Absolved from all Allegiance to the British Crown, and that all political connection between them and the State of Great Britain, is and ought to be totally dissolved; and that as Free and Independent States, they have full Power to levy War, conclude Peace, contract Alliances, establish Commerce, and to do all other Acts and Things which Independent States may of right do. And for the support of this Declaration, with a firm reliance on the protection of divine Providence, we mutually pledge to each other our Lives, our Fortunes and our sacred Honor.

The signers of the Declaration represented the new states as follows:

New Hampshire
Josiah Bartlett, William Whipple, Matthew Thornton

Massachusetts
John Hancock, Samuel Adams, John Adams, Robert Treat Paine, Elbridge Gerry

Rhode Island
Stephen Hopkins, William Ellery

Connecticut
Roger Sherman, Samuel Huntington, William Williams, Oliver Wolcott

New York
William Floyd, Philip Livingston, Francis Lewis, Lewis Morris

New Jersey
Richard Stockton, John Witherspoon, Francis Hopkinson, John Hart, Abraham
Clark

Pennsylvania
Robert Morris, Benjamin Rush, Benjamin Franklin, John Morton, George Clymer,
James Smith, George Taylor, James Wilson, George Ross

Delaware
Caesar Rodney, George Read, Thomas McKean

Maryland
Samuel Chase, William Paca, Thomas Stone, Charles Carroll of Carrollton

Virginia
George Wythe, Richard Henry Lee, Thomas Jefferson, Benjamin Harrison, Thomas
Nelson, Jr., Francis Lightfoot Lee, Carter Braxton

North Carolina
William Hooper, Joseph Hewes, John Penn

South Carolina
Edward Rutledge, Thomas Heyward, Jr., Thomas Lynch, Jr., Arthur Middleton

Georgia
Button Gwinnett, Lyman Hall, George Walton

CHAPTER 9

Ethical Infrastructure for Business with Special Emphasis on Poland: Designing for the Common Good

WOJCIECH W. GASPARSKI

> Before humankind learns to offer a heavenly smile,
> it first has to teach itself not to bare its teeth.
>
> — TADEUSZ KOTARBINSKI

1. Introduction

Let us start from the very concept of "common good". *The Human Good* is the title of the best elaborated monograph of the topic. The author Dr Bengt Brülde (1998) is a scholar of Gothenburg University, Sweden. He differentiates three kinds of *goodness-for-people-statements*: (i) "the particular situation X is good for the particular person P", (ii) "all particular situations of type X are good for the particular person P", (iii) "all particular situations of type X are good for all persons P"; situation X, type X, and persons P may be actual or hypothetical (Brülde, 1998, pp. 4–5). The third kind is the most fundamental, for the other two types can be deduced from it. According to the quoted author, "the question 'what types of situations are good for everyone?' is the central (fundamental) question of prudential value" (*op. cit.*, 5). Is it a statement that defines the common good? Brülde does not answer the question in a straightforward way. There is no "common good" item included in the Index of his book; therefore one is forced to guess how to understand the concept of the common good in the context of the human good as defined by the quoted author.

There is a dominating view in business that economics is a mechanism which converts invested capital, natural resources, labor and intangible factors into what is described in general terms as a "return on invested resources", and in addition this return should involve a surplus. Consequently, knowledge on the creation and functioning of such a mechanism, namely economics as a science, is treated as a kind of engineering that is free of any value judgment other than that made in monetary terms. Economics in this sense is placed close to the exact sciences, i.e. natural sciences for which physics is the model. Such treatment of economics distances it from studies on culture, and from the humanist factor that Florian Znaniecki highlighted as being the peculiarity of such studies.

The naturalistic approach to economics, though important in the modern-day economy practiced on a global scale, luckily is not the only approach. Nobel Prizes in economics are also awarded to economists who treat economics as a science of the processes of exchange accomplished by people, and thus as a science of a purposeful kind of conduct, i.e. of praxiological origin. The purpose of business activity, meanwhile, is the relation between the producer and the consumer, of which Adam Smith wrote that "Consumption is the sole end and purpose of all production; and the interest of the producer ought to be attended to, only so far as it may be necessary for promoting that of the consumer. The maxim is so perfectly self-evident, that it would be absurd to attempt to prove it." (Smith, 1954, II, p. 355; quoted from Zabieglik, 2003, p. 153).

Apart from its praxiological dimension (effectiveness and efficiency making up an action's efficacy), business activity, like any human activity, is subject to ethical judgment that reflects the framework of social acceptance for defining the objectives and using means to achieve them that are typical of the culture of the society whose members are involved in the activity in question.

The American author Lon L. Fuller (1969; quoted after the Polish edition 2004) distinguishes two kinds of morality: *morality of duty* and *morality of aspiration.* The morality of duty is the morality of the basic rules that organize social life. The morality of duty is a foundation essential for building social structures of a higher order. The morality of aspiration applies to those higher-order structures. Aspirations and the morality that goes with them are related to a drive for excellence, to all that is fair, to a fullness of skills that people are equipped with. Pointing to exchange as the essence of economics, on the basis of a praxiological premise, is close to the morality of duty, while the principle of marginal usefulness chosen as the core of economic reflection is close to the morality of aspiration.

Like a moralist of aspiration, economists of the latter school are unable to indicate the ultimate good. They will try to conceal this lack of knowledge by using the buzzword "usefulness". In this, the economist's weakness is the same as that of a moralist who aspires to show people the road leading to a decent life but is unable to specify what the ultimate purpose of life is or should be. Faced with the lack of some kind of highest moral or economic good, in the end – in both ethics and economics – we reach for the idea of equilibrium. This is not the seemingly easy "middle road", but the difficult Aristotelian golden mean, "dangerous to the indolent and unskilled", requiring "similar perceptiveness as efficient management", the quoted author points out.

The condition for success in an economy that is increasingly based on knowledge, which thus takes on the importance of a fundamental resource (Drucker, 1993), lies in expanding knowledge of what forms the core of the economy, i.e. economic knowledge, to include knowledge of the axiological context of the economy, which cannot be eliminated from a systemic point of view, i.e. knowledge on human activity taking into account not only the praxiological but also the ethical dimension (Gasparski, 2003).

Contributions to the issue of the *common good* start either from the concept and philosophy behind it, like the quoted treatise by Brülde, or from objects considered as the *good* itself by authors, activists, politicians etc. Both types of contributions deserve to be named the "what to ..." approach. This approach, which one may notice is of a consequentialist nature, dominates in the literature and in public debate. The other approach, let us call it the "how to ..." approach, is not so popular. There

are very few contributions to the topic trying to answer the "how to …?"
question, i.e. to point out the way towards protecting and/or creating the
entity agreed to be a common good. Incidentally, the paper "Designing
Human Society: A Chance or a Utopia?" that I wrote a quarter of a
century ago for a conference on design policy organized by the Design
Research Society in London, seems to be of that kind. It was published
in a collection of my praxiological-systemic contributions to the area
of design studies.[1] Since it is often said that "a novelty is the old stuff

1   "If we consider seriously and with responsibility the problem of survival, not as a
     problem of survival of 'us' at the expense of 'them', of 'our' generation at the expense
     of future generations, but as a problem concerning the survival of the species, then
     we should collectively initiate the work of creating a new culture, and taking into
     account the scarcity of resources, we should organize contemporary life in such a
     way that whatever is done should not threaten any future generation in any future
     time. The success of such an understanding will depend on joint action by all for
     the good of all … […] Therefore, just as Francis Bacon who centuries ago thought
     it necessary to give the Organum a new shape and created the famous Novum
     Organum, so we have to create a new Discourse of Method, a sui generis Novum
     Cartesianum.[…] Governed by microparadigms of science on the one hand, and by
     macroparadigms of art on the other, methodologically similar spectra of methods
     and techniques have been developed. They are concerned with the rational and
     emotional aspects of cognitive activities respectively. […] However, […] the two
     realms, science and art, do not encompass all activities. What remains is the prac-
     tice of biological existence and of individual and social life. This third developing
     realm was and remains to be an area of conquest for invaders from the other two
     worlds. […] The third world is the world of practical situations of people, a world
     of facts and of values according to which the facts are assessed. […] In simple […]
     cases […] we act according to our ability. […] In other cases, i.e., in cases of adequate
     time or great risk – in short, in cases of greater complexity – we prefer to prepare
     our actions. Among numerous kinds of such preparation […] I wish to distinguish
     one which consists of: developing patterns of actions, evaluating the patterns by
     considering various values which serve as a basis for appraisal, and selecting the
     pattern of highest relevance. Such a procedure, being in its essence a conceptual
     preparation of action, is design. […] Modern design […] would be concerned with
     the 'object of design' regarded as if it were linking together a given practical situation
     of a concrete subject (the core) with the remaining world (the complement). […]
     Design as a way of solving practical problems creates possibilities for overcoming
     our human inclination towards unreasonable or simply irrational behavior. This

forgotten long enough", it would be good (sic!) to re-visit the idea and re-examine the question of how to act with hope that the common good has a chance to be protected as it should be in the context of business activity with a special emphasis on Poland.

That paper presented the demands of business ethicists addressed to the business community regarding solutions fostering the ethical conduct of the stakeholders that form business organizations in a broad sense, i.e. companies *sensu largo*. Examples of solutions from business practice suggested what premises were adopted openly or implicitly, and illustrated the business community's response to those demands as well as the community's own initiatives.

2. The Premises, or the Intellectual Infrastructure of Business Activity

Let us start with the premises that form a kind of intellectual infrastructure of business activity. Many economists have the ambition to equal physicists and turn economics into an exact science, a kind of "social physics" which, like the natural sciences, would not be judgmental. "The belief in an external world independent of the perceiving subject is the basis of all natural science" (Einstein 1999, p. 97). Stanislaw Butryn (2006, p. 27), from whose work I quote Einstein's view, notes that the quoted

---

way necessitates an externalization of problem-solving process which, in effect is becoming transparent. Design as such a way enforces explicit presentation of all pros and cons of particular candidate solutions thus providing evidence to support the selected solution. [...] I have discussed [...] only the prerequisites, since that is all that can be done by those who are aware of the dangers. The remainder depends on whether the other members of human society understand the seriousness of the present situation or neglect the dangers with premeditation. They, the remaining members of society, acting consciously or unconsciously, in fact, take the responsibility for the fate of the human species" (Gasparski, 1984, pp. 194–209).

physicist related belief, whatever it may have concerned, with religion in his own special understanding of it: "If he thought (believed) that a certain view was right, but was unable to prove it, he would say that view was his religion" (Butryn, 2006, pp. 26–7). This exegete of Einstein adds that Einstein thought the view about the existence of an objective reality to be a thesis that was "completely random" from a logical point of view and impossible to prove scientifically. Butryn also adds that "today the belief that such is the nature of this particular view seems to be universal" (Butryn, 2006, p. 45). "Seems to be" is correct, as even outside physics and its consideration of the real world, researchers of human behavior, such as theoreticians of economics who are certain – or, as Einstein would have it, who believe – that economics free of any values exists in an ontological sense, are followers of exactly that kind of their own special religion. The recently deceased Milton Friedman was a supporter of precisely this type of economic "religion".

Those who polemicized with Friedman included Herbert A. Simon and Peter F. Drucker. At the Warsaw conference "Praxiologies and the Philosophy of Economics", organized in 1988 by the praxiological community grouped around the Praxiology Unit of the Institute of Philosophy and Sociology of the Polish Academy of Sciences, the former said:

> What is startlingly absent from the empirical literature of classical economics is evidence of optimization based on the direct observations of the behavior of economic actors. Milton Friedman (1953), of course, in his celebrated essay on methodology in economics, has sought to make a virtue of his deficiency. He argues that a theory cannot be judged by the realism of its assumptions, but only by its efficacy in making predictions. [...] The second flow in Friedman's argument in his claim that unrealism in the assumptions of a theory is a good thing, or that is even acceptable. [...] There is no support in any system of logic with which I am familiar, or in any school of philosophy of science, for Friedman's principle of unrealism (Simon, 1992, p. 36).

The other opponent of Friedman mentioned above, seeking to answer the question of what social responsibility was, pointed out that contemporary society was a society of organizations, and from this stemmed organizations' social responsibility for what they created, because:

And yet who else is there to take care of society, its problems and its ills? These organizations collectively are society. It is futile to argue, as does the American economist and Nobel Laureate Milton Friedman, [...] that a business has only one responsibility: economic performance. Economic performance is the first responsibility of business. A business that does not show a profit at least equal to its cost of capital is socially irresponsible. It wastes society's resources. Economic performance is the basis; without it, a business cannot discharge any other responsibilities, cannot be a good employer, a good citizen, a good neighbor. But economic performance is not the only responsibility of a business. [...] Power must always be balanced by responsibility; otherwise it is tyranny. But without responsibility power also always degenerates into non-performance. And organizations have power, albeit only social power. [...] But – and it is a big "but" – organizations of the Society of Organizations have a responsibility to try to find an approach to basic social problems which fits their competence and which, indeed, makes the social problem into an opportunity for the organization (Drucker, 1993, pp. 92–3).

The quoted authors most likely were not familiar with the *humanist factor* and thus did not invoke this concept put forward by Florian Znaniecki, though perhaps they should have, as Znaniecki lectured in America. Here is what this Polish sociologist wrote (Znaniecki, 1988, p. 25): "That feature of cultural phenomena as objects of humanist studies, that special quality whereby – while being objects of theoretical reflection – they are already objects given to someone as part of experience, or someone's conscious actions, could be called the humanist factor." Economics, meanwhile, belongs not to the world of nature but to the world of culture, i.e. the world of human creations, or artifacts, *ergo* it should account for the humanist factor, otherwise it could be offering theses very distant from economic practice.

(1) Economics had both a descriptive (positive) and a normative aspect; it describes how people behave in their economic decisions and actions, and it prescribes rational behavior. (2) Economics is a "science of the artificial", for it deals with systems that seek to adapt to their environments in order to reach goals survival goals. They may be subject to natural selection (Simon, 1992, p. 25).

Economics is therefore rooted in praxiology (praxiology is the theory of human action), as pointed out by Tadeusz Kotarbinski, Ludwig von Mises, Oskar Lange and others. This has its consequences that I have highlighted on many occasions, writing that business activities which are the subject of economics, are serious activities. As such, they should be performed effectively and efficiently (i.e. with a surplus of result over cost), and should take into account the axiological social context defining the framework of consent to the choice of these activities' goals and means used to achieve them.

Analyzing business activities according to any of the three dimensions: effectiveness, efficiency or ethicality, is methodologically justified. It is methodologically justified to express the dimensions of efficacy (effectiveness and efficiency) in monetary terms. Meanwhile, it is methodologically improper to design and carry out business activities, i.e. synthesize, without taking into account the "triple E", i.e. all three of these characteristics of action. It is methodologically improper to reduce ethicality to the measurable space, i.e. to express ethicality in monetary terms. Ethicality is the condition *sine qua non* that allows only for the performance of business activity that meets this condition. Ethicality of business activity, therefore, is a primary norm that defines the endo- and exo-morality of business activity, while economic efficacy, i.e. effectiveness and efficiency in monetary terms, is a secondary norm among the norms defining the social order of business.

Making the ethicality of business activities (or any other activities) conditional on their profitability makes no sense.[2] This found its formal though imperfect expression – essential for those who profess that "anything not forbidden is allowed" – in articles 17 and 18 of the Polish Law on Freedom of Business Activity from July 2004 (Box 1):

---

2   When a person acts, they choose some kind of good that becomes the purpose of their action. Karol Wojtyla distinguishes three kinds of good: (a) an honest good (*bonum honestum*); (b) a useful good (*bonum utile*); (c) a pleasurable good (*bonum delectabile*). If a person selects an honest good, the end result can be identified with the very essence of the purpose of the action, which makes the action honest. When a useful good is selected, the purpose is some kind of benefit. If the useful good is honest and the means are honest, then the purpose can also be considered honest. Utilitarianism has forgotten about the primary and fundamental dimension of good, i.e. *bonum honestum* (John Paul II, 2005, pp. 42–4).

Art. 17. Entrepreneurs shall conduct their economic activity based on the principles of fair competition and due respect for good practices and the legitimate interests of consumers.

Art. 18. Entrepreneurs shall meet all requirements related to economic activity set forth in legal regulations, and in particular requirements related to the protection of life, human health and public morality, as well as protection of the environment.

Box 1

This fulfils one of the demands related to shaping the ethical infrastructure of business activity practiced in Poland; in this case, the ethical infrastructure on the macro level, i.e. the national economy.

3. Material Ethical Infrastructure of Business

The ethical infrastructure in business that we will call material, as opposed to intellectual, is needed at all levels of economic activity, namely: (a) on the level of people's economic behavior, called the micro level; (b) on the level of the functioning of business organizations – companies, firms, corporations, called the mezzo level; (c) on the level of the economic system, or a region, country or economic community, called the macro level; (d) on the global level, or economic activity on a world scale. The mezzo level is the main area of interest for business ethics, which is thus identified with organizational ethics (the ethics of an organization) and management ethics (the professional ethics of managers), and this is the level primarily under consideration in the further part of this paper.

A major incentive to introduce ethical infrastructure in American business came with the publication in 1991 of special Federal Guidelines concerning judgments in cases against business as well as government and nongovernmental organizations, including schools and universities; these principles were amended in 2005 following a number of scandals involving U.S. business (Enron, WorldCom, Arthur Andersen etc.). Chapter eight on adjudicating in the case of organizations is especially important. These guidelines regarding offences committed by organizations – regardless of the individual perpetrators who acted on behalf of the organization – aim not only to mete out punishment for the offences, but also give organizations incentives to introduce internal mechanisms for preventing criminal actions, detecting such actions, and revealing them. The guidelines on adjudication offer possibilities of reduced punishment, up to non-application of punishment if the organization is able to show it has the appropriate corporate policy and an ethics program in place.

The requirements towards corporate ethics programs were expanded compared to the guidelines of 1991. Today they cover not only the obligation of good conduct preventing crimes and facilitating their detection, but also the duty of promoting an organizational culture encouraging people to comply with the law. In-house standards and procedures should guarantee internal control that reduces the probability of offences being committed. Direct responsibility for introducing and supervising the implementation of such norms and procedures rests with the organization's power organs (the board, the management etc.). The person (business ethics officer, compliance officer or similar) or unit (Ethics Office or similar) responsible for day-to-day running of an ethics program should have the necessary resources, enjoy considerable standing, and have direct access to the organization's leadership. No responsible position should be entrusted to someone who is known to have been involved in illegal activity or actions incompatible with the company's ethics program. Organizations are obliged to systematically train their staff, including top management, and to make sure that in-house channels of communications work properly. Moreover, organizations should conduct periodical audits related to compliance with legal regulations and ethical norms, evaluate the effectiveness of existing solutions, and ensure confidentiality of information on any offences. Improper conduct should be punished, while proper conduct should be an obligation supported by appropriate incentives. The ethics program should be analyzed periodically and modified as the need arises.

A demand that similar solutions be introduced in Poland[3] was first put forward by business ethicists a long time ago. Using foreign models

3   The history of the impact of European integration on Polish business conduct is rather short. It started on 1 May 2004 when the Republic of Poland became an EU member officially. But it does not mean that everything that has happened and is worthy to be mentioned is only a few years old. The pre-history of the integration in question or the way to integration is much longer. It began in the early 1990s with hope, belief and love for everything that was "Western" and was considered *the* remedy to the economy of shortage, of command, and of related politics. The so-called shock therapy was accepted in Poland for it was done with a surgical cut. It was introduced without pain during the operation (pain came later) and with almost metaphysical faith that the sun of solidarity would shine in full as was expected before the night of martial law and its follow-up period of the 1980s. It was a time of hope that moral standards would remove the bad practices of communist misbehavior, introducing ethical codes of best practices popularized by enthusiasts of transformation. It was a time of belief that the "invisible hand" of the free market would organize interrelations between enterprises becoming privatized and their stakeholders equitably. It was a time of love for advisors coming from the western side of the former Iron Curtain, considered as friends by definition; the adjective "Western" was considered almost a synonym of the "common good". It was expected that the EU be within arm's reach and would welcome Poland, a victim of the Yalta agreement, with understanding and help to overcome European separation that had lasted so many tough decades.

To be fair, some of the above hopes, beliefs and loves have happened but not as quickly as was expected (*"who gives quickly gives twice"* says a Polish proverb). Besides it happened with new types of business misbehavior, with some scandals and unfair exploitation. The worst thing was, and still is, that it happened not only because of "homo sovieticus" practices of local business people and politicians of the former "nomenklatura", but also because of the unethical conduct of Western companies many of which declare their CSR involvement. The way to Tipperary was apparently much longer and more difficult than the enthusiasts originally suggested. It created a larger number of Euro-skeptics in Poland than before, although the number of enthusiasts still prevails. Now even more than before the accession. It also causes that populists have come to the fore. Corruption, unemployment, the and their competent adjustment to Polish conditions met with verbal understanding, but in practice the reaction was, as people put it, that "the conditions are not ripe enough". Numerous negative examples publicized by the media, and other cases that were open secrets, supplied a *pars pro toto* negative example. Unfortunately it is not just in the past tense.

Given such a background, examples of solutions designed and implemented in Poland by individual companies as well as organizations grouping companies and corporations deserve a special mention. Let us add that elements of material ethical infrastructure are present to a much greater extent at large companies, chiefly multinationals, than at small and medium-sized enterprises. Multinational companies with subsidiaries in Poland usually implement a uniform policy in terms of compliance with legal norms, ethical standards, and corporate social responsibility (CSR) or accountability. Cases in point include companies that are partners of the Responsible Business Forum. Large companies (e.g. Orlen) try to adjust to the behaviors of similar companies in other countries. Small and medium-sized enterprises behave more spontaneously and in a less formalized way, as discovered by researchers from the Human Resources Management Department of Warsaw's Leon Kozminski Academy of Entrepreneurship and Management.

---

growing gap between rich and poor, exclusion and misconduct in the workplace are the main obstacles to enjoying the achievements to the full.

Nevertheless the achievements are authentic. They construct slowly but surely the foundation of better business operations. Education is the number one achievement, for knowledge is the most important resource in the era of the knowledge-based economy. One has, however, to take into account the very fact that technological knowledge and knowledge of economic science is not enough for a positive evaluation of business conduct in the "triple E" dimensions (effectiveness, efficiency, ethicality). It is social systems, which by their very nature give content to responsibility. It is for this reason that the knowledge-based economy must include knowledge of the axiological context of business activity. The concept of ethical programs and of ethical infrastructure of and for business activity is gradually becoming used, and programs introduced, by Polish businesses and business associations (Gasparski, 2005a).

One important element of the material ethical infrastructure normalizing corporate governance is the document titled *Good Practice in Public Companies*. This document, in essence a code, was introduced in 2002 by Warsaw's Corporate Governance Forum, also known as the Good Practice Committee. The document invokes a British solution from the early 1990s known as the Cadbury Report, after Sir Adrian Cadbury – chairman of a committee appointed by the Financial Reporting Council, the London Stock Exchange and the accountancy profession. This was a reaction to irregularities of corporate management occurring in Britain. The main issue was the conflict of interest involved in one person being a company's chairman of the board and CEO at the same time, becoming "a law unto themselves" or, as the Polish saying goes, "steersman, sailor and ship rolled into one".

And steering is what it is all about, as governance, like "govern" and "governor", come from the Greek *kybernetes* = steersman, *kybernan* = steer, guide. Corporate governance denotes steering a corporation – or more precisely, the system of exercising power by the appropriate bodies: the board of directors in a single-body system, or the management board and supervisory board in a two-body system. In Poland, this concept is translated as "corporate order" or "corporate supervision", though in fact it is about control in a corporation (Gasparski 2006a).

Good Practice in Public Companies was amended in 2005, and now includes: (a) a catalogue of general principles (company goals, rule of the majority and protection of the minority, honest intent and non-abuse of authority, court control, independence of opinions commissioned by a company; (b) good practice at general shareholders' meetings; (c) good practice for supervisory boards; (d) good practice for management boards; and (e) good practice in relations with external persons and organizations (48 norms in total).

Like the Cadbury report, *Good Practice in Public Companies 2005* was addressed to listed companies on a "comply or explain" basis, i.e. a company has to state clearly whether and which norms from this code it will follow in its practice, and which it will not and why. Such codes are also a model for other organizations to follow or a base for designing their own rules of conduct. The management of the Warsaw Stock Exchange has just prepared a new amendment of *Good Practice in Public Companies*, abandoning the "comply or explain" principle in the belief that mandatory regulations will ensure better corporate governance than rules adopted voluntarily. Does this not suggest smaller rather than greater trust?

Earlier than *Good Practice in Public Companies* is the Polish Bank Association's (PBA) *Rules of Good Banking Practice* adopted in 2001. This is a slightly modified document previously known as the *Code of Good Banking Practice* from 1995. The current document provides four groups of rules of conduct between: (a) the bank and its clients, (b) the bank and other banks, (c) the bank's employees, (d) the bank as an employer and its employees. The general provisions of this document require that banking activities be conducted in accordance with legal regulations, good banking practice, resolutions passed by banking self-regulation bodies, and good business customs. The detailed norms listed in the document include professionalism, diligence, a businesslike manner, care, knowledge. These norms are given an objectified interpretation in resolutions of the PBA Ethics Commission as well as decisions of the PBA arbitrator.

For comparison, note that the material ethical infrastructure of the banking sector in other countries includes the London Principles listing seven rules of sustainable development, and two codes introduced by the British Bank Association: (a) the *Banking Code* and (b) the *Business Banking Code* containing good practice standards in financial services. In Italy, the Associazione Bancaria Italiana is presenting a special educational package on corporate social responsibility (Zappi, 2006).

Based on the model of the PBA's *Rules* and advice from the Business Ethics Centre, the *Rules of Good Practice of the Conference of Financial Companies in Poland* (CFCP) was adopted in 2005. In the introduction to the published version of this code, I wrote as follows:

> The encyclopedic work Business: The Ultimate Resource contains a sizable section on "best practice" in business. This section comprises eleven chapters, each devoted to an issue important for business activity, such as: people and culture, marketing, strategy and competition, finance, information technology, systems, structure, leadership, renewal and growth, productivity, personal effectiveness in action. Among the best practices linked to people's conduct and culture, the authors mention action learning. This type of activity was introduced by Reginald

Revans, a British researcher and a friend of the Polish praxiological community. It involves a clever combination of knowledge and skills together with proper motivation. Other best practices listed in the above-mentioned work include a holistic approach to people as persons, care for people's dignity when reducing (which should be the exception rather than the rule) a company's size, investing in spiritual capital, avoiding negative behavior (mobbing, harassment), care for a high-standard corporate culture. The corporate culture is expressed not only in how employees are treated, but also in how all the stakeholders are treated. This particularly applies to difficult situations that financial companies face all the time (Gasparski, 2006, p. 4).

The *Rules of Good Practice of the CFCP* comprise three books: (1) general rules; (2) good practices in selling credit products; and (3) good practices in debt collecting. The general rules normalize: (a) conduct towards clients; (b) conduct towards partners and rival businesses; (c) financial companies' conduct towards employees; (d) the conduct of employees; (e) conduct towards the community and the environment; (f) sanctions; and (g) internal audits.

Ethics codes, also known as codes of conduct, are gradually becoming elements of the material ethical infrastructure. Some of them are directly modeled on foreign solutions, others make use of knowledge on ethics and corporate social responsibility and adjust it to Polish conditions of conducting economic activity. Some are extensive, others only cover the most important issues. One such document is the *Ethical Canon* adopted by the Polish Confederation of Private Employers ("Lewiatan"), developed in association with the Business Ethics Centre (Box 2). This canon is open to all entrepreneurs who are willing to declare they will follow it. This was confirmed by Mrs Henryka Bochniarz, president of the "Lewiatan", at a seminar preceding the official Gala of the *Pillars of the Polish Economy* awards by *Puls Biznesu* magazine in December 2006.

ETHICAL CANON FOR ENTREPRENEURS
of the Polish Confederation of Private Employers ("Lewiatan")

1. As entrepreneurs, we recognize that our responsibility primarily involves:
   - supplying clients and consumers with products (goods or services) of proper quality,
   - doing so in the long term,
   - ensuring appropriate relations with the company's main stakeholders,
   - conduct in accordance with the law and moral norms.
2. We aim to make sure that the companies we run enjoy the trust of all stakeholder groups, including clients and consumers, employees, managers, shareholders, suppliers and buyers, business rivals, and society.
3. In our decision-making, we give due consideration and take into account the opinions of people and groups that function within our companies' environment.
4. We develop the corporate culture of our companies so that it prominently features responsibility for employees and their responsibility for the tasks they perform.
5. We take care to ensure that our employees are not discriminated against for any reason, that their dignity as persons is respected, that their work is appropriately and promptly paid for, and their work environment is safe and healthy.
6. We do our best to make sure that management of our companies at all levels is conducted well and with due consideration for moral norms, so that it may serve as a model of conduct.
7. We carry out our production and trade activity and financial operations transparently, and we are prepared to suffer the consequences in case of errors.
8. We are reliable partners in activities involving the production of goods and adding value, while honest competition and generated profit testify to our ability to react creatively to changes occurring in the social environment in which we operate.
9. Out of concern for the common good, including the natural environment, we undertake important social initiatives and act as sponsors to the extent of our capabilities.
10. Our reliability is proved by the compatibility of our words and our deeds.

Box 2

During the ceremony, I highlighted the importance of democratization of the economy, in the sense of the participation of all stakeholders as a condition of identifying the common good and getting a greater number of entities involved in producing and protecting it. Below is an excerpt from what I said at the time:

> Democratization of the economy began in the economically most developed countries as they started becoming knowledge-based societies, because it is knowledge that increasingly decides about a company's value. This was expressed in the famous words of the U.S. president: "The economy, stupid!" Knowledge is not mechanisms, knowledge is free and aware people who have knowledge and know how to use it. Engaging in activity, people contribute their own personal stakes, investing intangible assets. This is expressed by the concept of "stakeholders". Stakeholders are all those without whom no organization would be able to function. Accounting for everything that individual stakeholders have invested is a prerequisite for companies' effective functioning in their relationship with the communities in which they operate, and the economy as a whole in its relationship with society. Here are two fundamental questions we need to answer: (1) Who is a genuine citizen of the economic republic? (2) What needs to be done to change the current economic "gentry" republic into a truly civil one? (Gasparski, 2006b).

The intention to introduce elements of ethical infrastructure in business organizations, according to research commissioned by the Business Ethics Centre and conducted by OBOP, was declared by 55% of respondents – company CEOs – in 2003, while 37% said they had no intention of introducing ethical standards in the companies they headed. As a result, in order to make it easier for business organizations to develop and introduce ethics codes, the Business Ethics Centre prepared its Ethical Company package for implementation of ethical standards in a small or medium-sized company. The package was presented at a conference on corporate social responsibility held by the Polish Chamber of Commerce in March 2005. Among other things, the package's authors wrote:

> Problems of business ethics are usually associated with large corporations. Meanwhile, the dangers and negative consequences of violating ethical principles are universal, and apply to all business entities. We believe now is a good time for implementing ethics programs at small and medium-sized enterprises in Poland, as a sizable number of them have achieved a high level of quality in terms of:

(a) offered goods and services, (b) personnel qualifications, (c) technology and equipment, (d) implementation of state-of-the-art financial systems with IT support, (e) applied organizational solutions and management methods. Moreover, the above qualitative changes find confirmation in contacts with growing international competition. For many Polish companies, the abolishment of the last restrictions on trade and investment after Poland's European Union accession became not a threat, but an opportunity to conquer new markets and therefore experience accelerated development. They are winning the respect of their business rivals, at the same time becoming sought-after partners for large organizations with a solid position in international business. We believe one cannot speak about the quality of a company without consistent implementation of high ethical standards in all key areas. They supplement the qualitative changes in offered goods or applied technologies, forming the backbone of a modern company (Cieslik and Gasparski, *op. cit.*).

Training courses are a particularly important element in creating ethical infrastructure. This has been proved by studies conducted by the Business Ethics Centre, according to which the condition of companies that held training courses was substantially better than that of companies which did not. Unfortunately the number of companies offering training, though on the rise, still only accounts for one-third of companies operating in Poland, including 11% holding courses several times a year, 12% once a year, 7% less than once a year. According to the study, 68% of organizations have not provided any training in business ethics.

Ethical infrastructure in the public administration of some OECD countries includes the following elements: (a) declarations of values or principles; (b) standards of conduct; (c) tools for promoting (disseminating) and increasing awareness of values; (d) means of controlling improper behavior; and (e) management and evaluation of ethics programs (Gasparski 2004, 218–23). Familiarity with these regulations is important in view of the experience of the developed countries regarding concern for ethical standards, but also because where administration and business meet, conditions exist for abuse resulting from treating administrative decisions that concern business activity as a kind of "goods", the price of which is corruption, bribes, or facilitating money. A study conducted a year ago shows how the meeting of business and administration is assessed in terms of the trust respondents place in business people and administration officials (Figure 1).

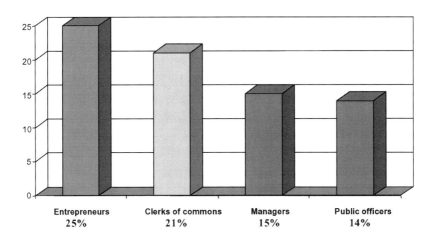

Figure 1: Opinions as to Honesty and Dependability [Source: CBOS 2006]

Forbes and Transparency International studies (Forbes, 2005/2006) show that personal contacts help in business deals according to 88% of respondents, while 59% think officials have too much influence over business activities, probably because they are the ones who interpret regulations, as 45% of respondents believe. Respondents said that barriers more important than corruption (13%) included ambiguous regulations (72%), the tax system (55%), faulty administration (26%), the political situation (23%), though as many as 35% said they knew someone who had given a bribe in connection with a public order, and 28% of respondents declared they knew someone who had taken a bribe. The latest research by the Transparency International Global Corruption Barometer places Poland among the countries where up to 5% of respondents declare they have given a bribe in the last 12 months. Perception of Poland as a country with high corruption has improved, but as this is not substantial improvement (from 70th to 61st place), it is no watershed. Concern for the ethical infrastructure of economic activity in Poland is a prerequisite for lasting improvement not of the country's image, but of the essence of such activity.

4. Conclusions

To conclude, it would be good to present the updated demands put forward for some time by business ethicists linked to the Business Ethics Centre of the Institute of Philosophy and Sociology of the Polish Academy of Sciences and the Leon Kozminski Academy of Entrepreneurship and Management. They are as follows:

Despite the introduction of certain elements of ethical infrastructure (the law on lobbying, establishing the Central Anti-corruption Bureau), the proper state institutions should undertake work aimed at improving legal regulations and defining the rules of adjudication on matters involving company operations, recognizing ethical standards as an important component of evaluating economic activity, introducing European standards of corporate social responsibility and business ethics, environmental protection, promoting and popularizing ethical behavior, for example by supplying good examples, supporting education on business ethics and corporate social responsibility, showing consideration for the honor of state administration and local government employees, primarily by ensuring the civil service its due rank and importance.

It is the duty of the business community to continue efforts where they have already started, and to begin where this has not yet happened, aimed at: introducing company ethics programs compatible with European and global standards of social responsibility, introducing ethics codes at companies and business organizations, encouraging companies to work for social responsibility certificates (e.g. SA 8000), conducting periodical ethical audits at companies and business organizations and preparing ethical/social reports according to Global Reporting Initiative (GRI) rules, showing proper care for the honor of entrepreneurs and managers and for subjective treatment of employees, and also concern for the natural environment.

Nongovernmental organizations and academic institutions should commit themselves to research, education and consulting on ethics, propagate European-standard business ethics, monitor corporate behavior, offer criticism and suggestions as to proper conduct, shape the factors of a civil society that are related to business ethics, undertake social initiatives, promote corporate responsibility compatible with European standards, organize competitions mobilizing companies to behave ethically and to become good corporate citizens in the regions where they operate.

Meeting these demands will mean that gradually, Polish business life will assume the character of an economic civic republic (Gasparski, 2005). This is important for reasons pointed out by such thinkers and men of action as Ralf Dahrendorf, who said that:

> [...] we are entering a time of ideological disputes over the shape of society, and also protests against something I call the excesses of capitalism. This contestation movement may start in the United States [...] not against capitalism as such, but for instance against increasing company profits at the cost of reducing the number of jobs. In Europe too, we can probably expect a return to policies that are not so much ideological as based on ideas. I think there is a growing dispute over our model of capitalism, over the fact that the rich are increasing their wealth with no limits, that the model of an entrepreneur who takes care of his business and profit but also shows concern for the social consequences of his operations, is disappearing (Dahrendorf, 2006).

Dahrendorf's words are supported by an article by the British Prime Minister, Gordon Brown, who discussed the works of Adam Smith, widely considered the founding father of modern economics, and wrote:

> [...] Many critics have claimed that these two [...] works are in conflict with each other. The Theory of Moral Sentiments favors altruism, while The Wealth of Nations assumes that all people are selfish. I have to question this interpretation. Adam Smith said clearly that the principle of "all for ourselves and nothing for others" was a despicable maxim. Being his compatriot, I had no trouble understanding that The Wealth of Nations was supported by The Theory of Moral Sentiments, that the invisible hand of the market depended on the existence of a helping hand (Brown, 2006, p. 26).

Significant support for business activity is provided, as a kind of helping hand, by ethical infrastructure, and this means its importance cannot be overestimated. Material infrastructure require appropriate intellectual infrastructure, namely knowledge – and not ideology – also about the axiological context of business activity, as one of the kinds of knowledge needed by an economy that is described more and more often as a knowl-edge-based economy. If this is to be more than just a slogan, lip-service, or a PR embellishment, it is worth recognizing that without sufficiently well developed infrastructure of both types the economic activity, we call business, will not enjoy the trust it needs to function properly, as pointed out not only by specialists from the academic world but also enlightened business people, e.g. those from the Caux Round Table (Young, 2004). This requires conceptual preparation of economic activities and activities that make up their social context, or design that leads to relevant solutions as a prerequisite of caring for the common good.

References

Alexandre, V., in cooperation with Gasparski, W., 2000, *The Roots of Praxiology: French Action Theory from Bourdeau and Espinas to Present Days*, New Brunswick (USA) – London (UK): Transaction Publishers.

Brown, G., 2006, "New Patron Adam Smith" (in Polish), *Dziennik*, n°50, p. 26.

Brülde, B., 1998, *The Human Good*, Acta Philosophica Gothoburgensia, Vol. 6, Acta Universitatis Gothoburgensis, Gothenburg.

——2002, in *Business: The Ultimate Resource*, Cambridge, MA: Perseus Publishing.

Butryn, S., 2006, *The Philosophy of Albert Einstein: An Overview* (in Polish), Warsaw: IFiS PAN.

Cieslik, J., Gasparski, W., 2005, "Ethical Firm" (in Polish), unpublished material, Business Ethics Centre (www.cebi.pl).

Dahrendorf, R., 2006, "The Open Society and Its Friends: An Interview by Marcin Bosacki" (in Polish), *Gazeta Wyborcza*, 6–7 May 2006, pp. 15–16.

Dow, S.C., 2002, *Economic Methodology: An Inquiry*, Oxford: Oxford University Press.

Drucker, P.F., 1993, *Post-Capitalist Society*, Oxford: Butterworth –Heinemann.

Einstein, A., 1999, *Philosophical Writings* (in Polish), Warsaw: IFiS PAN.

Fuller, L.L., 1969, *The Morality of Law*, Yale: Yale University Press (Polish edition: 2004, Warsaw: ABC Publishers).

Gasparski, W., 1984, *Understanding Design: The Praxiological–Systemic Perspective*, Seaside (CA): Intersystems Publications.

——1996, "Economic Activity as Seen by Philosophy: Between Praxiology and Ethics" (in Polish), *Prakseologia*, n° 1–4 (130–3), pp. 9–28.

——2003, "On the Need for Knowledge about the Axiological Context of Economic Activity", in W. Gasparski, J. Dabrowski, eds *Creating Knowledge-Based Economy*, Warsaw: LKAEM, pp. 19–32.

——2004, "Twix Cup and Lip There's Many a Slip: Ethical Aspects of Public Administration and Business Intersection", in Debicka, A., Dmochowski, M., Kudrycka, B., eds, *Professionalism in Public Administration* (in Polish), Association for Public Administration Education, Bialystok, pp. 211–23.

——2005a, "European Integration and Its Effect on the Ethical Dimension of Polish Business Conduct", contribution to the conference organized by the Institute of Business History and Raiffeisen Bank, Vienna.

——2005b, "Towards a Civil Republic of Economic Activity", in Banasinski, C., ed., *Competition and Consumer Protection in Poland and in the European Union: Legal and Economic Studies* (in Polish), Warsaw: UOKIK, pp. 231–40.

——2006a, "The Ethical Issue of Corporate Governance and Management Science Theories", in Rossouw, G.J. (Deon), Sison, A.J.G., eds, *Global Perspectives on Ethics of Corporate Governance*, New York: Palgrave Macmillan, pp. 91–104.

——2006b, "Address at the presentation ceremony of the Pillars of the Polish Economy awards", *Puls Biznesu*, unpublished material (www.cebi.pl).

——and Botham, D., eds, 1998, *Action Learning*, New Brunswick (USA), London (UK): Transaction Publishers.

—— , Lewicka-Strzalecka, A., Rok, B., Szulczewski, G., 2002, *Business Ethics in Practical Applications: Initiatives, Programs, Codes* (in Polish), Business Ethics Centre and UN Resident Coordinator's Office in Poland, Warsaw.

——, ——, ——, and ——, 2004, *Corporate Social Responsibility and Business Ethics in Polish Economic Life: An Infrastructure for Ethicality in Polish Business: A Survey Report* (in Polish), Research Group for Business Ethics of the Institute of Philosophy and Sociology, Polish Academy of Sciences and Business Ethics Centre, Warsaw.

John Paul II, 2005, *Memory and Identity: Conversations at the Dawn of a Millennium*, Polish Edition, Krakow: Znak Publishers.

Kotarbinski, T., 2002, "The ABC of Practicality", in Ryan, L., Nahser, F., Gasparski, W., eds, *Praxiology and Pragmatism*, New Brunswick (U.S.A.), London (U.K.): Transaction Publishers, pp. 25–60.

Simon, H.A., 1992, "Methodological Foundations of Economics", in Auspitz, J.L., Gasparski, W.W., Mlicki, M., Szaniawski, K., eds *Praxiologies and the Philosophy of Economics*, New Brunswick (USA), London (UK): Transaction Publishers, pp. 25–42.

Smith, A., 1954, *The Inquiry into the Nature and Causes of the Wealth of Nations*, Polish Edition, Vol. 1–2, Warsaw: PWN.

Young, S., 2004, *Moral Capitalism: Reconciling Private Interest with the Public Good*, San Francisco: Berrett–Koehler Publishers.

Zabieglik, S., 2003, *Adam Smith*, Warsaw: Wiedza Powszechna Publishers.

Zappi, G., ed., 2006, *Operational Guidelines on Banking Corporate Social Responsibility: Creating Values through Listening to Stakeholders – Strategies, Policies and Tools of CSR*, Rome: Bancaria Editrice.

CHAPTER 10

Profit, Partnerships and the Global Common Good

LAURA P. HARTMAN, SCOTT KELLEY AND PATRICIA H. WERHANE

> I do not know how to draw the solution to insoluble problems. It is
> still sleeping in the bottom of a box; but a box over which persons who
> have drawn close to each other keep watch. I have no idea other than
> the idea of the idea that one should have. The abstract drawing of a
> parallelogram – cradle of our hopes. I have the idea of a possibility in
> which the impossible may be sleeping.
>
> — LEVINAS, 1999, p. 89

Introduction

Let us consider a concept of the common good that lies within a Levinasian
box: a space that is not prescriptive in what it may contain but only by
reference to its context, defined, perhaps somewhat arbitrarily, by social
or cultural shifts such as a penchant for alleviating poverty, care of the
environment, or attention to national security. For example, a mental
model permeates an almost universal understanding of the common good
and corporate social responsibility practices on a global scale, in both the
corporate and non-profit communities. This model favors public sector
projects and pure philanthropy over a profit-maximizing shareholder
perspective as the only means by which to address global poverty (e.g.
Dunfee, 2006). This bias has served to trap us into imagining that global
poverty is endemic and unsolvable and that achieving a modicum of the
common good is impossible. As a result, this thinking constrains the

evolution of practices that might otherwise have allowed exponential improvement of living conditions in countless communities; and we are trapped in a Levinasian box.

We shall make three arguments in an effort to escape the box and to develop a potential within this impossibility. First, we contend that the common good, as a positive idea, cannot be articulated so as to fit across cultural or political domains. Second, we argue that, to the contrary, a focus on common "bads" is more properly within the domain of possibility. Focusing on one common "bad," endemic poverty, the alleviation of economic distress is served more effectively by reducing patterns of neglect or exclusion than by pursuing a common, clearly articulated shared notion of "public or common goods." Finally, the particular evils of economic distress can be reduced not merely by public works or philanthropy but, counter-intuitively, and not impossibly, through commerce.

1. Mental Models, Conceptualism and Common Sense

Let us begin by articulating an important assumption underlying these contentions. The assumption consists of a form of social constructivism, the view that all human experience is socially constructed. That is, human beings have mental representations, cognitive frames, or mental pictures of their experiences, representations that model the stimuli or data with which they are interacting; and these are frameworks that establish parameters through which experience or a certain set of experiences, is organized or filtered (Senge, 1990, ch. 10; Gentner and Whitley, 1997, pp. 210–11; Gorman, 1992; Werhane, 1999). Mental models or mind sets function as selective mechanisms and filters for dealing with experience. In focusing, framing, organizing and ordering what we experience, mental models bracket and leave out data, and emotional and motivational foci taint or color experience. These points of view or mental models are socially learned; they are incomplete, and sometimes distorted, narrow, single-framed. Nevertheless, because schema we employ are socially learned and altered through religion, socialization, culture, educational upbringing and other experiences, they are shared and often turn into culturally biased ways of perceiving, organizing and learning (Johnson, 1993; Werhane, 1999; Kelley et al., 2008).

Two particular kinds of mental models are helpful when examining our conceptions about the common good and the improbability of poverty reduction through for-profit initiatives, what Bernard Lonergan labels "the bias of conceptualism" and "the bias of common sense." One of the greatest dangers of addressing the problems of extreme poverty is the bias of conceptualism: the refusal to modify, adjust or abandon abstract concepts in light of emerging insights or failures of philanthropy or public policy. Conceptualism is "a strong affirmation of concepts, and a skeptical disregard of insights", which leads to "anti-historical immobilism", and "excessive abstractness" (Morelli and Morelli, 1997, p. 425). The bias of common sense also overlooks the importance of data by refusing to get beyond the familiar ways we have learned to frame our experiences (Morelli and Morelli, 1997, p. 97).

While all are bounded by mental models, some models are more attentive to data and to experience than are others. Language surrounding the common good must avoid slipping into conceptualism, that is, fixed social theories that assign exact responsibilities to clearly delineated institutions or individuals. It must also avoid slipping into a common sense bias that assumes one particular account of human flourishing is normative for all. Common good language must be attentive to particular experiences, yet intelligent in its ability to find common patterns. Only when common good language is attentive and intelligent will reasonable courses of action emerge.

2. The "Common Good"

Common good language has deep roots in Western philosophy and it includes long-standing disputes concerning social theory and the extent of moral responsibility. Manuel Velasquez and Antonio Argandoña offer two distinct interpretations of the common good and examine the usefulness of such an approach with regard to multinational corporations. Argandoña finds that the common good approach is liable to "vague and contradictory interpretations" and is not accepted by certain schools of thought (Argandoña, 1998). Velasquez argues that an overly strong conception of the common good reflects a particular worldview that does not respect cultural variation with regard to basic questions of human meaning (Velasquez, 1992). Furthermore, according to Velasquez, common good language must avoid two extremes. It must avoid collectivist attitudes that subsume individual interest entirely on one end. On the other end, it must avoid a concept of society that is oriented exclusively toward individual interest, which leaves little room for a coherent understanding of the global common good.

The most challenging critique of common good language is not its open-ended or contradictory approaches when it comes to social theory, as Argandoña identifies, but the overly strong conception that Velasquez critiques, which will be addressed further below. An overly strong conception of the common good is extremely difficult to identify "because cultures differ on their views of what conditions are necessary for humans to flourish" (Velasquez, 1992, p. 30), differences that are particularly acute when comparing cultures at the top of the economic pyramid with those at the base. Such strong, ideological conceptions of the common good have been used as justifications for establishing problematic economic policies that in some cases have exacerbated the effects of poverty.

Velasquez makes a significant, albeit challenging, contribution to common good discourse when it involves the complex realities of multinational corporations. Using the mental model of what he calls neo-Hobbesian realism, Velasquez contends that "the realist holds that it is a mistake to apply moral concepts to international activities: morality has no place in international affairs" (31), and Velasquez agrees with this conclusion. He critiques two versions of the common good, one acceptable to a realist and the other problematic. With an open-ended version of the common good in place, Velasquez then analyzes the circumstances and extent to which a multinational corporation is obliged to serve the common good. He concludes, closely following Hobbesian logic, that multinational corporations have no obligation towards the common good in the absence of an international sovereign, making the establishment of such an institution foundational and primary.

By differentiating a strong and weak conception of the common good, Velasquez makes a crucial contribution. Essentially, he identifies a contextual boundary for common good language to remain coherent. The strong conception, which Velasquez claims best represents "the Catholic conception", identifies a cluster of related terms that must be properly delimited and defined. It distinguishes common goods, which are universal and distributive in character, from private goods and collective goods, which can be either owned or divided up. While such a conception of the common good may be logically coherent, it does little to help clarify the complex matrix of responsibilities multinational corporations must navigate on a regular basis. Such a definition privileges logical coherence over the challenging appropriation of dynamic, global contexts. It does not adequately account for cultural variance with regard to human flourishing.

The weak conception of the common good, however, is far more useful, according to Velasquez. It does not seek to quantify which abstract goods are distributive or universal in character, but merely to identify those things that "diminish the sum total" of one's pains or increase the sum total of one's pleasures. Velasquez uses a utilitarian approach to identify those goods that increase pleasures and diminish pains, with the nuanced understanding that pleasure and pain are not strictly bound by colloquial usage. He argues that it is possible to identify some goods that qualify as global common goods, despite significant difficulties. Within a utilitarian mental model, he tentatively identifies some elements that constitute a global common good including a congenial global climate, safe transportation routes for the international flow of goods, and the avoidance of nuclear war (1992, p. 30).

A strength of Velasquez' approach is its refusal to allow substantive discourse over global concerns to slip into abstract, universal generalizations that do not adequately respect contextual differences regarding the criteria for human flourishing. The strong conception of the common good cannot be so strong that it fails to recognize legitimate variation when it comes to such basic questions of meaning. Conversely, two potential problems emerge with Velasquez' weak conception: first, it cannot be so weak that it fails to provide any substantive categories for moral evaluation. Second, it cannot be reduced to a "sum total" metric, as some utilitarian approaches are, that overlooks harms not immediately obvious in common poverty metrics such as purchasing power parity or gross domestic product. Though we are cognizant of the distinction made by Velasquez between a weak conception of the common good based on the utilitarian collective, and the strong conception based on the indivisible social benefits afforded to all members of society, both these conceptualizations remain tied to particular social contexts and thus rely on temporal and cultural interpretation.

3. A Modified Weak Conception of the Common Good

Antonio Argandoña uses the same definition of the common good from Catholic social teaching as Velasquez: "the overall conditions of life in society that allow the different groups and their members to achieve their own perfection more fully and more easily".[1] Argandoña's characteriza-

---

1   Cf. *Gaudium et Spes*, #26, cited in Argandoña (1998). Argandoña's reference has some differences from other translations. See for example, Vatican translation: http://www.vatican.va/archive/hist_councils/ii_vatican_council/documents/vat-ii_cons_19651207_gaudium-et-spes_en.html. Another version is found at: http://www.osjspm.org/majordoc_gaudium_et_spes_part_one.aspx.

tion of the common good, however, avoids the conceptual problems that Velasquez rightly critiques; it does not attempt to distinguish universal goods from private or collective goods. Rather, Argandoña offers some helpful clarifications. As a set of conditions necessary for members of society to realize their own personal objectives, this understanding of the common good follows Velasquez' weak conception that seeks to increase individual pleasure or decrease individual pain.

In addition, Argandoña points out that personal objectives operate within a common good that is inherently cooperative and transcendental. As transcendental, it cannot be fully expressed "in statistical terms"; although quantitative measurements contribute to its evolving realization. As cooperative in character, the common good is relational and dialogic. Argandoña's understanding is close to the weak conception Velasquez has in mind, but it avoids the danger of "sum-total reductionism" to which Velasquez' utilitarian approach is susceptible. Our approach brings both conceptions together, with a different perspective.

4. Social Goods and Common Evils

Defining the common good, even a weak definition is difficult in a culturally, socially, and religiously diverse planet. Should the common good be identified with basic rights and liberties, respect for community, meeting basic needs, equal opportunity, and/or economic well-being? It might turn out, for example, that, in some cultures, the community is prioritized above basic liberties or even meeting needs. In others, basic rights will be the trumping "good". Indeed, as Michael Walzer has demonstrated some time ago, what we call "good" or "goods" are socially defined such that there is no common definition or agreement (Walzer, 1983, Chapter One).

In the opening part of Plato's *Republic*, Socrates begins his investigation of justice by identifying particular instances of injustice. His initial "*via negativa*" approach seeks to identify those elements that frustrate the pursuit of justice, not yet fully defined at the beginning of the investigation. Following the *via negativa* and limiting our discussion to that portion of the common good that pertains to *economic* matters, we seek to create a starting point for common good discourse. Our aim is to identify those conditions that *preclude* individuals and groups from living decently so as to even begin to realize their potential. The starting point, therefore, is the experience of those living in poverty, those who are most harmed by patterns of economic neglect, and not an ideal, universal conception of human flourishing or a global common good. Borrowing a phrase from Muhammad Yunus, our starting point is the *worm's eye view*, not that of the bird's. As such, our conception is limited in that it is neither comprehensive nor exhaustive. From here, we will address those patterns of economic bias and neglect that, collectively, exacerbate the effects of poverty.

So we shall begin from another perspective. Even if we cannot definitely be clear about the common goods, we shall assume that there are some commonly agreed upon "bads". These might include murder, torture, arbitrary imprisonment, harms to children, etc. At least one other "bad" would the absence of the satisfaction of minimum basic needs, however those are socially defined. So the lack of food, shelter, access to worship, ability to move through the community or enjoy opportunities afforded some members of that community, and/or education, locally defined, are all candidates for creating conditions that are inhuman by any standards. That is, abject poverty, locally defined, would be considered bad.

It is on these "bads" we will concentrate in this essay. We contend that reducing poverty is both a moral and economic imperative, not merely for those in poverty, but for those of us in wealth communities. But, we will argue that commonly accepted solutions to abject poverty, e.g., through public or philanthropic endeavors have failed in many instances. We will propose, instead, a new mental model – that of for-profit initiatives aimed at creating new markets, encouraging micro-entrepreneurial ventures, and providing living-wage jobs in economically distressed communities. Such initiatives reduce poverty, help to create a sense of dignity and self-respect for those now engaged in these projects, and expand global economic well-being for future generations.

5. Patterns of Economic Bias and Neglect

From an economic viewpoint, the world looks like a pyramid. Of the world's 6.6 billion people, four billion live on less than $2 a day. The bottom half of the world represents only 1.1 percent of the world's total net worth (Davies, 2006). Despite such disparity, there is significant evidence to suggest the global economic pyramid is beginning to flatten into a diamond (*The Economist*, 2004, figure 1), especially since half of the world's population, located mostly in China and India, is experiencing economic development (Friedman, 2005). However, extreme poverty is rising in absolute numbers and a large share of that is in sub-Saharan Africa (Sachs, 2005, p. 20). One out of six in the global human population cannot meet the basic demands of survival (Sachs, 2005, p. 24). As a result, there are stark contrasts in life styles and life spans across the globe: a child born in Malawi, for example, has a life expectancy half as long as a child born in Japan (United Nations Development Programme, 2006).

From a numerical viewpoint, one could reasonably argue that the flattening trend of the economic pyramid is an expression of the "common good" because *the majority* is experiencing economic growth despite comparatively small, regional increases in extreme poverty. While one out of six cannot meet the basic demands of survival, five out of six can. One might also argue that the current population growth, expected to plateau at 9.1 billion around the year 2050 (Gore, 2006, p. 217) is evidence of a common good that is historically unprecedented. Such a collectivist and statistical interpretation of the common good makes no positive moral claim for those who live in moderate or extreme poverty. Here, a minimalist understanding of the utilitarian argument is insufficient.

To the contrary, there is a growing understanding that today's global economy is radically interdependent, such that extreme poverty anywhere is a threat to prosperity everywhere. As Tom Friedman declares, "[poverty] is the tragedy for the world because of the incredible lost contribution that all these people still outside the flat world [those living in abject poverty] could make" (Friedman, 2005, p. 468). Furthermore, most of the population growth in the next few decades will occur in the urban slums of the developing world since birth rates are inversely related to living standards and levels of education (Hart, 2005, p. 32). These megacities pose significant challenges to sustainability and to reducing global "bads": increased pollution from industrial emissions, diseases from contaminated water and lack of sewage treatment, unsustainable use of limited resources, and threats posed by high levels of unemployment to name a few (Hart, 2005, p. 43). What might be termed the "interdependence thesis" makes a positive moral claim for those who live in moderate or extreme poverty irrespective of the collective economic status of a statistical majority. The radical disparity of life styles and life spans across the economic pyramid, even if numerically small, pose a significant threat to global prosperity on a variety of fronts.

One of the most obvious threats comes from failed States. In 1994, the Central Intelligence Agency's State Failure Task Force found a strong connection between economic failure and State failure leading to mass migration, refugeeism, ethnic war, and even terrorism (Sachs, 2005, p. 332). The task force identified three significant explanatory variables in the 113 cases of State failure between 1957 and 1994: high infant mortality rates caused by low levels of material well-being increased the likelihood of State failure, greater economic linkages with the rest of the world decreased the likelihood of State failure, and democratic countries showed less propensity for State failure than authoritarian regimes. The connection between State failure and U.S. military engagements is also strong (Sachs, 2005, p. 333), which has not escaped the strategic planning of the U.S. Central Command.

Operating in Camp Lemonier, Djibouti, the U.S. Central Command's "Combined Joint Task Force – Horn of Africa" (HOA) combats terrorism by focusing on regional stability in some of the poorest parts of Africa: Djibouti, Ethiopia, Eritrea, Kenya, Seychelles, Somalia, Sudan and Yemen. Since regional instability provides a safe haven for transnational terrorist groups, no small part of HOA's efforts are focused on developing and increasing access to clean water, functional schools, improved roadways and improved medical facilities. HOA's mission is to create "a place where education and prosperity are within each person's grasp and where terrorists, whose extremist ideology seeks to enslave nations, do not infringe upon the right to self-determination". For the U.S. Central Command to send 1,500 people to the Horn of Africa attests to the strategic belief that extreme poverty anywhere is a threat to global security (Combined Joint Task Force – Horn of Africa, 2007). While the connection between extreme poverty and global security may be clear, it is not at all clear why economic development in the region has been left to soldiers trained for combat.

The stories of extreme poverty across the globe share some overarching trends and patterns that range from exclusion to exploitation on a spectrum of harm. Identifying and reducing patterns of neglect and exploitation create the conditions for alleviating economic distress. Systemic patterns of exclusion exacerbate the effects of extreme poverty. In *The Mystery of Capital*, the Peruvian economist Hernando de Soto examines why capitalism thrives in the West but tends to fail elsewhere. He argues that formal property titles "lead a parallel life as capital outside the physical world" by attracting and securing the interests of other parties through collateral (de Soto, 2000, p. 39). In many developing countries, however, much of the population is "barred from legally established social and economic activities" and must operate in the extralegal sector (82). Doing so is both restrictive and risky. Without property title and formal collateral, much of the developing world's capital is "hidden" or "dead." In Peru, for example, only thirty percent of homes built have legal title (85).

Given the anticipated growth trends of the urban demographic in the developing world, exclusion from the formal, legal economy is growing concern. De Soto found a critical moment in the history of the West that curbed the bifurcation of formal property rights into legal haves and have-nots; forward-looking minds decided that official law makes no sense if a sizable part of the population lives outside of it (106). Early in United States history the courts recognized the rights of squatters by arguing "possession was nine tenths of the law" and supporting "preemption", the legal innovation allowing a settler to purchase land he had improved before it was offered for public sale (114, 120). Such formal property rights are not extended to squatters in urban shantytowns of the developing world for various reasons. Prohibitive literacy requirements (Yunus, 2003, p. 52), gender bias (pp. 71–3), and a stifling bureaucratic process that can take decades to get legal title (de Soto, 2000, pp. 18–28) all preclude access to the life-blood of economic empowerment.

While bureaucratic patterns of exclusion may or may not be intentional, there are also active, intentional patterns of exploitation practiced by money-lenders, commodity traders, and public service providers. In rural Bangladesh, for example, creditors charge rates so usurious they are virtually impossible to repay (Yunus, 2003, pp. 48–58). In rural India, the creation of government-mandated marketplaces called *mandis* was intended to create more equitable distribution. In practice, however, they had the opposite effect presenting formidable challenges to farmers in every step of the supply chain. Without access to relevant information, competing markets, precise measuring instruments, or payment in full upon sale, farmers were systemically exploited by traders (Prahalad, 2005, pp. 323–9). For basic access to public services such as electricity, many consumers missed hours of work waiting in long lines to pay their monthly bills. For those who could afford it, "speed money" was the only way to avoid waiting in such long lines. As a result, the poor pay a heavy price for basic services, costing the citizens of one city $45 million in collective wage loss (Prahalad, 2005, p. 89). Many are able to exploit the asymmetry of access to markets and information that exist at the base of the pyramid.

Exclusion and exploitation are coupled with significant misconceptions concerning the role of large international organizations, which can lead to distortions in outcomes and forsake new possibilities. William Easterly argues that the $2.3 trillion in aid sent to less developed countries since the 1950's has had mixed results at best (2006). While IMF and World Bank efforts have been effective in parts of the world, they have done virtually nothing to change the economic landscapes in Africa, parts of the sub-continent of India, Pakistan and Bangladesh. Easterly makes a strong case that it was the sense of colonial-paternal responsibility coupled with the belief that the poor do not have the capacity for economic development that lead to such problematic consequences (Easterly, 2006, pp. 23–6). Joseph Stiglitz goes even further arguing that the IMF and World Bank reflect the commercial and financial interests of the G-7, the wealthiest industrial countries. Many of the IMF's policies, including premature capital market liberalization, have contributed to global instability (15). If Easterly and Stiglitz are correct, then the post-World War II era grand social-engineering projects share responsibility for today's economic disparity.

The most pernicious pattern, however, is a mental model that cannot envision latent opportunities in the base of the pyramid. The view that the poor lack resources and are irrevocably dependent on foreign aid skewed toward philanthropy, government and the public sector creates narrow or rigidly defined roles that often dismiss the variety of creative ways that different cultures respond to the demands of a flourishing society. The cumulative effect of such assumptions is that the private sector has avoided developing products and services for the poor because it seems risky and not worth the investment (Kelley, Hartman and Werhane, 2008).

6. Poverty Alleviation as Profitable Partnership

Considering the cumulative effects of exclusion, exploitation, and conceptualization, poverty alleviation is best served by removing the barriers that curb, stunt, or prohibit economic development. While we are uncertain about whether economic development serves the common good, we are certain that alleviating abject poverty reduces evil. This alleviation, we suggest, may be facilitated by the concept of the "profitable partnership", based on common economic foundations of incentives and vested interests. When incentives justify the investment of capital into a relationship in order to support long-term strategic interests of an organization, the organization is encouraged to enhance the ongoing investment. The resulting vested interest in the relationship creates a commitment based on aligned strategic objectives rather than charitable kindness.

This is not to say, of course, that public policy interventions and philanthropic contributions are without significant service to those most in need, but instead that the realignment of incentives can create a stable bond upon which those in need can most effectively rely for long-term planning and results. Ultimately, an equilibrium is possible – and in fact the ultimate goal – precisely because both partners are provided with what they seek most from a relationship: the organization invests in its future and receives value on that investment toward satisfaction of strategic objectives while the population served now has a reliable partner rather than a beneficent, though arguably somewhat subjective, if not arbitrary, donor.

This proposal would seem to pose an obvious connection – it permits someone to reap a value to which they will retain commitment and which has brought them value. However, reaping value, when perceived as taking advantage of someone else's vital need (as opposed to their "want"), is ethically offensive by social norms. Consider a doctor who responds to the familiar plea, "is there a doctor available?" at a restaurant where a child is choking. The doctor administers the Heimlich Maneuver and the child is immediately saved. Most, if not all, cultures would frown on the doctor if she or he were thereafter to submit a hefty bill for the life-saving few moments of assistance. Similarly, where a for-profit corporation has within it the power to alleviate the most intolerable forms of poverty by a relatively low cost investment, social norms have frowned on the corporation that instead reaps what are often alleged to be "unnecessary" or "excessive" profits.

But consider, however, the unfortunate doctor, who finds herself in the restaurant replete with choking children. Beyond the first few, many of the children will surely go without her valuable services and may suffer grave results. Moreover, the doctor herself will experience exhaustion and her regular patients will go underserved, resulting in an eventual loss of income to our doctor and those who rely on her. Similarly, a company that strives to serve the common good by continually and consistently doling out philanthropic remedies may find itself underserving stakeholders, depleting resources, and failing to appropriately position itself to achieve critical strategic objectives that would otherwise permit it to continue to meet the needs of those who rely on it. For better or worse, these contributions, whether at individual or organizational levels, do not always have the impact they intend nor are they immune from unforeseeable consequences of societal or temporal shifts. What was formerly valued as generous in the realm of corporate social responsibility, the purely philanthropic gift with no strings attached except the expectation of recognition, has proven in light of experience to be unreliable, at best.

In fact, it is precisely this type of dilemma to which Velasquez responds when he concludes that multinational corporations do *not* have a moral obligation to contribute to the international common good in the absence of international enforcement mechanisms. To the contrary, however, imagine how *common* objectives may be satisfied when a corporation's profit-maximizing incentives are aligned with the alleviation of extreme poverty. If we modify the mental models to embrace an incentive-based paradigm, and then utilize that paradigm to motivate those with power to effect the most significant change in the areas where they have the greatest opportunity and capabilities, we are creating a self-perpetuating system that reinforces the objectives of each partner while simultaneously meeting the needs of the most critical.

The above proposition is certainly not news to many of the world's most strategic minds. In his 2007 address to Harvard University's graduating class, Bill Gates reiterated the above analysis: "[i]f we can find approaches that meet the needs of the poor in ways that generate profits for business and votes for politicians, we will have found a sustainable way to reduce inequity in the world" (Gates, 2007). Similarly, Freeman, Velamuri and Moriarty (2006) take issue with the traditional model, termed the "separation thesis", as contrasted to the proposition described above, which is one instead of strategic convergence through profitable partnerships. Freeman et al. explain that, "by talking of business and social responsibility as if they are two separate things, we unintentionally promote the idea that they involve discrete thought processes and activities. The challenge is to promote a different way of doing business that integrates considerations of business, ethics and society" (2006; see also Freeman, 1994).

Several examples will serve to illuminate the value of strategic convergence as compared to the separation thesis. Each of these examples shares some basic challenges and solutions. The companies involved recognized that, though there was value in doing business in the particular environment discussed, there were also costs involved. For instance, in some cases, security might pose a risk, while in others the challenge might be related to consumer education. In most cases, a traditional response to these hurdles would likely reduce the incentives discussed above to such insufficient levels as to render the projects completely worthless *from a strategic perspective*. Instead, the projects below were not pursued according to the mental models of philanthropy nor were they abandoned – those involved applied innovative and creative paradigms that met the strategic objectives of the organization while satisfying the community needs of vested stakeholders.

Manila Water's experience in the Philippines is a prime example of a modification to the traditional approach to these challenges since the Philippines is not an economy that a business would traditionally consider to be high-growth and profitable. Ninety percent of its population earns an average of less than $300 a month per household and often had to stand for hours in order to access clean water, paying ten times a standard rate, if available. In addition, Manila Water's prime customer base did not even have the basic piping structure necessary to bring its product into their home. Customers had to pay almost half of their monthly income just to begin to access Manila Water's product.

How did Manila Water respond to these challenges? Through community engagement, Manila Water developed a process of customer options and collective billing through which customers may choose to participate in household group meter cooperatives. Each household's use is measured separated but billed collectively, with the entire billing group accepting financial responsibility for the full meter measurement. The group cooperative has reduced billing rates per consumer by as much as 60% and, in support of the profitable partnership theory, Manila Water has collected 100% of the money owed in communities where collective billing is used (with about 70% of the urban poor it serves). Manila Water has reported a 19% return over the past three years, with 600,000 households served. (Beshouri, 2006; Zobel de Ayala, 2006).

Cemex, a leading manufacturer of cement, is an example of a firm that simply capitalized on an opportunity to create a new market for itself, and happened to help a particular low-income community build their homes in the process. It is a prime model of a profitable partnership where all stakeholders are committed to the success of the venture through vested self interests towards common and valuable ends. About 2.5 million impoverished residents of Guadalajara, Mexico, live in extremely crowded and unfinished housing surrounding the city. The conditions give rise to other challenges and tensions that served as one of the catalysts to encourage Cemex to establish Patrimonio Hoy. "Imagine one room with ten persons living together, yelling and fighting all day long. So the children are propelled out into the streets at a young age. What do they learn in the streets? Vicious delinquency, theft and prostitution. If the first thing in your life is contact with the street, your future will be the street, with its related risks", says Israel Moreno, director and founder of the effort (Changemakers, 2002). Patrimonio Hoy is a for-profit project sponsored by Cemex that supports low income families (households with incomes of less than $5 per day) in financing the building or expansion of their homes.

After careful study of the micro-lending methods of the Grameen Bank, Cemex realized that homeowners simply were discouraged by lack of funding opportunities since it could take an average of thirteen years to finish building a small home. Therefore, the challenge of mental models existed on both sides; "Their mental model is 'We cannot do it, we cannot have a better life. This is my life, this has been my parents' life, and this will be my children's life'", says Moreno (Changemakers, 2002). Moreno and Cemex instituted savings groups of three "partners" each with well-established rules to assist the partners to participate in the borrowing process; and Cemex advanced credit to the group on the basis of participation. In line with the profitable partnerships concept, Cemex does not compete for Partners' purchases based on price but instead the partners receive benefits of membership such as technical assistance, educational programs, guaranteed quality materials and delivery, guaranteed price freezes on materials, and free storage of materials, among others. "I prefer to invest in helping our partners discover ways to live a better life", Moreno said. "I think that is a more responsible and intelligent way of doing business" (Changemakers, 2002).

As a primary consequence of the project, Cemex gains a foothold in a large and growing market segment, growth it could not achieve if it remained locked in a traditional mindset. According to Cemex' own forecasts, the world demand for cement through 2010 is expected to expand by 4% per year in developing countries, while it is anticipated that it will grow by only 1% annually in developed countries (Changemakers, 2002). These growth statistics have supported expansion of the Patrimonio Hoy program at a current rate of 2,000 new households per month serving a total of 150,000 families in 45 townships (Cemex, 2007), unquestionably impacting Cemex in ways that outright philanthropic donations could not have captured – the rate of cement used by low income homebuilders has tripled, increasing from 2,300 pounds consumed once every four years, on average, to the same amount being consumed in 15 months (Changemakers, 2002).

By 2005, Cemex reported a profit of $1.5 million and anticipated expansion into Colombia, Venezuela, Egypt and the Philippines (Johnson, 2005). Moreover, when combined with additional funding from Mexico's development ministry, SEDESOL, the program was able to enhance the number of people served by SEDESOL by three times and increase significantly the home equity resulting as a consequence of partner participation (Letelier and Spinosa, 2002, p. 35). Stunningly, Cemex reports an additional payoff not normally anticipated by multinationals when investing in developing economies. While traditional mental models prepare for instability of these markets based on security concerns or undependable individual finances, Cemex has found to the contrary that its low income market is far more reliable in times of economic fluctuation. When balanced in quantity against high cost developed markets, low income developing markets could therefore serve as extraordinary leverage against losses during periods of economic flux.

The equilibrium enabled by the profitable partnerships proposal in support of reducing poverty exists *only* because of the mutual reliance created by the interests vested between the stakeholders. Cemex invests in the builders' future and receives value on that investment toward satisfaction of its strategic objectives while the families served now have a reliable partner. The mutuality is evidenced by Moreno's common business-based anxieties. "This is not a charity organization", Moreno said. "We have to meet two objectives: we have to collaborate in providing a better life for these people and the next generations of their families, and we have to do business. If we achieve both these two objectives we will be OK. But you cannot manage this as only a business or a charity organization. This is my main concern: that we take both parallel courses. If you do only one of these, you will be out of business in less than six months. This is what wakes me up in the middle of the night" (Changemakers, 2002).

The third example of a sustainable, strategic profitable partnership between a for-profit corporation and a community is Hindustan Lever Limited's Project Shakti. The Project's stated objectives are "to create income-generating capabilities for underprivileged rural women by providing a small-scale enterprise opportunity, and to improve rural living standards through health and hygiene awareness" (Hindustan Lever Limited, 2004). However, also clearly articulated throughout all of the Project's materials is the Project's dual purpose to meet the strategic business purposes of Hindustan Lever Limited (HLL): "HLL has consciously woven India's imperatives with the company's strategies and operations" (Hindustan Lever Limited, 2004).

HLL recognizes that its efforts at rural development, health, hygiene and infrastructure development will be most successful and effective when linked to HLL's core business and in service to both the community stakeholders as well as to HLL. To those ends, Project Shakti established micro-enterprise opportunities for Self-Help Groups (SHGs) involving women from rural villages in India. HLL offered mass-market products, credit, training and other support to the SHGs in order to support the establishment of their enterprises. HLL benefits from the exchange in that they have access to a previously media-dark region; their products are now closely linked with a far more effective understanding of health and hygiene; and the women entrepreneurs have created a marketing access route that had never before existed for this population of consumers.

By creating jobs, it has not only created consumers, but has also created consumer purchasing power, as well. In 2000, alone, HLL claims 70% of India's £20 million shampoo market in rural India; and half of its $1.02 billion sales in soaps and detergents in India came from sachets in rural India. "Everybody wants brands. And there are a lot more poor people in the world than rich people. To be a global business [...] you have to participate in all segments", says Keki Dadiseth, who is responsible for HLL's global home care product division (Balu, 2001). "Even though developing markets use small quantities per capita, their huge population means a huge amount of fabric-washing products, shampoo, and so on. And even if you make modest profit levels on that, the gross profit can be much more than in the traditional markets".

Conclusion

Collaborative partnerships based on vested interests in profitable ends, however they may be defined by varied stakeholder objectives, suggest some appropriate parameters in delineating a space for poverty alleviating opportunities. Revisiting Levinas, we accept that Levinas is normally adduced to ethical discussions in order to interpret the value of only personal actions (Bevan and Corvellec, 2007): tacitly we maintain this corporate fiction but as one in which good may prevail.

> Commerce is better than war for in please the good has already reigned.
> (Levinas, 1981, p. 5)

References

Ahmad, P., J. Mead, P.H. Werhane and M.E. Gorman, 2004b, Hindustan Lever Limited and Project Sting, *Darden Case Study UVA-E-0269*, Charlottesville, VA: Darden Business School Publishing.

Argandoña, Antonio, 1998, The Stakeholder Theory and the Common Good, *Journal of Business Ethics*, 17: 1093–1102.

Balu, Rekha, 2001, Strategic Innovation: Hindustan Lever Ltd, *Fast Company*, 47: 120.

Beshouri, Christopher, 2006, A Grassroots Approach to Emerging-Market Consumers, *McKinsey Quarterly*, N° 4. http://www.mckinseyquarterly.com/article_page.aspx?ar=1866 (accessed 14 July 2007).

Bevan, David and Hervé Corvellec, 2007, The Impossibility of Corporate Ethics: For a Levinasian Approach to Management Ethics, *Business Ethics: A European Review*, 16: 3, 208–19.

Cemex, 2007, Crece Tu Patrimonio Hoy. http://www.cemexmexico.com/se/se_ph.html (accessed 18 June 2007).

Changemakers, 2007, Mosaic of Innovative Solutions: How to Provide Affordable Housing. http://www.changemakers.net/journal/300606/mosaic.cfm#cemex (accessed 17 June 2007).

Davies, James B. et al., The World Distribution of Household Wealth. http://www.wider.unu.edu/research/2006-2007/2006-2007-1/wider-wdhw-launch-5-12-2006/wider-wdhw-report-5-12-2006.pdf (accessed 14 December 2006).

De Soto, Hernando, 2000, *The Mystery of Capital: Why Capitalism Triumphs in the West and Fails Everywhere Else*, New York: Basic Books.

Donaldson, Thomas and Thomas Dunfee, 1994, Toward A Unified Conception of Business Ethics: Integrative Social Contracts Theory, *Academy of Management Review*, 19: 2, 252–84.

The Economist, 2004, Global Economic Inequality: More or Less Equal? 11 March: 84–7.

Freeman, R.E., S.R. Velamuri and B. Moriarty, 2006, Company Stakeholder Responsibility: A New Approach to CSR, *Business Roundtable Institute for Corporate Ethics Bridge Paper*. http://www.corporate-ethics.org/pdf/csr.pdf (accessed 21 June 2007).

Freeman, R.E., 1994, The Politics of Stakeholder Theory: Some Future Directions, *Business Ethics Quarterly*, 4: 409–21.

Friedman, Thomas L., 2005, *The World is Flat: A Brief History of The Twentieth Century*, New York: Farrar, Straus and Giroux.

Gates, W., 2007, Harvard University Commencement Address. http://www.news.harvard.edu/gazette/2007/06.14/99-gates.html (accessed 20 June 2007).

Gentner, D. and Whitley, E.W., 1997, Mental Models of Population Growth: A Preliminary Investigation. In *Environment, Ethics, and Behavior: The Psychology of Environmental Valuation and Degradation*, ed. M. Bazerman, D.M. Messick, A.E. Tenbrunsel, and K. Wade-Benzoni, San Francisco, CA: New Lexington Press, 209–33.

Gore, Al, 2006, *An Inconvenient Truth: The Planetary Emergency of Global Warming and What We Can Do About It*, New York: Melcher Media.

Gorman, Michael, 1992, *Simulating Science: Heuristics, Mental Models and Technoscientific Thinking*, Bloomington: Indiana University Press.

Hart, Stuart, 2005, *Capitalism at the CrossRoads: The Unlimited Business Opportunities in Solving the World's Most Difficult Problems*, New Jersey: Wharton School Publishing.

Herbst, Kris, 2002, Enabling the Poor to Build Housing: Cemex Combines Profit and Social Development, Arlington, VA: Ashoka. http://www. changemakers.net/journal/02september/herbst.cfm (accessed 14 July 2007).

Hindustan Lever Limited, 2004, Project Shakti. http://www.hllshakti. com/sbcms/temp. 5.asp (accessed 16 June 2007).

Johnson, Kay and Xa Nhon, 2005, Selling to the Poor, *Time Magazine*, (17 April). http://www.time.com/time/magazine/article/ 0,9171,1050276,00.html (accessed 14 July 2007).

Johnson, Mark, 1993, *Moral Imagination: Implications of Cognitive Science for Ethics*, Chicago: University of Chicago Press.

Kelley, Scott, Laura P. Hartman and Patricia H. Werhane, 2008, The End of Foreign Aid as We Know It: The Profitable Alleviation of Poverty in a Globalized Economy, in *Alleviating Poverty Through Business Strategy*, ed. Charles Wankel, London: Palgrave Macmillan.

Letelier, Maria and Charles Spinosa, 2002, The For-Profit Development Business: Good Business, Good Policy, Good to Foster. http://www. changemakers.net/cm/pointofview/forprofit.rtf (accessed 17 June 2007).

Lévinas, Emmanuel, 1999, *Alterity and Transcendence*, London: Athlone Press.

—— 1981, *Otherwise than Being*, Pittsburgh, PA: Duquesne University Press.

Morelli, Mark D. and Elizabeth A. Morelli, eds, 1997, *The Lonergan Reader*, Toronto: University of Toronto Press.

Prahalad, C.K., 2005, *The Fortune at the Bottom of the Pyramid: Eradicating Poverty Through Profits*. New Jersey: Wharton School Publishing.

Senge, Peter, 1990, *The Fifth Discipline*, New York: Doubleday.

United Nations Development Programme, 2006, "Malawi Data Sheet". http://hdr.undp.org/hdr2006/statistics/countries/data_sheets/ cty_ds_MWI.html (accessed 6 December 2006).

Velasquez, Manuel, 1992, International Business, Morality and The Common Good. *Business Ethics Quarterly*, 2: 1, 27–40.

Walzer, Michael, 1983, *Spheres of Justice*, New York: Basic Books.

Werhane, Patricia H., 1999, *Moral Imagination and Management Decision-Making,* New York: Oxford University Press.

Yunus, Muhammad, 2003, *Banker to the Poor: Micro-Lending and the Battle Against World Poverty*, New York: Public Affairs.

Zobel de Ayala, Fernando, 2006, The CFO Challenge to Sustainable CSR. Speech at *CSR Expo*, 23 September, Manila, Philippines, http:// www.ayalafoundation.org/news.asp?id=109.

PART III

Business and the Emerging Global Civil Society: Towards the Construction of a Global Social Contract?

CHAPTER 11

Reflections on Global Civil Society

JEAN-FRANÇOIS PETIT

Introduction

When we talk about international civil society, opinions diverge radically. The most optimistic show the numerous signs of its current strengthening. Just one example: in 1985, the solidarity concert Live Aid was seen by more than 1 billion people. It might have helped to make public opinion aware of the world starvation issue. These optimists point out that there are now more than 50,000 NGOs, which is for them an undeniable vitality sign. On the other side, pessimists will make another speech. Another example: despite demonstrations gathering more than 11 millions people in more than 80 countries the 15 February 2003, Iraq war could not be avoided. In these conditions, can we talk about a real global civil society?[1] The question I propose to deal with in this chapter is therefore quite precise: under which conditions could a global civil society be implemented, in particular to weigh on the constitution of a global government?

In the first place, it is useful, although it has already been done partially, to re-explore the origin, more European, of this global society concept. However, the growing interdependence and integration linked to globalization force us nowadays to reflect on the worldwide extension of this concept. Can its traditional components – associations, Churches, political or social movements – be re-thought in the dynamics of the

---

[1] Cf. M. Kaldor, H. Anheier and M. Glasius, eds, 2003, *Global Civil Society 2003*, Oxford: Oxford University Press.

current globalization process? The idea I will defend here is that there will not be a true global civil society without the implementation of a real global citizenship. This questioning, as we will see, is not new for philosophers. It raises the issue of the kind of world government able to support global citizenship. The discussion will probably be less easy at this stage, but let us start by clarifying this global society concept.

I. Clarifying the Global Civil Society Concept

During the 1990s, the term "global civil society" (or "worldwide", or "international") has become a neologism used without much care. Actually, it originates from three identified sources: the ancient law concept of *societas civilis*, the thought of the Prague 1968 revolution dissidents, and lastly McLuhan's "global village" idea.

In practice, its use is quite delicate. As noted by John Keane, it characterizes emerging social relations including new actors of globalization, multilateral institutions and international events.[2] This set is far from corresponding to a perfectly defined normative ideal. It includes different forms of actions, multiple interactions between voluntary groups such as NGOs, civil initiatives supported by transnational organizations, or movements like world social forums. It is therefore difficult to see clearly. Today, the extension of the concept's meaning is obvious. The "global civil society" idea has been re-examined, out of its original context. It is the subject of appropriations in various languages and differentiated elaborations according to interested authors. For that reason, getting back to its origin could prove quite illuminating.

The *societas civilis* concept was the expression of a law which organized society on an established order, in a system linked to one or several States. Such was for instance the conception of one of its first recognized

2   Cf. J. Keane, 2003, *Global Civil Society?*, Cambridge (UK): Cambridge University Press.

theoreticians, Emmerich de Vatel in his book *Le Droit des gens ou principes de la loi naturelle* (1758). But philosophically, it is Adam Ferguson who was the first to give the most important elements of this concept of civil society.[3] Like other Enlightenment thinkers, he tried to put forward his interest for situating relations between private life and political State. In his theory, the individual appears as a private and free owner, and this can explain his refusal of a new organization of society in which would remain a social system structured by relationships between masters and slaves. For Ferguson, civil society should not be analyzed only from the point of view of potential conflicts, divisions between social classes, inequalities, market anarchy, usurpation of the State by the rich or political apathy of the poor. One should rather pay attention to an anti-State form, even if it did not assure any supremacy in the social order. Consequently, it will be easy for the liberals to insist on market virtues, or on the contrary, for conservative philosophers to exaggerate the importance of the role of the State.

That is why, following Hegel in particular, this concept of civil society will be minimized. Above all in his *Philosophy of Right*, we can find a very elaborated theory. For Hegel, order is necessary for political life. It is the role of court, parliament and police to represent it. But civil society can contribute too, on the condition that the freedom given to everyone be compensated by a duty of participation to society's mediating institutions. Corporations in particular must have this mission. They can actually give consistency and opening to public deliberations. Thus, Hegel must not be considered as a bitter absolutist, in favor of a total subordination of civil society. He admitted that the ideas of individual, equality and solidarity could manifest themselves in it, even though he noticed that there was above all eccentricity and poverty, inequality and corruption. In the long run, it would be necessary anyway to put an end to this fragmentation between economic interests, ethnic solidarities or religious sensitivities. Ultimately, the State will realize this superior unity.

3   A. Ferguson, 1966, *Essay on the History of Civil Society*, Edinburgh: Edinburgh University Press.

Contemporary philosophy gave a major extension to this civil society concept. It is not understood in the same way by liberals, natural law supporters, Habermas' disciples or communitarians, to make reference only to a few streams of thought.[4] Nevertheless, for many, it is voluntary association that must be considered as civil society's base. Freedom to join or to retire from a group, without losing one's status or one's benefits, is regarded as its cornerstone. If civil society is too strong, government runs the risk of collapsing. In the opposite case, it becomes too weak without any possibility of being a counter-power. The establishment of its frontiers within each State is linked to history, to culture and political tradition, to the understanding of the common good. Therefore we do not find the same understanding of civil society in countries marked by Confucianism or Islam. It has been argued recently that the will to develop a very occidental understanding is not devoid of ulterior motives. In particular, the fact of considering civil society as a "third way" between State and Market does not seem to give a fair account of the variety of existing interactions in numerous countries. The market fosters voluntary association too, and the State, by its laws, can also render civil society more dynamic. That is why every oversimplification should be avoided.

Rather than Michael Walzer's definition, in which civil society means the space of irrepressible human associations and the series of relations formed for the good of family, faith, personal or collective interests and options,[5] I will choose Will Kymlicka's more precise definition, where civil society is characterized as a whole formed by:

– public interest groups, movements involved in democratic debate, which enable citizens to associate themselves and form public opinion;

4   N. Rosenblum and R. Post, 2002, *Civil Society and Government*, Princeton: Princeton University Press.
5   M. Walzer, 1997, "The Concept of Civil Society", in M. Walzer, ed., *Toward a Global Civil Society*, New York: Berghahn Books, p. 7 (Stockholm University lecture, October 1990).

– private groups in which members have more particular conceptions of the good (artist associations, Churches ...);
– the economic sector.

De facto, his definition excludes the State and the family which are, for him, based on other rules.[6] Even if Walzer's and Kymlicka's approaches are not identical, they manifest the same demand: to show how contemporary societies could strengthen the freedoms of individual choice, while helping to correct natural inequalities in the distribution of resources and opportunities offered to everyone. In our Western countries, we are used to family solidarities, mutual care and political organization. Those daily forms of cooperation between people are now attenuated, mostly because of individualism and the loss of civic sense. Relations through which this civic sense, this minimum of caring for others that is essential to social life, could be expressed, have to be completely thought again. For these two philosophers, citizens' desire to participate in the promotion of the common good, to take charge of issues concerning education, health or the environment, must be upgraded.

However, this action can be realized only if citizens also learn, in their requests, to dissociate what belongs to the public and private spheres, in order to avoid formulating unjustified claims or escaping from their personal responsibility. Indeed, civil society is especially built with daily life gestures (joining groups, protecting the environment, refusing discriminations in one's neighborhood) as much as with political life participation. But it does not lead to miracle drug. Voluntary association in civil society could participate in equality promotion, in particular for groups who fight against poverty or ignorance. An adapted legal framework could assist this expression of solidarity. The State and civil society should therefore not be opposed. In some circumstances, the State can help strengthen association life, enabling citizens to contribute to it. Nevertheless, Kymlicka rightfully notes that we cannot expect some groups to do everything in

6   W. Kymlicka, 2002, "Civil Society and Government, A Liberal Egalitarian Perspective", in N. Rosenblum and R. Post, *Civil Society and Government, op. cit.*, pp. 81–2.

civil society. For example, it is not the essential role of religions to encourage citizenship, to preach democracy or to ban discriminations, even though, de facto, some of them are involved in these actions.[7] In that case, it would rather be the State's role to demand necessary corrections to civil society, especially when discriminations arise.

This wish to constitute an international civil society is however regarded nowadays with suspicion by all those who consider it as the ultimate Trojan horse of the "americanization" or "protestantization" of the world. In fact, if this civil society chooses the promotion of individual freedom, tolerance and sexual equality as its priority goals, it is viewed as corresponding first to the experience of a particular way of life. We may seek elsewhere than in the US the way in which global civil society could be understood. The experience of Eastern Europe could be of interest here.

In Eastern Europe, the establishment of a true civil society by the dissidents, who came to power after the communist period, was perceived like a priority. This was meant to prevent any form of return to dictatorship. To reach this objective, Churches, trade unions, political parties were restored. But the action aimed at the State too. Indeed, according to leaders like former President Vaclav Havel, the State continues to be the first entity where we can be citizens, which means truly involved, taking part freely to the decisions, fully responsible. But living well in a State supposes to be politically active, to work with other citizens and to be collectively determined to build with them a common fate. For Havel, this presupposes to understand correctly the contrast between life, which is by essence plural and various and is constituted in an autonomous way, and a post-totalitarian system which promote more and more conformity, uniformity and discipline – or, as Foucault said, "blind automatic reflexes".[8]

But is it enough? We can find nowadays a revitalization of ethnic, racial, religious, feminist, environmentalist or "alterglobalist" identities,

7   W. Kymlicka, 2002, *op. cit.*, p. 95.
8   Cf. V. Havel et al., 1985, *The Power of the Powerless: Citizens Against the State in Central-Eastern Europe*, New York: M.E. Sharpe.

which act like centrifugal forces in a world that is already rather divided. Their claims go across traditional dividing lines. They challenge Churches, trade unions, political parties and traditional institutions, without always being able to make credible counter-proposals. To avoid the growth of a "balkanization" of the world, the birth of a global civil society has never been so necessary.

Some of the practices aimed at its strengthening are very ancient. We can mention here the campaigns organized in 1775 for slavery abolition in America, or the role played by NGOs quite active all over the world, such as *Médecins Sans Frontières* or OXFAM. Amnesty International gathers now more than one million members in 162 countries. The liberation of opinion prisoners, weapons control or the fight against all forms of slavery are powerful ways to constitute this global civil society. These actions at the international level are essential, but if they are not supported by similar actions at the local level, they run the risk of being doomed to failure. In the 1970s, American communitarians wanted to promote a civic virtue revival as an antidote to the growing fragmentation of society. During the same period, the power of the State increased hugely, partly to meet citizens' expectations, but the control mechanisms of its action were not always implemented. As a result, the space of civil society has been limited. Its actors are now more in a defensive position than in a real possibility to take part in decisions.

Yet, human being is social by nature. The quality of politics, of economic activity and of culture is related to a large extent to the vitality of associative ability. In a liberal society, market and State must be counterbalanced by a civil society. The plurality of private initiatives and associative relations prevent societies from being too polarized by the economic sphere or by the State. But is it enough to provoke the production or the reproduction of loyalty, civism or political competence? The aporia is obvious: a civil society cannot exist without a State. In other words, the apology of a civil society which would be constituted only on an "anti-State" basis is totally inconsistent. Only a democratic State can create a democratic civil society, which will be able to train citizens to act beyond their self-interest, to develop gratuitously associative relationships, and to take care of political life with equity. But can this model be extrapolated at the world level?

II. Fostering the Creation of a World Government Guarantor of Global Civil Society

At first sight, the emergence of a global civil society is not for tomorrow. The lack of common values and permanent violence on the worldwide scale make global civil society rather look like a freedom oasis in a vast injustice desert, to use an Arab metaphor which shows the difference between *al-mujtama' al-madani* (civil society) and *al sahara* (desert).[9] The first reality is that nowadays, many people have to fight first for their own subsistence and to assure their own security. Hence, the claim for a global civil society made by demagogues like extremists in the West or fundamentalists in the East becomes dangerous. When the French "extreme-right" leader Jean-Marie Le Pen talks about "euro-globalization", it is not in a favorable way. A pertinent global civil society concept should be able to contain the violence of de-globalizing speeches, but also this kind of speech which undermines peace and common welfare.

Besides, in Iraq for instance, military interventions do not convert miraculously survivors of an authoritarian regime into supporters of a pacified global civil society. According to Ralf Dahrendorf, it is possible to create new political institutions, to write a constitution and to establish electoral laws in six months, but six years are necessary to introduce a sustainable economy, whereas 60 years are required to create a real civil society in a country.[10] That is even more the case at the global level. How can it be envisioned to constitute a global civil society without a

---

9   J. Keane, 2003, *Global Civil Society?, op. cit.*, p. 141.
10   R. Dahrendorf, 1990, "Has the East Joined the West?", *New Perspective Quarterly*, February, p. 42.

common memory, without a way to think universal history as a union between peoples?

The emergence of a global civil society implies more than the awareness of a necessary world citizenship. It presupposes:

- decentralizing the world political organization, so that new opportunities can be given to citizens to take their own responsibilities in its activities;
- socializing the economy, so that a greater diversity of public and private agents can get involved;
- putting religious models into perspective, to show that there are different ways to realize and support historical and cultural identities.

In my view, all of this cannot be accomplished without the impulsion of a political and administrative power, resource holder, capable of supporting financially those associative activities that are the most useful on the global scale. Even better organized, a transnational government could not do everything alone. The constitution of families, children education and essential protections concerning security or health are also based on voluntary association. These actions, in reality very ordinary, require an implicit understanding of what civil society can represent as a potentiality for taking care of oneself. Nowadays, many people stay without resource to think what could be a global civil society. Therefore, the latter will be settled only of it is supported by various national or transnational groups, sometimes localized or temporary, but connected with each other, and which open to a wide sense of global responsibilities. It does not only presuppose sensitivity to what is local, contingent or specific, but also to what the acknowledgement of a "good life in fair institutions" (P. Ricœur) involves, including sometimes in the detail.

In practice, the constitution of this global society runs up today against significant difficulties: isolation, the lack of freedom and of resources are disabling for the poor, as well as the persistence of hierarchal, patriarchal, sexist, racist or nationalist structures prevents the emergence of fundamental human rights. Above all, there are divergences on what a fair society would be at a global level. Quite easily, some international associations based on sharing and consensus manage to get organized and provoke people's adherence. But cyber-crime, human traffics and nationalisms also manage to get organized efficiently. It is therefore important not to let future civil society constitute itself completely on its own without increasing the kind of political adjustment which it might need. Thus, world government and civil society must be thought in reciprocity on the basis of values that are precise enough. Otherwise, they will be taken for the last trendy utopian view.

To that end, a world government would precisely have the responsibility to foster association forms based on moral consensus, to encourage the right and dignity of their members, and to care for equity, justice and transparency of procedures. In that case, global civil society could be a fermentation place and provide necessary remedies, for example vis-à-vis international institutions which have no effect on political or economic inequalities. But its role would not only to be a safeguard against State or market trespassing, or against the dysfunctions of these institutions. It could also consist in generating, through discussions free of constraints, in the "spheres of justice" describes by M. Walzer, those models that are the most acceptable for life on earth. Civil society would consequently be precious for a world government effectively able to decode signals that it would receive. Thus, the issue here is not the setting up of a civil society "against" a world government or against States. This stance, shared by "ultraliberals" who think that civil society must be apolitical and private, as well as by some "alterglobalists" who cannot manage to understand it as something else than a counter-position, is no longer sufficient. In its organization, civil society can contribute to the reforms of its groups when their functioning needs to be revised, in order to better take into account the cultural, social or economic evolutions necessary for the persons.

Nevertheless, it is important to emphasize that finally, a global civil society will not really be able to emerge without the attribution of a genuine global citizenship.

III. Implementing a Genuine Global Citizenship

Whatever some philosophers may say, the idea of global citizenship is not completely utopist.[11] The inhabitants of the Earth are more or less aware that they already participate to the building of a global civil society. Whether they like it or not, a part of their powers has been transferred to international institutions. As for now, this idea of world citizenship has not attracted philosophers' interest or people's enthusiasm. Yet, it has already a long history in practice.

This awareness that the individual is a citizen of the State he belongs to, but also of the universal community, originates in Greek stoicism. We could as well find other expressions of it in different cultural areas, in China for example. Imported in Rome, the world citizenship concept has been developed in the Renaissance and the Enlightenment, particularly in Kant's philosophy. After 1945, the question of world citizenship attribution received new answers. Movements such as Robert Sarrazac's "World citizens' human front" or Garry Davis' "International register for world citizens" were introduced for this purpose, respectively in 1945 and 1947. They endorsed the system created by the UN in three well-known texts, which are the Universal Declaration of Human Rights, the International Convention on Civic and Political Rights, and its additive protocol. These three documents specify that citizens are allowed to take part in public affairs management, directly or via their representatives, that they can vote and be elected by universal suffrage for determinate periods, have equal opportunity of access to public services, and can resort to the United Nations Human Rights Commission. This movement for the constitution of a world citizenship is far from being achieved. In 1987 for instance, the Brundtland report on environment and development drew attention to the setting up of a true world ecological citizenship.

---

11   Cf. D. Miller, 1999, "Bounded Citizenship", in K. Hutchings and R. Dannreuther, eds, *Cosmopolitan Citizenship*, London: Palgrave Macmillan, pp. 60–80.

Traditionally, two approaches confront each other on this issue. On the one hand, federalist or internationalist "maximalists" advocate a sovereignty transfer to a world government. On the other, "minimalists" prefer to bet on a progressive enlargement of citizenship starting from local or national communities, fearing that its too rapid creation at the international level might lead to the setting up of inappropriate, uniform criteria, in a society not enough aware of global stakes concerning peace, justice and development that would nevertheless require its establishment. It is obvious that in practice, institutional changes within States are now necessary to try to implement it. If global citizenship was merely based on equality between citizens, China and India, which represent one third of the world's population, would be in a dominant position in a global State. We should not forget that citizenship pertains to the attributions of a State which often determines alone its modalities. Imagining that all the inhabitants of the Earth participate in a single political entity of which they would be members runs up against difficulties hard to overcome: how could the most vulnerable citizens be able to evaluate, negotiate, accept or refuse proposals linked to the concrete use of this sovereignty? If the attribution of this citizenship implied rights to vote, to stand for election, to have freedom of expression, to act in a reasonable way for the common good, how could it work at a global level whereas many Sates have already difficulties to implement this in their own country?

In fact, we have to distinguish here two traditions concerning citizenship. The first one, more "republican", pays more attention to how it could contribute to the good running of the State. The other one, more "liberal", stresses that, on the contrary, a free citizenship is necessary to make governments responsible of their actions. These latest years, this second option has been more present: world citizenship expressed itself in spectacular actions like demonstrations for nuclear disarming or respect for the environment, humanitarian commitment or participation to world social forums. International institutions have started to integrate in their functioning the numerous expressions of this new kind of citizenship. In 1975 already, on the occasion of its 30th birthday, the UN had implemented an assembly of the world citizens. In 1992, a parallel World Forum took place in Rio, during the United Nations Conference on

Environment and Development, gathering more than 1400 associations. A number of NGO actions, like that of the CAMDUN for a democratic UN, or those of the International Federalist Movement, contributed to substantial reforms of international institutions, making them closer to citizens, reinforcing their representative character, providing opportunities to other NGOs, and encouraging each person to behave like a "world citizen" in his daily life.

However, the creation of a genuine citizenship at the international level implies more, in terms of rights but also duties. Different models are in fact effective: Europe makes the experience of the constitution of a citizenship which preserves national citizenships. United States inhabitants regard themselves as citizens of one State, while belonging to a federation. These two models show that the issues of citizenship, State sovereignty, territoriality or nationality tend to overlap. A world citizenship seems therefore to have a reasonable chance of being constituted only if it enables the expression of different political loyalties, rather than an unconditional submission to a world authority perceived in an authoritarian or too distant way. A psychological approach to world citizenship shows that this idea corresponds for the moment to the ethos of people who have a very cosmopolitan life and take actively part in the world community. Strategies to enable a greater number of inhabitants of the planet to evolve from a passive citizenship to a more active one deserve further studies. Many perceive world citizenship like an antidote to nationalisms, to religious fundamentalisms or to the devastating effects of the market, but few are able to imagine concretely its shape. Yet, without any link to a legal and political frame or to international codes of conduct, it has for now little chance to materialize, especially since it would presuppose loyalty to a global authority.

Anyway, as noted by Will Kymlicka, a world citizenship is not impossible, provided that personal aspirations and specific needs are seriously considered.[12] Human beings are neither foreign to each other on earth,

---

12   Cf. W. Kymlicka, 1995, *Multicultural Citizenship: A Liberal Theory of Minority Rights*, Oxford: Oxford University Press.

nor at the mercy of economic and political powers, as illustrated by the creation of the International Criminal Court, but they do not all share the same level of responsibility. That is why the question is that of the necessary arrangements within each State, so that the distribution of advantages related to the attribution of a world citizenship can be beneficial to everyone, not only to a minority prepared for his practice.

Eventually, it seems difficult to ignore the historically located nature of the present claim for a world citizenship. It expresses a modality of the state of the relations and desires of our planet's inhabitants, in this beginning of the 21st century. It testifies to the way some people consider themselves as participants to global stakes and how they wish to translate their open-mindedness to human universality. Specific rights granted on behalf of a world citizenship show the desire that its structures of inclusion and exclusion (including geographical belonging, nationality, age, gender, religion, health or every other criterion) would no longer fall into the competence of the traditional national State. Likewise, the wish to avoid every kind of dissolution in globalization shows that this world citizenship cannot be considered without a strong rehabilitation of politics. The essential effort may perhaps be undertaken at this essential level. Most certainly, a difficult task is before us, but as Tocqueville would say, it is not absurd to wish to be "powerful and free".[13]

---

13   A. De Tocqueville, 1963, *De la démocratie en Amérique*, Paris: Union Générale d'Editions, p. 372.

CHAPTER 12

Can Governance Structures and Civil-Corporate Partnerships Manage the Global Commons?

ZSOLT BODA

Introduction

The lack of a global government, on one hand, and the need to sustain the global commons, on the other, make necessary the development of different forms of governance. Some promising examples of civil-corporate partnerships, like the Marine or the Forest Stewardship Council, and the growing number of multi-stakeholder management standards and codes raise the hope that governance without government could be possible, and that social and ecological sustainability could be achieved through agreement among the different social actors, even without state regulation.

The paper raises the issues of *legitimacy* and *effectiveness* of those governance structures. The first relates to the normative foundations of those governance structures and partnerships. What are the conditions which make them worth of recognition by the society? Why shall we accept and recognize as legitimate the agreement made by private companies and non-elected social activists? Are they representing the common good or just a contingent harmonization of particular interests? How are relevant stakeholders to be selected in order to promote their participation in governance systems? These problems of the governance model are difficult to solve. The paper suggests that the Habermasian discourse ethics and its implications could serve as normative underpinnings to the legitimacy of governance.

The second, the effectiveness problem relates to the issue of whether those non-governmental regulatory institutions are able to impose the needed strict norms and to implement them properly. Indeed, voluntary codes sometimes impose rather soft norms and enforcement can also lack effectiveness. The paper suggests that the implications of discourse ethics may also have a positive influence on the effectiveness of governance structures.

1. Regulating the Global Market: The Problem

Ours is the age of economic globalization. Although a glimpse of globalization had already appeared at the end of the nineteenth century, current trends differ considerably from past ones. The "globalization" of the nineteenth century was marked by strong movements of capital, labor and goods within the "world economy" of that time, which included only discreet portions of the globe. However, today's globalization is characterized by an unprecedented degree of free and fast movement of capital around the whole globe, and by the global institutions of a financial superstructure. Capital has acquired predominance over other factors of production. Economic activities are coordinated by globally integrated financial and capital markets.

The dominant development paradigm – preached by the International Monetary Fund, the World Bank, the World Trade Organization and global business organizations – advises countries to liberalize international trade, assist foreign investors, and privatize national assets; and to cut back government expenditures, including assistance to small farmers and spending on health, education and environmental protection. Economies all around the world are being reshaped under the pressure of global markets: "market economy" is being created on a global scale. And this has fundamental social and environmental consequences as well. There is evidence that national economic policies based on liberalization benefit international business, multinational companies (MNCs) and global financial markets. However, their effects on people, local cultures and the environment are many times more than dubious.

We know perfectly from economic theory that markets and private businesses work for the benefit of the society only under specific conditions. Those conditions include the transparency of the market, fully informed actors, non-existence of external effects and public goods, non-existence of monopolistic tendencies and power abuses, etc. If those conditions are not met, the activity of the private companies will not, or not necessary, serve the common good of the society as such. Some actors (successful companies, and some consumers) might be satisfied, others (cheated consumers, abused workers, polluted environment, ruined local communities, etc.) might be worse-off; and the overall balance might be negative. Since in real life those conditions are not automatically fulfilled, a complex regulatory architecture is needed to create them. Usually this consists of laws and authorities (like competition authority, consumer protection authority, environmental authority, etc.) created by the government. The government is supposed to collect the social needs through democratic political procedures, balance them, and find a feasible policy solution to the clash of interests. The legitimacy of the government in democratic welfare states thus depends on both procedural elements (which means the respect of democratic and legal norms), and on the outcome (social welfare) it is supposed to promote.

We know, of course, that beside market failures, we have to cope with government failures as well. Government interventions do not necessarily serve the common good either. Imperfect information might distort governmental decisions; powerful lobbies may be able to influence the regulation; bureaucracy has a tendency to expand; taxes (which are supposed to serve as financial basis for implementing the common good) may overburden the economy and destroy competitiveness, etc. A possible panacea for this is the *governance* idea (Calame, 2003; Hermet, Kazancigil and Prud'homme, 2005). Public policy should develop a new openness towards non-state actors, such as companies and civil society organizations (CSOs). Indeed, in recent times, forms of public-private partnerships have been spreading, and civil society forms are also flourishing at different levels of the policy making. Moreover, private organizations and CSOs are increasingly contributing to the regulation of the market. Companies are developing forms of self-regulations (ethical institutions of the companies, industry codes, environmental and social management standards etc.), while CSOs are developing the means of civil regulation, like boycotts, ethical consumerism, corporate criticism, etc. (Boda and Gulyás, 2006). Nevertheless, despite new governance structure, on one hand, and private and civil regulatory efforts, on the other, the backbone of market regulation still consists of norm-setting and norm-enforcement by the state.

Now, the well-known problem is that we do not have such a reliable regulatory framework on the global level. Global government does not exist. Although a complex institutional setting has been developed after World War II (international organizations and a huge body of international law), mainly, but not exclusively under the auspices of the United Nations, the institutions of global governance are still very weak compared to the effectiveness of a democratic government. We can go even further: not only are the existing global regulatory institutions weak, but they have been further weakened by the dynamics of globalization. Manuel Castells (1997) speaks about "global disorder". He argues that while during the twentieth century, states made considerable efforts to reduce international anarchy through the creation of global institutions (like the United Nations) and the development of international law, the appearance, and the growing power, of different kind of organizations in the international arena undermine their legitimacy. These international organizations, which include first and foremost multinational companies, but also non-governmental organizations (like Amnesty International and Greenpeace), and even government-founded institutions, like the International Monetary Fund (which have started to follow their own policy agenda), have become a major force in the international arena. Although their performance in attracting resources and managing issues is rather remarkable, their activity puts into question the sovereignty and the intervening capabilities of states, and the institutions (organizations and law) created by states. Nowadays many interests and values are represented by many agents in the international arena. Multinational companies promote their own interests, while Greenpeace tries to influence governments, business and the people in the name of environmental values, and so on. In this situation a state becomes just one kind of actor in a cast of many – and not necessarily the most powerful one (Boda, 2002).

We have to admit that "the usually reliable backdrop of national law, the local legal order which tends to ensure a minimum level of compliance for domestic corporations in domestic markets, is missing in the international scene" (Donaldson, 1989, p. 31). For international business, global disorder means first and foremost an insufficient regulatory framework; and, as a consequence, good opportunities to follow exclusively their own self-interest. This means that *the common good is not protected on the international level.* This statement implies two problems: the "what" and the "how". What is exactly the global common good and how could it be protected? The first problem is about the meaning of the common good on a global level. In a democratic society we have some procedural rules to aggregate the particular interests into a common will and define somehow the general interest of the society. However, we do not have such political institutions and rules on the global level. Who should decide about the content of the global common good? It might be relatively easy to define some general values, principles and objectives which could constitute the global common good, like global justice, the eradication of poverty, democracy, human rights, a healthy environment, development and quality of life for everyone, etc. UN documents and the preamble of international treaties abound in such statements. However, the *application and implementation* of those principles generate debates and dissent. How should we fight against poverty: by accelerating globalization or by restricting it? What does democracy and human rights mean (see the debate on "Asian values", Sen, 1999)? Who should bear the costs of stopping climate change (see the fact that the US did not sign the Kyoto Protocol)? Is a trade-off between job creation and environmental quality ethically acceptable (see the outrage caused by the ideas of Lawrence Summers, chief economist of the World Bank at that time)?

Ethics is always about action and behavior: norms, principles and values should guide us in our doings and makings. In the global, intercultural context the relationship between the meaning and the application of moral norms is a major problem – as illustrated by the above examples.

In a given moral culture we may have a general understanding about the expected behavior that moral values and principles imply. However, the complexity of globalization and the multiplicity of moral cultures imply that many different interpretations of the same norm may co-exist in the world. Later in the paper I will come back to this problem of defining the common good in the international level. But now let us consider the second problem related to the protection of global common good. This is the "how" problem, which is, as demonstrated, closely linked to the "what" problem. But it has another aspect as well. Let us suppose that we can find an acceptable definition of the global common good. Then the question is: how to ensure it in reality, given that there is no global government? In other words, and linking the problem directly to the topic of this paper: How to regulate the global market, if the existing institutions (like international treaties and organizations) of global governance are not strong enough to create and protect the needed balance between variegated values and interests?

2. Private Actors in Global Governance: A Solution?

As we referred to it above, the term of governance suggests that different kinds of social actors work together in order to develop common norms and rules. The term itself is an old one; however, it has acquired a noticeable popularity during the past two decades. One of its first usages in the 1990s was "global governance", a concept popularized by the Brandt Commission on Global Governance. The Commission's often quoted definition of governance goes as follows: "Governance is the sum of the many ways individuals and institutions, public and private, manage their common affairs. It is a continuing process through which conflicting or diverse interests may be accommodated and co-operative action may be taken. It includes formal institutions and regimes empowered to enforce compliance, as well as informal arrangements that people and institutions either have agreed to or perceive to be in their interest" (Commission on

Global Governance, 1995, p. 38). Indeed, if no ultimate political authority exists on the level of the global market, somehow market actors should regulate themselves, as the definition suggests. Is this possible?

The American political scientist James Rosenau (1997) uses the concept of "turbulence in world politics" in order to designate the same problem that Castells calls global disorder. Turbulence means the weakening of the traditional sources of authority and power (that is, state sovereignty and inter-national institutions), and therefore a growing uncertainty and unpredictability in international affairs. However, Rosenau argues that new actors, like MNCs and CSOs are not bringing just "disorder" into the system; they are bringing a new order as well. While MNCs create the rules of the games of the global market, the activity of CSOs and the fact that individuals can be and are actors on the international scene helps strengthening moral norms, like human rights, international justice, ecological sensibility, and so. Indeed, a growing literature about "private authorities" (Hall and Biersteket, 2002; Haufler, 2001), "global policy networks", "governance structures and international regimes" (Krasner, 1982; Petschow, Rosenau and Weizsäcker, 2005), "partnerships" (Bendell, 2000), or the emerging "global civil society" (Keck and Sikkink, 1999) suggests that globalization is not void of multifaceted regulatory efforts which come from different sectors. Besides international organizations, business and CSOs are also active in setting and promoting norms.

However, it is very important to make a basic distinction between two types of governance or regulatory systems. One type of regulation is intended to solve a coordination problem, while the other a collective action problem (Stein, 1982). The coordination problem means the lack of accepted regulation, where there is no distributional problem. Therefore once a regulation is somehow accepted, we can reasonable expect that the actors will follow the rules. The classical example is that of the traffic rules. Without those rules the traffic might be anarchic. However, if we decide that cars should fare on the right side and so about other rules as well, we can reasonably expect that drivers will – in most of the cases – follow the rules, because this serves their interests as well reducing the risks of driving. A collective action problem – or as Stein (1982) calls it, a collaboration problem – means that the distribution of a public good (or "bad") is at stake. In a collective action problem, incongruence exists between the common good and individual incentives: individually each of the actors is motivated to follow his/her self-interest, but this leads to a destruction of the collective good. The classical example is environmental protection: the best outcome for me is that I do not contribute to the costs of environmental protection, but the others do. In this way the environment is saved, and I do not have the bear the costs. However, the others have exactly the same rationale to follow – and the environment is destroyed.

Of course, most of the problems are not so straightforwardly either coordination or collective action problems. We should rather take them as the two extremes of a continuum, on which real life problems show more the characteristics of coordination or collective action problems. Actually, traffic rules are not so clearly only about coordination: sometimes we break the traffic rules, because, say, we are on a hurry, and we can do it relatively safely if we can trust the others will follow the rules. Traffic offers a lot of examples of collective action problems. Conversely, collective action problems sometimes bear at least partly the characteristics of coordination problems. Mancur Olson in his seminal work (Olson, 1965) pointed to the existence of "privileged groups" whose members do not have the same power, and where the most powerful actors may be both capable of and interested in securing the collective good on their own expenses.

Still, it is useful to differentiate between these two basic cooperation problems, because their logic is different and this has implications for real-life situations. Indeed, much of the "private regulation" praised in the literature (see for instance Haufler, 2001) happening in the global economy belongs to the first order of things. Companies, business associations, banks, accounting firms are apparently able to set the rules of quality management, commerce, communication, financing, assurance at the international level, without the necessary intervention of the states. The global economy is able to regulate itself to some extent; especially when it comes to solving coordination problems – that is, setting the terms for business. This certainly is the collective interests of businesses, but individual companies are also motivated to contribute to and respect the rules of the game, otherwise they are shortly driven out of business, since nobody will trade with them.

However, the real regulatory challenge is about collective action problems. Let us come back to the issue of environmental protection. The lack of global government means that companies are able to look for places where weak local regulation allows them to save on protection costs. Moreover, corporations with huge power are even able to influence the regulation in poor countries in a direction that fits their interests. Indeed, in the 1990s many developing countries relaxed their regulation concerning mining and forestry in order to attract foreign investors (Sampat, 2003). Although Vogel (1997) argues that the environmental performance of delocalized production is higher than the average environmental performance of the local companies in poor countries, i.e. that globalization has a positive environmental effect, it is also true that the environmental performance of delocalized production is generally lower than what would be required by the home country norms. It is generally recognized that globalization provides a low-cost ecological space for MNCs, and therefore the overall environmental balance of economic globalization is certainly negative (Rosenau, 2005).

The problem of labor standards is somehow similar to that of environmental regulation. Through outsourcing MNCs have the capacity to easily move production to places where the costs of labor are low. They are also able to generate hard competition among subcontractors. All this does certainly not help the protection of labor rights and labor standards. Indeed, many anecdotic evidences point to the fact that MNCs and/or their subcontractors – especially in the apparel, the shoe, and the toy industries – abuse the workers, who are generally young, uneducated women (Klein, 1999). It would be good to have a general and systematic account about the labor practices of MNCs, however, Sethi (2003) argues that we do not have such an analysis. His own estimation is that no more than 10% of the MNCs in developing countries do respect the labor standards of the given country. The others use their force and influence to bully regulation and – simply speaking – exploit the workers for their own benefit.

The similarity between environmental and labor standards of the production is that individual companies are not interested in raising their environmental or social performance, even if collectively the society – and even the companies themselves – would benefit from a higher performance. We can generally state that considering the interests, rights and claims of the stakeholders and respecting ethical norms might easily become a collective action problem, because doing so might be too costly for an individual company. Individual incentives are lacking – unless some "selective incentives" (Olson, 1965) motivate the companies. Now, it seems that public pressure, criticism coming from the media and CSOs and the endangered reputation of corporations might work as "selective incentives". But given the nature of collective action problems and the high possibility of free-riding, the governance problem does still exist. The question still holds: how to set and implement effective regulation in the global economy for collective action problems, such as environmental protection and labor standards?

Well, many of the existing governance structures do indeed address such issues. I will now focus only on those governance structures which deal with collective action problems of the global economy. I will use the term "code" for the regulatory efforts present in globalization, because codes are a typical and widespread manifestation of "private governance" in the economy. For the sake of this study, a code is any kind of standard, norm, or a collection of norms which aims at addressing an ethical issue. We may differentiate between the governance structures and regulatory efforts according to their source:

- *company codes* worked out by individual firms, which may or may not have included stakeholder dialogues;
- *codes of business associations*;
- codes promoted by *international organizations*, which may or may not be based on a partnership approach with other types of organizations;
- *multi-stakeholder codes*, that are based on the cooperation of different stakeholders, including firms, trade unions and/or CSOs.

The rest of the paper is concerned with the last category. My objective is to demonstrate that multi-stakeholder governance structures that include CSOs are a powerful source of global regulation: they are both legitimate and relatively effective. However, let us first make some short comments on the three other categories.

Company codes. It is widely recognized that since the mid 90's many large corporations have adopted ethical codes. This phenomenon is certainly a response to the growing criticism of business and alter-globalization movement and the serious scandals that have been made public about the activities of MNCs (see Klein, 1999). Many company codes have indeed been elaborated in the aftermath of a major public relations disaster. This is one of the main arguments against company codes: that most of the times they only come after a scandal has happened. In other words, without the media and CSOs, or trade unions which make the corporate behavior public, companies are reluctant to face their global responsibility. Another argument is that company codes reflect the positions and interests of the companies and they do not imply very strict rules upon the firm. Indeed, a study demonstrated that only 23–46% of company codes refer to the basic labor standards of the International Labour Organisation (ILO), like no forced labor, no child labor, no discrimination on the workplace, or freedom of association (Jenkins, 2002). Another problem is that company codes usually do not indicate the way they are enforced or monitored: it is up to the company to take or not to take seriously its own code. There is a fear that without external pressure – media and CSOs –, company codes remain only dead papers. Certification by third party is still an exception, not the rule. Pressure of the public might play an important role in forcing companies to develop and then enforce ethics codes. However, public pressure is effective only in the case of well-known brands and companies producing consumption goods. Nike, McDonald's or Shell could easily be hit by scandals and boycotts. But what about unbranded mining, fishing, and logging companies?

Codes of business association. The same study cited above argues that the codes of business associations are even weaker than those of individual companies, because they need to be accepted by the greatest number of

companies in the organizations concerned (Jenkins, 2002, p. 18). The already
mentioned criticisms hold here as well: most of the time the codes come
only *ex post*, and compliance is neither monitored, nor sanctioned.

Codes of international organizations. The OECD's Guidelines for
Multinational Enterprises, and the ILO's Tripartite Declaration of
Principles Concerning Multinational Enterprises (both codes were originally adopted in the 1970s), are two early examples of such international
codes. Given that they are intergovernmental codes, one would expect
them to have "teeth", to have some kind of enforcement mechanism.
Indeed, the OECD has established a complex institutional arrangement
which allows the application of the code to individual cases. In each
OECD member country there is a National Contact Point where trade
unions, CSOs or any stakeholder can file a complaint against a company
if it violated the OECD principles. The system and the working of NCPs
have been gradually developed and the code itself has been revised several
times. However, we still cannot say that the OECD has a strong and effective enforcement mechanism, partly because the means of the organization
are restricted in terms of taking actions against the violators.

The problem of the ILO is that it cannot make investigations at
individual companies. The organization (more precisely its predeces-
sor) was created at the beginning of the 20th century, where the main
concern of the states was to make sure that none of them was getting
unfair competitive advantage over the others by relaxing labor standards.
Therefore the mission of the ILO is to harmonize labor standards among
nations and to monitor compliance at the state level. Even there the ILO
has no power whatsoever to bind states to sign the basic ILO treaties,
or to respect them once they have signed it. What the ILO can do is to
"name and shame", that is, to exert some symbolic pressure on the states
(see Weisband, 2000).

A general problem of the OECD and the ILO codes might be formulated as follows. Seemingly they apply a top-down approach which
resembles the regulatory activities of governments inside their jurisdiction.
The codes contain formal norms and signatory states and their companies
are supposed to respect them. However, neither the OECD, nor the ILO

has real power to enforce their codes. They imitate legal regulation without its most basic feature: the enforcement power. This is certainly one of the reasons why international organizations are increasingly moving towards the *partnership approach*. The UN Global Compact is already deliberately based on the partnership approach. Although some elements of the top-down approach still remained, since the UN declared the nine basic principles of the Global Compact which should be acknowledged and promoted by companies, the adherence to the principles is voluntary and individual companies should develop on their own the specific means and projects through which they put the principles into practice. The partnership approach is a basic feature of multi-stakeholder codes as well. Now, if apparently the company codes, the codes of business association and the codes of international organizations are only insufficient means to provide an ethical regulation, can we expect something more from the partnership approach?

3. Civil – Corporate Partnerships: Merits and Limitations

In his study about the presence of basic ILO standards in codes, Jenkins (2002, 18) argues that "multi-stakeholder codes [...] are likely to be more demanding than either business association or individual codes since they are the result of negotiations with other stakeholders such trade unions or NGOs, which [...] are likely to make more stringent demands in terms of what they expect from codes". Indeed, 65–95% of the multi-stakeholder codes include the basic ILO standards. Now, evidence suggests that NGOs play a crucial role in the ethical regulation global business. Above we said that "selective incentives" represented by media scandals have certainly contributed to corporate code-writing activity. We know that from the Nestlé baby-milk case through the Shell Nigeria-scandal to the child-labor scandals of the footwear industry, NGOs have played an important part in raising negative publicity and campaigning against corporations. Now we learn that the NGOs participation in adopting codes also has a positive effect: the code will address more in depth the ethical issues at hand.

Indeed, theorists argue that in the post-modern era the civil movements are more and more motivated by inherently ethical values. According to the well-known post-materialization thesis of Ronald Inglehart (Inglehart, 1997), values in developed societies have moved from the so-called materialistic values (economic welfare, physical security) toward post-materialistic ones (quality of life, valuable human relations, self-expression, self-realization, responsibility towards the world etc.). Inglehart also argues that CSOs are paradigmatically representing those post-materialistic orientations: while people in Western countries have lost trust in political parties, political institutions and also business, the trust in civil society has increased dramatically during the 1990s (Inglehart, 1997, p. 296). This has an effect on CSOs as well: while the NGOs of the "modern society" might have well represented the interests of a given social group, the CSOs of today's "postmodern society" are typically organized around ethical values.

For instance Eder (1995) argues that the green movement is more and more values-driven and fuels a discourse about the "good society". Or let us consider the consumer protection movement, which has traditionally represented the interests of the consumers, and now moves towards the ethical consumerism, and, for instance, embraces fair trade – this shift is apparent even in the case of classical consumer protection organizations, like Consumers International (see Boda and Gulyás, 2006). Does all this mean that civil society and its organizations are the ultimate guardians of ethical values? Not necessarily. First, obviously CSOs are representing their own organizational interests as well. Second, they are obviously driven by the world views, commitments, visions of their members and leaders, which are, by definition, partial world views and commitments, even if they aspire to represent higher, or even universal values. The two cases described by Ali (2000) illustrate the point: in both cases a conflict emerged between environmental CSOs which opposed uranium mining projects and indigenous people who did not necessarily reject the projects as such, and were interested in job creation. It is difficult to say whether the environmental values propagated by the greens have automatically higher ethical stance than the social problems of local people.

Why shall we than accept and recognize as legitimate the agreement made by private companies and non-elected social activists? Are they representing the common good or just a contingent harmonization of particular interests? Critics, like Guy Hermet, indeed argue that the concept of *gouvernance*, which implies the cooperation and partnership of different types of social actors, is a very problematic one (Hermet, Kazancigil and Prud'homme, 2005). It builds upon the inclusion of stakeholders, but how are they selected and their representatives elected? New stakeholder groups can always be presented, or even created, and negotiations can be prolonged for the eternity, because new groups may present themselves as stakeholders. This is an arbitrary process of stakeholder selection, where those with greater resources have more chance to influence the policy outcome. In other cases stakeholders are somehow co-opted by the actors, but doesn't this lead to some kind of corporatist model? And isn't the whole partnership model about the privatization of the common good, since particular social actors are shaping the agenda, among them private organizations (corporations)? The partnership concept is based on negotiation, but who is the final decision maker? Negotiations can last for years if nobody is in a position to make decisions.

These criticisms have, of course, validity. But let us not forget, that there is a fundamental difference between talking about governance in the framework of the nation state and in a global context. True, the governance model is spreading inside the traditional political institutions as well – this may yield some benefit (growing flexibility or greater legitimacy of the public policy) and may have some problems as well (emptying democratic institutions, creating new power centers and institutionalizing the interests of some powerful social actors, like corporations). If I am right, Guy Hermet is first of all worried because of these new developments inside the democratic political institutions. He may or may not be right. But here we are talking about governance at the global level, where the problem is that there are no regulatory institutions which could be weakened by the governance or partnership model. It is an imperfect model, granted, but there is no other which could effectively regulate the global business. Another counterargument to the above criticisms might be that in the global risk-society (Beck), the risks associated with global business have also an arbitrary distribution in space and time. Hungary can be affected by GMOs, so why couldn't a Hungarian green or consumer organization join a global campaign against the American GMO-policy and the activity of US-based biotech companies? We live in a world of growing complexity, and governance models could be ways of managing this complexity.

Still, the criticisms of the partnership model should be taken seriously. However, there is no institutional framework under which the problems of representation, negotiation and decision making could be solved – the partnership model is itself a proposed solution to this lacuna. The only possibility is to follow some procedural rules when creating a partnership. Those rules could be the rules of discourse ethics, proposed by Jürgen Habermas and Karl-Otto Apel.

4. Discourse Ethics: A Foundation of Legitimacy and Effectiveness?

According to Karl-Otto Apel (1990), discourse ethics implies that only those norms that meet (or could be reasonably presumed to meet) the approval of all concerned in a real, rational debate can claim to be valid. The debate should be as close as possible to the "ideal communication situation" which is free of domination and argumentative inequality, and in which participants do not act in a strategic way but perform a real communicative action. Whereas in strategic action one actor seeks to *influence* the behavior of another by means of threatening sanctions or offering carrots, in communicative action one actor seeks to *motivate* another *rationally* by relying on the persuasive power of arguments (Habermas, 1990, p. 63). Ideally, the validity of speech lies in its *intel-*

ligibility (valid meaning), *truthfulness* (subjective authenticity), factual *truth* and *correctness* (normative justifiability).

The principles of discourse ethics imply that the actors should enter into fair negotiations with each other, and should involve all the parties concerned, or if it is physically not possible, should make a cognitive effort to consider their interests as well. Inclusion in practice could mean that companies should bear some costs of organizing the necessary stakeholder dialogues. This is not an unrealistic requirement: for instance the Aarhus Convention on public participation in environmental decision-making also prescribes "the empowerment of the stakeholders". Crediting the formal right to participate might not be enough, because resource-poor stakeholder might not be able to participate. Openness is a basic value which makes external accountability possible. That is, any partnership should be based on a fair negotiation among the participants, plus an open communication with the external world: a small and a large circle. The larger circle, the public opinion should serve as a final check for the agreement made by the parties. So that the "what" they define represents indeed an acceptable interpretation of the common good. In this way the lack of political legitimacy of the civil organizations and companies will be replaced by an ethical legitimacy. Their actions will become legitimate through the process of fair, valid discourse.

The normative foundations of discourse ethics have been reinvented in the theory of discursive or deliberative democracy (see Dryzek, 1990; Fishkin, 1991), which has the virtue of proposing a starting point for developing institutional solutions and arrangements. Indeed, new institutional inventions promoting public participation in decision-making, such as social forums or citizens' juries, have been spreading in the Western world in the past decade. The respect for the principles of discourse ethics might create the necessary legitimacy of the governance structure. Will it help its effectiveness? We should bear in mind that effectiveness is the biggest problem in global governance, since there is no ultimate political instance which could sanction non-compliance. Besides, it is also a problem in civil-corporate partnerships. The UN Global Compact has been severely criticized for its allegedly poor results in bringing change in corporate behavior. If we compare the effectiveness of multi-stakeholder governance structures to that of a government authority inside a country, we will certainly be disappointed. True, we will be disappointed also, if we compare it to the effectiveness of voluntary self-regulations of the coordination type. Business is able to monitor and sanction if it comes to, say, the abuse of ISO quality management standards. Why is it not so effective in terms of ethical standards? Again, because these bring about collective action problems.

So the effectiveness of governance structures is a delicate question and certainly needs more research. However, some evidences indicate that openness, inclusion and communication can help also the effectiveness of governance structures. Consider the two examples of the Forest Stewardship Council and the Marine Stewardship Council (for a description and analysis see Bendell and Murphy, 2000 and Fowler and Heap, 2000). The FSC is about institutionalizing sustainable forestry practices, while the MSC promotes sustainable fishing. Both the FSC and the MSC have developed standards and norms to be followed by the industry, and also a labeling scheme. Both of them were initiated by the World Wide Fund for Nature (WWF), but represent quite different approaches. The FSC is based on a "bottom up" approach, and inclusion: the most important stakeholders have been invited to join the FSC and its activity has been based on the deliberation and cooperation of the parties. The MSC was designed as a joint project of the WWF and Unilever, the market leader company in fish products. Other companies were invited to join, but after that the WWF and Unilever had already developed the MSC scheme, so the other potential parties could only "take it or leave it". Now, analysts say FSC seems to be more effective, just because the members consider the initiative as their own (Fowler and Heap, 2000). Of course, the general effectiveness problems we mentioned earlier arise here as well: the FSC cannot do anything with those businesses that do not join – for instance Japanese companies are not interested in the FSC.

Other factors than the structure of the governance model can also influence effectiveness. One could argue, for instance, that deforestation has been solidly established as a major environmental problem to which people are generally sensitive, while the problem of over-fishing has not got so much attention in public discourse. Therefore companies in the forestry industry are more vigilant of the public opinion and of their image than fishing companies. This is undeniably an important question. However, in this paper I am not so much interested in the sources of power CSOs have in trying to change the world (on this, see Arts, 2003), but in the normative foundations of their activity in regulating business. My argument is that solid normative foundations might have a positive effect on the effectiveness of the regulatory activity.

Breitmeier, Young and Zürn (2006) arrive at a similar result in their analysis about international environmental regimes. They have conducted an extensive and quantitative analysis of 172 "regime elements" of 23 international regimes, and they have been primarily interested in whether there are some institutional features (regime design) which increase the effectiveness of international governance structures. In fact, they have not been able to identify such features. But from our point of view, an interesting result of their analysis is that there is no decision-making rule which would have proven to be more effective than the others: regimes using the consensus or the unanimity rule are just as effectives as regimes built around the majority vote. Now, a general faith (and a general argument against discourse ethics) is that reaching a consensus is long and difficult, therefore not a very effective process. However, consensus creates a feeling of identification among the parties which increases the effectiveness of the regime in question. Again, let us not forget that we are talking about international regimes, where there is no final authority to enforce compliance. The perceived legitimacy (normative rightness and acceptability) of a regulatory framework indeed contributes to its effectiveness.

Conclusion

The regulation of global economy is still an unmet challenge. We know that without proper regulatory institutions, market activity has disastrous effects on the well-being of stakeholders and ecological systems. However, there are no effective regulatory institutions in the present global economy; therefore the global commons might be endangered by corporate activities. Civil society organizations play an important and ever increasingly essential role in regulating business. Evidence shows that governance structures in which CSOs are participating are more demanding in terms of their requirements and prescriptions – in contrast to many ethics codes developed by business, which are mere window-dressing even in terms of their content (not to mention the implementation problems).

However, governance models based on the cooperation of civil organizations and companies might have legitimacy problems. After all, neither the civil activists, nor the corporation leaders have been elected by the public – so who are they to make decisions about the public good? Some researchers have been interested by the sources of power that CSOs have in influencing business. In this paper I have been rather interested by the normative foundations of governance models. My argument is that discourse ethics and the theory of deliberative democracy may serve as normative foundations for those semi-public, semi-private governance structures. Participatory decision-making should be a basic model for the global economy. It has the merit of helping defining the meaning of global commons and the practical implications those definitions might bring about. Solid normative foundations might solve the legitimacy problems of governance models. Moreover, an institutional arrangement which is well-established in normative, ethical terms might even prove to be more effective in reaching its objectives.

References

Ali, S.H., 2000, "Shades of Green: NGO Coalitions, Mining Companies and the Pursuit of Negotiating Power", in Bendell, J., ed., *Terms of Endearment: Business, NGOs and Sustainable Development*, Greenleaf Publishing, pp. 79–95.

Apel, K.-O., 1990, "Is the Ethics of the Ideal Communication Community a Utopia? On the Relationship between Ethics, Utopia, and the Critique of Utopia", in Benhabib, S., and Dallmayr, F., eds, *The Communicative Ethics Controversy*, Cambridge, MA: MIT Press, pp. 23–59.

Arts, B., 2003, *Non-State Actors in Global Governance. Three Faces of Power*, Preprints aus der Max-Planck-Projektgruppe Recht der Gemeinschaftsgüter, Bonn, 2003/4.

Bendell, J., ed., 2000, *Terms of Endearment: Business, NGOs and Sustainable Development*, Greenleaf Publishing.

—— and Murphy, D.F., 2000, "Planting the Seeds of Change: Business-NGO Relations on Tropical Deforestation", in Bendell, J., ed., 2000, *op. cit.*, pp. 65–78.

Boda, Z., 2002, "Globalization and International Ethics", in Zsolnai, L., ed., *Ethics in the Economy. Handbook of Business Ethics*, Oxford: Peter Lang, pp. 233–58.

—— and Gulyás, E., 2006, "The Ethical Consumerism Movement", *Interdisciplinary Yearbook of Business Ethics*, Vol. 1, pp. 137–50.

Breitmeier, H., Young, O.R., and Zürn, M., 2006, *Analyzing International Environmental Regimes: From Case Study to Database*, Cambridge, MA: MIT Press.

Calame, P., 2003, *La démocratie en miettes. Pour une révolution de la gouvernance*, Paris: Descartes et Cie.

Castells, M., 1997, *The Information Age: Economy, Society and Culture – Vol. II: The Power of Identity*, Blackwell Publishers.

Commission on Global Governance, 1995, *Our Global Neighborhood – The Report of the Commission on Global Governance*, Oxford: Oxford University Press.

Donaldson, T., 1989, *The Ethics of International Business*, New York: Oxford University Press.

Dryzek, J., 1990, *Discursive Democracy*, Cambridge: Cambridge University Press.

Fishkin, J., 1991, *Democracy and Deliberation: New Directions of Democratic Reforms*, New Haven: Yale University Press.

Fowler, P., and Heap, S., 2000, "Bridging Troubled Waters: the Marine Stewardship Council", in Bendell, J., ed., 2000, *op. cit.*, pp. 135–48.

Habermas, J., 1990, "Discourse Ethics: Notes on a Program of Philosophical Justification", in Benhabib, S., and Dallmayr, F., eds, 1990, *op. cit.*, pp. 60–110.

Hall, R.B., and Biersteker, T.J., eds, 2002, *The Emergence of Private Authority in Global Governance*, Cambridge: Cambridge University Press.

Haufler, V., 2001, *Public Role for the Private Sector: Industry Self-Regulation in a Global Economy*, Washington: Carnegie Endowment for International Peace.

Hermet, G., Kazancigil, A. and Prud'homme, J.-F., 2005, *La gouvernance. Un concept et ses applications*, Paris: Karthala.

Inglehart, R., 1997, *Modernization and Postmodernization – Cultural, Economic and Political Changes in 43 Societies*, Princeton: Princeton University Press.

Jenkins, R., 2002, "The Political Economy of Codes of Conduct", in Jenkins, R., Pearson, R., and Seyfang, G., eds, *Corporate Responsibility and Labor Rights*, Earthscan, pp. 13–30.

Keck, M., and Sikkink, K., 1998, *Activists Beyond Borders. Advocacy Networks in International Politics*, London: Cornell University Press.

Klein, N., 1999, *No Logo*, New York: Picador.

Krasner, S.D., 1982, "Structural Causes and Regime Consequences: Regimes as Intervening Variables", *International Organisation*, 36 (2), pp. 185–205.

Olson, M., 1965, *The Logic of Collective Action*, Cambridge: Cambridge University Press.

Petschow, U., Rosenau, J.N., and Weizsäcker, E.U., eds, 2005, *Governance and Sustainability*, Greenleaf Publishing.

Rosenau, J.N., 1997, Along the Domestic–Foreign Frontier. Exploring Governance in a Turbulent World, Cambridge: Cambridge University Press.

—— 2005, "Globalisation and Governance: Sustainability between Fragmentation and Integration", in Petschow, U., et al., eds, 2005, *op. cit.*, pp. 20–38.

Sampat, P., 2003, "Scrapping Mining Dependence", in *State of the World 2003*, World Watch Institute.

Sen, A., 1999, "Human Rights and Asian Values", in Rosenthal, J.H., ed., *Ethics and International Affairs*, Washington: Georgetown University Press.

Sethi, P., 2003, *Setting Global Standards: Guidelines for Creating Codes of Conduct in Multinational Corporations*, John Wiley and Sons.

Stein, A.A., 1982, "Coordination and Collaboration: Regimes in an Anarchic World", in S.D. Krasner, *International Regimes*, London: Cornell University Press, pp. 115–40.

Vogel, D., 1997, *Trading Up. Consumer and Environmental Regulation in a Global Economy*, Cambridge, MA: Harvard University Press.

Weisband, E., 2000, "Discursive Multilateralism: Global Benchmarks, Shame, and Learning in the ILO Labor Standard Monitoring Regime", *International Studies Quarterly*, 44, pp. 643–66.

CHAPTER 13

Legal Aspects of the Respect for Environmental Common Goods: On What Foundations Does it and Should it Rely?

ISABELLE CADET

Introduction

The major interrogation about the foreseeable juridical foundations for "Environmental Common Goods" introduces this preliminary question: under international or national law, does the concept of "Environmental Goods" have meaning today? The immediate and simplest answer is to acknowledge that the very association of these terms is a juridical oxymoron. In legal terms, the word "goods" belongs to a precise terminology: it signifies anything a human being can appropriate. All things, then, are not necessarily goods. These other things are common in nature (*res communes*), as defined by article 714 of the French Civil Code. They include air, sunlight, the sea, and running water.

Furthermore, goods can only be classified according to their assimilation into the private or public sphere. In the French language, the concept of "environment" designates the totality of natural or artificial elements affecting human life, without reference to public or private. This chameleon-like idea (Prieur, 2004) embodies the natural sciences, ecology, natural resources, biological balance, biodiversity, city planning, landscape, regional development, rural life, agriculture, national landmarks, heritage, natural environment, and the setting and quality of life. Environmental law reflects this eclecticism. Although it is known mainly for risk prevention and repressing activities that cause extreme environmental damage, it assumed greater status in the eyes of the French people when the *Code de l'environnement* (environmental code) was enacted in 2000, bringing new weight and coherency to the laws. It is a discipline that essentially crosses both disciplines (civil, penal, administrative) and borders. And if environmental law represents a new subset of regulations, then the expression "environmental goods" is an emergent category, if it is one at all.

The investigation of the legal foundation of this new form of goods or law is obviously in its infancy. We must remember that the notion of "environmental goods" comes from management and economic sciences, which might explain both the varying opinion on which legal system applies here and the different foundational hierarchies. Yet we find the concept of "Global Common Goods" in a good many international agreements, in which a demand for absolute adherence to regulations on the part of the users and the obligation to work towards an equal repartition of goods that might benefit all, call for efforts to be made to create a public ecological order.

To this end, the United Nations Development Program (UNDP) is suggesting a new global approach to world crises – be they financial disasters, emergency humanitarian situations, global warming, the emergence of new diseases or the ever-increasing gap between rich and poor – the cause of which may be found in the quantitative insufficiency of "Global Common Goods". Water – the use of which has already been codified by regulation, public markets and international agreements – is labeled the "Heritage of Humanity". In more general human rights terms, the right to a healthy environment is now almost tantamount to the right to live, or quality of life.

This subject matter is so broad that it sometimes comes into conflict with the right to private property, an essential condition of freedom that is also considered to be an inalienable and sacred human right. Depending on the prevailing ideology, politics or idea of law, perspectives vary hugely. More specifically, this chapter will concentrate on the legal nature of our foremost natural resource – water – on which the human survival will depend in the decades ahead. The debate will focus on the various uses of water – on its production, circulation and distribution – that represent the stakes at hand not only in terms of quality (health) but also quantity (access to water, competition, and allocation).

All the major environmental pollution disasters – be they accidental or criminal – share the common vector of water: acid rains, eutrophication, heavy metal pollution (such as mercury – Minamata, 1966), disposal of waste water into rivers, marine oil slicks (Erika, 2006), etc. Another, more scientific reason justifies this choice: there is an extensive body of legislative work on this subject, and the intellectual construction of a universal environmental law that meets human and citizen rights via a transversal study of water has been successfully completed.

The symbolism of water in management models should not be left out of a consideration of universal needs. D. Desjeux (1985) reminds us that from a physiological point of view, living creatures need little water to exist; on the contrary, however, animal and vegetable products and industry consume large and ever increasing quantities of it. When it comes to the issue of access to drinking water, the collective imagination, hugely influenced by NGOs, focuses almost entirely on the power of international government organizations. The first paragraph of the 10 December 2003 Declaration of Rome states that "more than 1.4 billion people still have no access whatsoever to drinking water and more than 2.4 billion have no access to sanitary services, resulting in 30,000 deaths daily caused by diseases related to a lack of clean water or adequate sanitary services". And yet, the U.N. declared that the 1980s would be the Decade of Water and Sanitation (1981–1991), aiming to provide universal access to water by the year 2000 ....

The legal categorization of "Blue Gold" is an essential move in the attempt to prevent any iteration of that 21st century menace – the "Water War" – by determining both its legal status and the system of management appropriate to that status. This vital issue provides a window through which we can experience not only a redefinition of property, but also the increasing importance of international human rights. Water is legally defined in a host of ways. In the interest of being precise and getting quickly to the heart of the matter, we will be using the original French legal stance as a reference point. In environmental matters, this system is greatly influenced by EU law, a mixture of hard and soft law, and particularly by a resolutely modern conception of human rights.

It won't hurt for once: considering the close relationship between law and its neighboring disciplines, it would not be unreasonable to elaborate here juridical reasoning through a tripartite structure, especially since the relevant laws evolved in such a way: *water is not a good; water is a good; water is more than a good*. The following demonstration will thus comprise three parts: water as a "common thing", the common heritage of mankind (I); water as a private or global good (II); and water as a universal human right (III).

I. Water as a "Common Thing", the Common Heritage of Mankind

The term "common thing" still prevails: it justly implies that water is for the use of all (A). But as France realized the scarcity and the vital nature of some natural resources in the second half of the 20th century, it called for the international community to follow its example and, for the first time ever, qualify water as the "Common Heritage of Mankind" (B).

I.A. A Common Thing for the Use of All

Traditionally, Roman law placed all environmental goods – such as stream or sea water and air – in the category of *res communes*, because common things exist in such plentiful quantities that anyone may set apart what he needs without depriving anybody else. This negative definition implies that the exclusive – and to a greater extent absolute – use of some natural resources is forbidden.

Water use is subject to an immense number of regulations. In France, the modernized Civil Protection law took on the cause of access to drinking water. Article L.1321–1 of the French Code of Public Health states that "any person offering water for human consumption has to ensure that this water complies with sanitary regulations". Running water and source access are subject to covenants regarding right-of-way, which apply not to landowners but to the land itself (see articles 640 to 652 of the *Code Civil*, article 215–1 of the *Code de l'environnement* or articles 152–14 to 152–23 of the *Code Rural*). Water may be used under the condition that it is returned to its natural state of purity. It cannot be overdrawn: excessive irrigation is punishable by law. All such texts are ways to control water use and are derived from the original definition given by the *Code Civil* (article 714), and thus exclude any kind of human appropriation. Trail judges are authorized to take injunctive measures to stop temporary loss of use; they can then decide on any appropriate compensatory means if adjacent owners claim little or no access to water or if environmental pollution, whatever its cause, wrecks irreversible damage.

Preventative measures have come into being as well. Water use is closely monitored and its abstraction regulated, be it for industrial or agricultural use. Legal limits have been established for surface water, underground water, seawater and aquatic environments. As well as access rules, declarations of public interest and prescriptions for the respect of aquatic ecosystems, there is now extensive waste and water quality monitoring to combat pollution. In terms of a global evaluation of the vulnerability of manufacturing systems and water distribution, health and safety regulations have been enforced that cover water for human consumption. In order to achieve such objectives, various international agreements were made, particularly the EU Water Framework directive (23 October 2000) which aims to achieve a "sound ecological state" of water in all aquatic environments, including underground, before 2015.

The latest European directives insist upon a certain level of water quality, even if they still need to fully implement the polluter-payer principle adopted by the OECD in 1972. This principle, which the *Loi Barnier* included in article L.110–1 of the *Code de l'environnement* and which states that the cost of preventing, reducing and fighting pollution should be covered by the polluting party, is one of the essential founding principles of environmental politics in developed countries. It is now written into the French Constitution, and its logical application can be seen in the taxation of water sanitation and refuse disposal. When it comes to the environment, the preventative principle has been joined by a precautionary one. When these principles are not respected, the polluter-payer principle also applies. But the principle of precaution is the more demanding one. It's a new way of protecting society from the as yet unknown or uncertain risks that could result in irreversible damage to the environment and therefore to human health (the use of GMOs, for example). This principle is also recognized on the EU level (in article 174–2 of the Treaty of Amsterdam) and the global level (principle 15 of the Rio Declaration, and various international conventions on biodiversity, climate change, and the protection of cross-border rivers or lakes).

In order that water and air remain drinkable and breathable to all, we need to not only protect the thing itself but also its status: labeling them as common heritage is one way to make the idea of the common good consistent while protecting it from attempts to appropriate or destroy it. France has solidified its international position in the quest for the legal foundation of the environment by a juridical approach to the idea of national heritage (article L.110 of the *Code de l'urbanisme*). The consequent legal regulation of certain natural resources is an entirely original concept.

I.B. *The Common Heritage of Mankind*

Ecological awareness is ancient – consider the Babylonian Code of Hammourabi (17th Century B.C.) – various articles of which cover water management and the penalties to be inflicted should a neighbor complain. Several centuries later, under the Roman Empire (6th Century A.D.), the Digest defined the role of public authority (Adler, 2004). Domat states that "the sky, the stars, light, air and sea are goods so common to all mankind that no-one can be master of them". But this concept was not to outlast the belief that science could irremediably alter water or air quality. It was necessary to end or at least limit the destructive power of mankind. Now, "if something belongs to nobody, nobody can complain about its deterioration" (Rémond-Gouilloud, 1989).

Defining water as the heritage of mankind is thus a way of opposing the right to destroy or pollute. As with any kind of heritage, it implies a protection related to the recognition of its fragile state, such as locations considered to form part of our world heritage because of their aesthetics as ratified in the UNESCO Convention on Natural and Cultural World Heritage on 23 November 1972. It's a complex collection of unique sites, natural or urban landscapes that have been designed to be of public interest, in the protection of general interest, or of national heritage. European directives and French laws translate this right to a quality environment using architectural and urban regulations and special decrees governing facilities designed to protect the environment.

Water is not a good. As the heritage of humanity, there is an indissoluble link with the subject written into the texts (article L.210−1 paragraph 1 of the *Code de l'environnement*): water is no longer a thing, and it is even less an object that can be appropriated; it is, by nature, subject to legally binding rights and regulations. Heritage is a legal matter, and incurs certain obligations (Atias, 2003). This classification is most interesting because on the one hand, heritage is inalienable, and on the other, because it cannot be transferred from one living person to another. Yet heritage can be passed on after death, which assures that it is perennial. Indeed, if humanity is to survive, it is vital that heritage is not allowed to disappear.

Between French law and the complexities of EU regulation, we can finally come to a positive definition of environmental law that also contributes to the right to good health. Man cannot appropriate water on behalf of future generations. This issue encompasses the whole sustainable development problematic. The French Charter on the Environment voted by parliament on 28 February 2005 conferred a legal status on what had previously been but a symbol. All legal texts have to confirm to it, even if the constitutional value of the preamble cannot be directly invoked in a court of law. The French people must now consider the environment in its entirety as "the common heritage of humankind", and play a role in preserving it as they do for "other fundamental national interests", since in order to assure sustainable development, decisions made to answer today's needs cannot compromise the ability of future generations to satisfy their own. Water is not the only element that affects human development. All natural resources are covered by these constitutional measures. This proactive approach "will inspire European and international action" (article 10 of the Charter).

We must nevertheless remember that the consecration of common heritage appeared first in international law (Dupuy, 1985; Flory, 1995; Rémond-Gouilloud, 1998; Pacquerot, 2002) and that France could no longer ignore it. Natural heritage is declining, particularly mineralogical (article L.342–1 of the *Code de l'environnement*), biological (art. L.411–1s. of the same Code), flora and fauna (L.411–5), hunting (L.421–5), and piscicultural (L.430–1) heritage ... But the list is exhaustive: heritage has defined limits. The scarcity of drinking water and the risk of irreversible pollution confer upon it this limited character that is indispensable to the classification of "heritage" that enables the fight against opposing forces (Terré and Simler, 2002). While "common things" have become the heritage of humanity, fears about the "heritagization" of the environment have not disappeared. Paradoxical situations can henceforth arise: such is the case with greenhouse gas emission quotas that, while they aim to reduce CO_2 emissions into the atmosphere, have nonetheless led the EU to implement a sophisticated exchange system of negotiable and dematerialized units of value, each representing the equivalent of a ton of carbon dioxide (directive 2003/87/CEE, 13 October 2003).

Some analysts conclude that this is a "permit to pollute"; other, more purist authors believe it's a matter of restricting atmospheric use or the right to produce (Trébulle, note 38, pp. 8–9) – a simple administrative authorization to reject greenhouse gases that is subject to the regulations of listed facilities, and that does not challenge the principle of nonappropriation of common goods. But these latter authors cannot explain this securitizing movement that results in administrative authorization gaining the status of marketable goods (Jegouzo, 2004; Le Bars, 2004; Revet, 2004). All patrimonial rights are economic goods with pecuniary value ... If we accept this definition, the notion of an environmental good is no different. In classic doctrine, it's a kind of appropriation by occupation that justifies the re-categorization of water as a *res nullius*, or a thing without an owner. It entails admitting that, on the one hand, "using air or water in such a way that nobody else can do so at the same time, polluters are no longer the users of environmental goods, but the owners of them" (Martin, 1978); and on the other, that the abundance criteria is a very relative one.

The notion of humankind's common heritage is thus getting close to the definition either of a global public good – as humanity is not a legal entity (Terré, 1999; Hugon, 2003; Rémond-Gouilloud, 1998), it cannot therefore legally have a heritage – ; or of private good, as certain real rights can still be exerted on the very elements that make up common heritage. The legal links between passive and active heritage are not solid enough for this legal foundation to be sufficient to protect humanity itself.

II. Water: Private Good or Global Common Good?

A conception of the environment as a private good refers to liberal or neoliberal philosophy. Since the absolute right to private property is a guarantee of freedom against the attacks of public power, it fundamentally cannot be questioned. The right to the environment, as the stranglehold of the public domain over proprietary prerogatives, reveals the limits of the traditional concept of property without really being a revolution in legal thinking. The global interest at stake in the protection of natural resources is irreducibly opposed to existent institutional structures, be they private or public.[1] A reconsideration of ownership theory enabled the refinement of the concepts of public and private property but was

---

1   Conference 25–6 October 2001, Pau. http://www.hcci.gouv.fr/lecture/synthese/sy001.htm.

unable to classify "environmental goods" in one or other of the classic legal categories without ethical or economic reservations.

Certain scientists, economists and lawyers believe in ecological privatization as a new paradigm: in this definition, water could be a private good without being incompatible with the right to the environment (A). Nevertheless, the sycophants of private property as the foundational principle of water preservation are just as virulent as its denigrators. In order to limit the abuses, de facto appropriations and pollution, or to correct the perverse effects of the unequal division of natural resources, there are a great many authors who believe in the development of this idea of granting such goods, and particularly water, the status of global common good (B).

II.A. Private Good

The arguments in favor of private property or private management of water are certainly not lacking. Property rights often work for the environment: the State cannot do everything. The public/private partnership is one of the most realistic options available, since the State's command of land is sporadic. The most recent regulations in France call for competition between rural actors. In any event, even in communist countries, ecological catastrophes occur when the right to individual property is suppressed and the law of supply and demand outlawed.

Private goods actually represent individual and economic goods, since the right to dispose of ownership (*abusus*) is a result of the right to give up one's goods. Public goods, on the other hand, are the responsibility of the State, which does not usually have the financial means to exercise this capacity that it has through ownership; common goods, for their part, are not exclusively the property of any one person, and so it is difficult to envisage any kind of investment in preserving them for future generations. Within this framework there is also the risk of the superimposition of competing rights. All the *Ancien Regime*'s legal defaults resurge here: eminent domain and mortmain. One must be wary of attempts to dismember property (De Malafosse, 1973), proper to the feudal system, and have the prudence not to wage war against the *freehold*, the basis for democracy and the Republic. Even Proudhon, an early socialist, came to the same conclusion. Only a private good can have an effective social function.

Aristotle (384–322 B.C.) noted that "man takes best care of that which belongs to him and has a tendency to neglect what is common to all men". In other words, an awareness of environmental risks and a sense of responsibility are greater with privatized goods, whatever their nature. The notion of an environmental good finds its full expression. Natural resources are not necessarily any different from other economic goods when looked at in this way, and therefore call for identical treatment. There is no denying that the owners of material goods – such as land or natural resources – and immaterial goods – such as shares in commercial companies that strive to minimize their ecological footprint – contribute, whether they wish to or not, to the protection of the environment. There are a great many examples of cases where the extension of private appropriation has been a successful alternative to public regulation (Falque and Massenet, 1999). On the other hand, regulations to protect *res nullius* have almost always failed: how many species are endangered, despite considerable national and even international regulation? (Caballero, 1981).

There is no law against the association of economics and ecology. The management of rare goods is the subject of proven recipes. But the difficulty becomes greater when it's a matter of combining the right to the environment with the right to property. The "heritagization" of nature or the idea of private good is in part responsible for the difficulty of integrating this into the law (Romi, 1998). But sometimes the notion of private good is rather a source of complexity. In Morocco, for example, land ownership is even disassociated from individual ownership of water – in other words, water rights are sold as time periods of access to water for irrigation. Time slots are distributed according to the number of owners and the volume of available water. This extreme solution only ends up in conflict and contracts (Charmasson, 1995).

The definition of environmental responsibilities also poses several challenges to the very Cartesian French judges. Pollution can only be fought if we identify the ownership rights pertaining to the activities that cause it. And this can only be condemned if it affects the (ownership) rights of someone else (*abusus* thus remains intact). In the Roman legal tradition known as *immisso*, pollution issues were considered ownership violations. Who would be the subject or object of the damage? Lawmakers are at loose ends to define the very recent notion of environmental harm (that came from the classic framework of "harm unto others" from article 1318 of the French Civil Code), grant damages for the violation of objective rights (thus breaking with the affectation of damages law), and obtain compensation via rehabilitation in accordance with the criminal law of 5 March 2007.[2] The admissibility of legal action to defend a common good is a subject for caution in so far as *class action* is only grudgingly allowed under French law and is still not allowed when it comes to the environment.

The right to property is at the heart of the debate between directed and market ecology. According to the former, it is the cause of our environmental problems; the latter believes it to be the solution (Bramoullé, 1997; Bate, 1997; Falque and Millière, 1992). The World Bank denounces the perverse effect of undercharging for water and the supply subventions that result in the looting/wasting of water. The price we have to pay to move towards the sustainable development of water is to manage it as if it were an economic good (Centi, 156; Barde, 1999, p. 93). The French system has competition from regions all over the world (Malaysia, Argentina, India, Indonesia) because of the marked efficiency of contracted water management. In Germany, Brazil and Indonesia, mixed economy companies offer a successful private/public partnership. When purification entails costly infrastructure, it is necessary to resort to private companies. Such is the case in the Sahara, where the public sector contents itself with assuring the management and cooperation of different users: privatization has been relatively successful (Sow, 2001).

But if the limits of the Welfare State – or, conversely, the risks of a centralized and thus domineering State – have been much publicized

---

2   http://www.courdecassation.fr/IMG/File/pdf_2007/24-05-2007/24-05-2007_accueil_cotte.pdf.

by the fervent defenders of public freedoms, the assertion that the right to private property *alias* the market economy could be a cure-all for the environment has not been proven. In this time of globalization, when multinationals like Danone, Nestlé and Coca-Cola instill fear in citizens' hearts because of their total lack of transparency and their abuse of natural resources, many people are skeptical of their claims to be researching ways to improve the quality of human life in a monopoly situation that can be ill suited to balanced global governance. Privatization programs in the South have often brought about energy shortages and contamination (Amougou, 2001). Some authors see the market economy as a return to the state of nature (Paquerot, 2005). The "normative proliferation" (Dupuy, 1991) and the "floating perimeters of sustainable development" (Scarwell and Roussel, 2006) do not exist to reassure us. The fear of the "petrolization" of water, along with the inequalities that it causes and the total lack of respect for our ecosystem, bring us back to an antinomic conception of the global common good.

II.B. *Global Common Good*

The application of the global common good concept to the environment is new, but the notion of common good has been part of economic history since Adam Smith. In 1770 the English classical school assigned the care for national defense, the guarantee of justice, and the power to finance infrastructures to the public powers. Two centuries later, Samuelson developed the idea that a public (or collective) good is a pure one only if it benefits all without the exclusion of any. Water is filed in the category of impure public goods because men compete to use it although everyone should have access to it. Through the medium of international law, we can therefore assert that the notion of common heritage is not only inappropriate (Trébulle, 2005) but also unfit.

Global public goods are those goods and services that are indispensable to individuals and to the equilibrium of societies in both hemispheres. This classification, which is that used by the UN, translates into UNDP programs to fight the harmful effects of globalization, with the aim of identifying the global common goods capable of causing a large consensus and getting suggestions about how they should be preserved, produced, and managed by the international community. The solidarity criterion often justifies the qualification of something as a good. The evolution in the choice of legal terms reveals both social advancement and the reasons why goods exist. But classing peace, health, justice, the environment, water and education as global public goods neither determines their system nor confers any legal reality unto them. Indeed, the list is not an exhaustive one, and so the dilution of its contents into common law or even into discourse that has no legal weight is to be feared.

Furthermore, the global nature of this good far from simplifies the question, because it excludes both private and public appropriation, since only States and not their representative international institutions can be responsible for the public domain. Common property is not public property. On a global scale, the common good is not a legally recognized category, and States remain sovereign. Nonetheless, the term of a global common good is justified by an appeal to international cooperation (Kaul, Grunberg and Stern, 1999). The definition of a public good in administrative law is more elaborate, but it is symptomatic of a reminder of the general principle of private property. The good has to be specifically for public service, and directly for public use (Godfrin and Degoff, 2007). The most cited examples are the coastline, highways and byways, the surface and depths of the ocean, ports, havens and harbors, and streams, rivers and lakes that are navigable or have been thus classed "to satisfy public water needs".

In most of the world's countries including the USA, drinking water management is a public service distributed by municipal governments. France is the exception because it's the only country where private companies have played such a major role in water distribution, since the 19th century. These are mainly public service concessions and the State is responsible for regulating the whole affair. Several different ministries are involved: defense, agriculture, health, and the environment. But with this kind of administrative framework, the State still has the majority of control, since more than 500 different services are involved in water distribution and management (Giblin, 2003).

Would it be sufficient to create global legal regulations, which are themselves a global common good, that would go beyond the sovereignty of States? What kind of international jurisdiction would be able to preside in litigation cases over water use, in other words over the causes of war or peace? Which sources of global common goods would be considered to be legitimate? Would the source of public goods be a new *hegemony* (Neorealist American school) or a democratic authority? And would it ensure the stability of these goods?

Public goods are often assimilated into common goods (markets and public squares, streets, forests, pastures, etc.). In Muslim society, water belongs to God and thus to the community (Aldeeb Abu-Salelieh, 2005): sharing it to water livestock is a moral duty. The public fountains (*sbils*) in Tunisia, for example, are considered common goods. Global public good is also a collective good, not just an economic one. And that brings us back to the notion of *res publica*.[3]

But whether it is a private or public environmental good, the heritage of humanity or a global common good, a collective good in the singular or plural, water has always been defined in a logic of appropriation, whether that be by the State or by private owners. Now the right to property is not the good itself. In the same way that the right to property cannot be a real right (Zénati, 1993), water is not an environmental good. Water is a human right, like property. Both have an extra-patrimonial quality: if property is the daughter of liberty, water is the child of legal rights.

III. Water: Universal Human Right

Sustainable development is more than a lien. The European Court of Human Rights has followed in the footsteps of France and article 1 of the *Code de l'environnement* and has declared that we have the right to

3   http://www.iqhei.ulaval.ca/Pdf/ORIEPaquerot.pdf.

"a healthy and ecologically balanced environment." All the foundations have been laid for the right to water to be included in our fundamental human rights. The French Constitution and the European Legal system have taken the plunge: it's the genesis of a new human right (A). Are the right to property and the legal status of water today equal? A new balance is being sought between norms of the same value whose object may be contradictory: it's the birth of an ecological public order (B).

III.A. The Genesis of a New Human Right

In the concept of sustainable development, the right to the environment has found a solid international legal foothold and water can now be posited as a universal human right. A quick chronology deserves to be sketched to trace the evolution of the law relevant to this subject. In 1946, the World Conservation Union (IUPN) was created, made up of both governmental and non-governmental actors.[4] The 1960 Rome Conference denounced the exponential depletion of natural resources with economic and demographic growth. In Stockholm (1972), the UN Conference on the Human Environment implemented new strategies to protect the environment (UNEP) because of pollution caused by acid raid; for the first time, a link between basic human rights and the environment was officially established. The first international treaty to recognize this right was the 1981 African Charter on Human and Peoples' Rights (article 24).

Then, in 1987, the famous Brundtland report from the World Commission on Environment and Development (WCED), *Our Common Future*, saw the birth of the notion of sustainable development, which soon became a general principle of international law.[5] The 1992 Rio

---

4   It was renamed in 1956 and since 1996 has been known as the International Union for the Conservation of Nature (IUCN), cf. Olivier J., 2005, note 26, p. 12.

5   The International Justice Court at The Hague, Collection CIJ, 241–2 §29 commented by Dupuy P.M., "Où en est le droit international de l'environnement à la fin du siècle?," *RGDIP*, 1997–4, p. 887.

Declaration reformulated "the right to a healthy life ... in harmony with nature" and proposed that the right to the environment be equivalent of the right to development, and the systematic integration of the environment in all new public policy using two foundational proposals for international community action. The Commission for Sustainable Development (an organ of the UN's Economic and Social Council) watched over the implementation of the Agendas 21 in territorial and local collectivities. Next came the Johannesburg Declaration (2002) that defined the three pillars of sustainable development: economic development, social responsibility, and the protection of the environment.

The General Comment on the Right to Water, adopted by the Covenant on Economic and Cultural Rights (CESCR) in November 2002, is a milestone in the history of human rights. For the first time water was explicitly recognized as a fundamental human right, and the 145 countries that ratified the International CESCR are now compelled to progressively ensure that everyone has access to safe and secure drinking water, equitably and without discrimination. Not long ago, the right to water had been more or less implicitly recognized in the General Comment on the Right to the Best Possible State of Heath (2000), the Convention on Childrens' Rights (1989) and the Convention on the Elimination of All Forms of Discrimination Against Women (1979).[6]

On a regional level, the Maastricht Treaty (1992) adopted a sustainable development strategy that was then superseded by the Copenhagen Summit (1995) and the Göteborg European Council (2001), then several times by the European Parliament. The latter adopted a resolution on Corporate Social and Environmental Responsibility on 13 March 2007, following all relevant advances of European law. Now that the principles of sustainable development or the right to a healthy environment are announced in the first articles of all charters and resolutions and other international conventions are reiterating these principles or fundamental rights, sustainable development, health and the environment are no longer

6   Paragraph taken from the World Water Development Report (WWDR): "The Right to Water".

mere objectives: integrated into the Charter of Fundamental Rights of the European Union (Nice, 2000), they are now law. The Aarhus Convention on Access to Information, Public Participation in Decision-making and Access to Justice in Environmental Matters (1998) goes one step further, announcing both the fundamental right to the environment and a procedural right to invoke it directly in court.

On the national level, the forms that recognition of the right to the environment takes are varied and multiple. Sustainable development is now the norm in several States.[7] Its constitutionalization seems to be growing: article 225 of the Brazilian Constitution reclaims the right to an ecologically balanced environment for all; and ten European member States had integrated this right into their constitutions before 1 May 2004, including Germany and Belgium in 1994, Finland in 1999, and Greece in 2001. The newest members of the EU (Poland, Slovakia, Lithuania, Latvia, Estonia, and Hungary) have written the right to the environment directly into their new constitutions. In Africa a similar pattern can be seen in several recent constitutions (Prieur, 2003). In Uruguay, more than 60% of citizens voted to reform the Constitution in 2004 so that it declared water a "public good" and guaranteed user participation at all levels of water management: using democracy, access to water services and purification became a fundamental human right and a State-owned company was charged with implementing this right, thus avoiding new concessions being made to private industry in the future.

But between the constitutional recognition of a real subjective right – as in France (Van Lang, 2002; Drago, 2004; Jégouzo and Lolum, 2004) or Hungary, Slovakia, Slovenia, Belgium, Spain, Greece, Portugal, Finland and Uruguay –, and the State being deemed responsible for protecting the

---

7   In France, the Comité français du développement durable (CFDD) and Comité 21 were created in 1993. Several laws make reference to sustainable development, (loi sur l'eau, Barnier cited above, loi Pasqua in 1995, LOADDT called loi Voynet, Chevènement in 1999 which enable new technical and legal instruments, loi SRU of 2000 which plans sustainable development for SCOT and PLU), without forgetting the 2001 loi NRE which instigated a sustainable development report for public companies.

environment – as in Poland – or the citizens being charged with the same – as in Switzerland –, many States are still to take this step. A majority of them have only passed simple laws to promote sustainable development and insist that the right to the environment be respected (Canada,[8] USA, UK). The federal system and its complex division of labor could prove to be a hindrance to constitutionalization. Often a constitution was written at a time when the issue of sustainable development didn't exist, and this long-standing nature is invoked against change: in countries where the legal system is based on Common Law, only *soft law* allows for laws to be changed without modifying the original texts.

The contribution of jurisprudence, particularly European jurisprudence, since it serves as a precedent in countries under customary law, is in this fundamental legal and terminological construction. The European Court of Human Rights in Strasbourg has extensively interpreted certain similar rights that have been inserted into the European Charter of Human Rights, since in 1950 the latter did not make reference to a right to the environment. Several requests have been considered to be acceptable under article 8 of said Charter on private and family life and the home, which has been extended to environmental affairs, and some requests were deemed to be well founded under the right to life.[9] The Court has also extended the conditions of the beginning and admissibility of recourse. In addition to the 44 States between the Atlantic and the Oural that are parties at the Charter, any physical or moral person from one of these States could avail of the ECHR and file a legal action based on the text of the Charter in a national court of law. The notion

8   http://www.oag-bvg.gc.ca/domino/rapports.nsf/html/c007aa_f.html.

9   Arrêt Powel et Rayner, 21 February 1990; Hatton Affair and others in the EU, 2 October 2001; Lopez-Ostra Decree of 9 December 1994 recognising the right to quality of life; Guerra Decree of 19 February 1998 on information and impact study; Oneryildiz Affair of 18 June 2002 in Turkey, consecrating the right to life in the environment, commentary by Belaidi N., "Droits de l'Homme, environnement et ordre public", in *L'ordre public écologique*, p. 68 and by Tavernier P., "La Cour Européenne des Droits de l'Homme et la mise en œuvre du droit international de l'environnement", *Actualité et Droit international*, June 2003, www.ridi.org/adi.

of "potential victim" resulting from the *Soering* affair (art. 50 ECHR) represents the hope of recognizing future generations in a court of law and environmental damage.

Furthermore, the question was raised as to whether or not the environment should be protected as it is – in a more ecologist than environmental vision where man is just a link in the chain – or on the contrary whether the environment constitutes a human right, which would mean that nature should be subjected to human law or more accurately that the ecosystem and natural areas should be protected only to be of service to man's health, quality of life, and well-being. The second opinion is the one that currently prevails, which explains the recent emergence of the right of man to his environment (Ferry, 1992; Ost, 1995). Considering the urgency of the environmental issues at stakes, a new order is underway.

III.B. Public Ecological Order: A New Balance between Norms

The "globalization of law", particularly in terms of the broadcasting of human rights, tends to remove the State as a legal entity (Stern, 2000). But the pursuit of common projects has mainly come up against heterogeneous legal systems or the gaps inside them, and the increasing contestation of the dominance of industrialized countries over non-integrated poorer ones (Cadet, 2006). However, we can take some hope from the creation of the International Criminal Court on 11 April 2002, the jurisdiction of which is universal but limited (crimes against humanity). But the category of crimes against humanity could grow to include serious environmental attacks. The implementation of a global form of governance is even envisaged in article 1 of the ICC's statutes and the international legal and jurisdictional cooperation spearheaded by Europe (Dejeant-Pons, 1999). The institution of a European arrest warrant, which applies to crimes against the environment,[10] is of important note. As is the creation of the African Court of Human and Peoples' Rights (1998) which had its first

---

10   Art. 2§2 décision – cadre 2002/584 JOCE L190, 18/07/2002, p. 1.

meeting on 1 October 2007 in Banjul, Gambia. Another symbol might be the Valencia Water Tribune, a popular local institution in Spain that has been a legal entity since 1492.[11]

The capacity of decision makers to build frameworks on both a national and European level weighs heavily on the future of sustainable development on a global scale. The constraining character of European lawmaking is an advantage. French legislation, as a replica or complement to European legislation, also marks the way. In December 1964, water began to be taxed, in accordance with the principles of the OCDE (PPP). A 1976 law brought in water monitors for establishments undergoing impact studies, and danger studies were added after the Seveso II directive (1997). In 1999, the general tax on polluting activities was implemented, particularly with respect to phytosanitary products and cleaning supplies.

Prescriptions are numerous, eclectic and often heterogeneous. Some are more vital than others; they lead to the recognition of a public environmental order. In private law, the growing development of punitive damages in environmental affairs is very revealing (Loutant-Lapalus, 2005). In public law, the European Commission has once again used the European Court of Justice with regard to the surface water nitrate pollution affair in Brittany to fine and level significant daily constraints against France for being too late to implement the "Nitrates" directive 91/676/CEE of 31 December 1999. Public order covers both the notion of organization and the idea of tranquility, safety, public health. It is then both a "guardian of legal rights and situations" and, contrarily, "the possible limitation of these rights" (Kiss, 2005). We understand that it could come up against the right to property – as an individual liberty – when public interest justifies it. We can also understand that the preservation of certain natural areas and equitable access to natural resources calls for new and even surprising legal techniques in the service of humanity, such as a social (La Voilotte, 2005) or natural (Serres, 1992) contract bearing fundamental values: it's the birth of an environmental *jus cogens*, an ensemble

---

11   *Le manifeste sur l'eau*, p. iii.

of imperative norms and obligations opposable to all States and dealing with the right to a healthy environment as a basic human right.

Some view this as the fruition of an evolution in law (Apostolidis, 1991). Others believe that only the premises can be seen at this point (Picheral, 2001). Others are still doubtful, since even the criminal justice system can be the subject of a transaction after an infringement of the environmental code such as water pollution (Vincent-Legoux, 2005; Bertella-Geffroy, 2002).[12] Even if we are on principle incapable of derogating from public order via particular conventions, international law has weakened the law by tolerating numerous exceptions. There is then of course the risk that the most powerful will impose norms to which they will subject others (Ruzié, 2004). This is the main criticism of *soft law*, since the parties are not in a situation of de facto equality. The changes made to the Kyoto Protocol in 2012, which should include developing countries such as India, China and Brazil, will be a determining factor.

Even if a consensus is reached on the protection of people's security when it comes to natural or technological risks, public health measures taken against water or atmospheric pollution, or policing noise so that the public is not troubled by it, that is not the case for the Natura 2000 Birds and Habitats directives, which protect ecosystems as a fundamental source of life and which can enter into conflict with the right to property, protected as a fundamental freedom by the French Constitutional Council and the European Court of Human Rights. A hierarchy seems to be emerging even within the category of human rights. C. Mouly claims that "in terms of the environment, as elsewhere, property develops best alongside the other human rights, especially when you highlight the protection that property assures these rights. Less than a value in itself, property should be presented as the foundation of equality, human dignity, and personal freedom".[13] Property is a right; it should also, therefore, be a duty. A home, unlike water or air, is a building: it belongs to an owner, and the owner is responsible for it (article 1384 al.1 of the *Code Civil*).

12   Vincent-Legoux, 2005, p. 81; Bertella-Geffroy, 2002, chronique, p. 8.
13   "Place de la propriété parmi les droits de l'homme", in *Droits de propriété et environnement*, p. 40.

Land ownership therefore has a biological function, just as property ownership has a social function. In the interests of equality, it would be appropriate and fair that urban obligations be compensated (Hostiou, 1993). Hayek advocated coming out of tribal socialism and acquiring property as human progress: it was the very course of history (Smith, 1997). But when we take the lack of transparency and the abuses at the hands of the "water lords" into account, on the global level, the management of water, be it by a handful of private companies or by the States, has not given us the guarantees of good democracy and access to water for all current and future generations. Now, access to water is the right to life – individual, inalienable, and collective. The constitution of a network of water parliaments is a prerequisite to preserving the global right to that water.

In the name of human rights, the right to property can no longer be considered, as it was in the 19th century, as an absolute and exclusive right: it must be useful (Trébulle, 2005; Trotabas, 1930). Freedom, as we are constantly reminded by the European Court of Human Rights and the Constitutional Council of France, may still be the principle, but it cannot be limitless. This remark is as valid for private property as it is for public. If the right to property has never been an absolute anywhere but on paper, attacks on the right to property did not stop in the 20th century. Any expropriation would of course have to be justified in the public interest and compensated (art. 17 DHR). But many of the new constraints and pollution are not subject to indemnities. The exponential growth of environmental constraints (urbanism, nature and landscape protection, risk prevention) can, depending on the legal approach one takes, either seem a reassessment of an absolute and exclusive right (Trébulle), or, on the contrary, the intangible nature of a fundamental right that has not lost any of its strength (Libchaber, 2004; Revet, 2004).

On the European level, we are now witnessing the establishment of a source of public goods regulated by the subsidiary principle, to which the EU has added the principle of proportionality in its White Paper. In other words, the principle of private property would only become an issue if production and supply could not be met. At most, one might admit that the right to property is in the process of being redefined.

The public ecological order can justify a bracketing of individual freedom for the common good. Such thinking leads us to reconsider the notion of the right to property and to identify an environmental public domain in which community prerogatives prevail.

Conclusion

Access to water has been a source of conflict for almost 4000 years. The division and control of resources have become one of the keys in negotiating peace.[14] A real legal status for drinking water is needed, and this necessarily requires international law to be redefined in the interests of mankind (Paquerot, 1985, 2005). Legal theories and categories that have been proven over time and in practice are not as ripe for obsolescence as anti-liberals and headstrong militant ecologists who are hostile to financial capitalism would like to think. But change is necessary so that we can ascertain the hierarchy and monitoring of the appropriate norms.

Integrated water management has been possible within the framework of sustainable development. Similar approaches regarding air have been less visibly effective (Scarwell and Roussel, 2006). If pleading from the definition of global public good, the absolute necessity of public water and air management could be a deceptive pretext, since *res communes* are not goods, whether they be rare, expensive, or abundant. We cannot really appropriate water or air; at most we could possess and abuse our access to it. Its use must be regulated. Water is not just an economic resource, devoid of solidarity or responsibility. Rediscovering the social function of property is a way to reconcile individual freedom and the right to a healthy environment for all.

---

14   *Alternatives Sud*, Editorial, p. 15; Nguyen Tien Duc, "L'eau, enjeu politique important", in *La conquête de l'eau*, p. 81.

Lawmakers are too inclined to radicalize precaution beforehand or too caught up in posthumous legal battles, and their ignorance of the urgency of the situation is the assurance of the increasing "heritagization" of the environment. The waning attempts to legalize a right to water are revealing of the woefully mistaken division made between the idea of private and public goods. It is time to shake off these legal shackles and to dare to create an international constitutional right, which could be the foundation stone of global governance; but also to implement procedures to prevent pollution and shortages, to build on the *ratione materiae* capacities and the means of the International Criminal Court, so that we can begin to repair the damage of tomorrow, which is linked to the violation of all forms of this new kind of universal human right.

References

Books

Aldeeb Abu-Salelieh, S.A., 2005, *Introduction à la société musulmane, Fondements, sources et principes*, Paris: Eyrolles.
Apostolidis, C., 1991, *Doctrine juridique et droit international, Critique de la connaissance juridique*, Paris: Eyrolles.
Atias, C., 2003, *Droit civil, Les biens*, Paris: Litec.
Audrerie, D., Souchier, R. and Vilar, L., 1998, *Le patrimoine mondial*, Paris: PUF.
Bate, R., 1999, "La propriété comme préalable à la prévention de la pollution de l'eau", in Falque M. and Massenet M., eds, *Droits de propriété et environnement*, Paris: Dalloz.
Boutelet, M. and Fritz, J.-C., eds, 2005, *L'ordre public écologique*, Bruxelles: Bruylant.
Bramoullé, G., 1999, "Droits de propriété et biens environnementaux", in Falque M. and Massenet M., eds, *Droits de propriété et environnement*, Paris: Dalloz.
Caballero, F., 1981, *Essai sur la notion juridique de nuisance*, Paris: LGDJ.

Caïs, M.-F., Del Rey, M.-J. and Ribaut, J.-P., 1999, *L'eau et la vie, Enjeux, perspectives et visions culturelles*, Paris: Editions Charles Léopold Mayer.

De Malafosse, J., 1973, *Le droit à la nature*, Paris: Montchrestien.

Desjeux, D., ed., 1985, *L'eau, quels enjeux pour les sociétés rurales? Amérique centrale, Afrique, France, Moyen-Orient*, Coll. Alternatives paysannes, Paris: L'Harmattan.

Dupuy, G., 1991, *L'urbanisme en réseaux, Théories et méthodes*, Paris: Armand Colin.

Falque, M. and Massenet, M., eds, 1999, *Droits de propriété et environnement, Les ressources en eau*, Coll. Thèmes et commentaires, Paris: Dalloz.

—— and Millière, G., 1992, *Ecologie et liberté, Une autre approche de l'environnement*, Paris: Litec.

Ferry, L., 1992, *Le nouvel ordre écologique, L'arbre, l'animal et l'homme*, Paris: Grasset.

Godfrin, P. and Degoff, M., 2007, *Droit administratif des biens, Domaine, travaux, expropriations*, Paris: Sirey.

Golub, P. and Maréchal, J.-P., 2006, "Les biens publics mondiaux", in Laville, J.-L. and Cattani, A.D., eds, *Dictionnaire de l'autre économie*, Paris: Gallimard.

Harribey, J.-M., 2000, "Temps de travail et travail du temps: comment passer d'une mesure de la valeur économique à la prise en compte des valeurs non économiques?", in *Les temps de l'environnement, Paysage and environnement*, Toulouse: Presses Universitaires du Mirail.

Kaul, I., Grunberg, I. and Stern, M., eds, 1999, *Global Public Goods: International Cooperation in the Twenty-First Century*, Oxford: Oxford University Press.

Marsily (de), G., 2005, *L'eau*, Coll. Dominos, Paris: Flammarion.

Nérac-Croisier, R., ed., 2006, *Sauvegarde de l'environnement et Droit pénal*, Coll. Sciences criminelles, Paris: L'Harmattan.

Olivier, J., 2005, *L'Union Mondiale pour la Nature (UICN), Une organisation singulière au service du droit de l'environnement*, Université d'Aix-Marseille III, Ed. Bruylant.

Ost, F., 1995, *La nature hors la loi, L'écologie à l'épreuve du droit*, Paris: La Découverte.

Paquerot, S., 2005, *Eau douce: la nécessaire refondation du droit international*, Montréal: Presses Universitaires du Québec.

Petrella, R., 1998, *Le Manifeste de l'eau, Pour un Contrat Mondial*, Bruxelles: Labor.

Prieur, M., 2004, *Droit de l'environnement*, Paris: Dalloz.

Proudhon, P.-J., 1997 (1871), *Théorie de la propriété*, Paris: L'Harmattan.

Rémond-Gouilloud, M., 1989, *Le droit de détruire*, Paris: PUF.

Ruzié, D., 2004, *Droit international public*, Coll. Mémentos, Paris: Dalloz.

Scarwell, H.-J. and Franchomme, M., 2004, *Contraintes environnementales et gouvernance des territoires*, Editions L'Aube nord.

——and Roussel, I., 2006, *Les démarches locales de développement durable à travers les territoires de l'eau et de l'air*, Coll. Environnement et société, Septentrion.

Serres, M., 1992, *Le contrat naturel*, Paris.

Terré, F. and Simler, P., 2002, *Droit civil, Les biens*, Coll. Droit privé, Paris: Dalloz.

Trotabas, L., 1930, *La fonction sociale de la propriété: le point de vue technique, le régime administratif de la propriété privée*, Paris: Sirey.

Van Lang, A., 2002, *Droit de l'environnement*, Coll. Thémis Droit public, Paris: PUF.

Studies, Reports, Theses and Summaries

Gandin, J.-P., 1995, *La conquête de l'eau, Du recueil à l'usage: comment les sociétés s'approprient l'eau et la partagent*, Série Dossiers pour un débat, n°44, Paris: Editions FPH.

Gys, F., 1997, *Essai sur la notion juridique d'équilibre entre la propriété privée et la protection de l'environnement*, Université de Lille II, Diffusion ANRT.

Hugon, P., 2003, *L'économie éthique publique: biens publics mondiaux et patrimoines communs*, Paris: UNESCO.

Paquerot, S., 2002, *Le statut des ressources vitales en droit internationales, Essai sur le concept de patrimoine commun de l'humanité*, Bruxelles: Bruylant.

Picheral, C., 2001, *L'ordre public européen*, Paris: La Documentation française.

Articles

Adler, E., 2004, "La puissance publique, garante ou destructrice de l'environnement ?", *Environnement and Technique*, December, n°242.

Amin, S., 2001, "L'eau, bien commun des peuples", *Alternatives Sud*, Vol. VIII.

Amougou, J.-P.T., 2001, "L'eau, bien public, bien privé: l'Etat, les communautés locales et les multinationales", *Alternatives Sud*, Vol. VIII.

Barde, J.-P., 1999, "Le prix de l'eau", *L'eau et la vie*, OCDE.

Bergel, J.-L., 2001, "Paradoxes du droit immobilier français à la fin du XXe siècle", in *Le droit privé français à la fin du XXe siècle, Etudes offertes à P. Catala*, Paris: Litec.

Bertella-Geffroy, M.O., 2002, "L'inefficacité du droit pénal dans les domaines de la sécurité sanitaire et des atteintes à l'environnement, le point de vue d'un praticien", *Environnement*.

Cadet, I., 2006, "Du besoin au changement dans l'optique développement durable et responsabilité sociale de l'entreprise, la règle juridique comme passage obligé", *Colloque international ISEOR et Academy of Management USA*, Lyon: Editions ISEOR.

Centi, J.-P., 2006, "Le prix de l'environnement", *Colloque international ISEOR et Academy of Management USA*, Lyon: Editions ISEOR.

Dejeant-Pons, M., 1999, "Recueil d'expériences, La coopération juridique internationale: l'exemple européen", in Caïs, M.-F., Del Rey, M.-J. and Ribaut, J.-P., *op.cit.*

Drago, G., 2004, "Principes directeurs d'une charte constitutionnelle de l'environnement", *AJDA*, n°3, 26 January.

Dupuy, R.-J., 1985, "Réflexions sur le patrimoine commun de l'humanité", *Droits*, n°1.

Fabre-Magnan, 1997, "Propriété, patrimoine et lien social", *RTDCiv*.

Flory, M., 1995, "Le patrimoine commun dans le droit international de l'environnement", in *Droit et environnement*, PUAM.

Fontbaustier, L., "Environnement et pacte écologique, Remarques sur la philosophie d'un nouveau 'droit à' ", Etudes et doctrines, *Cahiers du Conseil constitutionnel*, n°15: 1–9.

Giblin, B., 2003, "Les pouvoirs locaux, l'eau, les territoires, L'eau: une question géopolitique, en France aussi!", *HERODOTE*, n°110: 3–9.

Hostiou, R., 1993, "La non-indemnisation des servitudes d'urbanisme; Droit de l'urbanisme, bilan et perspectives", *AJDA*, special issue, May.

Jégouzo, Y. and Lolum, F., 2004, "La portée juridique de la Charte de l'environnement", *Droit administratif*, n°3, March.

Jegouzo, Y., 2004, "Les autorisations administratives vont-elles devenir des biens meubles?", *AJDA*.

Kiss, A.-C., 1999, "L'environnement, sagesse de la propriété", in Falque, M. and Massenet, M., eds, *Droits de propriété et environnement*, *op.cit.*

——2005, "L'ordre public écologique", in Boutelet, M. and Fritz, J.-C., eds, *L'ordre public écologique*, *op.cit.*, pp. 155–67.

Lacoste, Y., 2001, "Géopolitique de l'eau", *HERODOTE*, 3rd quarter.

La Voilotte, M.-P., 2005, "La contribution de la technique contractuelle à l'émergence de l'ordre public écologique", in *L'ordre public écologique*, *op.cit.*

Le Bars, B., 2004, "La nature juridique des quotas d'émission de gaz à effet de serre après l'ordonnance du 15 avril 2004 – Réflexions sur l'adaptabilité du droit des biens", *JCP G*, I.

Libchaber, R., 2004 "La recodification du droit des biens", in *Le Code Civil*, Paris: *Dalloz*.

Loutant-Lapalus, C., 2005, "L'incitation à la reconnaissance et au respect de l'ordre public écologique par les sanctions civiles", in *L'ordre public écologique*, *op.cit.*

Martin, G., 1978, "Le droit à l'environnement, De la responsabilité civile pour faits de pollution", *PPS*, n°118.

Moreau, J.-P., 1991, "L'évolution de la propriété foncière", in *L'évolution contemporaine du droit des biens*, Paris: PUF.

Morin, G., "Le sens de l'évolution contemporaine du droit de propriété", in *Mélanges Ripert*.

Paquerot, S., 1985, "Quel droit international pour l'eau douce?", *Revue Pour*, n°185.

Prieur, M., 2003, "Droit de l'homme à l'environnement et développement durable", *AJDA*, n°8.

Rémond-Gouilloud, M., 1998, "L'autre humanité (remarques sur une homonymie)", in *Mélanges Kiss*.

Revet, T., 2004, "Le Code civil et le régime des biens, Questions pour un bicentenaire", *Droit and Patrimoine*, n°124.

——2005, "Les quotas d'émission de gaz à effet de serre", *D.*: 2632.

Romi, R., 1998, "Quelques réflexions sur l'affrontement économie-écologie et son influence sur le droit", *Droit et Société*, 38: 131–40.

Sériaux, A., 1995, "La notion de choses communes", in *Droit et Environnement, Propos pluridisciplinaires sur un droit en construction*, PUAM.

Smets, H., 2001, "Une Charte des droits fondamentaux sans droit à l'environnement", *Revue Européenne de Droit de l'Environnement*, n°4.

Smith, F.-L., 1997, "La protection de l'environnement par la privatisation écologique: un paradigme pour la réforme environnementale", in *Droits de propriété et environnement, op.cit.*

Sow, M., 2001, "L'accès à l'eau au Sahel à l'ère de la privatisation", *Alternatives Sud*, Vol. VIII.

Stern, B., 2000, "La mondialisation du droit", *Revue Projet*, n°262: 99–110.

Terré, F., 1999, "L'humanité, un patrimoine sans personne", in *Mélanges Ardant*.

Trébulle, F.-G., 2005, "L'environnement et le droit des biens", http://www.henricapitant.org/IMG/pdf/L_environnement_et_le_droit_des_biens.pdf

Vincent-Legoux, 2005, "L'ordre public écologique en droit interne", in *L'ordre public écologique, op.cit.*

Zénati, F., 1993, "Pour une rénovation de la théorie de la propriété", *RTDciv.*

CHAPTER 14

Business, Society and the Common Good: The Contribution of Paul Ricœur

JACOB DAHL RENDTORFF

Introduction

When we discuss corporate citizenship and business ethics in relation to the problem of the common good in international society we often forget to look at the philosophical foundations of our conception of the common good. The aim of this paper is to propose such a foundation. The argument is fairly abstract but nevertheless it is important to propose such a discussion in order to understand how a concept of the common good can be integrated into the political economy of business ethics. The following proposal of a theory of the common good of business in society is based on the philosophy of Paul Ricœur.[1] This analysis is grounded on the theory of republican democracy with respect for basic rights of citizens as the framework for theories of values-driven management, business ethics and corporate social responsibility (CSR).

When we use the concept of republicanism to define this approach to the common good in business ethics we refer to the classical political concept of republicanism, where republicanism is understood as a political theory that emphasizes liberty, people's democracy and civic virtue.

---

1   Paul Ricœur, *Du texte à l'action*, Paris: Editions du Seuil, 1987; Paul Ricœur, *Soi-même comme un autre*, Paris: Editions du Seuil, 1990; Paul Ricœur, *Lectures politiques 1*, Paris: Editions du Seuil, 1994; Paul Ricœur, *Le Juste*, Paris: Esprit, 1995; Paul Ricœur, *Parcours de la reconnaissance, Trois études*, Paris: Esprit, 2004.

In contrast to liberalism, republicanism emphasizes the importance of the common good for development of the best society. Republicanism emphasizes the need of citizenship based on liberty and civic virtue. When we talk about republican business ethics we refer to the engagement of the corporation as a good citizen that actively contributes with civic virtue and respects the laws of political democracy.

Such a conception of the common good integrates economic rationality into the larger framework of political community. With Ricœur we can define the ideal of politics as the realization of "the good life with and for the other in just institutions".[2] This vision of politics builds a close connection between a philosophical anthropology of existential commitment and a vision of the good life. Further, it provides an argument for the right formation of institutions and an outline of practical wisdom and judgments in the process and practice of law-making in democratic communities. Such a political theory of the social and economic ethics integrates economic rationality in ethics and economics.[3] The philosophy of Paul Ricœur helps to renew this concept of republicanism as the foundation of the common good concept in the international society. In the first part of the paper (I), I define the concept of the common good on the basis of Ricœur's political philosophy.[4] In the second part (II), I relate this concept to the idea of a *global civil ethos* as the basis of the common good in a global context. In the third part of the paper (III), I show how a concept of ethical judgment is the basis for the realization of the common good in international business and society.

2   Paul Ricœur, *Soi-même comme un autre*, Paris: Editions du Seuil, 1990, p. 276.
3   Jacob Dahl Rendtorff, "Critical Hermeneutics in Law and Politics", in Lars Henrik Schmidt, ed., *Paul Ricœur in the Conflict of Interpretations*, Aarhus: Aarhus University Press, 1996; Jacob Dahl Rendtorff, *Paul Ricœurs filosofi*, Copenhagen: Hans Reitzels Forlag, 2000.
4   Paul Ricœur, *One Self as Another* (K. Blamey trans.), Chicago: University of Chicago Press, 1992.

I. The Ideal of the Common Good within Just Institutions

With his reading of the debates between communitarianism and liberalism, Paul Ricœur contributes to a possible criticism of John Rawls' *A Theory of Justice*, which helps us establish some proposals for the development of a theory of business ethics and corporate social responsibility on the basis of our general formulation of the framework for business ethics in welfare economics.[5] The idea is that the ideal of ethics and justice should be based on the "aim of the good life with and for the other in just institutions".[6] Ricœur argues with the communitarian critiques of liberalism that the foundation of the rational choice behind the veil of ignorance in Rawls' theory is the commitment to a vision of the common good in universal institutions. This implies that it is presupposed in Rawlsian theory that a strict procedural conception of justice can be considered as formalization of the sense of justice that is founded in the ethical aim. Extended to society the mutual reciprocity of solicitude becomes a procedural concept of justice and the procedural concept of justice can be considered as a formalization of the concern for equality within the Aristotelian concept of practical wisdom and of the right middle. Of course this does not mean that Rawls' conception of justice is considered to be teleological. His concept of justice remains a sharp criticism of the utilitarian reduction of justice to utility. However, we should not forget that justice may still be conceived as a virtue as Ricœur reminds us referring to the opening declaration of the *Theory of Justice*: "Justice is the first virtue of social institutions, as truth is of systems of thought".[7]

The reason for this insistence on the close relation between the just and the good is that there seems to be no point in having a social contract without considering it as annulations of the ethical concern for the

5   Paul Ricœur, *Le Juste 1*, Paris: Editions du Seuil, 1994.
6   Paul Ricœur, *Soi-même comme un autre*, Paris: Editions du Seuil, 1990, p. 202.
7   John Rawls, *A Theory of Justice*, Cambridge, MA: Harvard University Press, 1971, p. 3; Paul Ricœur, *One Self as Another* (K. Blamey trans.), Chicago: University of Chicago Press, 1992, p. 197.

good. This may be an important addition to the social contract theory of business ethics.[8] The social contract may be considered as an effort to make the good a result of a deliberation between free and equal subjects. We may argue that the social contract of a theory of justice is based on the ethical conception of the respect for human beings as ends in themselves as what is the essence of a shared sense of justice. Accordingly, the foundation of the social contract is deliberation among individuals who are to find a shared conviction about the principles of justice in democratic societies. The basis of Rawls' formalization of the sense of justice is in this framework formulated in the following manner: "The foundation of deontology is the desire to live well with and for others in just institutions".[9] With this Ricœur refers to the idea that the starting point of individual choice must be a search for the good life of the individual. Accordingly, we can criticize the utilitarian concept of well-being as the foundation of economic action.[10] Well-being does not have to be reduced to utility but other things as human dignity, rationality, good life and democratic institutions may be included as important ethical justifications of fundamental preferences.

In contrast to hedonistic and utilitarian theories of well-being so popular in neo-liberal theory, the Aristotelian concept of the common good includes a complex view of preferences according to which pain and moments of unhappiness in the end may be integrated in the general view of the good life as the aim of human existence.[11] The idea of the good life may be conceived as an individual meta-preference that determines all other preferences of individuals. The use of the Aristotelian concept of preference contributes to the criticism of idiosyncratic preferences or asocial preferences like discrimination and racism. Using the concept of

8   Tom Dunfee and Thomas Donaldson, *Ties That Bind: A Social Contracts Approach to Business Ethics*, Cambridge, MA: Harvard Business School Press, 1999.
9   Paul Ricœur, *One Self as Another* (K. Blamey trans.), Chicago: University of Chicago Press, 1992, p. 197.
10   James Griffin, *Well-Being*, Oxford: Oxford University Press, 1986.
11   W.D. Ross, *Ethics*, in Jonathan Barnes, ed., *The Complete Works of Aristotle*, Princeton: Princeton University Press, 1984.

the good life as the foundation of preference it may be argued that it is rational to be socially responsible or to consider the primacy political rights as more important than utility, because this would ensure the good life of the individual. It is in this sense that Amartya Sen talks about capabilities or "functioning" as the foundation of economic rationality.[12]

We can argue that Rawls' theory has to be accomplished with a concern for common good as based on the good life of individuals in social institutions. Erwin M. Hartman explains how Rawls in *Political Liberalism* (especially Lecture VIII) refuses that there should be one particular conception of the good that political society should embrace.[13] Instead all citizens should have the right to pursue their own conception of the good and give others the same right. Rawls argues that the State should not be built on one conception of the good, but instead promote the right of different individuals to have their particular conceptions of the good. This criticism can be mobilized against a belief that there is one particular conception of the good. However, this is not what we mean when we make the vision of the good life in just institutions the aim of ethics. Rather what is at stake is the idea that a good society or organization is a society or an organization that helps different individuals realize their own conception of the good in accordance with their wishes and desires.[14] May we argue on this basis that it is really possible to combine the Rawlsian theory with the communitarian idea of the good life? Some liberals would argue that this impossible, because Rawls' theory concerns what is right and not what is good. In this perspective, the focus is on liberty and individualism. However, this is not exactly true. Rawls' theory may be said to imply a kind of liberal utopia where the good community supports individual rights and self-realization. It is exactly the ability of having different conceptions of the good life co-existing peacefully, that is important as the basis of such a community which should be based on a balance between individual liberty and public interest. The good

---

12   Amartya Sen, *Rationality and Freedom*, New York: Belknap Press, 2003.
13   Erwin M. Hartman, *Organizational Ethics and the Good Life*, Oxford: Oxford University Press, 1996.
14   Erwin M. Hartman, *op.cit.*, p. 41.

community is based on mutual openness, tolerance and willingness to discuss the good direction of society.[15]

This does not imply the abandonment of the universalistic and pluralist concepts of the just society. Nor does it have to be a rational return to desert and merit in contrast to the modern concept of rights.[16] What is important is the foundation of individual action in a vision of the good or of well-being conceived as happiness in human lives. Indeed, Ricœur also stresses the foundations of ethics in individual commitment and responsibility. This is important for understanding our discussion of economic anthropology. From the point of view of human existence, choices of economic preferences are secondary to a philosophical anthropology of human fragility and vulnerability. We can say that economic rationality is grounded in a philosophical anthropology of the human will.[17] Such an existential concept of humanity emphasizes ontological commitment in existential consciousness (*attestation et témoignage*) as constitutive of human subjectivity. Here, economics is secondary to the existential project of the human individual determined by his actions and passions. The economic projects of individuals should be considered as aspects of their visions of the good life with and for other persons. This does not have to undermine the Kantian and Rawlsian emphasis on universal morality, because individualist notions of the good life cannot be opposed to universal norms of justice in society.

Following Aristotle in *The Nichomachean Ethics*, the idea of the common good as based on the ideal of the good life is realized in the lifelong friendship with the other, based on difference, generosity and reciprocity in a mutual generous giving and receiving between free human beings. The ideal friendship is determined neither by common interest nor by utility, but by the common vision of the good life, founded on real need of and

---

15   Erwin M. Hartman, *op.cit.*, p. 177.
16   Alasdair MacIntyre, *After Virtue – A Study in Moral Theory*, London: Duckworth, 1985, p. 252.
17   Paul Ricœur, *Le volontaire et l'involontaire*, Paris: Aubier, 1947–48; Paul Ricœur, *L'homme fragile*, Paris: Aubier, 1960; Paul Ricœur, *La symbolique du mal*, Paris: Aubier, 1960, p. 21.

concern for the other as a happy, independent and responsible human being. According to Paul Ricœur, ethics is basically grounded in mutual estimation and reciprocity with the other, and the idea of self-estimation and ontological commitment precedes the idea of the other as an absolute imperative of the other, which is proposed by Lévinas to be the absolute source of morality.[18] The foundation of ethics is not an unconditional duty, but mutual affection, where the concern for the fragility of the irreplaceable other is the condition of personal and mutual happiness.[19] Universal duty comes only afterwards when we have to test whether our concepts of the good life can be combined with those of other human beings in society.

In Ricœur's interpretation of Aristotle's ethics, the search for the common good as founded in the idea of the good life is considered as the true foundation of *vouloir-vivre-ensemble* in a political community or in another social context, e.g. a corporation. We can argue that Aristotle is addressing the problem of the relation between community and individual in his discussion of the common good as the aim of ethics. Although there is a possible tension between the good of community and the good of the individual the two concepts of the good are mutually dependent. By saying that the vision of the good life must include the other, we aim at addressing the importance of community for personal fulfilment. With the words of Erwin M. Hartman: "In a good community, the interests of its participants must not be narrowly self-regarding or entirely self-less. Instead, the citizens must want what will preserve the commons; in the long run the community serves their interests will in part because it shapes their interests well, within limits".[20] Accordingly, it is important to stress that the good life with and for the other in just institutions aims at bridging the gap between individual and community without destroying the individual's rights to have personal conceptions of the good life.

18   Emmanuel Lévinas, *Totalité et Infini – Essai sur l'extériorité*, La Haye: Martinus Nijhoff, 1961.
19   Paul Ricœur, *Soi-même comme un autre*, Paris: Editions du Seuil, 1990, p. 236.
20   Erwin M. Hartman: *Organizational ethics and the good life*, Oxford: Oxford University Press, 1996, p. 185.

From the point of view of the common good, the foundation of
politics is not technological rationality, strategic calculation, or a rational
natural law theory, where societies are justified as the result of a contract
between egoistic and fearful individuals in an unbearable state of nature,
but the genuine desire to live together in stable and just institutions. A
basic condition for the political community is not a rational consensus,
but rather common sympathy and understanding based on the ideal of
common realization of freedom in enduring political life and institutions. Although politics primarily must be seen in relation to economic
factors, determined by human interaction with nature to satisfy basic
needs, economy is an external human relationship governed by technology, while politics concerns internal relationships between citizens in a
specific historical community. However, modern welfare economics is
characterized by a dangerous tendency to dissolve political deliberation
in economical rationality and to forget the importance of public space
in community, reducing human beings to mere working machines seeking their private happiness and the meaning of life in work and endless
consumption.

Ideal political praxis is in opposition to the inequalities of economic
relations of work and private intimacy, founded on the open discussion
between free and equal citizens in a public space characterized by respect
for differences and concern for the common good. Erwin M. Hartman
helps us to understand what is meant in this context by the common
good and the good life. He emphasizes that a good organization or a
good society exactly is a society or organization that opens for personal
autonomous search for the good life.[21] Accordingly, when we talk about
the common good, it should only be understood as a result of autonomous deliberation among free and equal individuals, not as the result
of some predetermined objective account of the good of human nature.
When an organization or a community finds principles for the good life
they are results of deliberation not of pre-given rationality or objectivity.
And when such principles concern many individuals they should give

21   Erwin M. Hartman, *op.cit.*, p. 43.

the frame for their search for the good life rather than impose particular conceptions of the good upon them. The aim of ethics of the good life is to develop "virtues, rules, agreements, and institutions" that contribute to value-creation and realization of the good life.[22]

In this very Aristotelian vision of the political community, justice, that is founded in the vision of the common good, can be seen as the search for the right proportion between extremes, determined by the particularity of experiences, situations and involved persons. This idea includes a teleological concept of justice as equity, as the right middle between extremes in the distribution of the goods in society. The equality of distributive justice concerns primary as well as secondary goods, basic political liberties as well as the social and economic situation of the citizens. Although it includes a dimension of abstract equality, the concept of equity admits the heterogeneous character of the goods which means that the idea of the common good emerges out of the concrete aspects of justice in culture and society. From this point of view, it is also important to be aware that the Aristotelian concept of the good life of the aim of the just community constitutes a vision of the good that can said to be the foundation of concepts of universal justice in the sense that the driving force of the theory of justice is the concern for the good society. Therefore, it is not surprising that we can argue that it is necessary to limit the contextual vision of the common good with a test of the possible universality of moral norms and principles for the social contract.

Accordingly, we may consider the foundations of common good for business and society in the international community as based on the "vision of ethics as the good life with and for others in just institutions".[23] According to Ricœur's concept of ethics, such limits on corporate action are based on the view of corporations as institutions which should contribute to the good life in society. However, ethics face the problem of the relation between community and universal norms of society. If we

22   Erwin M. Hartman, *op.cit.*, p. 60.
23   Paul Ricœur, *Soi-même comme un autre*, Paris: Editions du Seuil, 1990, p. 202; Jacob Dahl Rendtorff, *Paul Ricœurs filosofi*, Copenhagen: Hans Reitzels Forlag, 2000.

follow Aristotle's economics, the market system is nothing but a means to facilitate exchange in order to create a good political community. Such a virtue ethics would consider every firm and organization as a part of a broader social context. The firm may be viewed as "a form of life", a community of excellence based on virtuous and good behavior, building moral character through experience. The aim of work is not primarily to earn money but to cultivate an ability contributing to the good life of community. Individuals are required to act according to the virtues and to fulfill required standards of conduct as participants of the firm which develops a culture of excellence.[24] This communitarian approach to ethics is based on the view of the firm as belonging to a culture and to a society with particular traditions and standards of excellence which are required to be respected in corporate economic action.

II. The Importance of Shared Values and Mutual Recognition for the Common Good

Ricœur's vision of the good life in just institutions implies a criticism of the neo-liberal theories of absolute liberty, because those theories do not work with any concept of a common good. Welfare economics is also too limited to the optimization of resources and it implies a too simple concept of preferences, so that it cannot grasp the importance of community. Kant and Rawls contribute with important concepts of moral norms and ideas of justice as fairness, but they do not help with a concrete conceptualization of the virtues of a just community. In contrast, Ricœur's approach uses the criticism of liberalism of Alasdair MacIntyre and Michael Walzer to promote local culture and historical tradition as important sources of the good life.[25] Such narrative representations of

24   Henri Denis, *Histoire de la pensée économique*, Paris: PUF, 1966, pp. 36–54.
25   Paul Ricœur, *Du texte à l'action*, Paris: Editions du Seuil, 1986.

visions and aims of the good are necessary for the development of ethics. However, the universalism of Kant and Rawls also sets limits to possible visions of the good life, because their concepts of society imply that individual concepts of morality must be compatible with Kantian universal and cosmopolitan ideals of equal social and political rights to all citizens, according to practical reason and categorical imperative.[26]

Consequently, we have to find the right balance between extremes, in the space embracing abstract concepts of justice of fairness and universal norms, respect for human dignity, responsibility and freedom in a *Rechtsstaat* built on the rule of law on the one hand; and visions of a common praxis for the community, a concrete morality of society on the other. In fact, what we look for may be a kind a "Post-Hegelian Kantianism", open to concepts of community and social coherences within the Hegelian concept of *Sittlichkeit* (global ethical life) which is a necessary foundation for political community in modern society. *Sittlichkeit* means concrete ethics or ethical life in community, and in international society we may talk about "global ethical life". Charles Taylor interprets Hegel's concept of *Sittlichkeit* in the following way: *"Sittlichkeit* is the usual German term for 'ethics', with the same kind of etymological origin, in term 'Sitten', which we might translate 'customs'. But Hegel gives it a special sense, in contrast to 'Moralität' ... *Sittlichkeit* refers to the moral obligations I have to community of which I am a part".[27] We may say that this is an ethical definition of the idea of the common good. In search for the common good we can define *Sittlichkeit* as the necessary *common global ethos* that is behind the creation of the vision of the common good in international business and society. Indeed, we can integrate the discussion of ethical life in the framework of a political philosophy and theory of business ethics. In his later work Ricœur enters into the debate about the concept of recognition with regard to the constitution of the self and

---

26　Jacob Dahl Rendtorff, *Paul Ricœurs filosofi*, Copenhagen: Hans Reitzels Forlag, 2000.

27　Charles Taylor, *Hegel*, Cambridge (UK): Cambridge University Press, 1977, p. 376.

society, and he argues that the relationship of recognition is important for social, legal and political integration.[28]

In this way Hegel tried to solve the problem of formal and abstract morality in Kant's philosophy by proposing the concept of ethical life indicating the idea of common ethical life of community as an expression of the vision of the common good.[29] This idea of a common morality emerged out of Hegel's critique of abstract Kantian morality and can be considered as an attempt to define the common good. When practical reason cannot be in harmony with concrete reality it has no value. An abstract concept of liberty is totally formal and cannot govern the reality of political life. The Hegelian attempt is to make a reconciliation of freedom and community in the realization of objective morality through the concept of ethical life, expressed in concrete mediations. By ethical life Hegel refers to the norms of practical, social and political life of a society. Those norms are the foundations of the interactions between individuals in that society.

The German philosopher and sociologist Axel Honneth contributes to the clarification of the concept of *Sittlichkeit* in modern society. He argues for the need for a conception of community in modernity and in this sense he contributes with a new approach to the debate between liberals and communitarians. Like Ricœur, Honneth maintains that we need to work with a concept of the good life or rather with a vision of the common good in modern society. We cannot restrict ethics to a formal theory of rights and justice, but we need an account of concrete visions of the good life in society, because society is characterized by concrete processes of fight for recognition where different social groups are searching to be recognized as respectable participants of the political community.[30] Honneth states that society may be characterized by many different groups with different conceptions of the good life. Those different groups have to be recognized in their dignity and integrity in order to be considered as members of the community. Modern society is not determined by homogeneous ethics,

28   Paul Ricœur, *Parcours de la reconnaissance, Trois études*, Paris: Stock, 2004.
29   Paul Ricœur, *Soi-même comme un autre*, Paris: Editions du Seuil, 1990, p. 279.
30   Axel Honneth, *The Struggle for Recognition*, Cambridge: Polity Press, 1995.

but it is a pluralistic society with many different conceptions of the good. Honneth thinks that the debate about liberalism and communitarianism is a debate about what kind of values are needed, and how they should be, in order to get a sufficient basis for the norms of a common social order of modern society.

In fact, we can say that it is possible by characterizing the particular democratic global ethos with Rawls and Arendt as a *conflictual-consensual* society, where there is always disagreement about distributive justice in concrete cases, but where an agreement prevails about certain basic legal and constitutional procedures.[31] In practical political life, government is based on the formation of public opinion, the irreducible plurality that cannot be overcome in philosophical idealizations of political life. The boundaries of political community are no others than this *conflictual consensus* determined by a sense of community and by the willingness to test personal conviction in the confrontation between opinions in a public space of discussion. The reason is that the possibility of violence in discourse is the other side of political language.[32] Language can be seen as an overcoming or reduction of violence, because the appeal to understanding and reason is implied in language as opposed to the mute character of violent force. The democratic process of deliberation leads to the transformation of potential political violence into peaceful disagreement in discussion, whereas the totalitarian use of language implies the transformation of language into an instrument of manipulation.

However, no democratic communication is without difference and power. In Ricœur's perspective, conflict is an essential and basic aspect of communication. Communication takes places as a *loving struggle* (*combat amoureux*)[33] between particular peoples with different convictions that imply certain openness, because they expose their convictions to the argumentative force of language and the rationality of discourse. The argumentative force of language cannot be reduced to the violence of instrumental calculation, and the reduction of language to calculation

31   Paul Ricœur, *Lectures 1. Essais politiques*, Paris: Editions du Seuil, 1990, p. 219.
32   Paul Ricœur, *op.cit.*, p. 132.
33   Paul Ricœur, *op.cit.*, p. 137.

leaves no room for critical reflection on the ends of actions. At the same time, political language should not become pure rhetoric, seeking only to impose a hidden goal without appealing to reason and a vision of the common good. Even if one cannot overcome personal convictions, commitments and beliefs, the responsibility towards the other, due to respect for the moral norm, implies the willingness to engage in an open debate about the argumentative validity of personal convictions. This respect for the presence of reason in the diversity of languages implies a non-violent attitude regarding the plurality of discourses and convictions.[34]

On this basis with Ricœur we can reject the Hegelian attempt to seek an objective morality, but emphasize however two other aspects of the idea of ethical life in a democratic society as expression of the common values of respect for individual autonomy and common political ideals. We can mention the tension between the Aristotelian vision of the good life and with the Kantian moral norm that may be present in the political and social culture of society.[35] In particular, we can recognize the existential tension between the individual and the State, between private and public, between the commitment to the other, to the family, and the commitment to the values of the State, where the personal obligations and devotions of the citizen are designated to enter into insoluble conflict with the law and the morals of the State. The private sphere of commitments, responsibilities and beliefs can never totally be integrated into the morals of the political community. The finitude and tragedy of action signify that human beings on the political as well as the personal level are continuously confronted with destiny and never for certain have awareness and transparent knowledge of all the consequences of their actions. Moral choices, determined by ignorance, passion or emotional blindness lead to wrong actions and consequently the moral destruction of the self.

---

34   Paul Ricœur, *op.cit.*, p. 140.
35   G.W.F. Hegel, *Grundlinien der Philosophie des Rechts*, Stuttgart: Reklam Universal-Bibliotek, 1981; G.W.F. Hegel, *Phänomenologie des Geistes*, Hamburg: Felix Meiner Verlag, 1988 (1807); Paul Ricœur, *Du texte à l'action*, Paris: Editions du Seuil, 1987, p. 237.

Ricœur draws attention to Hegel's interpretation of the Greek tragedy of Sophocles, *Antigone*, as an example of how even morally superior human beings can be caught in the game of destiny, the contingency and unexpectedness of human life.[36] Kreon, a tyrant, the leader of the Polis, forbids Antigone to bury her brother at the burial place, because the brother has acted contrary to the wishes of the State. Antigone must make a choice between loyalty towards her brother and loyalty to the laws of the State. She chooses to bury her brother and therefore does not obey the law and institutions of the State. She is committed to a divine law, her own ontological commitment, and promise to her brother, which overrides her duty to respect the positive legal code of the State. The tragedy illustrates the priority of the personal commitment in relation to the objective legal code, and the possible oppositions between profound individual beliefs and State institutions.

Political communities, even democratic societies obeying the rule of law are never totally free of such moral conflicts. Personal ethical convictions, actions and responsibilities happen to be in insoluble conflict with the norms and ethical life of the community. Such a conflict implies contradiction between universal principles of morality, the vision of the good life of the community and the ethical commitment of the individual in promise and responsibility to a divine law. Even the most well-founded consensus would turn into totalitarianism, if it did not allow the emergence of dissent as a possibility that would always be real. Therefore, a realization of a final, universal, objective ethical life is impossible and there will always remain a potential gap between positive and divine law.

Furthermore, some situations show tragic dilemmas where there is no satisfying outcome of the conflict. Here, the respect for the legal rules of the State, personal conviction and the respect due to the other person are in insoluble conflict. Consequently, society must always recognize the eternal tension between the human being and the State. In this context Ricœur emphasizes the respect for the individual and the importance of conflict in the Hegelian definition of the ethical life where individual

---

36   Paul Ricœur, *Soi-même comme un autre*, Paris: Editions du Seuil, 1990, p. 281.

freedom and subjectivity are essential parts of modern society. Justice and law cannot be totally founded on culture and tradition, but a universal dimension is acquired in the philosophy of law. By the continuous recognition and acceptance of the possibility of conflict as an essential dimension of democracy, the republican notion of peoples' sovereignty, e.g. respect for autonomy and fair legal procedures as founded in the constitution and institutional political or organizational praxis, can mediate between individual, universal and community norms, in opposition to the terror and technological rationality of a totalitarian society, reducing the individual to an abstract function of the State.

The character of this institutional praxis can be illustrated by the concept of authority.[37] In opposition to a totalitarian political institution or a bureaucratic private enterprise with strong hierarchical management structures, we may say with Ricœur that real authority presupposes the recognition of the political community in a democratic process of legitimization. Authority is neither based on the natural will of God, nor on the laws of a totalitarian regime, but is founded on the decisions of the political community. Authentic political authority must be distinguished from domination and force, because it relies on the common power of the participants of the political community. Authority in open institutions relies on the shared understandings of the *vivre ensemble* in the political community.[38]

In conclusion, the concept of ethical life or global shared values expresses the necessary global ethos that is an important dimension of the search for the common good in international business and society. This idea of a common ground of shared understandings and ethical life is important for the development of a global vision of the common good. Without a firm foundation in shared understandings of democratic civil life in respect for liberty and rights it is very difficult to create a vision of the common good for the international community that can be promoted through business practices and codes of conduct for organizational and

---

37   Paul Ricœur, *Lectures 1. Essais politiques*, Paris: Editions du Seuil, 1990, p. 19.
38   Paul Ricœur, *Soi-même comme un autre*, Paris: Editions du Seuil, 1990, p. 27.

corporate ethics. However, there is no common good without individual responsibility and judgment.

III. Business in Global Society: The Role of Reflective Judgment to Achieve the Common Good

With these reflections about the foundations of the common good in modern society we will therefore formulate a theory of judgment as the general framework for business ethics and corporate citizenship as based on "the aim of the good life with and for the other in just institutions". With the reference to the concept of global ethical life we can argue that the ethics of community is where the concrete dialectics between the good life and the moral norm is realized. With judgment and practical reason global ethical life represents the concrete institutional mediation of morality in which practical wisdom is exercised. In these concrete mediations in institutions abstract moral principles and principles of justice are related to concrete cases in what Ricœur calls a "hermeneutic style philosophy of good government". Accordingly, judgment and practical wisdom deal with concrete justice in concrete cases and we can say that concrete cases of business ethics articulate the tensions between deontology and teleology. From the perspective of business ethics it is the task of ethical judgment to operate in the space of expression in reflective equilibrium between the ethics of argumentation and considered convictions.[39]

The starting point is the pluralism of ethical values within economic systems, which, however, includes utility and efficiency as predominant values. After this we can conceive the ethical foundation of economics with the principles of democratic values as external limitations of economic action. Ethics may be conceived as a kind of political theory of

---

39 Paul Ricœur, *op.cit.*, p. 289.

market economics and we cannot ignore the perspective of the State.[40] Business ethics is not only about the relationship between ethics and economics, but it is also about finding the right balance between political governance of market economies and legal incentives for economic behavior. In this way we can say that the main issue of business ethics is the problem of ethical behavior of the firm in relation with its surroundings in the market and in society at large. The firm is placed in the context of the political economy of society. Business ethics and corporate citizenship are about the right values at the micro-level of organizations, but also about individual behavior at the macro-level. In this sense business ethics is about defining acceptable ethical positions of the firm within society and in relation to the State. Business in the ethical perspective is not only a descriptive and positivist discipline about the factual values of organizations, individuals and market systems, but it also concerns the normative question of which values should be promoted regarding the relation between organizations, individuals, and market economies in a broader social and political context.

Thus, business ethics can be conceived as based on an interdisciplinary approach to social sciences integrating views from economics, sociology, political science, law, organization theory and ethics, in order to discuss the right values and ethical principles to be promoted in business life. When we deal with the concept of the common good we propose a vision of *social man* as the foundation for economic anthropology, which is much broader than the limited idea of *economic man* only following self-interest. Utility-maximizing individuals are not guided by absolute principles of utility, but personal preferences only get meaning within the context of a "vision (aim) of the good life with and for the others in just institutions".[41] Within this view of economic action, rationality in economic theory is not based on "homo œconomicus maximizing individual

---

40   Jacob Dahl Rendtorff, "Critical Hermeneutics in Law and Politics", in Lars Henrik Schmidt, ed., *Paul Ricœur in the Conflict of Interpretations*, Aarhus: Aarhus University Press, 1996; Jacob Dahl Rendtorff, *Paul Ricœurs filosofi*, Copenhagen: Hans Reitzels Forlag, 2000.

41   Paul Ricœur, *Soi-même comme un autre*, Paris: Editions du Seuil, 1990, p. 202.

preferences", but on individuals who are integrated in social relationships of reciprocity and exchange. This social notion of rationality places the economic actor within an ethical community of values and visions of the common good and therefore the firm must be conceived in the perspective of broader institutional and social dimensions.[42] It is the reciprocity and the exchange of social man in community which constitute the basis for understanding economic action. We may say that it is the task of judgment in business ethics to find good and right decisions concerning action in economic affairs. Here, business ethics can learn a lot from the concept of legal and political judgment in philosophy of law.[43]

In his analysis of judgment, Ricœur combines Aristotle and Kant.[44] Practical reason assures the respect for the moral norm and the recognition of basic procedural rules in a society. But, because of the possible exceptions to the rules and the particularity of situations, practical wisdom and judgment is required as a necessary supplement to practical reason. Practical wisdom is needed in exceptional situations of difficult tragic dilemmas where universal norms are difficult to apply. However, in many cases concrete judgment is required to intervene in the application of general rules and values. So both faculties of human deliberation contribute to the work of the unfinished mediation between the ideal of the good life, universal principles in relation to concrete situations and social traditions. Ricœur uses the concept of judgment in Kant's *Critique of Judgment*, inspired by Hannah Arendt in *Lectures on Kant's Political Philosophy*.[45] The Kantian understanding of judgment is as such, an effort to approach the formalistic concept of practical reason to the situation and tradition of the political community. Ricœur defines in law judgment as a peaceful way of solving

42 François-Régis Mahieu, *Éthique économique, fondements anthropologiques*, Paris: L'Harmattan, 2001, p. 314.

43 Hannah Arendt, *Lectures on Kant's Political Philosophy*, in Ronald Beiner, ed., Chicago: University of Chicago Press, 1982.

44 Paul Ricœur, *Du texte à l'action*, Paris: Editions du Seuil, 1986, p. 237.

45 Immanuel Kant, *Kritik der Urteilskraft*, Frankfurt: Suhrkamp Werkausgabe, 2004 (1794).

social conflict.[46] Here general understandings and principles of justice are applied to concrete situations. The legal system, autonomous, different from and yet mediated through public debate and political legislation, implies a rational discourse about justice, where minimum mutual respect, human punishment and recognition of basic rights even of those to be punished replace pure violence.

Accordingly, judgment is an important faculty to promote mediation and decision-making in the application of ethical principles in relation to concrete situations of economic decision-making and action.[47] The Kantian concept of judgment extends the Aristotelian idea of practical reason, phronesis, which is the capacity of deliberation and reasoning for the good life in community according to the moral sense and habitus of the experienced moral actor. In this context judgment finds the right course of action, the means of virtue and consistency between extremes. Kant does not only consider the importance of the means for finding the good life, but he also points to the moral sentiments and common morality of human beings, sensus communis.[48] Moral judgments find universal validity in the appeal to common sense and to the shared values of human beings.

Determinate judgment is the capacity to apply already established general rules to concrete cases. Reflective judgment is the ability to find new rules for new cases where there are no pre-established rules or principles that are intuitively given or self-evident. Judgment in business ethics is not only the application of ethical principles to factual cases. Rather it should also be responsible for mediating between ethics and economics in relation to other disciplines of social sciences which are important for decision-making and research. What is required in reflective judgment is moral imagination and the ability to integrate and weigh in judgments different disciplines and viewpoints in regard to concrete decision-making.

46   Paul Ricœur, "Juger", *Esprit*, 1992.
47   Lynn Sharp Paine, "Law, Ethics and Managerial Judgment", *The Journal of Legal Studies Education*, Vol. 12, n°2, 1994.
48   Paul Ricœur, "Juger", *Esprit*, 1992; Immanuel Kant, *Kritik der Urteilskraft*, Frankfurt: Suhrkamp Werkausgabe, 2004 (1794).

The faculty of judgment – applied to decisions-makers in the good citizen corporation – can be said to have two major finalities. The first one is the finality of economic efficiency and the second one is the finality of contributing to the integration and development of society towards the ideal of a community of ends in themselves.

Although the reflective judgment in Kant's *Critique of Judgment* primarily concerns aesthetics and natural teleology, one should not forget its significance for the concepts of political rationality and jurisprudence.[49] There is a logical and structural analogy between aesthetical, political and judicial judgment. The characteristics of judgment are mediation between particularity and universality in a space of intersubjective, public deliberation and communication concerning judgments of opinion and taste related to particular cases, and founded on the common under-standing of validity and shared values. Judgment as formation of political opinion, legislative act and concrete legal processes can be conceived as an interaction between understanding, imagination, reason and *sensus communis*. We may emphasize the distributive character of judgment as being a peaceful way to solve conflicts of ownership in a discursive rather than in a violent way. It distributes things and goods among individuals. It decides conflicts of ownership among individuals taking part in soci-ety as a system of exchange of goods. Here judgment contributes to the delimitation between spheres in society. As a contributor to social peace, judgment presupposes a vision of society as fundamentally cooperative, so that the communitarian vision of community as a fragile and vulnerable context of *vouloir-vivre-ensemble* is behind the very exercise of judgment to maintain social peace.

But conflicts about repartition of the good in different spheres of justice often also transcend shared understandings. Common visions of the good are often realized to be inadequate, and must be confronted with universal standards and individual autonomy. Disagreement with State policy can lead to civil disobedience in the name of the divine law, and

---

49   Paul Ricœur, *Le Juste 1*, Paris: Collection Esprit, 1994; Paul Ricœur, "Juger", *Esprit*, 1992; Immanuel Kant, *Kritik der Urteilskraft*, Frankfurt: Suhrkamp Werkausgabe, 2004 (1794).

the corresponding *hard cases* that, according to Ronald Dworkin's analysis in *Taking Rights Seriously*, are an appeal to rights and principles which must be seen as the foundation for innovation and reform insuring legal coherence. This conception of judgment focuses on the concrete conflicts in society, assuring the right balance between shared understandings and *judicial* universality in opposition to ideology and contingent interests of power. We can refer to Dworkin's hermeneutical-narrative understanding of law as integrity (*Law's Empire*) concerned with the respect for principles of political morality and progressive innovation according to the principles of equality, fairness and impartiality, based on a permanent reinterpretation of the constitutional basis and emergent legal practice. We can say that reflective judgment constitutes the mediating bridge between micro-economic rationality of free market economics, based on individual economic actors on the one hand, and macro-economic rationality of welfare and rights in political community on the other.

Moreover, we neither opt exclusively for an ethics of the lonely *moral manager*, nor solely for an ethics of the economic market or of the business system as a structural totality, nor for an ethics of political welfare economics, based on the allocation of goods and services by democratic political authorities. To focus exclusively on one of these fields of ethics may lead to negligence of important knowledge. Republican business ethics uses the faculty of judgment in order to celebrate the internal ethical dynamics of micro-economics, but also to impose external ethical limits on economic actions in order to contribute to social justice in community. This means that business ethics does not only operate on the micro-level of ethical behavior of individual rights and ethics in firms. It also operates at the level of organizational behavior and more broadly at the level of market institutions. But business ethics also goes further and takes the point of view of State regulation and macro-economic ethics concerning the significance of the organization of market economies for the general development of society.

Conclusion

In this paper we have focused on the foundations of the common good in business and society. This idea of the common good can be considered as the theoretical ground of arguments for corporate social responsibility (CSR), corporate citizenship and of the concept of the good citizen corporation. The idea of the common good also represents the foundation of the social contract between society and business corporations. We have conceptualized this idea of the common good in republican democracy by referring to Paul Ricœur's concept of the "good life with and for the other in just institutions". According to Ricœur the common good is based on this combination between happiness and justice. At the level of global society this means that the common good combines cosmopolitan ideals of universal respect for rights with concern for the particularity of the concrete ethical life of particular cultures.

The idea of ethical life (*Sittlichkeit*) in a republican democracy, proposed by the philosopher Hegel was in this sense used to propose a necessary concrete foundation of the vision of the common good. In order to develop the common good in global society we need to find a common ethical life that is based on shared democratic and social values. It is finally the task of reflective judgment to mediate between different ethical fields. It is, in the perspective of business ethics, the role of business institutions to contribute to the realization of the aim and vision of the good life within just institutions, and to help to improve fair co-existence in the framework of a human community based on the vision of the common good, in a republican democracy conceived as a kingdom of ends in themselves respecting human freedom and autonomy.

CHAPTER 15

Corporate Responsibility and Global Social Contract: New Constructivist, Personalist and Dialectical Perspectives[1]

JEAN-JACQUES ROSÉ

Introduction

This chapter attempts to summarize and to expand upon a recent collection of essays entitled *Responsabilité sociale de l'entreprise. Pour un nouveau contrat social* (*Corporate Social Responsibility. Towards a New Social Contract*, J.-J. Rosé, ed., 2006) which may be considered as a starting point to show the necessary links between Responsibility, Social Contract and Justice. Why have we run the risk of choosing a title that could be understood as a paradox or even an epistemological transgression? How and why do we dare to reconnect, in a research project, an ordinary management science's concept (corporate social responsibility) with the founding notion of modern political philosophy (the social contract) and an ancient concept of Greek and medieval metaphysics and ethics, (the Common Good)? This may be a paradox, but if it is a transgression, it is voluntary and out of necessity. The purpose of this essay is to demonstrate this statement.

In his *Esquisse historique sur le mot responsable* (*History of the Word Responsible*), M. Villey (1977) declares: "I'm surprised that, while it

---

[1]   English version written in collaboration with Abby Shepard. Except when the English reference of a quoted text is given, the translation is our own.

constituted the primary focus of the field in Rome, the sort of responsibility that we call 'contractual' has not held your attention". According to Villey, it is a question of analyzing compensation for harm in the sense of Roman law inspired by Aristotle's theory of "corrective justice", where its contractual character is strongly emphasized. The link between responsibility and justice is historically rooted in two periods:

– the common religious origin of the two notions, and
– their progressive secularization.

Ethnographers and sociologists like L. Lévy-Bruhl (1884) and P. Fauconnet (1928 – who belonged to the Durkheim school) have retraced the process by which responsibility and justice evolved from religious and collective cults into individual and subjective duty and awareness. The philosopher P. Ricœur (1960) followed the succession from impurity to sin to misdeed in Greek (Moulinier, 1952) and Biblical texts, and analyzed how these notions were historically constructed through legislation, litigation and judges' sentences. His analysis leads us back to Aristotle's text which specifies how compensation balances out the harm done to the "Other":

– the obligation to compensate still exists whether or not the damage was caused voluntarily,
– precisely because "corrective justice" consists of returning to the state prior to the injury.

Throughout history, being responsible has always signified justice and contract between moral and physical persons. In the cities emerging from the 12th century, M. Weber (1998) and J.-L. Génard (1999) have observed the transformation of a feudalism characterized by asymmetrical pledges of allegiance into a modern society where citizenship replaced allegiances with new social relationships between equal individuals. These historical facts were formalized into the theories of civil contracts (Pufendorf) and social contracts (Hobbes, Locke). Therefore it is not possible to separate social responsibility from the theory of political sovereignty: both come from the same ideological source, much like Siamese twins. It was not only by chance that the noun *responsibility* appeared immediately after the height of the expression of the Social Contract as the modern principle of political legitimacy in the English and French languages.

Henriot (1977, 1990) cites the *Dictionnaire critique de la langue française* (*Critical Dictionary of the French Language*, 1787–1788), to illustrate the first occurrences of the word responsibility:

– in English, attributed to Hamilton in the preparatory writings for the Federal Constitution,
– and in French, attributed to Necker in reference to paper money ("Trust in this paper which comes from government responsibility").

Contrary to the cliché, it was the Frenchman who established responsibility's origin in monetary exchanges, while the American traced it back to political philosophy. In fact, its historical origin is the verb *respondere* ("to answer for") in Roman law, which means to act as guarantor. This shows that the legal codification of the verb occurred in response to economic and commercial constraints and realities of the time (Andreau, 2001). The modern evolution, according to Henriot, is the result of the new connections between responsibility, the right to property, and human rights in the context and even the texts of the American and French Revolutions:

– representative democracy is based on the political responsibility of government;
– responsibility is based on voluntary and reciprocal trust according to social contract theories.

During the same period, Adam Smith wrote separately *The Theory of Moral Sentiments* (1759) and *The Wealth of Nations* (1776), and only the epistemological rupture[2] between economics and ethics could have

---

2   This was very clearly formulated in a general way by D. Hume (see infra section 5). A. Smith and D. Hume met around 1750 and became close friends over the course

generated such prolific literature about the famous "Adam Smith's problem". Moreover, this period of modernity produced, as everyone knows, the epistemological autonomy of political economics, then of economic science and finally, in the 20th century, management sciences. From these ruptures on, and correlatively, the two terms of *responsibility* and the *social contract* would indeed be deployed in spaces that no longer intersect: they are surplus, both foreign to the disciplines of political economics and management. This is what explains the paradoxical character today of the link that we propose to establish between corporate social responsibility and the social contract. This is the "modern" history of the separation between disciplines (ethics, politics, economics, management), which imposes, from an epistemological point of view (in the sense of the ever existing disassociation between these disciplines), the heavily problematic character of the link between responsibility and the social contract.

The goal of this chapter is to interrogate some major works by such authors as Rousseau, Durkheim, Donaldson and Dunfee and Ricœur. We have thus assembled texts produced in seemingly historically and culturally heterogeneous spheres, but whose aim is common: to connect what was separated by Hume's epistemological rupture (between the "is" and the "ought") as well as to find a possible foundation for transcendence (without which there is no ethics). The declared intention of these very ambitious authors is to explore the paths to overcome the *aporias*[3] that characterize the "modern" era in a way that makes a new teleological phenomena approach possible.

In other words, it develops a critique of the "modern" paradigm which is epistemologically split into economics and management on the one hand, and ethics and politics on the other. The reading of Donaldson and Dunfee's *Ties That Bind – A Social Contracts Approach to Business Ethics* (1999b) as an application of Rawls' procedural theory of justice in the field of economics is the cornerstone of the thesis presented here. We will

---

of the years and their many fervent discussions. Hume eventually made Smith the executor of his will.

3   *Aporia*: etymological Greek root: absence of passage. Thus by extension: raising questions without necessarily answering them.

use Ricœur's very subtle analysis to claim that all forms of procedural and deontological ethics presuppose or imply finality as a hidden principle or assumption. Rousseau's *The Social Contract* explicitly permits the General Will to define the Common Good: "Only the general will can direct the powers of the state in accordance with the purpose for which it was established, which is the common good".[4] This movement is the opposite of mainstream 20th century ethics, which tends to push the idea of Good out of Philosophy. On the contrary, we try to show how it is not possible to articulate any sort of discourse relative to human action (even when it concerns its economic dimension) without it at least being implicitly conceived before concepts of a teleological nature.

Our starting point is Durkheim's reading of Rousseau's social contract which establishes social bonds as the new foundation of moral transcendence (section 1). With Donaldson and Dunfee, we see how a contractarian approach is mobilized to respond to the challenge resulting from the relative failure of business ethics attributed by them to the insurmountable separation between works of normative dimension and empirical research[5] (section 2). To evaluate the aptitude of the "Integrative Social Contracts Theory" (ISCT) to truly overcome this challenge, we follow Ricœur in his reading of John Rawls, who shows how the idea of good is preconceived in the theory of justice (section 3). On the contrary, the interpretation Ricœur gives of finality in *The Nichomachean Ethics* allows for the validation of Donaldson and Dunfee's central idea of coexistence between the micro-social contract and the macro-social contract (section 4). A close rereading of a few passages from Rousseau's *The Social Contract* leads from the foundation of individual ethics in Aristotle's and Ricœur's works to the foundation of just institutions for modern society (section 5). Since any affirmation of a teleological phenomena approach is justly suspected of masking forms of manipulative ideologies, it is necessary to disarm this trap before designing any new perspective

---

4   Rousseau J.-J., 1984, *The Social Contract*, New York: Penguin Books, p. 69.
5   Donaldson and Dunfee (1999b), p. 9: "These two approaches to business ethics, which we will call the 'empirical' and the 'normative', have produced two powerful streams of business research."

today of a social contract on a global scale by mobilizing in particular the results of empirical studies conducted to test the feasibility of ISCT theories (section 6).

To conclude, by referring to a certain number of contemporary works within several disciplines, we will attempt to trace the axis of research that redefines corporate social responsibility in a global social contract.

1. Social Contract, Legitimacy and Issues Concerning the Modern Foundations of Normative Ethics Theories

At the beginning of the 20th century, Durkheim provided a new philosophical and epistemological interpretation in addition to his reading of Rousseau's *The Social Contract* (Durkheim, 1918, p. 7):

> It is impossible not to be struck by the resemblance between this method and Descartes'. Both esteem that science's first procedure must consist of a sort of intellectual purging, having the effect of throwing all the indirect judgments that have not been scientifically proven out of the intellect, in a way that uncovers the confirmed proposals from which all others should be derived. On the one hand and on the other, it is a matter of clearing the ground of all the inconsistent dust that encumbers it in order to bare the solid rock that the edifice of all knowledge should rest upon, here theoretical, there practical. The conception of a state of nature is therefore not simply, as sometimes believed, the product of a sentimentalist reverie, a philosophical restoration of ancient beliefs relative to the golden age; it is a methodical process.[6]

In general, Rousseau is seen as one of the principal theorists of modern democratic legitimacy. Durkheim uses the comparison of Rousseau and

6   Our translation based on Durkheim's text, *Le contrat social de Rousseau*, published for the first time after his death in the *Revue de Métaphysique et de Morale*, Vol. XXV, 1918, pp. 1–23 and 129–61. An electronic version is available on the following website: http://classiques.uqac.ca/classiques/Durkheim_emile/durkheim.html.

Descartes' analytical methods to show that it is impossible to establish political legitimacy without having first characterized the nature of social bonds.[7] Durkheim and Rousseau's identical position on this theoretical foundation is more important than choosing between the natural and conventional characters of social bonds. As explained by Goyard-Fabre (1990):

> The issue of society's origins and foundations has received two responses from classical philosophy: naturalist and constructivist.[8] Thus the idea of the social contract was born in the sophists' circles of the 5th century B.C., while throughout the centuries, the naturalist thesis – of which Aristotle is the most illustrious representative – diminished (despite several recurrences), the contractarian thesis underwent considerable development. But the contractarian inflation of modern times goes hand in hand with formidable problems.

For a sophist like Protagoras, the conventional origin of the idea of citizenship embodies the crucial separation (or rupture) of the political from nature, religion and myth (Guthrie, 1971; Romilly, 1988). However, in Plato's as well as in Aristotle's works, both the naturalist and contractarian theses are largely presented and discussed in such a way that it seems difficult to attribute to each author one position or another. The contract (or pact or convention) amongst individuals is of fundamental importance to the creation of social bonds, citizenship, morality and the economy, as we have previously seen in the theory of corrective justice. One of the strong points of Durkheim's article is that he shows how Rousseau renewed the research on the normative foundation of social bonds: Rousseau not only explains the origins of political sovereignty with the myth of social contract but also logically deduces that it is the driving force behind all economic activity.

After having analyzed Rousseau's quest for a foundation of normative transcendence, Durkheim shows how the separation from the state of nature necessarily leads to the social contract and, consequently, to Man's invention of an economic age. This myth explains the origins of

---

7   For Durkheim, social bonds are always moral.
8   The French term used in Goyard-Fabre's text is: *une réponse artificialiste.*

inequality and injustice, codified by the right to property: "It is evidently against the law of nature, however defined [...] that a handful of people gorge themselves on surplus while the starving multitude is in want of basic necessities".[9] The singular relevance of this terrible sentence to the beginning of the 21st century is that it allows us to better understand how, far from being a dusty concept, Aristotle's corrective justice constitutes a pertinent and urgent injunction today. The objective of the social contract is the same for corrective justice: to re-establish a natural equilibrium (for Rousseau it is the equilibrium of the state of nature) unbalanced by a freely consented-to contract.

2. Donaldson and Dunfee's Rawlsian Response within Normative and Empirical Business Ethics

At the end of the 20th century, Donaldson and Dunfee's work *Ties That Bind* (1999b) addressed the dichotomy brought up by Durkheim in his analysis of Rousseau. The first chapter starts off by challenging both scholars and business managers to find a solution to the ethical dilemmas that multinationals face when trying to apply vague normative theories of business ethics. A couple of well-known cases are Shell in Nigeria and at Brent Spar in the North Sea, which are used to demonstrate two key ideas:

– obligations must be far more precise when applied to ethics in economics than to ethics in general. This first idea ties into Durkheim's view (2004, p. 113): "there is one rank of values which cannot be detached from concrete experience without losing all significance: these are economic values";

9   Rousseau, 1992. These are the final lines of the *Discourse on the Origin of Inequality.*

– concrete ethical obligations vary according to each culture where they are formed and applied, rendering the situation even more complex for multinationals, which have to change their moral judgments depending on the location where they operate.

With this introduction Donaldson and Dunfee clearly show how the ethical dilemmas that multinationals must respond to, constitute an exemplary demonstration of the concrete current circumstances of theoretical questions resulting from by the epistemological rupture noted by Hume at the beginning of modernity (no possible passage between is and ought) and to which Rousseau, Kant and Durkheim have each attempted, in their own way, to respond. For Donaldson and Dunfee, like for Durkheim, the root of the contradiction lies in the necessary empiricism of values in the economic domain. The spectacular way by which *Ties That Bind* shows the variation of moral prescriptions from one culture to another renders this aporia even more intense and more intolerable because it poses a daily challenge to multinational companies. The diversity of ethical prescriptions according to each culture is not, of course, a new phenomenon in history, as different cultural norms have always existed, but distant economic exchanges presupposed long voyages from one corner of the world to other, totally separate ones, assuming specific risks which, since antiquity, have been instruments of economic development such as insurance and credit (Andreau, 2001; Weber, 1998).

Globalization's current form is characterized by technology and information, as well as by the speed of transportation: it consists of the creation of one single space – of a simultaneity that causes the differences in norms to become intolerable (Scholte, 2000, 2005). Thus the differences in cultural norms automatically generate confrontation (not to be confused with the so-called *clash of civilizations*). Multinationals have fewer and fewer opportunities to ignore or to escape from these contradictions because they are "forced"[10] by civil and political society to take them into account. If scholars and academics cannot rise to the challenge of finding a solution, then their intellectual function will lose all purpose. Globalization has intensified the pressure of ethical constraints on multinationals due to the diversity of culture-specific applications of normative theories. This pressure is present in business ethics literature, for example, in the necessity of a change in moral perception (Werhane, 2002, 2008; Hartman and Arnold, 2004; French, 2005).

Donaldson and Dunfee's originality is that they have gone beyond the field of business ethics to seek a pre-existing solution in modern political philosophy. Traditional medieval philosophy established the origin of citizens' obedience and the justification of the state's monopoly of violence in a divine transcendental authority. The crumbling of modern political philosophy's foundation led to the necessity of finding a substitute, thus the political social contract became the philosophical foundation for modern democratic regimes. Even though this concept is hypothetical, Donaldson and Dunfee note that it not only worked within theoreticians' texts, but also in the functioning of political institutions after the English, American and French Revolutions. This sort of pragmatism incited the authors to attempt the *transposition* of the social contract from the political to the economic field: since it was successful in another field, why shouldn't it succeed in this one? Nevertheless, Donaldson and Dunfee go beyond the pragmatic dimension in order to legitimize this transposition through the only possible shared epistemological origins of politics and economics: ethics. Their transposition is not only an analogical one, but also constitutes a philosophical reflection on the foundation of norms in general. This explains why in the index of the book the most commonly cited authors are John Rawls (15 references, and 21 references to his *Theory of Justice*), Kant (17 references), Aristotle (8 references), and major American business ethics authors averaging 5 references each.

---

10   The authors express this pressure in a quasi-obsessive way on pages 5 and 6 where the term "forced" is repeated 6 times.

To construct the Integrative Social Contract Theory (ISCT), Donaldson and Dunfee's text follows in Rawls' footsteps, and specifies where they do and do not agree with classic contractarians in general (i.e. Locke and Hobbes) and with Rawls in particular. The ISCT is a theoretical architecture built upon both micro-social contracts between economic actors and rooted in the empirical, and upon macro-social contracts (hypernorms) where the norms are hypothetical and operate at the global level according to the social contract paradigm. The definition of these hypernorms constitutes a detailed discussion[11] which provides a means of escaping relativism and dogmatism by proposing a form of procedural ethics which is found directly in John Rawls' and Amartya Sen's hereditary line of thought:

> We assume then, with Rawls and Sen, that fairness and aggregative welfare constitute necessary goods for any society, no matter how that society is constituted.[12] Other *necessary goods* may exist, but we assume at least these two. Hence, we may conclude that efficiency in the pursuit of fairness and/or aggregative welfare is desirable.[13]

Hypernorms have the ability to accept multicultural content because "the generic form of the hypernorm is independent of culture or economic system".[14] Globalization requires an ethical form of reference compatible with the morals of the entire planet's cultures and subcultures, and which the peoples of each of these cultures may fully recognize. This justifies its designation as a meta-ethic. In his *Globalization: A Critical*

---

11 Habermas (1983), Principe U cited by Apel (1994, p. 78): "Any valid norm must satisfy the condition according to which the consequences and secondary effects result, in a foreseeable way, from the universal observation of the norm with a view to satisfying the interests of everyone, and which could be accepted without constraints by all concerned."

12 Donaldson and Dunfee (1999b, Chapter 5, note 1, p. 266): "The same basic notion of aggregative welfare functions in Rawls' concept of the 'difference principle', which relies on the notion that some *goods* (called '*primary goods*') are the sort that we all want more of, not less of." Our emphasis in italics.

13 Op. cit., p. 121.

14 Op. cit., p. 131.

Introduction, J.A. Scholte's definition of a meta-ethic coincides with the objectives laid out by the ISBEE at its First World Conference in Tokyo in July 1996 (Wokutch and Shepard, 1999): "This conference brought together leading business ethics scholars and theologians from around the world, as well as Japanese business and government leaders, and it demonstrated a far greater interest in Japanese business ethics than had formerly been evident."

"Meta-ethic" signifies that each culture is based upon one *Universal* or upon several, but far from being identical, these Universals are in fact heterogeneous. Therefore a meta-ethic can only result in the construction of a Universal common to all cultures. Hence the foundation of a meta-ethic must be conceived within a contractarian tradition. The utopia of this construction is actually a new social contract between the planet's heterogeneous cultures. In this sense, *Ties that Bind* is a direct philosophical heir to John Rawls' theory of justice and an indirect heir to Kant (in whose thought, as we know well, Rousseau holds an important place).[15]

3. Ricœur's Critical Reading of John Rawls' Procedural Ethics

Donaldson and Dunfee explicitly found their theoretical approach on Rawls' theory of procedural ethics. We have chosen to use Ricœur's critical reading in an attempt to evaluate how Donaldson and Dunfee's contractarian and procedural solution allows for the circumvention of CSR

---

15   V. Delbos, 1964, "La Morale de Kant", Introduction to *Fondements de la Métaphysique des mœurs*, Paris: Librarie Delagrave, p. 24. Our translation: "The handwritten thoughts thrown out by Kant in his copy of Observations on the Feeling of the Beautiful and Sublime, bear witness to what point the action exerted upon him by Rousseau was profound ... *Rousseau is the Newton of the moral world.*" Our emphasis in italics.

aporias. This consists of understanding how (and if) the social contract theory can function as the foundation of ethics today. Indeed, it is from this angle that Ricœur in *Soi-même comme un autre* (*Oneself As Another*, 1992) proceeds with his analysis of John Rawls' theory of justice:

> The aim and the function of the fiction of a contract is to separate the just from the good, by substituting the procedure of an imaginary deliberation for any prior commitment to an *alleged common good*. According to this hypothesis, it is *the contractual procedure* that is assumed to engender the principle or the principles of justice.[16]

The idea of separating the just from the good (which is implicit in all procedural ethics) brings us back to a major axis of twentieth century philosophy, which was the eviction of the idea of good from philosophy, its historical dwelling (Auroux, 1990, p. 231):

> The traditional issue of Good has little place in contemporary philosophy. It was a certain way of unifying thought in different domains of human life, stemming from a unitary metaphysical aim in so far as it has been based, since Plato, on the issue of *dependence between Good and the Being*. This dependence alone can ensure a foundational role to a theory of Good, and when it is no longer perceived as essential, philosophy can be considered to no longer be preoccupied with a theory of Good as such.

The big question is knowing if it really is possible at the same to evict the good from its dwelling, and to recover forms of ethics without transcendental foundation.

The shared idea of a 20th century philosophy that would have succeeded in evicting the good is based, in fact, on a historical interpretation according to which ethics was transformed in successive stages: from teleological (Aristotle), it would have become deontological (Kant), then procedural (Rawls). Ricœur's key position is the rejection of the evidence of an apparent chronology by considering, conversely, that *ethics is by necessity at once teleological and deontological*. John Rawls' text *A Theory*

---

16   P. Ricœur, 1992, *Oneself as Another*, Chicago: The University of Chicago Press, p. 228.

of Justice illustrates how procedural construction *cannot operate alone* without the implicit reintegration of the teleological dimension. The demonstration is founded upon the observation of "the lexical order" of John Rawls' text: the principles of justice are in fact developed prior to the definition of the procedural rules which are supposed to produce them. In other words, the process is based on a "pre-understanding of what is meant by the unjust and the just".[17]

This process has its origins in the Kantian formalism defined by pure universal criteria: "Act only on that maxim which you can at the same time will to become a universal Law". In fact, this attempt is limited by another of Kant's famous texts, the first sentence of *Groundwork of the Metaphysics of Morals:* "It is impossible to conceive anything at all in the world, or even out of it, which can be taken as *good* without qualification [ohne Einschränkung], except a *good will*".[18] Instead of a limitation, it is a question for Ricœur of an "anchoring in the ordinary moral experience. As in Aristotle, moral philosophy in Kant *does not begin from nothing*; the task is not to invent morality but to *extract the sense of the fact of morality* ...".[19] We rediscover here the dialectic between empirical fact and the normative universal presented by Durkheim and also by Donaldson and Dunfee as the major obstacle to be overcome in order to make the credibility of business ethics possible – that is, both theoretically founded and applied in practice.

17   P. Ricœur, *op. cit.*, p. 237; see also note 54, p. 236: "In an article entitled 'Cercle de la démonstration dans Theory of Justice (John Rawls)' (Esprit, n°2, 1988, p. 78), I note that the work as a whole does not obey the lexical order prescribed in its statement of principles but follows a circular order. In this way, the principles of justice are defined and even developed (§§11–12) before the examination of the circumstances of choice (§§20–25) consequently, before the thematic treatment of the veil of ignorance (§24) and, even more significantly, before the demonstration that these principles are the only rational ones (§§26, 30)."

18   I. Kant, 1964, *Groundwork of the Metaphysics of Morals*, New York: Harper and Row, p. 61.

19   P. Ricœur, *op. cit.* p. 205, note 2.

4. From Dispersed Finalities in Everyday Life to Revisiting the Aristotelian Concept of the "Good Life"

It is a matter of a separation that spoils any attempt of applied philosophy through the creation of an impassable gap between:

- the golden perfection of the multiple established ethics theories generally referred to by business ethics authors,
- and the absence of a concrete response to practical moral questions.

This dichotomy erases all substance from business ethics and this impossibility which has strongly marked modern philosophical thought is precisely the one accepted by Donaldson and Dunfee (1999b, p. 9): "To suppose that one can deduce an 'ought' from an 'is', or, what amounts to the same thing, that one can deduce a normative ethical conclusion from empirical research, is to commit a logical mistake".

On the contrary, Ricœur purely and simply refuses this prohibition of "all that precedes only in the tradition of thought stemming from Hume, for which 'ought' is opposed to 'is'" (Ricœur, 1994, p. 169). He rejects this opposition of "ought" and "is" which forbids any path leading from "being" and the empirical to "ought" and obligation. Establishing all possible paths between the empirical and normative domains constitutes Ricœur's goal in his work *Oneself as Another*, which delineates his contribution to ethics, or, in his own words, his *petite éthique* (1995, p. 13). His strategy is founded upon a succession of scrupulous examinations of empirical disciplines by considering the works of multiple authors belonging to the humanities and other social sciences, language philosophy, but also, which is rare for the French, to analytical Anglo-Saxon philosophy. In fact, the first six studies in *Oneself as Another* are Ricœur's meditations on his previous works consecrated to contemporary social sciences, in order to extract the construction of the human personality and postulate the existence of a moral dimension: one which constitutes an exemplary path from the empirical towards the normative.

The process used in "the present work recognizes that it belongs to what Jean Greisch has called the hermeneutical age of reason".[20] This hermeneutic approach helps to detect within discussion and take action for what we could call a human disposition (difficult to perceive, but impossible to deny) toward the necessity of ethics: "What we are summoned to think here is the idea of a higher finality which would never cease to be internal to human action" (Ricœur, 1992, p. 179). This type of finality does not take the classic form of a supreme, transcendent and universal value, but is unveiled (or constructed) throughout the life of each person, all while forming, nevertheless, a *final* perspective which gives meaning to an entire life remaining forever open until the discovery of the *ultimate end*, which can only appear during the reading of Marcel Proust's *Finding Time Again*. Indeed, the hermeneutic metaphor functions here as a decoding of a text where each chapter cannot be understood without understanding the piece as a whole, which is the singularity of the "*ergon* of man" and also in a certain way the substratum of Proust's masterpiece.

In order to attempt the transition between re-reading his meditations on the empirical (Studies 1–5 in *Oneself as Another*) and the definition of ethics' aims, Ricœur relies upon two authors who are not usually associated with each other. Proust appears in an elusive but very strong way as a reference to "true life's" prolific hermeneutics that the *Search for Lost Time* would be, on the condition that it be considered from the point of view of *Finding Time Again*. This evocation of Proust's "true life" theme is a means of shattering the character of Aristotle's concept of the "good life" which has become, alas, academically conventional. This is a very efficient means of renewing commentary on the opening lines of *The Nichomachean Ethics*[21] which, after centuries of controversy, still remain enigmatic today. To follow the thread of the enigma, Ricœur explicitly

---

20   This is the final sentence at the end of his introduction to *Oneself as Another*, p. 25.
J. Greisch, 1985, *L'Âge herméneutique de la raison*, Paris: Editions du Cerf.

21   Ricœur, *Oneself as Another*, p. 172, note 1: "The opening lines of the Nichomachean Ethics set us on the path: 'Every art [tekhnē] and every inquiry [methodos] and similarly every action [praxis] and pursuit [proairesis, preferential choice] is thought

identifies Aristotle's "good life" with Proust's "true life" in a gripping formula (1992 p. 172): "Whatever the image that each of us has of a full life, this apex is the ultimate end of our action".

The question about this text that has survived throughout the centuries is how to order the chain of finalities which defines good as an attribute of life. It is important to note that in Aristotle's text these finalities are initially dispersed because they are always connected to concrete, daily activities. It is in the description of these daily activities that we can discover how "prescription" is inseparable from the ordinary unfolding of all human activity. According to Ricœur, these dispersed finalities find adequate expression in Alasdair MacIntyre's "standards of excellence"[22] which are explicit or implicit judgments of daily life allowing us to speak of a "good" doctor, a "good" baker, a "good" architect, etc. The identical analyses found in Aristotle's and MacIntyre's texts separated by a distance of more than twenty centuries forces us to hunt for the foundation of the normative in simple, spontaneous words spoken countless times throughout the day (Ricœur, 1992, p. 177):

> Standards of excellence allow us to give a sense to the idea of internal goods immanent to a practice. These *internal goods* constitute the teleology immanent to the action, as is expressed on the phenomenological plane by the notions of interest and satisfaction which must not be confused with those of pleasure [...] In this sense, the idea of *internal goods* occupies a twofold strategic position in our undertaking.

MacIntyre's concept clarifies the audacity of Aristotle's use of the idea of the "good life" in which he reunites the two traditionally separated poles of teleology, before and after him:

– limited finalities of daily life, subordinated to other partial finalities, or chained to one another in an infinite and therefore inconsistent process;

---

to aim at some good; and for this reason *the good has rightly been declared to be that at which all things aim.*" Our emphasis in italics.

22 A. MacIntyre, 1981, *After Virtue: A Study in Moral Theory*, Notre Dame: University of Notre Dame Press.

– "ultimate ends" or the end itself of each individual's life, then of the city.

To this first audacity that reunites two opposite attributes in the definition of human action, Aristotle adds two generally "separated" couples which can never "go together":

– both the immanent and transcendent character of these finalities;
– the profoundly personal but necessarily social character of the perception of these finalities by each and every person in a given society.

To the reader familiar with the successive books of *The Nicomachean Ethics*, these couples of "modern," explored, then overcome contradictions propose the happiness of perusing a well-known and oft-analyzed landscape, which is suddenly being placed among the most burning contemporary philosophical events: moral prescription is imposed as an inescapable fact, profoundly internal, but radically social (in the sense of Durkheim and Rousseau). "Social" meaning shared with another. Solipsist ethics could not exist even if it were profoundly rational or even spiritual. This double marking of profound interiority and of sharing with others is the place where together Ricœur's and Aristotle's ethics intertwine "a good life in just institutions" – according to the most well-known formula of *Oneself as Another*, clearly leading to a new theory of justice as the foundation of the social.

5. From Ethics of the Other to an Outline of the Global Social Contract

On the institutional level, the necessary opening up towards the other in the definition of the "good life" is a process of defining the social contract at the dawn of each nation's[23] modernity. Globalization marks the moment when this social contract (which founds the democracy of modern times) erodes (or collapses) faced with the upheld planetary power – who knows exactly which one? – by multinational firms and/ or financial markets. Yet be it for Hobbes or for Rousseau (even if in each one of their theories the processes are apparently opposite)[24] *the social contract is the foundation of humanity as it is.*[25] The rupture with

---

23   J.-J. Rousseau, 1762, *The Social Contract, or Principles of Political Rights*, Book I, Chapter VI: "If then we discard from the social compact what is not of its essence, we shall find that it reduces itself to the following terms – 'Each of us puts his person and all his power in common under the supreme direction of the general will, and, in our corporate capacity, we receive each member as an indivisible part of the whole.' At once, in place of the individual personality of each contracting party, *this act of association creates a moral and collective body*, composed of as many members as the assemble contains votes, and receiving from this act its unity, its common identity, its life and its will. *This public person*, so formed by the union of all other persons formerly *took the name of city, and now takes that of Republic or body politic*; it is called by its members *State* when passive, *Sovereign* when active, and *Power* when compared with others like itself. Those who are associated in it *take collectively the name of people*, and severally are called *citizens*, as sharing in the sovereign power, and subjects, as being under the laws of the State. But these terms *are often confused* and taken one for another: it is enough to know how to distinguish them when they are being used with precision." Our emphasis in italic. http://www.fordham.edu/halsall/mod/rousseau-contract2.html.

24   For Hobbes, the way out of the state is war, where every man is against every man; for Rousseau, on the contrary, the way out the state is through reestablishing the unbalance created by leaving the state of nature.

25   J.-J. Rousseau, 1762, *op. cit.*, Book I, Chapter VIII: "The passage from the state of nature to the civil state *produces a very remarkable change in man*, by substituting justice for instinct in his conduct, and giving his actions the morality they had

the social contract thus constitutes a calling into question of our Western civilization in the sense of "modern" political, economic and social institutions. Consequently, the ethics worksite imposed today is the necessary transposition of the social contract from the scale of nations where it was conceived and partially put to use over the last centuries but today progressively "neutralized", to a radically new scale, that of "all" the nations. Nevertheless, that new scale is where the *conditions of possibility* for the achievement of the social contract are not reunited in the political sense of a supranational sovereignty: and perhaps the evocation of such an idea would dramatically summon the worst ghosts of Huxley or Orwell.

If the political dimension of a planetary social contract is in itself frightening, the only possible way out for a societal ethics that responds to current and future stakes, is the collective construction of a *contractual ethics on a social and economical level*. Now, today, it is not a question of a pure abstraction. When the French government had just discretely liquidized the prospecting institution that was the National Plan,[26] F. Lépineux (2006) suggested that we return to the source along the lines of Gaston Berger's correct forecasting: he tried to decode the inescapable forces of change through seven fields of observation in French society. Departing

---

formerly lacked. Then only, when the voice of duty takes the place of physical impulses and right of appetite, does man, who so far had considered only himself, find that he is forced to act on different principles, and to consult his reason before listening to his inclinations. Although, in this state, he deprives himself of some advantages which he got from nature, he gains in return others so great, his faculties are so stimulated and developed, his ideas so extended, his feelings so ennobled, and his whole soul so uplifted that, did not the abuses of this new condition often degrade him below that which he left, he would be bound to bless continually the happy moment which took him from it for ever, and, instead of a stupid and unimaginative animal, *made him an intelligent being and a man*." Our emphasis in italic. http://www.fordham.edu/halsall/mod/rousseau-contract2. html.

26   On 27 October 2005, the Prime Minister announced the transformation of the *Commissariat Général du Plan*. This institution had a significant ideological reputation domestically and internationally. The *Centre d'analyse stratégique* took over on 6 March 2006. See www.strategie.gouv.fr.

from the organization of work and the repartition of time, he placed at the center of his procedure:

- transformations of modes of exercising solidarity (passage from a centralized Jacobin State model towards a plural model of volunteering);[27]
- CSR and sustainable development in the principle of redefining the corporation itself and in its relationship with other fields.

This analysis tends towards identifying in each of these fields, a *declining model* and an *emerging model* which both contribute to a change in the social contract and to a paradigm shift. This is perceived even more clearly in the last two observed fields: the institutional logic of actors and ways of thinking.

L. Hartman and D. Arnold (2006) have shown how multinationals and NGOs maintain a dialectical relationship made up of confrontations and partnerships. This tendency is reinforced by triangular partnerships where public authorities (national and/or multilateral) come to reinforce this new direction of trans-organizational or even multi-field action.[28] These actions of triangular partnerships set up today could be read as the beginning of a process of questioning the founding epistemological rupture of political economy, then of economic and management sciences; in this geometric place, the transformation of the logic of action and models of thought cross paths. Francois Perroux is without a doubt

---

27 For a critique of the French perception of philanthropy, through the filter of the operating preemption in France, the monopole of the State on the "general interest" (the distinguished, the elites, cultural bureaucracy over the common, commerce, business, cultural sponsorship, associations), by application of Pierre Bourdieu's categories, the distinguished-noble and the ordinary-commoner, see Rosé (1986).

28 Among other terms, is it not too utopist to think that the created dynamism could generate "homologue positions in different fields", "effects of synchronization", and "relationships of objective orchestration" (Bourdieu, 1984, p. 228) in crisis solutions, or negotiated and contractual processes that no longer obey the fatality of revolutionary violence, but are constructed in contradictory forums?

one of the first, in the sphere of economic sciences to have made a dent with an acuity often forgotten today[29] (1958, Vol. III, p. 611):

> believing we were dying for Class, we died for the people of the Party. Believing we were dying for the homeland, we died for the Industrials. Believing we were dying for people's Liberty, we died for the Liberty of dividends. Believing we were dying for the Proletariat, we died for its Bureaucracy. Believing we were dying for state order, we died for the Money it has. Believing we were dying for a nation, we died for the bandits that gagged it. Believing – but why believe – we are in such deep shadow? Believe, die? ... When is it a question of living?

These lines taken from *La coexistence pacifique* (*Peaceful Coexistence*) were cited by Herbert Marcuse (1964) with the following commentary: "Here is a good translation from the reified form of the universals into a truly concrete form and nevertheless it recognizes the reality of the universal because it calls it by its real name". The strength of Marcuse's text is in superimposing onto one sole denunciation:

- the observation of empirical phenomena that force us to deny the epistemological rupture that tore economics and management science from their origins,
- and the seemingly abstract philosophical notions (like the universals) that are operative in the social critique of the *Ideology of Advanced Industrial Society.*

What is observed today across the dialectics of struggles and partnerships must be clarified by the relevance of these "substantial universals" – "like Beauty, Justice, Happiness and their contraries" – (Marcuse, *op. cit.*, p. 233) which obstinately reappeared throughout the 20th century in empirical management studies (ibid., p. 234):

29   Except, of course, for the members of ISEOR, the international research center that today in France and around the world works at the arduous task for which Perroux was the precursor. See for example H. Savall and V. Zardet, 2004 and 2005, and the website http://www.iseor.com.

If these untranslatable universals persist as sore points of thought, they reflect the unhappy conscience of a divided world where "what is" is above "what could be", refuses it, even. [...] In the same idea, the universal comprehends the possibilities that are achieved and at the same time frozen in reality.

This contradictory way of relating has been extensively developed and expressed in varied vocabularies. "Civil regulation" or "world systems of private regulation" have been discussed.[30] In *The Age of Paradox*, Charles Handy (1994) exposes that the necessary dialectic dimension of these phenomena – "living with these contradictions, not necessarily resolving them" – is a steady action to reduce the worst and find the best in the foundations of progression. A similar contradictory structure characterizes the analyses of fields such as businesses' codes of conduct, voluntary initiatives, different systems of internal evaluation and reporting, specialized agencies' ratings, and the assessment of ethical or sustainable development funds. In *Business Responsibility for Sustainable Development*, P. Utting (2000) attempted an inventory where he denounces:

- the weakness of the criteria that the United Nations and other organizations often use to choose their commercial partners, the way that NGOs and United Nations institutions silence all the most vehement critics when they approach businesses, and the problem of businesses who come to excessively influence the public interest;
- certain forms of spontaneous initiatives and partnerships [because] they can serve in weakening powerful motors of accountability, like the government regulation of collective negotiations and certain forms of civil society militancy.

Taking into account the prudence acquired in a reputable study that commits the author only, but published, nonetheless, in the sphere of the UN, the "worries" expressed by Utting form a good evaluation of the permanent risks of seeing the best intentions in the world for *responsibility* return to the hell of *window-dressing* ... in such a way that the conclusion

---

30   Applied by organizations like the Forest Stewardship Council (FSC) or the Marine Stewardship Council (MSC).

"invites the rethinking of regulation and partnership". To be more precise: "certain forms of co-regulation could play a major role", for example

> a civil regulation[31] in which NGOs, consumers and unions would have a considerable influence, contribute to the establishment of rules and norms reacting to businesses' relationship to society and the environment. [...] The success of this co-regulation depends not only on *dialogue and compromise* that could be characterized as *soft characteristics*,[32] but also as *hard characteristics*, such as *government sanctions, laws*."

The same dialectic structures function at the level of territories. A very empirical example is given by the sociologist L. Draetta (2006), who puts the toppling of paradigms (in economics, management and sociology) to the test of field research by creating a grid of fine analysis of business actors' logic in their institutional field. In the example of ecological modernization, three outlines concentrate the results:

- inductive forces of ecological action (the social institutional web) or external forces (judicial, social, market and organizational forces);
- internal company variables (according to Maslow's hierarchy whose base remains the financial situation);
- the logics of actions (economic-utilitarian, strategic-utilitarian).

None of these three systems of forces could be explanatory alone: each business' behavior is a specific result of the combination of these forces; the results are classed, in turn, in an interesting trilogy of "macro-categories": first, those of "commercial influence", and then that of "regulatory constraint." Transdisciplinarity is not a vain word here since, from a departure point that is both institutional and social-constructive, this sociological

---

31   This goes back to the question asked with irony by Y. Dezalay and B. Barth in the title of their article: "Will the International Civil Society be Washington's New Avatar of Consensus?", *Le Monde Diplomatique*, May 2002, and *Actes de la Recherche en Sciences Sociales*, March 1998. The response is played out in debates, conflicts and negotiations that engage and pursue each other ... in many instances.

32   On this very complex point see S. Guinchard (2002).

interpretation integrates two categories borrowed from management science and economics.

Nevertheless, these two categories are not sufficient to address all actors' language because they would not be able to explain voluntary actions, for which a third category is required – that of moral obligation which must address (Draetta, 2006):

> businesses that themselves construct a constraint to conform to an entire system of social and organizational norms, laws, collective dispersed representations, incorporated into businesses via the socio-institutional web. From this point of view, moral obligation takes place on a cultural and political-social horizon, and not only economic-judicial. This third explanation goes back to a civic dimension which falls under the social and political responsibility that business recognizes as vital.

This is without a doubt a remarkable example in literature: attempting to discover CSR while not even looking for it, never considering it as a given fact or a departure point for research. It is, on the contrary, an unexpected but necessary by-product: a form of the logic of action that is imposed at the end of an empirical analysis of businesses' behaviors and decision-making processes.

6. How Do We Overcome the Risks of Ideology and Effects of Domination?

It is necessary to take the Marxist and institutionalist critiques as they are summarized by M.T. Jones (1996) in his article "Missing the Forest for the Trees". For Jones CSR is the tree in this analogy: an ideology whose function is to morally legitimize the continuation of the rationality of capitalist accumulation (maximizing profit). In this article, the right to property is directly connected to "the fact that management constitutes the legal representative of ownership interests [which] enables it to decide what's what in the firm; employees and communities have only tenuous legal status in terms of challenging managerial prerogatives". Jones demonstrates how the successive phases of capitalism's evolution (Fordism, Postfordism, multinational corporations, globalization, networking organizations) have changed nothing for this capitalist logic: the increasing hegemonic influence of the financial sector renders the interpretation of economic reality by the CSR and stakeholder theories impossible ... The logical conclusion from these analyses is therefore summarized by M.T. Jones:

> – a manager is breaking the law if he or she does not prioritize the interest of the shareholder;
> – "to posit a capitalism voluntarily acting in accordance with the tenets of social responsibility is absurd".

This sentence could have been written by Milton Friedman ... but it is Jones'! This apparent but paradoxical convergence between Jones and Friedman is explained by the fact that CSR is nothing more than applied philosophy, and all applied philosophy is halted by the aporia which is at the center of our analysis:

> – either it is normative – but Jones shows that in the complex system of constraints in which the manager makes decisions, CSR is *not powerful enough to be effective*;
> – or it is empirically effective, but in this case according to Jones, it is "redundant with good business practices and thus unnecessary." And therefore *useless* because it does not change the capitalist logic of accumulation.

This absence of effectiveness leads Jones to interpret CSR as an ideological concept whose conditions constitute a system studied by neoinstitutionalists and empirically observed by L. Draetta in the functioning of businesses over a three-year period. Neoinstitutionalist Jones recognizes that contractarians take the concept of CSR out of the realm of ideology and models, and ground it with material content by accepting that Donaldson and Dunfee in *Ties That Bind* undertake the challenge of the applied philosophy (normative/empirical) aporia by proposing the solution of the ISCT.

Donaldson and Dunfee's work presented at the beginning of this chapter is the outcome of several years' work in collaboration with Preston. Jones thus summarizes one of the stages of this theory: "Donaldson and Preston (1995) [...] argue that contemporary property rights theory based on the notion that property rights are embedded in human rights [...] can be used to undermine shareholder primacy and promote stakeholder management".[33] At this stage in the analysis, it is necessary to revisit this text because Jones admits to their position as the best possible foundation for CSR and stakeholder theory, opposing it nonetheless to two forms of refutation: the growing *financialization*, and the institutionalists' argument against CSR as a way of calling functionalist theory into question. Property rights cannot be conceived without binding them to the theory of justice.

According to the functionalist paradigm, the social spheres (i.e. economy and society) are distinct and conflicts have to be settled at the core of each sphere: if the manager is the arbitrator between the interests of all the stakeholders, an economic agent is seen to possess social, ethical and political functions for which he has no legitimacy. This major objection to the paradigm of the social contract or ISCT is discussed in *Ties That Bind*, which is a constructivist attempt to escape the debate between skeptical relativism and universalistic dogmatism through contractualism. As analyzed above in section 2, the authors propose to integrate the normative and the empirical through a repartition of the "Social Contract for Business" into two spheres that do not come under the same procedure of legitimization (or foundation, or justification), the hypernorms or macro-social contracts and the tacit micro-contracts that translate the actually existing contracts into different social levels (industrial sectors, businesses, NGOs, unions, etc.).

---

33   T. Donaldson and L.E. Preston, 1995, pp. 83–4: "The notion of property rights is an integral part of human rights and the limitations of its harmful uses are integral parts of this concept that clearly include the rights of others (that is to say, those of stakeholders, not owners)."

As shown by the lexical analysis of the EBSCO database, the tendency toward empirical verification of the theses presented in the field of business ethics has grown over the years (Rosé and Delanoë, 2008, Annex 1 and 2). In the last year of the selected database, A. Cava and D. Mayer (2007) offer an empirical retrospective of the use of Donaldson and Dunfee's theoretical constructions in a 2006 article from the *Journal of Business Ethics*: "Integrative Social Contract Theory and Urban Prosperity Initiatives" or UPIs. This contribution constitutes a test of the contractualist hypotheses as a model for understanding the societal commitment of American multinationals in their support for UPIs which are attempts to respond to the phenomenon of desertification and impoverishment of megalopolis and city centers by heavy investments in a set of actions for urban restoration, business startups, creating employment, access to health and education services, etc. These programs are initiated by concerned community political powers throughout the entire American territory, which have called on the businesses present in the territory of these communities.

From 2002 on, an extensive study has been conducted on 3,000 businesses operating in 50 urban communities to evaluate the results of these "public – private – civil society partnerships", under the direction of D. Guthrie, Professor of Sociology and Business at NYU and Director of the "Program on the Corporation as a Social Institution" at the Social Science Research Council (SSRC) of New York, which is the emblematic association of the social sciences in the USA. At the time of the association's 50th anniversary in 2001, its president, sociologist C. Calhoun, acknowledged the interdisciplinary work of Berle and Means as a significant step in the history of the social sciences.[34] The particular interest of Cava and Mayer's article is in fact a very strong clarification of the transdisciplinary mobilization required to measure, in an empirical fashion, the tangible commitment of businesses to significant public (or general) interest programs. Donaldson and Dunfee's "hypernorms"

---

34   Calhoun C., 2001, "Social Science Research Council: The First Fifty Years", Foreword, *SSRC Annual Conference*, New York.

function as hypotheses that *help to show how socially-integrated business concepts better explain these behaviors than Friedman's definition of business for profit.*

This partition of the social contract into two spheres of legitimacy allows it to escape the most radical institutional critiques by moving closer to the multiple localizations of power in society (M. Foucault). The forever persistent risk for ethics to sink into ideology (and become an instrument of domination) would not be able to abolish all possibility of ethics in postmodern societies, and even less of corporate responsibility: in the opposite case, the effect of the critique goes back to the consequences of a particular (but always renewable) form of economic liberalism justly named savage, that of the "robber barons". On the contrary, would it be necessary to regard as acquired and necessary that "the instrumentalization of the ethics sphere to the ends of human resources management is immediately recognizable to those who give so much or so little attention to the literature produced on the subject"?[35] At the risk of being accused of naïveté, I propose to take seriously the plurality of available texts to affirm that their proteiform content asks a crucial methodological question: what is the magnitude of the theoretical context that *must be summoned as a foundation upon which to construct the tools of their own analysis?* How can the very subtle analyses by A.O. Hirschman relative to the relationship of capitalism with morals be ignored:

> That capitalism might have the capacity to be both reinforced and undermined is not more contradictory than the fact for a business to have both an inflow and outflow of money [...] Understanding these two things at once is perceiving that the moral base of capitalist society is constantly eaten away and at the same time no less constantly restored?[36]

The prolongation of this dialectic is found in L. Boltanski and E. Chiappello (1999, p. 670):

35 Salmon A., 2002, *Ethique et ordre économique – Une entreprise de séduction*, Paris: CNRS Editions, p. 7.

36 Hirschman A.O., 1984, *L'économie comme science morale et politique*, Paris: Gallimard, Ch. 1. English text in the *Journal of Economic Literature*, December 83.

> We reuse Hirschman's (1984) solution here, when, confronted by apparently irrec-
> oncilable theories concerning the impact of capitalism on society, he shows that
> they can be made to coexist in the same representation of the world as far as the
> idea is accepted that capitalism is a contradictory phenomenon which has the
> capacity to self-limit and be reinforced at the same time.

This attitude authorizes the separation of "oppositions" between these currents where "the description of the world appears too black to be true" and those where "the social world is a little too rose to be credible" (Boltanski and Chiapello, 1999, p. 68). The function of the critique that plays, according to these actors, *a driving role in the change of capitalism* is from now on, in part, institutionalized in the stakeholder theory; this institutionalization in turn takes place in a diplomatic-economic practice by applying Agenda 21, in the form of a contractual mobilization in the sense of sustainable development (Utting, 2007).

Conclusion

The German current of *Unternehmensethik* has linked Donaldson and Dunfee's contractualism (Grabner-Kräuter, 2000) to Appel's and Habermas' discursive ethics about where foundation and practice are connected by the search for a "rationally motivated consensus". A textual analysis of the Second ISBEE Conference proceedings (Rosé, 2005) shows an essential symmetry in the long process of founding the normative, not in an absolute *a priori*, but according to the perspective of critical dialogue: *the validity of the moral norm is defined by the consequences of actions on those who are affected by them,*[37] indeed, in very close terms to those used by Appel and Habermas (*cf.* section 2). Discovered here is a

---

37   See Lozano, 2000: "In discourse ethics the consequences of actions are taken into
      account, and are the core of the validity of moral norms. If all those affected by
      the norms are in agreement with them, they will be moral".

requirement close to what has appeared as a salutary process proposed by Yvon Pesqueux (2002, p. 31):

> An essential question inherent to the question of representation is to know where one is speaking from. It is indeed typical to speak about the "inside" of the organization and "up above" the organization [...] which is the common position of economists when they speak to us. The authors who attempt to speak about those that are "outside" or "below" are rare. The organization as seen by the excluded does not interest anyone.

The absolute outside is the South. From the irrefutable observation according to which "seen from developing countries, CSR appears like a protectionist arm serving the rich countries", Jean-Michel Severino[38] (2005) vigorously pleads for a "worldwide extension of CSR, [...] an urgent but crushing task" as "all diffusion of CSR is based on a broader, tacit social contract". Currently "in certain countries this contract is so fragile that it seems non-existent"; but he concludes: "our common future depends on the management of this antinomy". In terms of destiny, the spheres of business, ethics and politics cannot be separated: that is the ultimate justification of the necessity to accomplish the paradigm shift in management science. Indeed, well-understood CSR entails a change in the global social contract. This new phenomenon has barely been outlined, but as P. de Woot recently concluded (2005, p. 184):

> The key role that the avant-garde movements could play is clearly seen, like those of Corporate Responsibilities on the condition of being generalized and taking place in a political and legal framework that supports and orients them. This is where the transformation of business rejoins that of the development model.

One of the goals of a global social contract is to make the establishment of a real form of economic democracy possible. The *conditions of possibility* have been analyzed in particular by L. Bouckaert (2004) in the

---

38   J.-M. Severino is CEO of the *Agence Française de Développement*. I wish to thank F. Lépineux, to whom I owe my acquaintance with this article.

perspective of the personalist philosophical current[39] (Ricœur was its last major representative in the 20th century in philosophy, as was Perroux in the economic field):

> The search for economic democracy was more than an intellectual debate. A lot of experiments were set up, mostly in the form of co-operative associations. Some could survive as the Mondragon complex in Spain, for instance, most of them were less successful. Undoubtedly shareholder capitalism has got the upper hand today and the cooperative movement has lost its vitality. But at the same time it seems to me that the idea of stakeholding and Stakeholder Corporation reanimates the dream of economic democracy ...

Bouckaert perceives correctly; the utopias of French socialists in the 19th century can indeed find a new form of concrete actualization in an interpretation he calls a "strong version" as opposed to a "weak version" of stakeholder theory, the difference being no longer reserving the decision-making power for those with property rights, but spreading it out amongst the different organizations' stakeholders. Lépineux (2005) explains this by clarifying the respective right of stakeholders in comparison to the social finalities of the common good in question. Thus the passage from the traditional social contract to the new global economic social contract presumes a redefinition of the right to property (and not its suppression).

The planetary transformation of business' functions in the societies of the 20th then 21st centuries is common knowledge, but nevertheless questions the concepts and practices that are often grouped under the single expression *social contract*. Companies of all sizes, from small businesses to multinational corporations, are inevitably transformed by the

---

39   In one of the first articles (chronologically) categorized by the EBSCO database, R.W. Faulhabert connected precisely, in the economic field, the notion of common good with the personalist current. His article, published in 1954 in the *American Journal of Economics and Sociology*, referred in particular to the *Economy and Humanism* Manifest of 1942 (F. Perroux being mentioned as one of the founders), and to the piece by J.-L. Lebret, 1947, *Découverte du Bien commun*, Paris: Editions Economie et Humanisme.

same forces causing the shift at the global level. Consequently, it becomes necessary for academics to break with obsolete traditional management models, to embark upon new research pathways, and, as their civic duty to NGOs, unions, and the businesses themselves, to bear witness to the planetary changes in three respects:

– the diversity of professions which the transformation affects (finance, human resources, marketing, etc.) should save them from being excessively monolithic;
– the variety of research subjects brings about diverse epistemological constraints;
– and the increase in the need for qualified professors to train future business managers must lead to abolishing the Malthusian temptation of each academic discipline to section off its intellectual borders like a sovereign territory.

As J.-L. Le Moigne (2006) writes very well:

This may be one of the great merits of contemporary CSR development that having publicly "twisted the knife in the wound" of contemporary management sciences, by emphasizing the denial of epistemic responsibility that they have committed since their academic institutionalization: to fragment into further and further sub-disciplines the intellectual discipline that mobilizing knowledge requires in order to take responsible action, they have, in some way, inhibited the social responsibility of organizations by subcontracting it to the human resources department or to "coaching" consultants. Will "his loss of memory, these errors of perspective" be able to make us forget over time that human organizations are constructed precisely on the conscience of their responsibility and solidarity, as much endogenous as exogenous [...] We must re-conceptualize these "evolving artifacts"[40] that are social organizations rather than claiming to be able to "analyze in as many elementary pieces as could be ... as would be arranged afterwards into long chains of quite simple reasoning". For over half a century, Herbert Simon and Edgar Morin have provided us with enough epistemic and ethical material to "work on thinking cor-

---

40   Cf. Simon H.A., 2004, *Les sciences de l'artificiel*, Paris: Gallimard, Chapter 6: "An Evolving Artifact".

rectly about these intelligent uses of reason in human affairs"[41] [...] These are the epistemological resources that allow the experimental research carried out today on the reluctant renewal of the social contract to take more explicitly into account the collective aspiration for responsibility and solidarity.

International academic literature is characterized by the proliferation of heterogeneous concepts and theories developed by members of academic associations such as the Social Issues in Management (SIM) Division of the Academy of Management and the Society for Business Ethics (SBE) in the USA, as well as the European Business Ethics Network (EBEN), the European SPES Forum, and at the global level the International Society of Business, Economics and Ethics (ISBEE). The conceptual foundations for the institutional construction of a pertinent framework at the global scale can be found in G. Enderle's opening text as president of the Second ISBEE Conference in Sao Paolo (2000) – in the perspective presented here at the conclusion of this chapter, a process that is both constructivist, close to the ethics of discussion, and susceptible to providing guidelines for the *social contract* in the search for a new paradigm necessary for imagining the present and future relationship between business and society:

> While giving equal importance to the cognitive and normative dimension, the "two-leg approach" strives to integrate them in a balanced way. By doing so, it necessarily affects the understanding of business and ethics as well. On the one hand, the structuring of the field of business ethics outlined above poses numerous complex questions to ethics such as the moral status of organizations and systems, the relationship between personal, organizational and systemic ethics, the legitimacy of particular ethical theories in the global context, and the foundation of a global ethic, to name a few. On the other hand, ethics challenges the paradigms of business disciplines. If management theory, marketing, accountancy, economics, and finance are basically "value-free", integration from within the disciplines is excluded. Ethics has a role to play, at best, from outside [...] The distinction between the "engineering approach" and the "ethics-related approach", proposed by Amartya Sen, the Nobel Laureate in Economics 1998, proves helpful in this regard

41   Simon H.A., 1983, *Reason in Human Affairs*, Stanford: Stanford University Press.

(Sen 1987) [...] The "ethics-related approach" involves a broader understanding of economics and other business disciplines. It also comprehends the problems of human motivations and judgments of social achievements which cannot be disconnected *from the ethical questions of the good and the just: How should one live and what is a just society.*

It is noteworthy how much G. Enderle's definition of a "good life" is similar to P. Ricœur's words analyzed in this chapter. This speech which opened one of the first planetary conferences on this subject leads us to a final note that everyone has already heard, at the very least in the media: from now on, no longer does the right to give the world lessons on intercultural dialogue and general management, nor on responsibility and ethics, in particular, belong only to the "good conscience" of the West. Since the beginning of the sixties, for example, the first redefinitions of corporate social responsibility have been modeled on the Hindu tradition in particular (Virmani, 2006):

> The ultimate motivation of the West has always been to dominate nature, in order to acquire wealth and pleasure through scientific or technological inventions and achievements, whatever the cost. In contrast, the Hindu schools reject this separation between Man and his biotope, accentuating the reconciliation of the ideal and the real, and the collective effort of the human species to make progress for all its members.

This chapter's only ambition was to find new perspectives in several major texts on a global social contract. It will be necessary to go beyond those perspectives to the construction of a new paradigm as much at the theoretical level and in empirical research as at the level of praxis. This objective has already been defined by H. Bartoli, an economist strongly present in the personalist current, when he spoke at the conclusion of a UNESCO conference (2000):

> The "new paradigm" pursued by international experts is not exclusive to the scientific community. It calls on all actors in economic, social, political and cultural life; it requires us to rise to the challenges of our times. What is needed is not so much an "example" as a "portrayal of development" centred on a guiding principle; not so much a "disciplinary" as a "pluridimensional" matrix in which all facets of

development find expression. It is neither doctrine, ideology nor "world view" in the Schumpeterian sense that should dictate the interpretation of development. It is with reference to the actual state of the world, with a view to seizing and transforming it through the creative skills of men and women, that the "new paradigm" must be considered, and economics consigned to its role as an instrument in the service of all aspects of life, with human objectives.[42]

Annex 1

Interdisciplinary Construction of CSR over the Last Thirty Years of the 20th Century: Keyword Search

All EBSCO notes are classified by a certain number of keywords. The search field is identified by the "subject" category, allowing rapid observation of the related fields of management. Having extracted all of the notes concerning the concept of CSR, a tally of the principal terms used is crossed with the years in order to obtain the variations of the subjects concerning CSR year after year.

Figure 1:

- In the left-hand column, the table displays the notions subsumed by CSR in order of their respective chronological emergence;
- The table shows the progressive saturation of CSR in a growing number of notions (diagonal Northwest / Southeast) or a chronological diversification of the themes that concur with the construction of the notion;

---

42   Bartoli H., "Human Rights, the Basis of Sustainable Development", in Bartoli (2000).

	1999	2000	2001	2002	2003	2004	2005	2006	Total	Catégorie
business	25	32	73	173	260	346	437	435	1781	Gestion de l'ent en général
social	0	27	69	158	243	324	418	423	1662	Macro-économique
responsibility	0	27	67	157	235	319	410	414	1629	Macro-économique
ethic	0	0	0	34	103	187	216	180	720	Macro-économique
corporation	0	0	0	29	68	129	178	149	553	Gestion de l'ent en général
industrie	0	0	0	28	57	108	133	124	450	Gestion de l'ent en général
management	0	0	0	47	61	90	98	78	374	Gestion de l'ent en général
personne	0	0	0	27	28	46	53	73	227	Disciplines
environment	0	0	0	0	37	42	63	56	198	Macro-économique
enterprise	0	0	0	0	49	60	100	94	303	Gestion de l'ent en général
economic	0	0	0	0	34	26	53	52	165	Macro-économique
development	0	0	0	0	35	30	50	43	158	Macro-économique
administration	0	0	0	0	33	32	36	35	136	Gestion de l'ent en général
sustainable	0	0	0	0	25	0	0	31	56	Disciplines
public	0	0	0	0	0	38	49	37	124	Macro-économique
relation	0	0	0	0	0	28	39	38	105	Disciplines
service	0	0	0	0	0	34	49	42	125	Disciplines
corporate-social-responsibility	0	0	0	0	0	33	71	62	166	Macro-économique
international	0	0	0	0	0	31	46	33	110	Disciplines
executive	0	0	0	0	0	32	32	29	93	Disciplines
capital	0	0	0	0	0	30	40	42	112	Disciplines
organization	0	0	0	0	0	0	26	29	55	Disciplines
human	0	0	0	0	0	0	27	28	55	Disciplines
plan	0	0	0	0	0	0	38	0	38	Disciplines
culture	0	0	0	0	0	0	57	47	104	Disciplines
consumer	0	0	0	0	0	0	34	28	62	Disciplines
investment	0	0	0	0	0	0	0	28	28	Disciplines
Total occurrences	25	86	209	653	1268	1965	2753	2630	9589	

Figure 1: The occurrence rate of article keywords per year (source Ebsco).

– This is confirmed by the very clear growth of the total occurrences
of terms per year (last horizontal line).

Finally, the interpretation of the totals (corresponding to the last
column on the right) results from the construction of notion categories
according to their relative degree of decreasing generality and increasing
specialization by specific, identifiable disciplines:

– macro-economics;
– general business management;
– disciplines identified in the academic field.

From 1999 to 2006, the number of terms grew to specify the field of application of CSR: in 1999 CSR related to "general business management",
then spread to a macro-economic sphere before progressively penetrating
into different management disciplines from 2002 on.

Annex 2

Each journal is categorized by a certain number of subjects and interests.
It is possible, then, to determine which fields the journals publishing articles on CSR belong to. The result of this crossed cataloging (category of
journals / years) is shown figure 2.

Figure 2: The total number of relationships between categories and
years shows a clear quantitative growth (by number of occurrences for
each category) but also a qualitative diversification (by number of different categories); however with a slowdown beginning in 2005.

	1999	2000	2001	2002	2003	2004	2005	2006	Total	Méta-catégorie
business	15	15	35	56	124	162	207	177	791	Gestion de l'ent en général
general business	3	1	0	0	1	2	5	7	19	Gestion de l'ent en général
management	2	1	6	39	20	36	32	16	152	Gestion de l'ent en général
accounting	2	5	5	13	8	14	2	5	54	Disciplines
economics	1	0	4	1	5	19	24	34	88	Macro-économique
law	1	0	3	1	1	6	10	9	31	Disciplines
sociology	1	4	1	3	3	3	1	4	20	Macro-économique
politics	1	0	1	1	4	2	0	8	17	Macro-économique
computer science	1	1	0	0	2	2	3	4	13	Disciplines
banking, finance	0	2	2	8	10	7	24	23	76	Disciplines
sales	0	0	13	28	23	26	27	26	144	Disciplines
communications	0	0	1	4	12	10	9	5	41	Disciplines
medical sciences	0	1	0	0	0	0	0	0	1	Disciplines
engineering	0	0	1	4	2	2	2	9	20	Disciplines
consumer education	0	0	1	0	3	2	5	0	11	Disciplines
agriculture	0	0	1	0	0	1	0	4	6	Disciplines
industry	0	0	0	6	14	26	25	20	91	Gestion de l'ent en général
hospitality	0	0	0	2	3	2	2	11	20	Disciplines
trade	0	0	0	2	1	1	1	1	6	Disciplines
environmental studies	0	0	0	1	4	1	5	6	17	Macro-économique
general interest	0	0	0	0	1	1	3	0	6	Macro-économique
chemistry	0	0	0	0	4	3	0	4	11	Disciplines
transportation	0	0	0	0	2	2	2	3	9	Disciplines
general science	0	0	0	0	2	1	1	0	4	Macro-économique
food science	0	0	0	0	1	0	2	4	7	Disciplines
area studies	0	0	0	0	1	1	3	0	5	Macro-économique
consumer health	0	0	0	0	3	0	0	0	3	Disciplines
marketing	0	0	0	0	0	4	0	1	5	Disciplines
public administration	0	0	0	0	0	2	0	1	3	Macro-économique
international relations	0	0	0	0	0	0	10	1	11	Macro-économique
Total occurrences	27	31	74	170	254	338	405	383	1682	

Figure 2: The occurrence rate of category sources per year (source Ebsco).

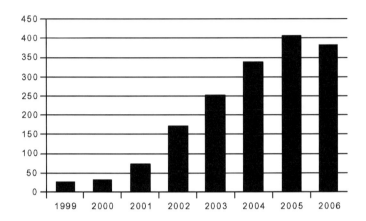

Histogram 4: Occurrence rate of all categories together per year.

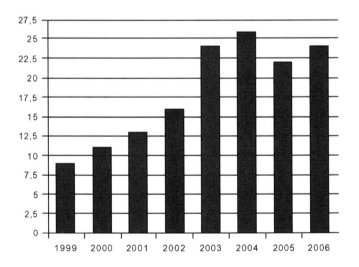

Histogram 5: Number of categories per year.

The two preceding histograms clearly indicate the growth and the diversification of the terminology and disciplines that CSR has integrated over the course of the years. Nevertheless, it seems useful to research which dynamic has fed this process of concept construction.

A new graph representation was necessary and can be found below (graph 6: CSR tree). This graph was created through a matrix of co-occurrences of "support categories" and "years". This means that the higher the point, the more the term is represented in the database. The correlations between lexical categories and year are represented by the lines between points. The thicker they are, the stronger the correlation is between year and term.

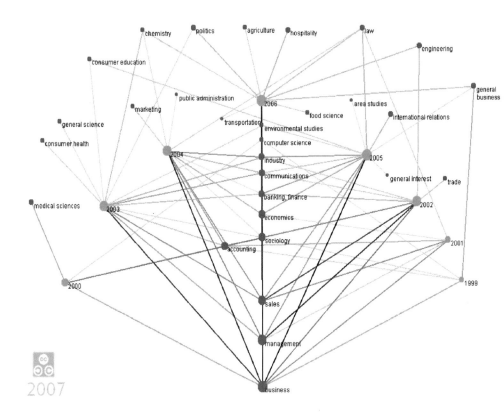

Graph 6: The CSR Tree (Corporate Social Responsibility), from 1999 to 2006
(obtained with Visugraph, Tétralogie module)[1]

"Business", "management" and "sales" make up the trunk of the tree: as it gets bigger
over the years, branches grow to make all the ramifications towards a growing specialization of CSR in a very large number of disciplines appear in a bush-shape.

1   We have eliminated non-representative data, that is to say, those whose number of itera-
     tions is less than 10% of the whole database; in doing this, we increase the visibility of
     the entire process from 1999 to 2006.

References

Andreau, J., 2001, *Banque et affaires dans le monde romain. IVe siècle avant J.C. – IIIe siècle après J.C.*, coll. "Points Histoire", Paris: Editions du Seuil.

Appel, K.O., 1994, *Ethique de la discussion*, Paris: Editions du Cerf.

Aristote, 2002, *Ethique à Nicomaque*, 4 Volumes, Leuven: Peeters.

Aristotle, 2003, *The Nichomachean Ethics*, Cambridge: Harvard University Press.

Auroux, S., ed., 1990, *Encyclopédie philosophique universelle*, Vol. II, *Les notions philosophiques*, Paris: PUF.

Bartoli, H., 2000, *Rethinking Development: Putting an End to Poverty*, Paris: UNESCO and Economica.

Baudrillard, J., 1970, *La société de consommation*, Paris: Gallimard.

Boltanski, L. and Chiapello, E., 1999, *Le nouvel esprit du capitalisme*, Paris: Gallimard.

Bouckaert, L., 2004, "Spirituality and Economic Democracy, A Personalist Approach", in L. Zsolnai, ed., *Spirituality and Ethics in Management*, Boston: Kluwer Academic Publishers.

Bourdieu, P., 1984, *Homo Academicus*, Paris: Editions de Minuit.

—— 2000, *Les structures sociales de l'économie*, Paris: Editions du Seuil.

Cava, A. and Mayer, D., 2007, "Integrative Social Contract Theory and Urban Prosperity Initiatives", *Journal of Business Ethics*, Vol. 72, pp. 263–78.

Chauveau, A. and Rosé, J.-J., 2003, *L'entreprise Responsable*, Paris: Editions d'Organisation.

Debord, G., 1992 (1st ed. 1967), *La société du Spectacle*, coll. "Folio", Paris: Gallimard.

Delbos, V., 1964, "La Morale de Kant", Introduction to *Fondements de la Métaphysique des mœurs*, Paris: Librarie Delagrave.

Donaldson, T. and Preston, L.E., 1995, "The Stakeholder Theory of the Corporation: Concepts, Evidence, and Implications", *Academy of Management Review*, Vol. 20, n°1, pp. 65–91.

Donaldson, T. and Dunfee, T.W., 1999a, "When Ethics Travel: The Promise and Peril of Global Business Ethics", *California Management Review*, Vol. 41, n° 4, pp. 45–63.

—— and —— 1999b, *Ties That Bind: A Social Contracts Approach to Business Ethics*, Boston, MA: Harvard Business School Press.

Draetta, L., 2006, "On n'est pas des repris de justice ! Pour une sociologie de l'environnementalisme industriel", in J.-J. Rosé, ed., *Responsabilité sociale de l'entreprise. Pour un nouveau contrat social*, Brussels: De Boeck.

Durkheim, E., 1918, *Le contrat social de Rousseau*, coll. "Les classiques des sciences sociales", http://classiques.uqac.ca/classiques/Durkheim_emile/durkheim.html.

——2004, (1st ed. 1924), *Sociologie et philosophie*, coll. "Quadrige", Paris: PUF.

Enderle, G., 2000, "A Conceptual Framework for Business Ethics in the Global Context", paper presented at the *Second ISBEE Conference*, Sao Paolo.

Fauconnet, P., 1928, *La Responsabilité, étude de sociologie*, Paris: Librairie Félix Alcan.

French, P.A., 2005, "Inference Gaps in Moral Assessment: Capitalism, Corporations and Individuals", *International Social Science Journal*, Blackwell Publishing for UNESCO, Vol. LVII, n° 3, *Moralizing Capitalism*, September, pp. 573–84

Galbraith, J.K., 1958, *The Affluent Society*, Boston: Houghton Mifflin.

Génard, J.-L., 1999, *La grammaire de la responsabilité*, Paris: Editions du Cerf.

Gernet, L., 1917, *Recherches sur le développement de la pensée juridique et morale en Grèce*, Thèse de doctorat ès lettres, Paris: E. Leroux.

Goldschmidt, V., 1985, *Le paradigme dans la dialectique platonicienne*, Paris: Librairie Philosophique Vrin.

Guinchard, S., 2002, "L'émergence d'un droit procédural mondial", in D. Soulez-Larivière and H. Dalle, eds, *Notre Justice – Le livre vérité de la justice française*, Paris: R. Laffont.

Goyard-Fabre, S., 1990, Article "Contrat social", in S. Auroux, ed., *Encyclopédie philosophique universelle*, Vol. II, *Les notions philosophiques*, Paris: PUF.

Grabner-Kräuter, S., 2000, "*Unternehmens Ethik* in German-Speaking Countries: Discourse Ethical Versus Contractarian Approaches to Improving the Ethical Quality of Business Decisions and Actions", paper presented at the *Second ISBEE Conference*, Sao Paolo.

Greisch, J., 1985, *L'Age herméneutique de la raison*, Paris: Editions du Cerf.

Guerrette, R.H., 1994, "Management by Ethics. A New Paradigm and Model for Corporate Ethics", in A. Lewis and K. Warneryd, eds, *Ethics and Economic Affairs*, London: Routledge.

Guthrie, W., 1971, *The Sophists*, Cambridge: Cambridge University Press.

Habermas, J., 1992, *De l'éthique de la discussion*, coll. "Champs", Paris: Flammarion.

Handy, C., 1994, *The Age of Paradox*, Boston: Harvard Business School Press.

Hartman, L. and Arnold, D., 2006, "Multinationales et avenir des sweatshops", in J.-J. Rosé, ed., *Responsabilité sociale de l'entreprise. Pour un nouveau contrat social*, Brussels: De Boeck.

Henriot, J., 1977, "Note sur la date et le sens de l'apparition du mot responsabilité", *Archives de Philosophie du Droit*, Vol. 22, Paris: Dalloz.

—— 1990, Article "Responsabilité", in S. Auroux, ed., *Encyclopédie Philosophique Universelle*, Vol. II, *Les notions philosophiques*, Paris: PUF.

Hirschman, A.O. (1984), *L'économie comme science morale et politique*, Paris: Gallimard, Chap. 1, English text in the *Journal of Economic Literature*, December 1983.

Jones, M.T., 1996, "Missing the Forest for the Trees – A Critique of the Social Responsibility Concept and Discourse", *Business and Society*, Vol. 35, n°1, pp. 7–41.

Kant, I., 1964, *Groundwork of the Metaphysics of Morals*, New York: Harper and Row.

Klein, N., 2000, *No Logo*, Toronto: Alfred A. Knopf.

Lefebvre, H., 1962, *Introduction à la modernité*, Paris: Editions de Minuit.

—— 1968, *La Vie quotidienne dans le monde moderne*, Paris: Gallimard.

Le Moigne, J.-L., 1977, *La Théorie du Système Général, théorie de la modélisation*, Paris: PUF.

—— 2006, "L'expérience de la responsabilité appelle l'éthique, qui appelle l'épistémique, qui appelle la pragmatique", Postface, in J.-J. Rosé, ed., *Responsabilité sociale de l'entreprise. Pour un nouveau contrat social*, Brussels: De Boeck.

Lépineux, F., 2005, "Stakeholder Theory, Society and Social Cohesion", *Corporate Governance: The International Journal of Business in Society*, Vol. 5, n°2, pp. 99–110.

—— 2006, "La RSE et le modèle socio-économique émergent", in J.-J. Rosé, ed., *Responsabilité sociale de l'entreprise. Pour un nouveau contrat social*, Brussels: De Boeck.

Lévy-Bruhl, L., 1884, *L'idée de Responsabilité*, Paris: Librairie Hachette and Cie.

Lozano, J.F., 2000, "Rational Discourses as a Foundation for Ethical Codes", paper presented at the *Second ISBEE Conference*, Sao Paolo.

MacIntyre, A., 1981, *After Virtue: A Study in Moral Theory*, Notre Dame (Ind.): University of Notre Dame Press.

Marcuse, H., 1964, *One-Dimensional Man. Studies in the Ideology of Advanced Industrial Society*, Boston: Beacon Press.

Moulinier, L., 1952, *Le pur et l'impur dans la pensée des Grecs d'Homère à Aristote*, Paris: Klincksieck.

Morin, E., 1973, *Le paradigme perdu: la nature humaine*, Paris: Editions du Seuil.

—— 2004, *La Méthode, Vol. 6 – Ethique*, Paris: Editions du Seuil.

Perroux, F., 1958, *La coexistence pacifique*, Vol. III, Paris: PUF.

Pesqueux, Y., 2002, *Organisations: modèles et représentations*, Paris: PUF.

Ricœur, P., 1960, *Finitude et culpabilité*, Vol. I and II, Paris: Editions Aubier Montaigne.

—— 1992, *Oneself as Another*, Chicago: The University of Chicago Press.

—— 1995, *Le Juste*, Paris: Editions Esprit.

Romilly (de), J., 1988, *Les grands sophistes dans l'Athènes de Périclès*, Paris: Editions de Fallois.

Rosé, J.-J., 1986, *L'Or pour l'Art, de Mécène aux sponsors*, Paris: Flammarion.

—— 2005, "Faisabilité de la RSE: entre dénonciation, légitimation et médiation – Une analyse lexicale des actes du deuxième Congrès de l'ISBEE", *Proceedings of the Third ADERSE Conference*, Lyon: ISEOR.

—— ed., 2006, *Responsabilité sociale de l'entreprise. Pour un nouveau contrat social*, coll. "Méthodes et Recherches", Bruxelles: De Boeck.

—— and Delanoë A., 2008, "La nature transversale de la RSE dans la littérature managériale", paper presented at the *Fifth ADERSE Conference*, Grenoble, January.

Rousseau, J.-J., 1984, *The Social Contract*, New York: Penguin Books.

—— 1992, *Discours sur l'origine et les fondements de l'inégalité parmi les hommes*, Paris: Flammarion.

Roustang, G. et al., 1996, *Vers un nouveau contrat social*, Paris: Desclée de Brouwer.

Salmon, A., 2002, *Ethique et ordre économique – Une entreprise de séduction*, Paris: CNRS Editions.

Savall, H. and Zardet, V., 2004, *Recherches en Sciences de Gestion: Approche Qualimétrique. Observer l'objet complexe*, Paris: Economica.

—— and —— 2005, *Ingénierie stratégique du roseau*, Paris: Economica.

Scholte, J.A., 2000, *Globalization: A Critical Introduction*, New York: Palgrave.

—— 2005, *The Sources of Neoliberal Globalization*, Geneva: United Nations Research Institute for Social Development (UNRISD).

Sen, A., 1993, "Codes moraux et réussite économique", *Actes de la Recherche en Sciences Sociales*, n°100, pp. 58–65.

—— 1999, *L'économie est une science morale*, Paris: La Découverte.

Severino, J.-M., 2005, "Des entreprises 'responsables'?" *Le Monde*, 1 June.

Touraine, A., 2005, *Un nouveau paradigme: pour comprendre le monde d'aujourd'hui*, Paris: Fayard.

Utting, P., 2000, *Business Responsibility for Sustainable Development*, Geneva: UNRISD.

——2007, "Fair Trade, Corporate Accountability and Beyond: Experiments in Globalizing Justice", paper presented at the *Fair Trade Workshop "Regulations for Social Development: The Potential and Limits of Corporate Responsibility and Accountability"*, Melbourne Law School, The University of Melbourne, 19–20 December.

Villey, M., 1977, "Esquisse historique sur le mot responsable", *Archives de Philosophie du Droit*, Vol. 22, Paris: Dalloz.

Weber, M., 1998, *Economie et Société dans l'antiquité*, Paris: La Découverte.

Werhane, P., 2002, "Moral Imagination and Systems Thinking", *Journal of Business Ethics*, Vol. 38, pp. 33–42.

——2008, "Mental Models, Moral Imagination and System Thinking in the Age of Globalization", *Journal of Business Ethics*, Vol. 78, pp. 463–74.

Wokutch, R.E. and Shepard, J.M., 1999, "The Maturing of the Japanese Economy: Corporate Social Responsibility Implications", *Business Ethics Quarterly*, Vol. 9, n°3, pp. 536–40.

Woot (de), P., 2005, *Responsabilité sociale de l'entreprise – Faut-il enchainer Prométhée?*, Paris: Economica.

Contributors

HELEN ALFORD is Dean of the Faculty of Social Sciences at the Pontifical University of St Thomas – Angelicum in Rome (Italy). She originally trained as a manufacturing engineer at Cambridge University, and her PhD thesis concerned "human-centered technology" and its potential for the "humanization of work" in manufacturing. At present, she is Director of the international research project "Ethics and CSR" which involves universities and businesses in the US, EU, post-communist and economically-developing worlds. She is co-author with Michael Naughton of the book *Managing As If Faith Mattered: Christian Social Principles in the Modern Organization*, University of Notre Dame Press, Notre Dame, 2001; and co-editor of the volume *Rediscovering Abundance: Wealth Creation and Distribution in the Christian Social Tradition*, University of Notre Dame Press, 2005. Her most recent publication, edited with Francesco Compagnoni, is *Preaching Justice: Dominican Contributions to Social Ethics in the Twentieth Century*, Dominican Publications, Dublin, 2007.

HENRI-CLAUDE DE BETTIGNIES is the Distinguished Professor of Globally Responsible Leadership at the China Europe International Business School (CEIBS), in Shanghai where he has created the Euro-China Centre for Leadership and Responsibility (ECCLAR). He is also the AVIVA Chair Emeritus Professor of Leadership and Responsibility and Emeritus Professor of Asian Business at INSEAD. Between 1988 and 2005, with a joint appointment at Stanford University (Graduate School of Business), he shared his time equally between Europe, California and the Asia Pacific region. Professor de Bettignies started the development of the Ethics initiative at INSEAD, and pioneered a new approach (AVIRA) to enlighten business leaders. Over a 16 year period the AVIRA program brought together 900 Chairmen and CEOs from 60 countries, keen to

enrich their vision and enhance their "responsible" leadership competence. Henri-Claude teaches MBAs, E-MBAs and executives at CEIBS
and at INSEAD in the areas of ethics and CSR, HR management and
corporate transformation. On the editorial Board of 5 academic journals
he has published many articles and 5 books on management in Japan, in
Asia, and on business ethics.

ZSOLT BODA was born in 1969 in Budapest, Hungary. He holds an MA
in economics and a PhD in political science. He is Research Fellow at
the Institute of Political Science, Hungarian Academy of Sciences, and
Associate Professor at the Business Ethics Center, Corvinus University of
Budapest. He has co-edited and written books in Hungarian on corporate
ethics, political theory, and environmental policy. He has published several
papers in academic journals and books on international ethics involving
the fair trade problematic, trade and environmental issues, and the politics of global environmentalism. His publications in English include the
following: "Globalization and International Ethics", in László Zsolnai,
ed., 2002, *Ethics in the Economy: Handbook of Business Ethics*, Oxford:
Peter Lang, pp. 233–58; "Global Environmental Commons and the Need
for Ethics", *Society and Economy*, fall 2003, pp. 213–24; and "The Ethical
Consumerism Movement", *Interdisciplinary Yearbook of Business Ethics*,
Vol. 1, 2006, pp. 141–53.

ISABELLE CADET is Doctor in Law and Associate Professor at ESDES,
Catholic University of Lyon (France). She is a member of the Board of
ADERSE (*Association for the Development of Education and Research on
Corporate Social Responsibility*), Managing Director of the French South-
East Committee for Civil Defense, and Town Council member. Her publications include the following articles: "Prévenir les risques: une nouvelle
forme de responsabilité juridique, quel impact pour l'entreprise ?" *La
lettre du management responsable*, n°8, 2007, www.esdes-recherche.net; "Le
droit de la responsabilité des entreprises: entre la prévention des risques
et l'idéologie de réparation", *La Revue des Sciences de Gestion*, n°211–12,
2005; "Time, Rule of Law and Sustainable Development", *Sciences de
Gestion*, Ed. ISEOR, n°49, 2005, pp. 39–59. Her research interests focus

on the fields of risk, responsibility, governance, and on the relationship between soft law and hard law (international law).

JEAN-MARIE FÈVRE is a Senior Lecturer in Management at the University of Metz, France. A graduate of the College of Europe in Bruges, Belgium, he received his PhD in Economics at the University of Aix-la-Chapelle (Aachen), Germany. A French citizen, he has lived twenty-four years abroad and has had work experience in sixteen countries. He speaks seven languages and is a court interpreter for German. He is a member of the "Görres-Gesellschaft zur Pflege der Wissenschaft" (Köln). His areas of interest focus on intercultural management, logistics and corporate social responsibility. His recent publications include: "Peut-on concilier performance logistique et responsabilité sociale de l'entreprise?", *5th ADERSE Conference*, University of Grenoble, France, January 2008; and "Logistics as a Key Factor for Disaster Management", *3rd International Conference on Integrated Natural Disaster Management*, University of Teheran, Iran, February 2008, Book 1: Full Papers, pp. 212–23 (book supported by UNESCO). He received decorations in France: *Chevalier dans l'Ordre National du Mérite* (2008), and in Germany: *Verdienstkreuz am Bande des Verdienstordens der Bundesrepublik Deutschland* (2000).

WOJCIECH W. GASPARSKI, Professor of Humanities, Dr Sc., Director and founder of the Business Ethics Centre, immediate past vice rector for research of the Leon Kozminski Academy of Entrepreneurship and Management, Warsaw. Professor emeritus of the Institute of Philosophy and Sociology, Polish Academy of Sciences (PAS) where he chaired the Academic Board and headed the Department of Praxiology. His publications on human action theory (praxiology), business ethics, methodology, science studies, and systems theory are numerous. He is a member of the Warsaw Learned Society, Learned Society of Praxiology (Honorary President), Polish Philosophical Society, ISBEE, Academy of Management (USA), EBEN Poland, Caux Round Table Poland (Vice-President), Society of Business Ethics, Science Studies Committee PAS (Honorary Member). Editor-in-chief of *Praxiology: The International Annual of Practical Philosophy and Methodology* (Transaction Publishers).

His recent books include: *Ethics and the Future of Capitalism* (with L. Zsolnai, 2002), and *Praxiology and the Philosophy of Technology* (with T. Airaksinen, 2007). In 2006 he was nominated to the European Faculty Pioneer Awards for Business in Society by Aspen Foundation (USA) and EABIS.

KENNETH E. GOODPASTER earned his A.B. in mathematics from the University of Notre Dame and his A.M. and PhD in philosophy at the University of Michigan. His research has spanned a wide range of topics, from conceptual studies of ethical reasoning to empirical studies of the social implications of management decision making. Goodpaster taught graduate and undergraduate philosophy at the University of Notre Dame throughout the 1970s before joining the Harvard Business School faculty in 1980. At Harvard, he taught both MBA candidates and executives and developed the second-year elective course, *Ethical Aspects of Corporate Policy*. In the fall of 1989, Goodpaster accepted the David and Barbara Koch Endowed Chair in Business Ethics at the University of St Thomas, Minneapolis, MN. He is co-author with Laura Nash and Henri-Claude de Bettignies of the 4th Edition of the well-known casebook *Business Ethics: Policies and Persons*, along with the *Instructor's Manual* on CD Rom (McGraw-Hill, 2006). His newest book is *Conscience and Corporate Culture* (Blackwell Publishers, 2007).

LAURA P. HARTMAN is Associate Vice President for Academic Affairs and a Professor of Business Ethics and Legal Studies in the Management Department at DePaul University, Chicago, USA. She also serves as Research Director of DePaul's Institute for Business and Professional Ethics. She is the Gourlay Professor at the Melbourne Business School/ Trinity College (2007–2008), and has been a visiting professor at INSEAD (France), HEC (France), the University Paul Cézanne Aix-Marseille III and Grenoble Graduate School of Business. Hartman's academic scholarship focuses on the alleviation of global poverty through profitable corporate partnerships as well as the ethics of the employment relationship. She has been published in *Business Ethics Quarterly*, *Business and Society Review*, *Business Ethics: A European Review*, and the *Journal of Business Ethics*. Her research and consulting efforts have also garnered national media attention by publications such as *Fortune Small Business* where she was named one of the "Top 10 Minds for Small Business", as well as the *Wall Street Journal, BusinessWeek*, and the *New York Times*. She has also written or co-written a number of texts, including *Effective & Ethical Practices in Global Corporations, Rising Above Sweatshops, Employment Law for Business*, and *Perspectives in Business Ethics*.

SCOTT KELLEY is a Visiting Assistant Professor in the Religious Studies Department and Research Fellow for the Institute of Business and Professional Ethics at DePaul University in Chicago. He received a PhD in Theological Ethics from Loyola University Chicago. Prior to that, he taught English in Tokyo, Japan and was a volunteer in Pohnpei, Micronesia with *Jesuit Volunteers: International*. His has authored and co-authored a number of publications, including: "Subsidiarity and Global Poverty: Development from Below Upwards", in *Vincentian Studies*; "Saint Vincent De Paul and the Mission of the Institute for Business and Professional Ethics: Why Companies Should Care About Poverty", in *Vincentian Studies*; and "The End of Foreign Aid as We Know It: The Profitable Alleviation of Poverty in a Globalized Economy", in C. Wankel, ed., *Alleviating Poverty through Business Strategy*, New York: Palgrave Macmillan, forthcoming. His research interests include global poverty alleviation strategies, Vincentian Heritage, and moral discernment.

FRANÇOIS LÉPINEUX is Professor and Head of the Center for Responsible Business at Rennes School of Business (in Brittany, France), and Research Fellow at INSEAD. After graduating from HEC Paris School of Management in 1990, he has carried on various research and consulting activities, and received a PhD in Management Science at the Conservatoire National des Arts et Métiers (CNAM, Paris). He is co-author of the book *Sustainable Development and Corporate Governance* (Paris: Editions d'Organisation, 2003, in French) and has produced a number of other publications. His areas of interest include the relationship between business activities and the search for the common good, ethical issues in the financial services industry, as well as stakeholder theory, the emergence of a global civil society and the shift in the social contract. François Lépineux is co-founder and past-President (2002–2005) of ADERSE (Association pour le Développement de l'Enseignement et de la Recherche sur la Responsabilité Sociale de l'Entreprise), the French academic association for the development of education and interdisciplinary research on CSR.

JOSEP F. MÀRIA, S.J., is Lecturer in Social Analysis and in Corporate Social Responsibility at ESADE (Barcelona). Member of the European Business Ethics Network, he received a PhD in Economics and a Degree in Theology. He has been Development Worker with the Jesuit Refugee Service in the DR of Congo (2004), Visiting Professor at the Universidad Centroamericana de Managua in Nicaragua (2005 and 2006), Visiting Researcher at the CEPAS (Centre d'Études Pour l'Action Sociale) in Kinshasa, DR of Congo (2007). His areas of interest include globalization, development studies and spirituality. Recent publications: "The Many Faces of Globalization", in L. Bouckaert and L. Zsolnai, eds, *Spirituality as a Public Good*, Antwerp: Garant, 2007, pp. 69–78; and "Traineeship as Vocational Training in Catalonia: Between the Law, the Actors and the Market" *European Journal of Vocational Training*, n°38, 2006/2, CEDEFOP, Thessalonica, pp. 39–48.

HENDRIK OPDEBEECK is Professor of Philosophy and Economics at the University of Antwerp where he is affiliated to the Centre for Ethics. He studied philosophy and economics at the Universities of Leuven and Gent where he obtained a PhD with a dissertation on E.F. Schumacher (1911–1977) and the polyparadigmatic discourse in economics. His research interest is focused on the cultural-philosophical backgrounds and effects of globalization with special attention for the role of spirituality and technology. In 2000 together with Luk Bouckaert (K.U. Leuven) he founded the SPES forum for Spirituality in Economics and Society which nowadays has also a European branch. His publications in English include *The Foundation and Application of Moral Philosophy* (Leuven: Peeters, 2000); *Building Towers, Perspectives on Globalisation* (Ethical Perspectives Monographs Series, Leuven: Peeters, 2002); and together with L. Bouckaert and L. Zsolnai: *Frugality, Rebalancing Material and Spiritual Values in Economic Life* (Oxford: Peter Lang).

JEAN-FRANÇOIS PETIT belongs to the catholic community of the Assumption, and is a Lecturer at the Department of Philosophy and Theology, Institut Catholique de Paris (France). Member of the "Association des amis d'Emmanuel Mounier", he is currently in charge of editing the *Carnets* of this philosopher. He collaborates on a regular basis to the book review pages of the newspaper *La Croix*. His recent publications include: *Penser après les postmodernes*, Paris: Buchet-Chastel, 2005; *Agir avec Mounier. Une pensée pour l'Europe*, Chronique sociale, 2006; *Philosophie et théologie dans la formation du personnalisme d'Emmanuel Mounier*, Paris: Cerf, 2006; *Individualismes et communautarismes. Quels horizons aux Etats-Unis et en France?* Paris: Bayard, 2007; and *Saint Augustin et l'amitié*, Paris: DDB, 2008.

JACOB DAHL RENDTORFF is Professor of Ethics at Roskilde University, Denmark. He is Director of Studies and Director of Research for the section of Business Ethics and Philosophy of Organization at his department. Rendtorff has been educated from Universities in Denmark, Germany and France and he has been visiting professor in Utrecht, Freiburg, Rome, Boston, Santa Clara, Stanford and Louvain. He has been director and co-director on several research projects; in particular, he was reporter to the European Union as a member of a BIO-MED II Project. Rendtorff has in Danish, English, French and German written more than 50 articles, authored 7 books, been editor or co-editor on more than ten other books; in particular, *Basic Ethical Principles in European Bioethics and Biolaw*, Copenhagen and Barcelona (with Peter Kemp, 2000). His work covers issues of existentialism and hermeneutics, French philosophy, ethics, bioethics and business ethics as well as philosophy of law. He is currently member of the board of the Danish Philosophical Forum and he is vice president of the Danish Association for philosophy in French language. He is also a member of the international group on reflection about ethics, Eco-ethica, founded by Professor Tomonobu Imamichi.

JEAN-JACQUES ROSÉ is a Senior Research Associate at the Sociology, History, and Anthropology of Cultural Dynamics research center (SHADYC), an institute of the Ecole des Hautes Etudes en Sciences Sociales, Centre de la Vieille Charité, Marseille, France. He is a former Associate Professor at University Paris IV – Sorbonne and CEO of ID FORCE – FCA communications consulting, France. His publications include the following books: *L'Or pour l'Art: de mécène aux sponsors*, Paris: Flammarion, 1986; *L'Entreprise responsable*, Paris: Editions d'Organisation, 2003 (www.lentrepriseresponsable-lelivre.com); and the collection *Responsabilité sociale de l'entreprise: Pour un nouveau contrat social*, Brussels: De Bœck, 2006. He is Vice-President of the *Association for the Development of Education and Research on Corporate Social Responsibility* (ADERSE, http://www.aderse.org). He is particularly interested in the application of lexical analysis methods to business ethics, corporate social responsibility and sustainable development literatures.

YULIYA SHCHERBININA is currently a Lecturer in Critical Perspectives on Management at the Business School of the National Academy of Management (Kyiv, Ukraine). A graduate in Industrial Management from the Taras Shevchenko University (Kyiv), Yuliya worked in several international companies, including Kraft and Arthur Andersen. She holds a Doctorate degree in Social Sciences from the Pontifical University of St Thomas Aquinas (the "Angelicum", Rome, Italy), where she is a member of the international research project "Ethics and CSR". She has a particular interest in the idea of organizational social capital, its link with CSR and the philosophical underpinnings of the CSR concept.

PATRICIA H. WERHANE is the Peter and Adeline Ruffin Professor of Business Ethics and Senior Fellow at of the Olsson Center for Applied Ethics in the Darden School at the University of Virginia, with a joint appointment as the Wicklander Chair of Business Ethics and Director of the Institute for Business and Professional Ethics at DePaul University. Professor Werhane has published numerous articles and is the author or editor of over twenty books including *Ethical Issues in Business* (with T. Donaldson, eighth edition), *Adam Smith and His Legacy for Modern*

Capitalism, Moral Imagination and Management Decision-Making (Oxford University Press). She is the founder and former Editor-in-Chief of *Business Ethics Quarterly*, the journal of the Society for Business Ethics, and currently a member of the academic advisory team for the Business Roundtable Institute for Corporate Ethics housed at the University of Virginia. Her present work focuses on poverty alleviation through for-profit initiatives.

NOEL KEIZO YAMADA, S.J., is Emeritus Professor of Economics at Sophia University, Tokyo (Japan). Since 1960 he has been involved in solidarity activities with Asian neighboring people, then in Latin America, and then with the African Jesuit Refugee Service. Since 1989 he has been a member of the Peace Research Center of the World Council on Religion and Peace. Between 2002 and 2004 he served as a missionary in East Timor; he is now Campus Ministry of the Sophia Junior College. His main books include: *Liberation Theology in the Modern World*; *Church Responding to the Challenge of 21st Century*; and *Japanese Church Living with Asian Neighboring People*.

LÁSZLÓ ZSOLNAI is Professor and Director of the Business Ethics Center at the Corvinus University of Budapest (Hungary). He is chairman of the Business Ethics Inter-faculty Group of the Community of European Management Schools (CEMS). László Zsolnai was born in 1958, in Szentes, Hungary. He has a master's in finance and a doctorate in sociology from the Budapest University of Economic Sciences. He received his PhD and DSc degrees in economics from the Hungarian Academy of Sciences. His books include the following: *The European Difference*, Boston, Dordrecht and London: Kluwer Academic Publishers, 1998; *Ethics and the Future of Capitalism* (with Wojciech Gasparski), New Jersey and London: Transactions Publishers, 2002; *Ethics in the Economy: Handbook of Business Ethics*, Oxford and Bern: Peter Lang Academic Publishers, 2002; *Spirituality, Ethics and Management*, Boston, Dordrecht and London: Kluwer Academic Publishers, 2004; and *Business Within Limits: Deep Ecology and Buddhist Economics* (with Knut Johannessen Ims), Oxford and Bern: Peter Lang Academic Publishers, 2005.

Index

Frontiers of Business Ethics

Series Editor
LÁSZLÓ ZSOLNAI
Business Ethics Center
Corvinus University of Budapest

This series is dedicated to alternative approaches that go beyond the literature of conventional business ethics and corporate social responsibility. It aims to promote a new ethical model for transforming business into humanistic, sustainable and peaceful forms. The series publishes monographs and edited volumes with fresh ideas and breakthrough conceptions relevant for scholars and practitioners alike.

VOLUME 1

László Zsolnai and Knut Johannessen Ims (eds):
   Business within Limits: Deep Ecology and Buddhist Economics. 2005.
   324 pages. ISBN 3-03910-703-8

VOLUME 2

Luigino Bruni and Stefano Zamagni:
   Civil Economy: Efficiency, Equity, Public Happiness. 2007.
   282 pages. ISBN 978-3-03910-896-1

VOLUME 3

Stig Ingebrigtsen and Ove Jakobsen:
   Circulation Economics: Theory and Practice. 2007.
   349 pages. ISBN 978-3-03911-089-6

VOLUME 4

Luk Bouckaert, Hendrik Opdebeeck and László Zsolnai (eds):
   Frugality: Rebalancing Material and Spiritual Values in Economic Life.
   2008. 322 pages. ISBN 978-3-03911-131-2

VOLUME 5

Forthcoming.

Volume 6

Henri-Claude de Bettignies and François Lépineux (eds):
   Business, Globalization and the Common Good. 2009.
   447 pages. ISBN 978-3-03911-876-2